The Thought of Bal Gangadhar Tilak

The Thought of Bal Gangadhar Tilak

An Intellectual Biography

ROBERT E. UPTON

OXFORD
UNIVERSITY PRESS

OXFORD
UNIVERSITY PRESS

Great Clarendon Street, Oxford, OX2 6DP,
United Kingdom

Oxford University Press is a department of the University of Oxford.
It furthers the University's objective of excellence in research, scholarship,
and education by publishing worldwide. Oxford is a registered trade mark of
Oxford University Press in the UK and in certain other countries

Published in the United States of America by Oxford University Press
198 Madison Avenue, New York, NY 10016, United States of America

British Library Cataloguing in Publication Data

Data available

Library of Congress Control Number: 2023947571

ISBN 978-0-19-890065-8

DOI: 10.1093/oso/9780198900658.001.0001

Printed and bound in India by
Replika Press Pvt. Ltd.

Links to third party websites are provided by Oxford in good faith and
for information only. Oxford disclaims any responsibility for the materials
contained in any third party website referenced in this work.

In memory of Isaac and Elizabeth

Acknowledgements

This work has its somewhat remote origins in a doctoral project undertaken at the University of Oxford, culminating in the award of the DPhil in 2013. Thanks are due to my supervisor, Polly O'Hanlon, who gave generously of her time and considerable expertise on the social and intellectual history of Maharashtra, greatly enriching the thesis which is the foundation of this work.

Among the History Faculty at the University of Oxford, I am also indebted to Judith Brown and Faisal Devji for making such constructive comments on that thesis's final shape. Nandini Gooptu's comments were also valuable in setting out my initial research path. St Antony's College provided a congenial home and considerable intellectual stimulation throughout my time there. I am grateful to the College's staff and Fellows, and in particular I must thank the then College Warden, Margaret MacMillan, for discharging her duties graciously and taking time to meet with and interest herself in the research of the College's students. My College advisor, Michael Willis, was kind and supportive beyond the call of duty. Jan-Georg Deutsch was a valued part of the community of global historians among whom I developed, and his insights and encouragement are much missed. It is with more unalloyed pleasure I take the opportunity to put on record my enormous intellectual debt to those others who from the beginning of my time at Oxford were responsible for my development there, and I offer my warmest thanks to David Rundle, Zoe Waxman, and John Darwin.

For helping me negotiate the transition to postdoctoral life—which is so often a difficult one—I owe a huge debt of gratitude to Maria Misra, and to David Priestland. Maria was kind and supportive, beyond the norm, of my forays into teaching, and her guidance, encouragement, and support of my career in the years since have been indispensable. For these things, as well as her interest in my work, and the time she has given to provide her scholarly insights, I am immensely grateful. David Washbrook, who as an exacting but fair-minded DPhil examiner improved my thought on Tilak, was also generous afterwards with thoughts and ideas for post-doctoral research, in roving conversation in his study at Trinity College, Cambridge. Those who knew David appreciated his humour as much as his enormous learning and intellectual brilliance, and it feels inadequate to note here what a sad loss he is to the field and the community. My thesis's other examiner, William Gould, also gave superb advice as to my developing my work for publication when we were subsequently teaching colleagues at University of Leeds, and I am most grateful for his time and support. I am also grateful to my other colleagues there for creating a warm and sociable environment for the exchange of research ideas. Advice on publication—so important for a first-time author—was also offered by Tamson Pietsch, Erica Charters, Faisal Devji, and in great detail by William Whyte: the assistance of all was doubtless more helpful than they know. Yasmin Khan, my then colleague at the University of Oxford's Continuing Education Department, was both shrewd and generous with her advice. At 'Conted' I also drew on the good counsel of Tom Buchanan. My thanks extend to all.

I am grateful to Shruti Kapila for her special invitation to attend the conference 'The Bhagavad Gita in Modern Times' in Cambridge (2008), and to the other participants. I found receptive audiences for some of the ideas in this thesis at the conference of the Association for the Study of Ethnicity and Nationalism (2010) and at the Copenhagen South Asia Workshop (2012), where Thomas Blom Hansen was particularly generous with his scholarly guidance. I am also grateful to the community of graduate students of South Asian History at Oxford, in particular the participants of the South Asian History Seminar, where I presented early research. The organizers of the Graduate Colloquium, Liz Chatterjee and Sneha Krishnan, did an excellent job in encouraging the sharing of research in a supportive environment. I am also grateful to the organizers and participants at the stimulating and enjoyable Princeton South Asia Conference on 'Technologies and Traditions' in April 2015, and to Manjiri Kamat for inviting me to give a workshop offering centenary reflections on Tilak's later career in Mumbai in December 2016.

In the course of my research, I relied upon the assistance of staff at many archives and libraries. I wish to thank the staff at the following: the Bodleian family of libraries in Oxford, in particular the library of the Oriental Institute; the British Library, in particular the Asia and Africa

Reading Room; the National Archives, Kew; the Centre of South Asian Studies, Cambridge; the library of The School of Oriental and African Studies, University of London; the Sydney Jones Library at the University of Liverpool; the Orient Institute, Istanbul; and SALT, Istanbul. In India I was assisted by staff at the Nehru Memorial Museum and Library, the National Archives of India, the Mumbai Marathi Grantha Sangrahalaya, the Maharashtra State Archives, the Deccan College Library, and the archive of the Kesari-Mahratta Trust. At the latter in particular I must thank Rohit Tilak, the cotrustee, for his interest in and support for my project.

I am also very grateful for the dedication of my various Marathi tutors. Shreeyash Palshikar helped guide my first steps in formally learning the language. The intensive course in Marathi at the American Institute of Indian Studies, which I took in 2008 at the Deccan College campus, Pune, provided a great boon. I am hugely grateful to the director of the course, Sujata Mahajan, who gave of her time freely, and very kindly, to help me. I also wish to thank the course tutors, Shantanu Kher and Kalika Mehta. I am indebted to the Marathi-speakers who have assisted me in various difficulties of translation, particularly Sumeet Mhaskar, Niranjan Joshi, and Prashant Potnis. Avelina Kuenzel helped with my comprehension of German-language scholarship cited in this thesis.

In a work that traverses many intellectual fields, aiming to track Tilak's own roving interests and wide impact, assistance from experts in them is absolutely necessary for scholarly orientation. Figures who furnished me with much-appreciated scholarly guidance on hitherto unfamiliar areas were Madhav Deshpande, Christopher Minkowski, Tania Saeed, and the late Chris Bayly. Their generosity helped enrich the work and avoid many a naïve error.

I have relied upon the miscellaneous support, moral, material, and intellectual, of many good friends while I undertook this demanding project, from an editorial eye to some sympathetic conversation or the offer of a necessary sofa or air mattress while on a research trip. I must first mention Rob Fletcher, so often my first port of call for advice and a prod in the right direction, a friend from our earliest graduate student days and an exemplar as a researcher and scholar. To him and Christine Boyle, I am grateful for support and friendship over the years. Megha Kumar is another whose long friendship has involved intellectual assistance and practical help of various kinds to me (some of which must be acknowledged separately on another occasion), and I offer my warmest thanks to her and Jonah Wilberg. Other friends I must single out for kindness (among others who I hope will forgive my oversight) include Marcus Edwards, Edward Arden, Joseph Dunlop—a true friend of the vagrant scholar—Tom and Gill Ambrose, Michael Derringer, Sylvy Anscombe, and Karlin Younger, not only a dear and supportive friend, but a kindly and perceptive proofer. For the gentle understanding of his pastoral support I am grateful to Revd Gregory Platten, and I extend thanks to the broader chapel community of Lincoln College, Oxford. William Thomas and Rob Saunders were also splendid hosts, their thoughtfulness matched with sparkling conversation. Tom Brodie, another battle-hardened Teaching Fellowship veteran, and Jennifer Wunn, offered a cherished mix of wisdom, humour, and kindness. Back home, I could rely on the diverting conversation of Rowan Dyer and James Lydon, particularly on movie nights which gave my mind a regular excursion from the lifeworld of Bal Gangadhar Tilak. I am also grateful to my parents for the unquestioning support and encouragement they have given to my academic career, and for patiently housing me during several periods of writing-up over the course of the project.

The rigours of a teaching timetable back at Oxford from 2017 were made more bearable thanks to the good company and conversation of George Artley, James Wakeley, Mike Nixon, and David Tweddle, much of it enjoyed at The Bear, in sessions during which the world was put firmly to rights. Simon Faulkner's catering and warm cheer behind the bar of Lincoln College's Deep Hall were appreciated in equal measure. George's kindness, and that of Tom Daggett, in hosting me umpteen times during research trips to London, before and since, has been exceptional, and is acknowledged with very many thanks.

Support for my research was provided by an Oxford University History Faculty Designated Studentship, support from the Beit Fund, and a bursary at St Antony's College. I am grateful to the trustees of all these funds for their confidence, and for all who wrote in my support. I also wish to thank the British Association of South Asian Studies for funding my language study in India. The work has been brought into its final shape thanks to a Marie Skłodowska-Curie postdoctoral fellowship held at Ca' Foscari University of Venice, which I gratefully acknowledge.

It remains only to state that this work could not have been written without the practical support of so many of the above, and it is certainly a better work for the intellectual assistance I have received: but the errors and fallacies that remain in it are mine alone. As I close these acknowledgements I remain in the thick of researching Maharashtra's early twentieth-century politics through my current fellowship: and although a host of new debts have already accrued to me in connection to it, to be properly acknowledged elsewhere, it would perhaps be appropriate to briefly express gratitude not only to those at Ca' Foscari—in particular Prof. Matteo Legrenzi for his stewardship, and the administrative staff for all their assistance—but also for the gracious hosting of the Netaji Institute for Asian Studies, Kolkata, and its Honorary Director, Prof Suranjan Das, whose agreement to enter into partnership with Ca' Foscari to host the project's phase in India has enabled me to continue research into such richly rewarding, and often no less controversial, themes in the political and cultural history of modern India.

Delhi, November 2022

This project has received funding from the European Union's Horizon 2020 research and innovation programme under the Marie Skłodowska-Curie grant agreement No 101031636.

Contents

List of Illustrations

Abbreviations

AH	B. G. Tilak, *The Arctic Home in the Vedas* (Poona; Bombay, 1903).
BC	*The Bombay University Calendar*. Published annually, Bombay; references are given by year, for example, *BC*, 1873.
CWMG	Gandhi, M. K., *The Collected Works of Mahatma Gandhi* (Electronic Book), 98 vols (New Delhi, 1999).
GR	B. G. Tilak, *Sri Bhagavad Gita Rahasya*, trans. Bhalchandra Sitaram Sukthankar, 2 vols (Poona, 1935).
NCERT	National Council of Educational Research and Training
Report DPI	*Report of the Director of Public Instruction in the Bombay Presidency*. Published annually, Bombay; references are given by year, for example, Report DPI, 1861–1862.
RNPB	Report on the Native Press in the Bombay Presidency. Reports are referred to by week ending, unless otherwise indicated.
SLT	*Samagra Lokmanya Tilak* [Tilak's collected works], ed. B. K. Kelkar, D. N. Shikare, and B. D. Kher, 8 vols (Pune, 1974–1995). References to volumes 3–6, in which the articles are numbered, are given by volume and then article number, for example, SLT I, 54.
TOI	*Times of India*

Introduction

Approaching the many Tilaks of today: memory, politics, and global intellectual history

In the *Oxford Dictionary of National Biography*, Bal Gangadhar Tilak is described as an 'icon of modern India'.[1] Whatever our opinion of Tilak's ideas, this seems a reasonable assertion; and given that it is made in a collection of studies of the lives of men and women who have 'shaped British history and culture, worldwide', it encapsulates the global influence of Tilak's career, and the critical importance of the milieu—and his part in it—in the development of the colonial relationship. Yet we would be misled to think that Tilak, the icon, has an evident meaning. For Tilak is a polysemic icon. In his own career, he showed himself a deft manipulator of historical symbols: history's revenge on Tilak has seen a cacophony of claims to his own symbology in the century since his death, though perhaps it is an irony he would have appreciated.

Tilak, the firebrand nationalist, pioneering journalist-editor, and dominant political impresario of western India in the forty years before M. K. Gandhi's rise to national leadership, was significant enough in his day to have been named a 'maker of modern India' by Gandhi on his death.[2] Following the Mahatma, Ramachandra Guha, modern India's 'preeminent chronicler', named Tilak more recently as one of his own nineteen modern India-makers.[3] His is still a name to be dropped by Indian prime ministers. Yet there has been a curious lack of serious study of his ideas. Tilak, indeed, has not really been seen as a thinker. Even his own former newspaper, *Mahratta*, editorialized on his second death anniversary in

---

[1] The assessment is from the venerable historian of western India, Jim Masselos, 'Tilak, Bal Gangadhar (1856–1920)', *Oxford Dictionary of National Biography* (2007), https://doi.org/10.1093/ref:odnb/41085 (hereafter, Masselos, 'Tilak').
[2] *Young India*, 4 August 1920, *CWMG*, vol. 21, 112.
[3] Ramachandra Guha, *Makers of Modern India* (New Delhi, 2010) (hereafter, Guha, *Makers*).

The Thought of Bal Gangadhar Tilak. Robert E. Upton, Oxford University Press. © Robert E. Upton 2024.
DOI: 10.1093/oso/9780198900658.003.0001

1922 that he did not 'waste time or energy in academical discussions of political dogmas and hollow theories of political conduct'.[4] And the idea that Tilak was a man of practical action has militated against serious study of his thought; his major published works on Aryan history and his treatise on the Bhagavad Gita (the *Gita Rahasya*) are often seen as an aside or perhaps a footnote to the thrust of his career, and one of his biographers was even criticized for wasting space on a discussion of them.[5] Yet on the facing page to the editorial just mentioned, his disciple M. R. Jayakar made the recurring claim that Tilak in fact would rather have been a scholar and philosopher than an agitator; this was echoed the same year by Professor Sarvepalli Radhakrishnan (more famous as the second President of independent India), contributing to a work on *Eminent Orientalists*.[6] It also clashed with Tilak's own self-conception as founder-editor of that same newspaper in its earliest days in 1881: *Mahratta* might have been criticized as theoretical, visionary, or chimerical, he claimed, but he vowed to continue in the vein, offering ranging discussions on topics such as the 'future of India' or the permanence of British rule.[7] It is the contention of this work that Tilak's thought is worthy of serious study, and that the lack of this is a noticeable hole in our understanding of the political and intellectual history of modern South Asia. Tilak's views on the historically important questions of the nature of the Indian polity, the reform of Hindu society, and the conduct of politics—the three areas that are the core concern of the book's central chapters—were pivotal in their ongoing discussion in India, not least because of the period he inhabited. As an intellectual active from 1880 to 1920, he necessarily grappled with these questions at a time when they became more urgent and vital, from the emergence of organized 'nationalist' politics, through to its bourgeoning during the Swadeshi agitation from 1905, and onwards to the dawn of Gandhian nationalism. This work above all offers an excavation of his answers to these questions as a contribution to understanding

---

[4] 30 July 1922, 358.
[5] The biographer was his long-standing friend and lieutenant N. C. Kelkar, *Lokmanya Tilak Yanche Charitra*, vol. 3 (Poona, 1928); the criticism was in Kelkar's own biography, R. M. Gole, *N. C. Kelkar* (New Delhi: Sahitya Akademi, 1976) hereafter, Gole, *Kelkar*).
[6] *Mahratta*, 30 July 1922, 359; Sarvepalli Radhakrishnan, 'Bal Gangadhar Tilak', in [editor unknown] *Eminent Orientalists: Indian, European, American* (Madras: Natesan and Co., 1922) (book hereafter, *Eminent Orientalists*), 327 ff.
[7] *Mahratta*, 22 May 1881.

more fully the trajectories of politics, processes of identity formation, and the negotiation of social relations in modern India.

Today's Tilak: patriot, dissenter, fighter, terrorist, anti-reformer, reformer, Hindutva ideologue, secularist ... ?

Tilak is, of course, still deeply relevant as a symbol today in India's politics and culture. Today, indeed, there seems to be a Tilak for everyone. To take some of the more prominent, he is a heroic patriot, the 'father of the Indian national movement', and revivifier of Indian political and spiritual traditions; patron of good, ethical governance, or even far-left resistance to the postcolonial state; exponent of sturdy, muscular politics; a violent extremist; a deplorable high-caste chauvinist; a patriarchal politician, using nationalist language to entrench a subservient social and political position for women; contrastingly, a 'legendary social reformer', forward-thinking and progressive; and most importantly, perhaps, a Hindutva-pioneering ideologue (or a conscientious secularist—or a combination of both). An aim of this work, then, is not only to study what Tilak's own intellectual positions were in their own time, but to trace the process through which Tilak was reworked into so many different guises, and how he came to be the iconic representation of various groups and causes at the heart of modern India's culture. Our final chapter, 'Remembering Tilak', therefore follows the journey through the century from Tilak's death up to today to trace this process of his remembrance.

To dig a little deeper into these various present-day Tilak personas, we find Tilak's reputation as a pioneer patriot is such that India's government-owned broadcaster Doordarshan describes him as the 'father of the Indian national movement'.[8] Seen as the progenitor of nationalist politics who pointed the way for M. K. Gandhi, he is (inaccurately) up to prime ministerial level described as the 'instigator' of the Ganesh Chaturthi, the public celebrations in honour of the Hindu deity, seen as integral to the

---

[8] Their video (via DD News) marking Tilak's 93rd death anniversary was propagated by the Ministry of Information and Broadcasting. See '93rd Death Anniversary, "Lokmanya" Bal Gangadhar Tilak' (1 August 2013), https://www.youtube.com/watch?v=TucoZsr0CFE, accessed 20 November 2020 (hereafter, DD News, 2013).

'mass movement' to independence he inaugurated—and he is invoked at its celebration not only in Bhusawal, but also in Bracknell.[9] A recent popular biography claims that 'if even one per-cent of [Tilak's] love fills every Indian's heart, the country can progress to achieve greater heights and power', adding that he should have been awarded India's highest military decoration, the Param Vir Chakra.[10] The well-received 2015 Marathi biopic *Lokmanya: Ek Yugpurush* ('the man of his age') suggests India's development challenges could be overcome if 'Tilak [became] known to the people'; the film rails in particular against Indians leaving after their education to seek enrichment overseas, the antithesis of Tilak's vision. His famous slogan 'Swaraj is my Birthright and I shall have it', so closely associated with him, was marked with special state commemoration in 2016.[11]

And though the state continues to laud him and foster association with him, his name is also associated with patriotic good governance in a way which involves a potentially subversive critique. Prime Minister Narendra Modi, on India's Independence Day in 2017, might have evoked Tilak by adapting his slogan to '*Surajya* [good governance] is my birthright', but he had also previously used this as an attack line against the governing Indian National Congress.[12] Tilak's ideals are sometimes directly juxtaposed with contemporary corruption, to biting effect. The 2005 film *Shobhayatra* (dir. Vijay Ghatge), based on the long-running Marathi play by Shafaat Khan, leavens its critique by exploiting the comedy in the contrast of contemporary vice and historical greatness: Tilak is one of six historical figures (the Rani of Jhansi, Jawaharlal Nehru, Gandhi, Subhas Bose, and the lesser-known Babu Genu being the others) played by pettily corrupt everyday people for a 50th anniversary

---

[9] 'Full text of PM Narendra Modi's 46th Mann Ki Baat', *Indian Express*, 29 July 2018, www.indianexpress.com (hereafter, 'Mann Ki Baat 46'); also 'Lokmanya Bal Gangadhar Tilak, the architect of present day Ganesh Chathurthi celebrations', *India Today*, 5 September 2016, http://indiatoday.intoday.in.

[10] Nandini Saraf, *The Life and Times of Lokmanya Tilak* (New Delhi: Ocean Books, 2012) (hereafter, Saraf, *Tilak*), 10.

[11] 'Lokmanya Tilak Remembered on Centenary of "Swaraj My Birthright" Slogan', 23 July 2016, http://www.india.com (hereafter, 'Tilak Remembered'). The history of the expression and its origin in 1916–1917 are discussed in Chapter 3.

[12] ' "Chalta Hai Attitude Must Go, Should Be Badal Sakta Hai": PM Modi', *Indian Express*, 16 August 2017, www.indianexpress.com; 'Need of the hour is to bid goodbye to the Congress, which has failed on all fronts: CM at BJP public meeting in Pune' (narendramodi.in) (14 July 2013).

independence parade; 'Tilak' is in fact a university professor, seen frantically burning newspaper copies to hide the disclosure of his role in an exam paper scam. In other hands the critique is harsher: by contrast to his ideals, an introduction to one book on him asserts 'corruption has now become part of the Bureaucracy'; *Ek Yugpurush's* introductory voiceover bemoans the new Indian Gita, in which the Pandavas and Kauravas are in a fetid power-sharing arrangement, with government still nonetheless unstable.[13] 'Even today we do not have Swaraj' is its melancholy conclusion: the *Times of India* review, recording a standing ovation, added that 'probably the power has changed but we are still being ruled and exploited'.[14] It is natural enough for those finding themselves in opposition to the state, indeed, to invoke Tilak in support—pointing to how the state in India rests on anti-colonial acts of resistance. After being charged with sedition in 2016, the CPI (M) (that is, the Communist Party of India [Marxist]) leader Sitaram Yechury claimed, 'I am in great company', 'national stalwarts' like Tilak being charged under the same clause.[15] Tilak continues to be prominently named in accounts criticizing the modern-day operation of Section 124A of the Indian Penal Code, under which he was convicted, and which is interpreted as still stifling anti-state dissent.[16] Even the view of the bench of the Supreme Court of India, that 124A is used to 'implicate the opposition groups and silence them', is editorialized by the *Times of India* with the observation that '[a] law, once used by the colonial state against the likes of Tilak and Gandhi, really has no place in today's India'.[17] And the danger that the COVID-19 pandemic could likewise be used as an occasion for oppressive anti-press measures by the Indian state has also been seen against the background of Tilak's groundbreaking conviction for sedition in 1897, itself during a previous 'serious plague epidemic in India'.[18]

[13] Saraf, *Tilak*, 10.

[14] 'Lokmanya Ek Yugpurush', *Times of India* (hereafter, *TOI*), 21 April 2016, https://timesofindia.indiatimes.com/etimes.

[15] 'In Great Company of Bhagat Singh, Mahatma: Yechury on Sedition Charges', *Hindustan Times*, 29 February 2016, https://www.hindustantimes.com.

[16] 'The Second Coming of Sedition' (Bhairav Acharya), *The Wire*, 18 February 2016, https://thewire.in/law/the-second-coming-of-sedition.

[17] 'Supreme Court: Why Keep Colonial Sedition Law Used Against Mahatma Gandhi, Tilak?', *TOI*, 16 July 2021, https://timesofindia.indiatimes.com/etimes.

[18] Abhinav Chandrachud, 'Plague of 1896 Redefined Sedition. Coronavirus Mustn't Bring In Laws That Outlive Crisis', *The Print*, 24 March 2020, https://theprint.in/.

Tilak's home region of Maharashtra has seen, especially since 2014, a flowering of its perennial celebration of his muscular patriotism, and occasionally outright endorsement of his violence. A clear example of this is *Ek Yugpurush*. The film imagines a recórding of a speech by Tilak being discovered: in it, he is given Gandhi's famous 'do or die' exhortation, adding a clarification that 'it is better to kill'; Tilak is even given a conversation with Gandhi in which he scathingly dismisses Gandhi's mendicancy, instructing him that 'we must shed blood for Swaraj', otherwise 'we will not value it'. He is also specifically shown encouraging Damodar Hari Chapekar (the assassin of an unpopular government plague commissioner in 1897), euphemistically, to meet the Queen's jubilee with 'fireworks'; the film even includes a song ('Powada ... ' [a Marathi historical ballad form]) celebrating the subsequent assassination. Tilak is, indeed, represented as a serial conspirator in violence; and his justifications are made explicit in a speech which offers a pastiche of Tilak's historic statements on violence. Maharashtra's float for the 2017 Republic Day parade, meanwhile, saw a tableau of Tilak accompanied, notably, by Pehlwani wrestlers, significant in reflecting the historic lilt of Maharashtrian politics, perhaps, but also as a manner of stridently representing Maharashtra's peculiar martial values vis-à-vis the rest of India (see Figure I.1).[19]

Petitions deploring Tilak's being described as an 'extremist' (or as a terrorist) have, meanwhile, been frequent in recent years—such as that to the Delhi High Court by Dina Nath Batra, an official of the Hindu nationalist Rashtriya Swayamsevak Sangh ('National Volunteer Association, or RSS) education wing Vidya Bharati, and serial objector to publications in India, in 2011, regarding an Indian Certificate of Secondary Education textbook.[20] Such controversies have the power to reach the highest levels, with Union cabinet minister Smriti Irani intervening to lament that Delhi

---

[19] 'Republic Day Parade: Which States Had the Best Tablèaux and Which Had the Weirdest Ones?', *India News, Firstpost*, 26 January 2017. There is indeed often a sense that these peculiar Maharashtrian virtues are unrecorded and unhonoured in modern India, something also seen in the 2009 film *Me Shivajiraje Bhosale Boltoy* ('This Is King Shivaji Bhosale Speaking') (where the spirit of Tilak incidentally is also, fleetingly, associated with a resurgent and martial Marathi identity).

[20] 'ICSE Calls Shahid Bhagat Singh "Terrorist", Court Says Change It', *Daily News & Analysis*, 9 May 2011, http://dnaindia.com. Batra filed the case that led to the removal by Penguin of Wendy Doniger's *The Hindus* in 2014. See 'Dinanath Batra: Here Comes the Book Police', *Mint*, 13 February 2014, https://www.livemint.com/.

Figure I.1 The Maharashtra tableau featuring Tilak, along with a printing press and wrestlers, passes down New Delhi's Rajpath during India's 68th Republic Day Parade (2017). Image courtesy of Ministry of Defence, Government of India.

Government-prescribed schoolbooks for her children describe Tilak as an extremist, just as newspaper reports they might read describe Osama bin Laden: they 'would obviously ask how one extremist is different from another extremist'.[21] Such sensitivity to criticism of the violence of Tilak's politics is mostly associated with the Hindu right. But the tables can be turned by their political opponents to demonstrate ostensibly superior patriotism: a textbook used by schools affiliated to the Bharatiya Janata Party (BJP) -controlled Rajasthan Government was similarly denounced by the local Congress committee chief in 2018 for calling Tilak the 'father of terrorism', decrying this 'insult to the nation'—'so much', he added, 'for a self proclaiming "nationalist" BJP government'.[22] These objections have certainly been taken seriously, even before Irani's

---

[21] 'Express Adda: We Have to Understand That Children Cannot Be Vote Banks, Says Smriti Irani', *Indian Express*, 24 April 2015, www.indianexpress.com.
[22] 'Rajasthan: Chapter Calling Tilak "Father of Terrorism" Is an Insult to Nation, Says Sachin Pilot', *Scroll, in*, 12 May 2018, https://scroll.in; Sachin Pilot went on to become Deputy Chief Minister of Rajasthan seven months later.

ministerial intervention, and representatives of the National Council of Educational Research and Training (NCERT) for instance have given assurances, without court instruction, that such 'mistakes' as the inclusion of 'objectionable lessons' branding Tilak (among others) a 'militant' had been rectified through changes to their textbooks.[23] Newer NCERT textbooks appear more careful, referring to such figures, Tilak foremost among them, as 'Radicals'.[24] It is notable in this context that recent memorializations of Tilak by Doordarshan have referred to Tilak as one of the 'hardliners' or 'nationalists', in distinction to moderates (though it is unclear where this leaves the 'nationalist' content of the thought of, for example, G. K. Gokhale).[25]

At the same time, media organs ostensibly dedicated to social justice, particularly in relation to caste and gender, show a resilient and hostile memory of Tilak, as witnessed by a web article from March 2016 noting the 'social harm done by Tilak and his think-alikes now found in the [Rashtriya Swayamsevak] Sangh and elsewhere', and scorning Tilak for 'offering a textbook defence of the caste system that would have made Manu proud' and 'claiming Aryan supremacy while Hitler was not even 5 years old'. Describing him as an opposer of female education, it adds that 'amidst the marital rape controversy we face today, we can revisit its source in Tilak's ideology'.[26] Tilak's stance is also used as a stick with which to beat the whole tradition of Indian nationalism from other quarters: for example the Pakistani newspaper *Dawn* carried a piece by its Delhi correspondent in October 2015 entitled 'The Nationalist Heritage of Rape', citing the 'widespread rape of young girls in India' and asking 'is there a political collusion with regressive social practices today just as leading Indian nationalists had fought British steps to protect infant girls from brutal marital assault?' Clearly implying an affirmative answer,

---

[23] 'Mistakes Rectified, Says NCERT', *Hindustan Times*, 31 January 2008, https://www.hindust antimes.com. Bipin Chandra Pal and Lala Lajpat Rai, Tilak's most familiar associates, were also mentioned.

[24] National Council of Educational Research *Our Pasts III*, Ch. 9, 'The Making of the National Movement 1870s–1947', revised ed. November 2021 (first published 2008), 113 ff, https://ncert.nic.in/textbooks.php.

[25] DD News, 'Birth Anniversary of Bal Gangadhar Tilak Today', 2016, https://www.youtube.com/watch?v=XfnnefRHjIg (hereafter, DD News, 2016); DD News, 2013.

[26] Gaurav Somwanshi, 'Bal Gangadhar Tilak: Teaching English Would Prove to Turn Out Girls to Be a Dead Weight on Their Husbands', 16 March 2016, https://counterview.org (hereafter, 'Teaching English'). Counterview.org describes itself as a 'voluntary platform for peace, equality and social justice'.

the article names only one such figure: Tilak, 'who became the first "iron man" of Indian nationalism to back the right of Hindu men to take a bride of 10 years'.[27] Even the contemplative milieu of the university seminar room struggles to contain such revulsion for Tilak: for instance at a workshop at the University of Mumbai in December 2016, the present author's motives in trying to 'revive Tilak' were questioned (the author in fact has no such motive); one audience member even quoted the Preamble to the Indian Constitution, declaring its aim to secure for all its citizens 'JUSTICE, social, economic and political' to angrily indict Tilak's caste politics by that yardstick, before abruptly leaving the gathering. Such criticisms are enough to ask his sympathizers how this 'terrific person' has 'become a villain in the eyes of his countrymen suddenly?', and to couch praise of him in the form of response.[28]

The response is vigorous, from various quarters. It is also diverse: *Ek Yugpurush*'s opening montage describes the scandalous immodesty of women's clothing in contemporary India, contrasting the India Tilak represented with it, suggesting the superior, and much missed, cultural standard of gender norms that Tilak in fact represented. But there is, more simply, an increasing tendency simply to reinvent Tilak as a leading exponent of reform: the response alluded to above for instance focuses on his brief stance in favour of raising the age of sexual consent for girls from 10 to 12 in October 1890 (before he in fact came out emphatically against the reform in question, that winter).[29] The 2010s, indeed, witnessed an efflorescence of such readings of Tilak. He was invoked in the context of social justice in the 2012 introduction to the television talk show *Satyamev Jayete*, focused on social issues; the *Times of India*, in reporting in 2015 on the renaming of Tilak's cremation ground, called him a 'veteran freedom fighter and social reformer'; on his following birthday Doordarshan switched the order of primacy ('B. G. Tilak was a social reformer and freedom fighter'); their video heralding him as the 'father of the national movement' (from 2013) had similarly called him a 'committed social

---

[27] 'The Nationalist Heritage of Rape' (Jawed Naqvi), 27 October 2015, http://epaper.dawn.com/DetailImage.php?StoryImage=27_10_2015_008_001.
[28] Saraf, *Tilak*, 167.
[29] Ibid., see 9, 28–32, 134.

reformer, writer and a journalist', who was 'against early marriages'.[30] In the ultimate expression of this tendency, the *Indian Express* in 2012 referred simply to 'Legendary social reformer Bal Gangadhar Tilak': this, rather than any other aspect of his career, attached to his name.[31] And almost a decade later it could be echoed by Prime Minister Modi's tweet in honour of Tilak's birthday, singling out his views on 'women's empowerment' for praise.[32]

And by far the most prominent critiques of Tilak relate to his 'communal' politics. On the occasion of his 100th death anniversary in August 2020, Shashi Tharoor, the Congress politician with a notable online following, raced out of the traps to 'pre-empt any attempt to appropriate' Tilak's legacy 'by the Hindutva brigade' with a piece posted to his 7 million Twitter followers emphasizing instead Tilak's religious inclusivity.[33] But BJP President Vijay Sahasrabuddhe within hours had justified Tharoor's fears by hailing Tilak as the 'first political leader in modern India to appreciate the importance of identity'—reflecting how the party's mouthpiece the year before had celebrated Tilak's birthday by saluting him as 'the real father of India, [which] messed up the entire freedom movement by ignoring the essential Hindu character of the movement and unnecessarily emphasising the Muslim element in Indian politics'.[34]

Tilak is also consciously linked to a range of Hindutva symbols which are much in evidence thanks to the renewed vigour of Hindutva politics, especially since the run-up to the BJP's election victory of 2014. Most prominent is Gandhi's killer, Nathuram Godse (a figure whose association carries special condemnation from Hindutva's opponents).[35] Godse's

---

[30] 'Maharashtra Government to Rename Garden at Mumbai's Girgaum Chowpatty as 'Swaraj Bhoomi', *TOI*, 18 March 2015, https://timesofindia.indiatimes.com/etimes (hereafter *TOI*, 18 March 2015); DD News, 2016; DD News, 2013.

[31] '92 yrs [sic] after Death, Lokmanya Tilak to Come Alive on Reel', *Indian Express*, 19 September 2012, https://indianexpress.com/.

[32] 'PM Modi Pays Tributes to Bal Gangadhar Tilak and Chandra Shekhar Azad on Their Birth Anniversary', *Outlook*, 23 July 2021, https://www.outlookindia.com/.

[33] https://twitter.com/shashitharoor/status/1289385923881209858, 1 August 2020.

[34] 'Lokmanya Tilak: Father of the Indian Renaissance', *Hindustan Times*, 31 July 2020, www.hindustantimes.com; 'Tilak: The Father of Indian Renaissance', *Organiser*, 11 September 2012, (Jay Dubashi), https://organiser.org/.

[35] The link between Tilak and Godse has long been advanced: in a preface written by Godse's brother Gopal to a reprint of Godse's statement at trial for killing Gandhi—revealingly published the year of the Janata Party's first election victory in 1977—Tilak's position in a tradition incorporating Savarkar and Godse is suggested. *May it Please Your Honour: Statement of Nathuram Godse* (Pune: Vitasta Prakashan, 1977), xiii. Tilak seems to have been influential to Godse, though he is in fact barely mentioned in his statement.

prominence rose significantly during the 2010s, with statues erected, a 'temple' inaugurated in Gwalior (Madya Pradesh), and the Chief Minister of Uttar Pradesh calling for the renaming of Meerut as 'Nathuram Godse Nagar'.[36] His association with Tilak is strong, and is attested in writings which are not obviously sympathetic to Hindutva. Christophe Jaffrelot, for instance, in the *Indian Express* summarized in 2015 that

> by his own admission, Godse belonged to an ideological stream fed by Hindu nationalism and political violence against Gandhi, a school of thought that began with B.G. Tilak and was perpetuated by 'Tilakites' such as V. D. Savarkar, Godse's mentor.[37]

Similarly, an article on the resurrection of the 'Hindutva icon' B. S. Moonje in the *Times of India* in 2015 contained a thumbnail description noting that he was 'an acolyte of Tilak and a firm believer in imparting military training to the Hindu youth'.[38] Tilak himself remains a symbol to invoke for the Hindu right today, something witnessed by Prime Minister Modi's tweets and statements about him, Modi's endorsement of the Ganesh *utsav* indeed specifying it as 'non-communal' (and anti-casteist).[39] And as alluded to in relation to debates over Tilak as 'extremist', there has also been an increasingly bold activism over the last decade from Hindutva-aligned figures to shield him from possible criticism regarding 'communalism' in educational materials: in 2016 controversy flared over a textbook, *Modern Indian Political Thought* (2012), produced for the MA in Political Science at the University of Mumbai, which termed the 'Ganesh *utsav* and use of Gita' as 'categorically anti-secular', and supported this by noting (somewhat elliptically) that Tilak 'was fond of the

---

[36] 'Hindu Mahasabha Sets Up Godse Temple in MP's Gwalior, Sparks Political Controversy', *Hindustan Times*, 15 November 2017, https://hindustantimes.com; 'Meerut to Be Named as Pandit Nathuram Godse Nagar? UP Government Seeks DM's Nod', India TV News, 17 December 2019, https://www.indiatvnews.com/news/india/meerut-renamed-pandit-nathuram-godse-nagar-up-government-yogi-adityanath-571896.

[37] 'The Retrial of Nathuram Godse: Gandhi Assassin's Political Audience', *Indian Express*, 30 January 2015, www.indianexpress.com.

[38] 'BJP Plans Dec 12 Event to Resurrect Hindutva Icon Balkrishna Moonje', *TOI*, 20 November 2015, https://timesofindia.indiatimes.com/etimes.

[39] See 'Mann Ki Baat 46'. *Utsav*, meaning festival, is a common description of the Ganesh celebrations.

intelligence and activities' of Savarkar.[40] Significantly, the *Times Now* news report glossed the accusation of anti-secularism as an accusation of anti-nationalism, a rigid framework to which all such disputes over cultural politics in India are increasingly subjected—and despite the overt criticism of secularism by such Hindutva supporters themselves.[41] Among all this, and perhaps most astonishingly, it is often forgotten that the Supreme Court of India's own understanding of Hinduism itself derives substantively from a (glibly miscited) Tilak *shloka*, such is his resonance and assumed authority.[42]

Taken together, this is an exhaustingly pluralistic set of readings. But it is no mere smorgasbord of interpretations, with Tilak representing—to adopt the old cliché regarding Indian culture—everything and its opposite. It is because Tilak is central to a deeply formative period of India's political culture that he has such continued importance as a symbol.

Tilak reconsidered

Tilak's historical importance and modern-day symbolic resonance make excavating him—and his remembrance—an important task. Most particularly, his assumed, only sometimes contested, importance as a progenitor of Hindu nationalism, so dominant in modern India's political culture, is central to his relevance: and on this crucial issue, this work marks a departure from much of the existing scholarly literature, which argues, *pace* Tharoor, that Tilak is a proto-Hindutva thinker. Tilak, this book argues, has been misunderstood or mispresented as such. It is

---

[40] 106 ff. A National Congress Party member of the Maharashtra Legislative Assembly met with the University of Mumbai Vice-Chancellor over the textbook, leading him to form a committee to review its content. This information is taken from the *Times Now* report, published 18 May 2016, https://www.youtube.com/watch?v=j46c0yvB3Mc, accessed 23 January 2017 (hereafter, *Times Now* report). The video has since been made inaccessible, as 'private': for reportage of the controversy, see 'Experts to Judge if Mumbai University Textbook is Objectionable', *Mid-Day*, 18 May 2016, https://www.mid-day.com/mumbai/mumbai-news/article/experts-to-judge-if-mumbai-university-textbook-is-objectionable-17244169.

[41] *Times Now* report.

[42] This is discussed further below, in 'Remembering Tilak'. Tilak's definition was approved in the landmark 1966 '*Satsangi*' case, which in turn was cited, with Tilak's definition, *inter alia*, in the so-called Hindutva judgement of 1995 [1996 SCC (1) 130], which asserted that 'Hindu', 'Hinduism', and 'Hindutva' could not be defined exclusively of the broader culture and heritage of India.

the absence of a systematic treatment of Tilak's ideas that has allowed the growth of sometimes simplistic historiographical assumptions regarding them, drawing on selected parts of his thought and political practice, and this is perhaps most marked in regard to current assumptions on Tilak's Hindutva.[43] Tilak's subsuming into a Hindutva narrative is in fact, time-honoured: descriptions of Tilak as a 'religious nationalist' were expounded during his own lifetime, and long before the flowering of systematic analysis on Hindutva from the 1980s.[44] But much modern scholarship on Hindutva, even the most sophisticated, places Tilak in a curious position, considered as a 'nascent shape' of an ideology that nonetheless is only seen to crystallize with the output of other figures such as V. D. Savarkar in the decade after his death.[45] This ambiguity enables an assumption that Tilak fits into such a narrative, while betraying an uncertainty, often unexamined, as to exactly how.[46] Some other authors have argued more definitely for Tilak's full membership of a Hindutva school of nationalism, based on his 'synthesis of archaic primordialism with politicised devotionalism'.[47] The conviction draws in particular on Tilak's 'Aryan' ideology expressed in his Vedic history works, and his rallying round Ganesh in the public celebrations he encouraged from the 1890s. Much of the stimulating historiography on the Aryan idea itself only underlines this.[48] For those most overtly ideologically opposed to Hindutva, Tilak is a whipping boy, and a criticism of his religious politics

---

[43] A precise example of this tendency is Sanjay Seth, 'The Critique of Renunciation: Bal Gangadhar Tilak's Hindu Nationalism', *Postcolonial Studies*, 19/2 (2006) (hereafter, Seth, 'Critique'), looking at the *Gita Rahasya* through a set of unsubstantiated assumptions relating to Tilak's conception of society and nation.

[44] J. N. Farquhar, *Modern Religious Movements in India* (New York, 1915); see also Stanley Wolpert, *Tilak and Gokhale: Revolution and Reform in the Making of Modern India* (Berkeley, 1962) (hereafter, Wolpert, *Tilak and Gokhale*).

[45] Christophe Jaffrelot (ed.), *Hindu Nationalism: A Reader* (Oxford, 2007) (hereafter, Jaffrelot, *Reader*), 1.

[46] Christophe Jaffrelot, *The Hindu Nationalist Movement and Indian Politics, 1925 to the 1990s* (London, 1996) (hereafter, Jaffrelot, *Movement*), 17. For Jaffrelot, he was one of 'the principle Indian leaders with Hindu leanings' in the nineteenth century.

[47] Chetan Bhatt, *Hindu Nationalism: Origins, Ideologies and Modern Myths* (Oxford, 2001) (hereafter, Bhatt, *Hindu Nationalism*), 3. Only a small number of authors explicitly dissent, insisting (though without giving space to demonstrate it) the pluralism of Tilak's views on Indian society, notwithstanding his Hindu devotionalism: see Thomas Blom Hansen, *The Saffron Wave: Democracy and Hindu Nationalism in Modern India* (Princeton, 1999) (hereafter, Hansen, *Saffron Wave*), 75–76.

[48] M. Deshpande, 'Aryan Origins: Arguments from Nineteenth-Century Maharashtra', in E. F. Bryant and L. L. Patton, eds, *The Indo-Aryan Controversy: Evidence and Inference in Indian History* (London, 2005) (hereafter, Deshpande, 'Arguments').

is folded into a survey of his apparent reactionary chauvinism, and/or the physical violence of his politics (an ironic echo of the criticisms levelled against him by the colonial state).[49] The further irony of such modern critique is how it is complementary to that of Hindu nationalists claiming Tilak as part of a grand narrative for their ideology—including for instance a post-2014 government-published biography of Keshav Baliram Hedgewar, founder of the RSS, which simply refers to him as a disciple of Tilak.[50] That Tilak, this work argues, appears so because he has been viewed through the wrong end of a telescope—a teleology that distorts our image of him—therefore has significant implications for our ideas of Hindutva's origins and trajectories.

This work eschews examining the bleeding chunks, but looks at the whole body of Tilak's work in order to understand both the parts and the whole better. In the account that follows, Tilak emerges in his conception of community and nation as a majoritarian pluralist, rather than as a genuine cultural nationalist; and as a form of radical liberal, attached deeply to counter-autocratic politics in defence of natural rights, specifically representative self-government. His legitimation of political violence should be understood in that context, not as a break with liberal thought in advocating loyalty to the primordial community over obedience to the state. And in all his prescriptions for India Tilak was self-consciously a modernist, advocating a revived, muscular Hindu society for the conditions of modernity—though he remained rooted in, even intellectually hemmed in by, nineteenth-century frameworks, and an assumption of atavistic Brahminic preponderance in society.

In terms of Tilak's view on Hindu society's relation to the Indian nation, Tilak conceived of Hinduism's claims as at best majoritarian, not integral. For all that Tilak, long before V. D. Savarkar, did employ and explicate the term 'Hindutva', Tilak subscribed, in classically colonial terms, to a view of India as largely composed of two unitary and primordial communities, Hindu and Muslim, each of which would have a distinct position in the

---

[49] See Parimala V. Rao, *Foundations of Tilak's Nationalism: Discrimination, Education and Hindutva* (New Delhi: Orient Blackswan, 2010) (hereafter, Rao, *Foundations*); Jose Kuruvachira, *Hindu Nationalists of Modern India: A Critical Study of the Intellectual Genealogy of Hindutva* (Jaipur, 2006) (hereafter, Kuruvachira, *Hindu Nationalists*).

[50] Rakesh Sinha, *Dr. Keshav Baliram Hedgewar* ('Builders of Modern India' series) (New Delhi: Publications Division, Ministry of Information and Broadcasting, 2015) (hereafter, Sinha, *Hedgewar*).

polity. This informed his agreement with the Muslim League at Lucknow in 1916 on the separate representation of Hindus and Muslims in future legislatures and councils. Tilak's writing on Aryan history, meanwhile, maintains a studied and political silence on the controversial 'Muslim' period of history often held to be responsible for India's historic decline from Aryan values. Further, in its insistence that the Vedic Aryans themselves originated outside India, his interpretation was diametrically opposed to the emerging Hindutva interpretation of Indian history, even during his lifetime.

Tilak emerges from this study as an intellectual self-consciously attempting to construct a modern India. This is notable, given the classic emphasis, articulated during his life by Aurobindo Ghose, that he was able to 'bridge the gulf between the present and the past and to restore continuity to the political life of the nation'.[51] Modernity for Tilak was characterized by modern political forms like democratic nationalism, and a revitalized and remilitarized Hindu society (a preoccupation that has not only a fascinating transnational context in the period, but also explicitly found encouragement in the contemporary Japanese example, among others). In order to achieve this, Hindu dharma itself would be explicated anew, as Tilak attempted in his commentary on the Gita to espouse a highly gendered 'activist' form of Hinduism that could respond to the challenges of the age of the New Imperialism and global conflict, and in particular respond to late-colonial fears of India's 'emasculated' weakness. The democratic element to his political vision was in an unresolved tension with his concern, running through his output, to justify an elevated Brahmin role in society and polity. This was in part conditioned by the historical conditions of the Brahmins of Maharashtra from the mid-nineteenth century: a loss of political power and a felt need, indeed opportunity, to re-establish social and political authority. This concern—particularly manifested as a hostility to non-Brahmin political participation—is one of the ways that Tilak remained hemmed in by his nineteenth-century and regional antecedents. Tilak grappled with the problems of how to extend his Brahminism into a wider reimagined Hinduism, his natural

---

[51] Aurobindo Ghose, 'An Appreciation by Babu Aurobindo Ghose', in *Bal Gangadhar Tilak, His Writings and Speeches* (Madras: Ganesh and Co., 1918), (hereafter, Ghose, 'Appreciation'), 6.

elitism into the foundations of a representative form of government, and his Maharashtrian patriotism into broader Indian nationalism. In this, he is expressive of time and place; and his solutions, for all their flaws and tensions, were intellectually committed and highly influential.

In our final chapter we see through our study of Tilak's remembrance in the century since his death that the modern historiography on Tilak is closely related to the popular conceptions of Tilak that emerged in the various socio-cultural contexts in which he has been deployed since 1920. In describing these socio-cultural contexts, therefore, this final chapter also produces what Sumit Sarkar has described as 'a social history of historiography', enriching the understanding of the historiography with which this book engages. Indeed, a major feature of this section is the close relationship between popular, official, and academic history in India (and more widely), (mis)apprehensions about Tilak trafficking between the three. Critically, the chapter discusses the mid-1920s as a pivotal moment in cementing Tilak's memory to the Hindu right, despite his opposition only a few years previously to many of the same figures who did so: this appropriation of Tilak by Hindutva casts its shadow over academic accounts, many of which are strangely assumptive.

Approaches to Tilak's global intellectual history

Tilak also offers further insights into the 'global' intellectual history of modern South Asia, something which has seen a scholarly upsurge, amid disagreements concerning those categories' implications and relevance. Tilak's conscious engagement with cosmopolitan intellectual frameworks, most obviously in his English-language writing on the history of the Aryan race, as crucial to European as Indian identities in the period, speaks to what Kris Manjapra has described as an aspirational cosmopolitanism, a pursuit of conversations across lines of difference; indeed as we shall see he reflects the practice of Manjapra's subjects in drawing on traditions of exegesis that fashioned an account of history to burnish Indo-Aryan prestige while undermining the universalist claims of colonizers, in an intellectual framework in which the distinction between 'western' and 'autochthonous' knowledge cannot be sustained.[52] Tilak also reflects the importance of tracing the trans-temporal connections, as much as those across space, in the writing of global history, something that emerges strongly in other writing on concepts of sovereignty, with which Tilak was much concerned, in modern South Asia—to capture in that case what Jonathan Spencer has described as the 'nuances of sovereignty' in 'what we might call the vernacular past'.[53] There is much more than linguistic and conceptual translation of trans-local concepts into local idioms in Tilak's work, situated though it is in a global intellectual context and coeval, globally operating colonial political conditions. These conditions gave rise to urgent refashionings of existing notions of power and authority in society, and of dharma: Tilak's ideas of *Swarajya*, of Brahmin assumption of 'Kshatriya' power, and the ethical implications of Hindu conceptions of cosmic time—specifically the evil age of the *Kaliyuga*, which frames the political ethics of Chapter 5—show a precolonial provenance, often (as in the first two of these) a specifically Maharashtrian one, to thought which contested the authoritarianism of the colonial state. Thus we may transcend the model of 'truncated universalism' in which the role of non-European actors is merely to fulfil, sometimes through dissenting within, conceptual frameworks formed in Europe.[54] And the work echoes, from a somewhat different perspective, Andrew Sartori's non-diffusionist argument concerning Bengali 'culturalism', that convergent modern intellectual forms might emerge by simultaneous and non-directional processes: there were similar, indeed convergent conditions of plausibility for concepts given the contemporary socio-political pressures.[55] Indeed, Tilak's alignment with parallel global ideas of militarism also echoes C. A. Bayly's earlier observations

---

[52] See especially the 'Introduction' to Sugata Bose and Kris Manjapra, eds, *Cosmopolitan Thought Zones: South Asia and the Global Circulation of Ideas* (Basingstoke, 2010).

[53] Jonathan Spencer, '*Afterword: We Have Other Ideas*'. *South Asian Sovereignty* (India: Routledge, 2019), 216–226, 11; see also Milinda Banerjee, 'Sovereignty as a Motor of Global Conceptual Travel: Sanskritic Equivalents of "Law" in Bengali Discursive Tradition', *Modern Intellectual History*, 17/2 (2020), 487–506 (hereafter, Banerjee, 'Sovereignty'), 503.

[54] This concern is forcefully articulated by Samuel Moyn, 'On the Nonglobalization of Ideas', in Samuel Moyn and Andrew Sartori, eds, *Global Intellectual History* (New York: Columbia University Press, 2013), 187–204; my response echoes that of Banerjee, 'Sovereignty'.

[55] This might be seen as parallel to Sartori's Marxian analysis based on globally operating capitalistic conditions in his *Bengal in Global Concept History: Culturalism in the Age of Capital* (University of Chicago Press, 2009).

on nineteenth-century global uniformities.[56] Tilak also reminds us of the importance of registering these refashionings while observing that they may overlap with relatively undifferentiated acceptance of frameworks of colonial knowledge, as seen in his assumptions regarding the fundamentally communal character of Indian civilization, along with aspects of his historical consciousness and assumptions regarding political progress. And attentiveness is also necessary to the moments when ideas or concepts of 'external' provenance contribute to the renewal of aspects of vernacular thought, often indeed because of real and perceived commonality with the historical socio-political conditions that gave rise to those concepts (an implication, for instance, of Tilak's engagement with vernacular ideas of representative government while invoking the notion of 'birthright', discussed in Chapter 3), while avoiding a mere reinscribing of influence of the European 'centre' against the 'periphery'.[57]

It may also be noted that there has been a tendency to exaggerate the foreignness of India's historical setting to the writing of intellectual history, seen to draw its techniques and approaches from a European setting dominated by 'great thinkers'.[58] Because of the course of his peculiar career, Tilak is a canonical thinker with canonical texts, especially the *Gita Rahaysa*, but he also contributed in a more quotidian manner to the intellectual culture of western India, and provides materials and glimpses into it through newspaper editorials and speeches.[59] As such he is suggestive of the means by which such a history can be written, and this book offers a contribution to it, here blending the canonical and the quotidian, understanding his main historical/philosophical texts in the context of his journalism and prolific political speeches. We also have rich information on Tilak's 'lifeworld', the scarcity of which for early modern Indian intellectuals, as Sheldon Pollock notes, renders the study of Indian intellectual history in that period so different from that of Europe.[60]

---

[56] C. A. Bayly, *The Birth of the Modern World, 1780–1914: Global Connections and Comparisons* (Blackwell, 2004).

[57] On that latter tendency, see Sanjay Subrahmanyam, 'Global Intellectual History beyond Hegel and Marx', *History and Theory*, 54/1 (2015), 126–137.

[58] Shruti Kapila, 'Preface', *Modern Intellectual History*, 4/1 (April 2007) ('A New Intellectual History for India'), 5; reflected by C. A. Bayly, 'Afterword', ibid., 167.

[59] A measure of this canonicalness is the English Heritage blue plaque commemorating Tilak at his London residence, 10 Howley Street (now Howley Place), near Maida Vale, styling him as a 'philosopher' as well as a patriot.

[60] Sheldon Pollock, *The Ends of Man at the End of Premodernity* (Amsterdam, 2005) (hereafter, Pollock, *Ends*), 80.

Tilak is also, simply, a prominent discussant of ideas with a vital global life in the period, and his intervention offers a distinctive contribution on racial superiority, the foundations of ethical reasoning, and political liberalism. Naturally, it would have been possible to pursue some of these ideas among, for instance, circles of Brahmin nationalists in western India during the period. While remaining aware of Tilak's intellectual peers and collaborators, this study has tried, on the contrary, to specify his in-dividual contribution to his milieu. This is for many reasons: Tilak is of course already personally invoked in the historical remembrance we have described, popular and scholarly; as a discrete individual, he is powerful today. But perhaps the most powerful reason for choosing a study of this nature is to see how one intellect, in as much as it can be delineated and observed, is able to negotiate the tensions and contradictions of such an ecumene as Tilak's.

This work adopts a contextualist approach to Tilak's output, looking at particular of Tilak's linguistic contexts and audiences to work out what his statements were trying to 'do', in Quentin Skinner's terms, in and to their political world—or, what he could have been intending to communicate by the utterance of a given utterance.[61] This means tracking Tilak closely in terms of his contribution to particular contemporary debates, and involves an in-depth appreciation of the vernacular political culture of Tilak's region, Maharashtra. It means, further, that each of the three main themes of this study—the nature of the Indian polity, reforming Hindu society, and the conduct of politics—are approached from a study of Tilak's interventions in controversies across his career that relate to them (the treatment of individual themes, rather than the work as a whole, being largely chronological), viewed in relation to the 'major' works, *Orion*, *Arctic Home*, and *Gita Rahasya* ('Secret Import of the Bhagavad Gita'). The most important advantage of focusing on specific moments in Tilak's career is the greater understanding possible of the context of Tilak's statements. Intermittently a journalist for over thirty years—all his career apart from when imprisoned—Tilak's statements touching all of these concerns are profuse. Yet without an attempt to isolate moments,

---

[61] Quentin Skinner, 'Meaning and Understanding in the History of Ideas', in James Tully, ed., *Meaning and Context: Quentin Skinner and His Critics* (Princeton, 1988), esp. 63, classically terming this 'illocutionary force'.

we may be deprived of understanding the meaning of these statements, through an inability to sufficiently recreate salient elements in their context. It should be emphasized that it is Tilak's explicit reflections upon these themes that the study will uncover; it is as intellectual expressions that they are studied, though to do so their nature as political acts in themselves, most obviously in the cases of his editorials and speeches, is borne in mind. There is a particular challenge in writing the intellectual history of a politician, given the practical imperatives to adopt certain positions at different times, and here again an appreciation of Tilak's situations helps us to understand his thought as it emerged from them. It is certainly possible to draw a great deal of long-term continuity in Tilak's thought, which informed many of his responses to clear and sometimes shifting political imperatives. It is also important to try and determine the relation of his major texts to the rest of his political thought. *Orion, Arctic Home*, and the *Gita Rahasya* are in a different order to his more quotidian statements; a central problem of the study is how his modes of thought may have differed between the two, and how he intended them to relate to one another.[62] Prolix and recondite, they are, classically, overlooked in attempts to understand the totality of his career, either uncomplicatedly collapsed into the rest of his political practice, or else seen as incidental diversions from it, something this study aims to remedy.[63] As far as is possible, this study also attempts to adduce different materials in each chapter, though some material is touched on again, as especially germane to more than one area of his thought.

Sources

It is worth for a moment reflecting further on the material used for this work. Tilak edited the newspapers he cofounded, the Marathi *Kesari* and the English-language *Mahratta*, at various stages in his career, and as well

---

[62] B. G. Tilak, *The Orion: Or Researches into the Antiquity of the Vedas* (Bombay, 1893) (hereafter, *Orion*); B. G. Tilak, *The Arctic Home in the Vedas* (Poona, 1903) (hereafter, *AH*); *Srimad-Bhagavadgita-Rahasya: athava Karma-Yoga-Shastra*, (SLT I) (first published Poona, 1915).

[63] For the former view, see especially Wolpert, *Tilak and Gokhale*; for the latter, Jim Masselos' reference to them as an afterthought in his brief account (Masselos, 'Tilak') is emblematic, as is the classic biographical account by D. V. Tahmankar, *Lokamanya Tilak: Father of Indian Unrest and Maker of Modern India* (London, 1956) (hereafter, Tahmankar, *Tilak*).

as this wrote for them sporadically when not editing, from 1881 to the last months of his life in 1920. They are of crucial importance to this study. The history of Tilak's involvement with the papers, and his other major texts, is discussed more in Chapter 2; but it should be noted that Tilak was editor of *Kesari* in total for around nineteen years (interrupted by imprisonment and terminated by his advancing years and other duties after his final release), whereas he edited *Mahratta* for around six, and hence care is taken over glibly attributing Tilak's authorship of anything written in either paper during his lifetime. Tilak composed his English-language treatise *The Orion, or Researches into the Antiquity of the Vedas* in 1893, the fruits of his long, precocious engagement with questions of Vedic history. *The Arctic Home in the Vedas* followed a whole decade later, in 1903, aided by a spell of imprisonment which gave him leisure to study. Similarly, the *Gita Rahasya* was composed in exiled imprisonment in Mandalay, and was published a year after his 1914 release. As Tilak edited neither newspaper after 1908, his speeches (reported diffusely and later collected) become an increasingly important source for this post-release period, as it was into this propagandizing work that he put most of his energies. His letters, meanwhile, throw light on incidents and circumstance, but are not revealing of a great deal of his thought. The majority of Marathi sources have been studied in the original. The *Gita Rahasya* exists in both original vernacular and English translation, made fifteen years after Tilak's death. The translation is of invaluable help with such a prolix work, but where necessary it has been compared with the original Marathi, and some commentary on terms, and occasional retranslation of the original, have been supplied. Page references are given to the English edition for convenience.[64] *Kesari* has been largely freshly translated from Tilak's collected works published by the Kesari-Mahratta Trust between 1974 and 1976. The poor physical condition of many of the original surviving *Kesari* hard copies, and the microfilms of some of them, renders this preferable, although where possible original issues have been consulted. In this, it should be noted, *Kesari* has fared better than most of its contemporaries: the sad state of preservation of printed literature from western India in this period, some housed in the

---

[64] *Sri Bhagavadgita-Rahasya: Or Karma-Yoga-Shastra*, trans. Bhalchandra Sitaram Sukthankar, 2 vols (Poona, 1935) (hereafter, *GR*).

Maharashtra State Archives alongside alarmingly crumbling official records, is an unavoidable conclusion to be drawn from such a research project.[65] Tilak's broader milieu has also been shown through reference to contemporary intellectuals and writers, in both English and Marathi.

Outline of chapters

The first chapter will survey the educational milieu in colonial Maharashtra and its evolution from the mid-nineteenth century, including a survey of the institutions—the English-medium high school and above all the Deccan College—that had a formative effect on Tilak. It will also include an account of the early life and education of Tilak himself. The 'Europeanized' milieu of Sanskrit studies Tilak encountered is significant, as is the anglicized historical consciousness that these institutions propagated. Of particular importance in this milieu is the nexus of Bombay-based missionaries and orientalist scholars who developed and disseminated the Aryan theory of race in western India, a crucially important cosmopolitan intellectual framework that Tilak inherited. Indeed this Bombay-based nexus developed the standard applications of the Aryan theory to India—including the development of caste as a consequence of a prehistoric Aryan invasion—something not fully grasped in current literature.

Chapter 2, 'Tilak as a Writer', will give a general account of Tilak's major texts and his newspapers. For the major texts, *Orion*, *Arctic Home*, and the *Gita Rahasya*, a conspectus of his aims and influences in composing each is offered, situating them in the context of his career and in the context of contemporary debates, particularly surrounding Aryanism. It will also give an account of Tilak's career as a newspaper editor and journalist, tracing the concerns and content of the

---

[65] MSA Judicial Department records bearing on the Ganapati 'festival' of 1894, for instance, were already in shreds when delivered to the present author, and fell apart further in his hands as he attempted to piece them together. They are utterly unique records of an important moment in Maharashtra's public culture, yet they cannot long survive under current conditions. What could be gleaned is presented in Chapter 3. 'Tilak's Library', housed at the Deccan College, Pune, has also fared poorly: though under lock and key, most of the texts in it were published from the 1920s onwards, an apparent attempt by curators at some point to bulk out a depleted collection with texts relevant to his interests.

newspapers during his editorship, and their response to contemporary controversies, as well as examining the issues on which Tilak appears to have written most personally.

The controversies and events engaged with in the central chapters are taken from the whole length of Tilak's career, though especially from the period after 1890, when he assumed a more singular and prominent role. We begin in Chapter 3 with a study of Tilak's views on 'The Nature of the Indian Polity', investigating Tilak's conception of the constitution of Indian society as a political unit, and the ultimate origin of legitimate political authority: in its investigation of Tilak's understanding of 'communal' politics it establishes parameters for the next chapter on Hindu society, while setting out in its discussion of legitimacy the preconditions for legitimate violence Tilak espouses in Chapter 5. The chapter focuses on Tilak's communitarian vision, consistent from the aftermath of the Hindu-Muslim Bombay riots of 1893 and still present in his response to the *Khilafat* agitation at the end of his life, in which the polity was a site of competing, enumerated, primordial religious communities: his concern for the consolidation of the Hindus of western India within this framework prompted his promotion of the festival in honour of the elephant-headed deity Ganesh in Maharashtra in the mid-1890s. The chapter will also consider the problematic nature of Tilak's attempts, hemmed in by his Maharashtrian Hindu antecedents and imaginative resources, to fashion all-Indian nationalist symbols, focusing on his celebration of the seventeenth-century warrior-king Shivaji as far afield as Bengal in the early 1900s. Lastly, it will consider Tilak's conception of the ultimate origin of legitimate political authority in representative government, influenced by English radical and liberal thought, and precolonial Maharashtrian political history, and resting on his Vedantic understanding of the self.

The fourth chapter, 'Reforming Hindu Society', looks at Tilak's efforts to revive Hindu society, with a focus on caste identities and their relationship to social power and authority. It examines Tilak's espousal of a radical *kshatriyatva*, 'warriorness' among all castes, a highly gendered identity reflecting concerns over lost manliness within Hindu society. The chapter is thus concerned with Tilak's conception of masculinity and its relationship to individual and social power: it forms a complement to studies examining Tilak's dismissive views of the education of women, which it therefore does not discuss.[66] Tilak's martializing agenda, very prominent in the *Gita Rahasya*, also informed Tilak's consistent calls for the military enlistment of Indians, even urging them immediately after his release from imprisonment for sedition to fight in the King-Emperor's armies in the Great War. This was no egalitarian conception of caste identity, for Tilak was in fact hostile to the claims to social authority of self-professed Kshatriyas themselves, and to distinct non-Brahmin political organization and representation. Rather, Brahmins, appropriating aspects of Kshatriya identity, were the natural leaders of Hindu society, which would maintain distinctions between varnas, as shown by Tilak's coolness to the eradication of untouchability and hostility to inter-caste marriage.

Chapter 5, 'The Conduct of Politics', examines Tilak's reflections upon political conduct (rather than dwelling on the political conduct of his own career per se). Tilak emerges as a theorist of opposition to autocracy, and of civil disobedience in the assertion of the rights of representative self-government—the end that was outlined in Chapter 3. It first tackles Tilak's espousal of political violence, a dominant historiographical preoccupation—and in this it complements a growing strain of historiography on anti-colonial violence in India.[67] It focuses on the material for which he was indicted on sedition charges, from 1897 and 1908, looking at its rationales for political violence. In looking at the 1908 trial, a significant moment for Tilak as political propagandist, we can view Tilak's views on the freedom of the press, once more informed by a reading of a British liberal tradition, which Tilak weaponized in an intellectual contest with the colonial bureaucracy and its apologists, thus further sharpening its radicalism within his own thought. During his subsequent imprisonment, Tilak's thought on political conduct informed his *Gita Rahasya*, and we shall see how it closely related, at such an emotional and physical distance, to the rest of his career. We shall also examine his conception of 'passive resistance', looking at the moment of its inception in the Bengal partition agitation from 1905, in so doing seeing the larger political implications of Tilak's conception of boycott. We shall trace how

---

[66] Rao, *Foundations*, gives a recent and full account of Tilak's stance on female education.
[67] See, for instance, Durba Ghosh, *Gentlemanly Terrorists: Political Violence and the Colonial State in India, 1919–1947* (Cambridge, 2017) (hereafter, Ghose, *Gentlemanly Terrorists*).

his conception shifted after his release in 1914, from an initial continued avowal of non-cooperation to 'responsive cooperation', even in the face of Gandhi's calls for non-cooperation in the opening months of 1920, just a few months before his death. Much as Tilak's ideas on violence or passive resistance related to practical action, they were always anchored in ethical justifications: his political rootedness in arguments within the *dharmashastra* is striking, nowhere more so than the *Gita Rahasya*. Tilak stands as one self-consciously developing a Hindu language and ethos for politics in the modern age.

The final chapter, 'Remembering Tilak', shifts away from intellectual history towards a cultural history, surveying how Tilak's legacy has been contested and transmitted in politics and the public imagination since his death, and how the range of bitterly contested popular readings described above emerged. It offers, in addition, a contextualization of the historio-graphical response to Tilak we have examined, through illustrating the porous boundaries between official, popular, and academic accounts. In addition, it aims to enrich our understanding of later phenomena, in par-ticular incipient Hindutva and the early post-1920 leadership of Gandhi, by referring to the use made there of Tilak's memory. Beginning with his remarkable initial remembrance as national 'founding father' from 1920 within India and its diaspora (a fact with implications for how we under-stand India's 'imagining' in this period), and the relevance of the 'charis-matic' suffering of his sedition imprisonments for this, it then describes Gandhi's appropriation of Tilak's memory for his non-cooperation agenda, and the subsequent remembering of Tilak as Gandhian, even so far as his would-be celibacy. It also describes how Tilak's endorsement of violence was conversely celebrated by many, particularly on the emer-gent Hindu right in Maharashtra in the 1920s, and how this helped to cement posthumously his credentials as a Hindutva ideologue, some-thing involving a reworking of his ideas. Meanwhile, non-Brahmin pol-itical organization has helped to concentrate both popular and academic attention upon his 'casteist' and 'Arya-supremacist' politics, while there has been a fruitful exchange between women's activism and the academy in India more recently in interrogating (often vociferously) his gendered understanding of Indian society—just as there has been a largely correla-tive response in increasingly insisting baldly that Tilak was a 'legendary social reformer'. In the same vein, while the post-independence state has used Tilak's patriotic memory for legitimization, burnishing the popular sense of his heroism, others, following the Gandhian pre-independence Congress lead, have used him to critique and resist state power. Criticism of Tilak on grounds of religious politics or 'extremism', often denounced as 'anti-national', has become more strenuously resisted, with increased use of the power of the state through legal actions—often aimed at school textbooks—to silence his critics being perhaps the most startling feature of recent years, tied in with the growth in power of the Hindu right. This regime of proscription operates strongly today: and the potential influence of his remembered politics in India is all the greater because of the use of the courts to silence textbooks seen to imply the illegitimacy of his violence or his 'communalism'.

1

Intellectual Formation

This chapter surveys the educational milieu of Maharashtra from the mid-nineteenth century, with a focus on the institutions—the English-medium high school and above all the Deccan College—that had a formative educative effect on Tilak. It will situate these institutions in the broader history of education within the Bombay Presidency, and the effects there of the 'Anglicizing' turn of educational policy from the 1830s, and the ultimate decision to reorder educational provision, establishing a full Education Department in 1860 administering English-medium higher schools and a presidency university at Bombay, to which Tilak's Deccan College would be affiliated. Among the most important developments we will examine is the deliberate inculcation of an anglicized historical consciousness through high school education in the Presidency in the 1860s. This was an important component of Tilak's intellectual conditioning and resources, forming his responses (ironically, of course, in opposition to the colonial state) on many questions of political thought to be examined later. Changes in Sanskrit scholarship in the Presidency, whose 'modern institutions' rendered it a world centre for Sanskrit studies according to the 'European method', are vital to grasp. The work of this 'Bombay school' of Sanskritists was one Tilak, not uncritically, would imbibe. The Bombay-based nexus of professional Sanskritists and missionaries was also vital in developing and disseminating the Aryan theory of race in western India. This was a crucially important cosmopolitan intellectual framework that Tilak inherited. We shall therefore also devote independent space to examining the 'Aryan' idea, its origin and impact, observing how all of the main debates around the direction of society under colonial rule in western India were inflected with the idea and its different implications. It was in fact in this Bombay-based nexus that the standard applications of the Aryan theory to India—including the development of caste as a consequence of a prehistoric Aryan invasion—were

The Thought of Bal Gangadhar Tilak. Robert E. Upton, Oxford University Press. © Robert E. Upton 2024.
DOI: 10.1093/oso/9780198900658.003.0002

developed, something not grasped in current literature. The survey will end with an account of Tilak's own education.

Before beginning this survey of the educational milieu, however, we will introduce some important social and historical features of Tilak's vernacular region, Maharashtra. It had, both before and after the Company's takeover, a distinctive regional vernacular culture—indeed, it was a distinct cultural locale. Crucially, some of the fiercest controversies that Tilak was to engage in during the course of his career had a special meaning and relevance for Maharashtrian society, which also gave him a set of understandings regarding them. We will examine Tilak's own specific antecedents, looking at the fraught position of Tilak's community, the Chitpavan Brahmins, upon losing political pre-eminence in Maharashtra to the British in 1818, their responses to it, and the characteristic position of eminence alloyed with official suspicion that they had achieved by the mid-century; and we will situate Tilak's own family within this.

Maharashtra in the mid-nineteenth century

Maharashtra, an area defined by the prevalence of Marathi and by its associated vernacular culture, extends from India's western coast to the central highlands in the east; and from the Satpura mountains in the north to the Andhra plains in the south. In some ways a pivotal region between the Hindustani-speaking culture that abutted it to the north and east and the Kanarese and Telugu cultures of the south, the region historically expressed a substantial degree of cultural and linguistic homogeneity, and boasted a venerable vernacular literary culture.[1] Its major geographical cleavage is between the Konkan littoral, a long, thin coastal stretch with rich tropical vegetation, and the parched inland Deccan areas (from which it is screened off by the *sahyadri* mountains), consisting of flat plains, dominated by occasional rocky outcrops, heavily dependent on the annual monsoon rains—though Tilak's own family history was

---

[1] See M. S. Gore, 'Identifying Maharashtra as a Cultural Region', in N. K. Wagle and A. Kulkarni, eds, *Region, Nationality and Religion* (Mumbai, 1999).

testament to the ready migration between the two.[2] The coastal strip, of course, also contained Bombay, western India's main entrepôt from the late eighteenth century, and handling enormous volumes of global trade after the opening of the Suez Canal in 1869. Its population was already seven times that of a large Maharashtrian city like Poona in 1872, giving it a population density greater than London; and its whole career as an East India Company trading port and its magnetism for migrants, especially from other parts of western and northern India, gave the city an atypical character in Maharashtra, and a unique urban culture of its own, heavily influenced by Gujarati mercantile communities.[3] The Deccan, meanwhile, had a population of almost 8 million by 1872; and of particular importance in Maharashtrian cultural terms, and in terms of Tilak's own life and career, was its the western portion. Not only did this contain some of Maharashtra's major urban centres, Belgaum, Nasik, and above all the former seat of the Peshwa Maratha rulers, Poona, its administrative unity in the nineteenth century, as the southern part of the Bombay Presidency, provided a particular cohesion in patterns of social and cultural association.[4] The eastern parts of Maharashtra, meanwhile, fell into the administrative units of the Central Provinces and Berar, and also the Princely state (that is, governed by a nominally independent Indian 'prince') of Hyderabad, by mid-century. One other Princely state survived within Maharashtra by the time of Tilak's birth: Kolhapur, the seat of Bhosle rulers tracing their line back to the illustrious Maratha warrior-king Shivaji Bhosle (ruled 1674–1680).

At the start of the nineteenth century, the whole region, except for the East India Company's earlier outpost Bombay, had effectively been under the sway of the Peshwa in Poona, heading a 'confederacy' of Maratha rulers; at its height around 1760, Maratha power extended

---

[2] It should be noted though that the dialects of the Maharashtrian Konkan differ from 'standard' Marathi: what is often today referred to as 'Maharashtrian Konkani' straddles the boundary of Marathi and Goan Konkani.

[3] *Census of India 1871–1872: Bombay Presidency Pt II, General Report and Tables of the Population, Houses, &c. Enumerated* (Bombay, 1875) (hereafter, 1872 Census), 12 and 14. This census—the first full census of western India, an important and overlooked resource—listed Bombay's population as 644,405. On the development of the city's character, see Sharada Dwivedi and Rahul Mehrotra, *Bombay: The Cities Within* (Bombay, 2001).

[4] The 1872 Census had the population of the Deccan within the Bombay Presidency as 7,966,061 (4–5), or roughly the combined population of Wisconsin, Alabama, Iowa, Illinois, and Michigan. The Konkan, including Bombay, had a population of 3,259,776.

from the Deccan to the Indo-Gangetic plain, and eastwards to the Bay of Bengal—a dominance Maharashtrians have always tended to remember. (It might be helpful to note at this point that 'Maharashtrian' carries a sense of regional connection; 'Marathi'—when used to describe people— a more strictly linguistic one; and Maratha, in one of its various spellings (such as Mahratta), as well as giving its name to the historical 'Empire', and sometimes being used to describe all Marathi-speaking people, also carries another distinct meaning, connoting a specific Maharashtrian community, with a contested membership regarding caste, as we shall discover below.)[5] Recurrent conflict between the Maratha Empire and the Company culminated in decisive defeat for the army of the last Peshwa Bajirao II in 1818.[6] The former Maratha heartlands were consolidated into the Bombay Presidency, headed by its first governor, Mountstuart Elphinstone, the former British Resident at the Peshwa's court. One im-mediate consequence of the Company's takeover was a diminution in the prestige of—and a measure of official hostility to—the region's Chitpavan Brahmin community, from which the Peshwas had been drawn for over a century, and which Tilak would be born into. Chitpavans were a tiny proportion of Maharashtra's population. They constituted around 12% of Maharashtrian Brahmins, who in total accounted for merely 4–5% of the population of the region; Chitpavans numbered, therefore, no more than 80,000 or so by the 1880s (from when the first reliable figures are available).[7] The greatest proportion of Brahmins, around 37%, were *deshasthas*, hailing originally from the *desh* (or 'country'), that is, the in-land regions, whereas Chitpavans (or *konkanashthas*) originated on the Konkan coast.[8] The bulk of Maharashtra's population, meanwhile, be-longed to the Maratha-Kunbi complex of castes. Kunbi referred to any

---

[5] There is also no agreement as to the nomenclature of the Maratha 'Empire'; its unusual structure does not fit many established imperial models, and 'confederacy' is also often seen as unsatisfactory.

[6] A classic account of this from an official British perspective is James Grant Duff, *A History of the Mahrattas*, 3 vols (first published 1826; reprinted Bombay, 1864) (hereafter, Duff, *History*).

[7] According to the 1872 Census (135), Brahmins were 4.28% of the population of the Deccan, and 1.14 of the Konkan whereas 'Maharashtra' Brahmins were listed in 1881 as 5.53% of the Hindu population of the whole Presidency: *Imperial Census of 1881: Operations and Results in the Presidency of Bombay, Including Sind By J A Baines* [With Maps], 2 vols (Bombay, 1882) (here-after, 1881 Census), i, 118. The community's strength throughout India was calculated as 86,596 in 1881, listed as present in Bombay, Madras, and Baroda. See Eustace John Kitts, *Compendium of the Castes and Tribes Found in India* (Bombay, 1885), 34.

[8] 1881 Census, i, 118.

caste whose livelihood was tied to the land, whereas Maratha—a term which bore increasing importance and contestation as the century wore on—carried with it an association of an elite, and usually Kshatriya, status.[9] In practice, mobility was common within the complex. The lower castes, Shudras and *ati Shudras* ('beyond Shudras', commonly known as untouchables), formed around 10% of the population. Maharashtra was therefore predominantly Hindu, around 90% by the 1872 census.[10] But even this early census figure reflected a significant and lasting change during Tilak's early life: the historically small, predominantly Sunni, Muslim population concentrated in Deccani centres such as Aurangabad had been augmented by a surge in Muslim migration to Bombay city by that date, tens of thousands of Pathans and others being drawn to work in its booming cotton mills—an unprecedented mass Muslim presence in the region.[11]

The eighteenth century had seen a Chitpavan windfall, as following the accession of the first Chitpavan Peshwa Balaji Visvanath in 1713 they spread into the *desh* and its administrative centres, encouraged by tax breaks and grants of land to the Peshwa's caste-fellows.[12] The new administration of 1818 not only deprived them of this century-old distinction of political pre-eminence and its perquisites, however. It also viewed them in particular as a dubious quantity; and its hostile critique impacted the community's perception and bearing through the mid-century. The tone was set early. 'The Bramins [sic], who have long conducted all the business of the country, are correctly described', said Mountstuart Elphinstone himself in his report on the Company's new territories, as 'an "intriguing, lying, corrupt, licentious, and unprincipled race of people"!'[13] Grant Duff, Elphinstone's appointee as Resident to the short-lived Bhosle court

---

[9] The changing tenor of Maratha identity is mapped out in Rosalind O'Hanlon, *Caste, Conflict and Ideology: Mahatma Jotirao Phule and low Caste Protest in Nineteenth-century Western India* (Cambridge, 1985) (hereafter, O'Hanlon, *Caste*), Ch. 2.

[10] Calculated from 1872 Census, 87.

[11] The 1872 Census (89) had Bombay city at 22% Muslim; nowhere else in Konkan were they above 7%.

[12] Maureen Patterson, 'Changing Patterns of Occupation Among Chitpavan Brahmans', *Indian Economic & Social History Review*, 7/3 (January 1970); and Gordon Johnson, 'Chitpavan Brahmins and Politics in Western India in the Late Nineteenth and Early Twentieth Centuries', in Edmund Leach and S. N. Mukherjee, eds, *Elites in South Asia* (Cambridge, 1970) (hereafter Johnson, 'Chitpavan Brahmins').

[13] Mountstuart Elphinstone, *Report on the Territories Conquered from the Paishwa* (Calcutta, 1821), 7–8. Elphinstone quoted 'Mr. [William?] Chaplin', another Company servant.

at Satara, and the progenitor of the official British view of Maratha history, popularized the narrative of a polity highjacked and ruined by self-serving Brahmins.[14] He even besmirched Chitpavan ritual status, citing a Puranic creation account—which he added was carefully suppressed by the Chitpavans—in which the sage Parashuram created them from bodies washed up on the Konkan sea shore before later cursing them on account of sinfulness to be the servants of others.[15] Duff's work, translated into Marathi, exerted an influence on mid-century Marathi critiques of Chitpavans' historic failure of leadership (among other failures), notably by the polemicist Gopal Hari Deshmukh, alias Lokahitawade, whose *Shatapatre* ('one hundred letters', published between 1848 and 1850) was a landmark in social commentary in western India's emergent print culture.[16] Although in fact Elphinstone did reconcile Chitpavans to the new administration, and many retained significant positions within it, there is broad evidence that in the wake of the fall of the Peshwas in 1818, many Chitpavans left Poona and other urban centres for their ancestral lands.[17]

Historians have noted the community's heightened concern with asserting Brahminic status at the expense of the region's non-Brahmins in a series of '*gramanyas*' or 'caste disputes'—specifically refusals by the Chitpavans to carry out ceremonies for non-Brahmins according to the Vedas, the most sacred of all Hindu texts. This refusal was intended to emphasize exclusive Brahmin access to the Vedas on account of an exclusive Brahmin ritual status as *Arya* varna: all others (even those claiming the identity of the other *Arya* varnas—particularly in this case Kshatriya but also potentially Vaishya) would only have access to the Puranas, texts appropriate for mere Shudras. At stake was also a broader social authority. Chitpavan keenness to assert it did not end with the ebbing of these controversies by the 1840s: as we shall see, it would permeate Tilak's own career.[18] Yet by the beginning of that career in 1880, the

---

[14] Duff, *History*, i. 8n.

[15] Ibid. The text is found in the *Sahyadri Khanda* of the *Skandapurana*, possibly an interpolation by a Deshastha hand. The text is discussed in John Wilson, *Indian Caste*, 2 vols (Bombay, 1877), ii. 19–21.

[16] The *Bakhar Marathyanci*, a translation of Duff's work by Capt. David Capon, was published in Bombay in 1830.

[17] Kenneth Ballhatchet, *Social Policy and Social Change in Western India 1817–1830* (London, 1957), 77 ff and esp. 93–94. The 1881 Census reflected their preponderance in their ancestral lands: the Konkan held 586/1,000 Konkanasthas; the Deccan 354/1,000 (i, 118).

[18] This controversy is given a full treatment in Rosalind O'Hanlon, 'From Ritual Status to Political Conflict: Brahmans and Marathas in Southern Maharashtra Under Early East

Chitpavans, despite their fall from grace, would, as officially noted by the Bombay government, continue to follow 'almost all callings and generally with success', with a particular liking for government service, 'from the humblest village accountant, schoolmaster, and clerk, to very high and responsible posts'. It described them as a 'very frugal, pushing, active, intelligent, well-taught, astute, self-confident, and overbearing class'; its men were 'handsome', its women 'graceful and refined'.[19] For all that, and perhaps because of it, they would continue to inspire deep suspicion and hostility in some quarters of government.[20] Their traditional contentment with varied forms of employment—while it may have contributed to their lowly ritual status in the eyes of some of Maharashtra's other Brahmin communities—seems to have been a major factor in enabling them to thrive in the new, colonial milieu.[21]

Tilak's own family broadly fits into this pattern. *Khoti* (revenue collecting) rights had been vested in the family in the person of Tilak's great grandfather Keshavrao (born 1778) in his ancestral village of Chikhalgaon, whence he returned in 1818, devoting himself to religious rites.[22] His son, Tilak's grandfather Ramachandra, was born in 1802, and had a somewhat peripatetic career in the government survey department.[23] Tilak's family, like many *khots* or upper landholders, continued to act as moneylenders, as Tilak's father Gangadhar (born 1820) did.[24] But the Presidency Government's attempt to regularize the tenure system and reduce the *khots'* proprietary rights, leading to protracted legal struggles

India Company Rule', in Kenneth Ballhatchet and John Harrison, eds, *East India Company Studies: Papers Presented to Professor Sir Cyril Philips* (London, 1986); see also N. K. Wagle, 'Ritual and Change in Early Nineteenth-Century Society in Maharashtra: Vedokta Disputes in Baroda, Poona and Satara, 1824–1838', in Milton Israel and N. K. Wagle, eds, *Religion and Society in Maharashtra* (Toronto, 1987).

[19] *Gazetteer of the Bombay Presidency*, vol. 10 (Ratnagiri) (Bombay, 1881),113.
[20] Ibid. See also Temple to Lytton, 9 July 1879. G. R. G. Hambly, 'Mahratta Nationalism before Tilak: Two Unpublished Letters of Sir Richard Temple on the State of the Bombay Deccan, 1879', *Journal of the Royal Central Asian Society*, 49 (1962), 154.
[21] See Johnson, 'Chitpavan Brahmins'.
[22] To this Keshavrao later added the *mamlat* (another revenue office) of Anjanwel. See the first volume of Kelkar's biography of Tilak (in English translation): Kelkar, N. C., *Life and Times of Lokamanya Tilak*, trans. D.V. Divekar (Delhi, 1987) (hereafter, Kelkar, *Tilak*), 8–10. Kelkar, who knew Tilak for at least twenty-four years and was his key lieutenant, is the best-placed source for this information.
[23] Ibid., 11.
[24] Ibid., 22.

with the administration for Tilak's family and many others, seems to have assisted the fresh migration, which Gangadhar himself exemplified, of Chitpavans back to urban centres such as Poona, as their rural livelihoods were threatened.[25] Before turning to Tilak's own early life, we will now investigate the development of the educational milieu in Maharashtra which would shape it.

Colonial education in the Bombay Presidency

By the time Tilak entered high school, public instruction had been under what its director called 'systematic control' for thirty years.[26] In 1818, the Company had proclaimed that it would not interfere in the cultural or religious life of the people: as Duff had it, in a classic statement of its kind, 'to attempt no innovations, and to endeavour to show the people that they were to expect no change but the better administration of their own laws' was the prime policy.[27] One important emblem of this, as early as March 1818, was the distribution by Elphinstone's government of *dakshina*, a payment made under the Peshwas (and before) to Brahmins, commensurate to their learning in the Vedas and *shastras*.[28] The Poona Hindu College was established in 1821 from *dakshina* funds in further-ance of this, for the youth to 'acquire instruction in their own way' in fields such as astronomy, mathematics, and medicine.[29] This early trend was, of course, to be overshadowed by the 'Anglicizing' bent of colonial educational policy from the 1830s. In fact, this had been foreshadowed in the 1820s in western India: it was 'teaching the English language, and the Arts, Sciences, and Literature of Europe' for which Professorships were endowed at the Elphinstone Institution, founded in Bombay upon the Governor's retirement in 1827 by public subscription, subsequently

---

[25] Ravinder Kumar, *Western India in the Nineteenth Century: A Study in the Social History of Maharashtra* (London, 1968); Kelkar, *Tilak*, 8, 16–18.
[26] Bombay (Presidency) Director of Public Instruction, *Report of the Director of Public Instruction in the Bombay Presidency* (Bombay, 1859–1960 [&c.]) (hereafter, *Report DPI*), 1869–1870, 49.
[27] Duff, *History*, iii. 346.
[28] Edward Moor, *The Hindu Pantheon* (London, 1810), 376–378; Duff, *History*, iii. 355–356.
[29] Ibid.

supported by an annual subscription from the government of Rs. 22,000.[30] The triumph of the 'Anglicists' was no absolute rupture.

The stance of early British colonialism in India, and of the institutions propagated under Elphinstone in the Bombay Presidency, did, however, change with the decisions of the Company's outgoing governor-general Lord Bentinck in 1835. The minute prepared for him by Thomas Babbington Macaulay, setting out the hostility of the Anglicists to 'Oriental' knowledge, epitomizes, in its now famous words, the desire to create a class of persons 'Indians in blood and colour, but English in taste, in opinions, morals and intellect'. The Anglicists' victory was expressed in the resolution that 'all the funds appropriated for the purposes of education would be best employed on English education alone'.[31] Institutions outside the government's purview, such as the Sanskrit *pathasalas*, were able to continue according to their own scholarly norms, even in an unpropitious environment, but without official financial support. The effects of this Anglicizing turn on the Bombay Presidency's government institutions were also marked. The history of the Poona Hindu College itself shows this most clearly. In 1837 its curriculum was revised, English and Marathi introduced, and some 'branches of Hindu learning' dropped.[32] In 1851, it was amalgamated with government English schools, all placed under the stewardship of Major Thomas Candy. In 1857 it branched into a college division and a school division. This division effectively created a major new institution of higher education in Poona, which was renamed the Deccan College after its move to spacious buildings away from the centre of Poona at Yerwada, in 1864.[33] Thus by incremental developments the Poona Hindu College, established to employ *dakshina* in a more efficient manner in the 1820s, was turned into the outstanding vehicle for Western-style education in Poona, which Tilak would attend in the 1870s. The new Deccan College hosted, in its splendid neo-Gothic buildings, tuition along Western lines; and among its first principals were Edwin Arnold, future Editor-in-Chief of the *Daily Telegraph* and author

---

[30] *The Bombay University Calendar for the Year 1873–74* (Bombay, 1873 [&c.]) (hereafter, *BC*), 1873, 219.

[31] Reproduced in Baman Das Basu, *History of Education in India under the Rule of the East India Company* (Calcutta, 1922), 84–85.

[32] *BC*, 1873, 226.

[33] Ibid., 227. James Nelson Fraser, *Deccan College: A Retrospect* (Poona: The Author, 1902).

of the *Light of Asia*, and William Wordsworth, grandson of the illustrious Romantic poet.[34]

The Elphinstone College in Bombay, which Tilak would attend for his LLB, similarly arose after a separation of the high school from the existing Elphinstone Institution, and was another emblem of new educational policy.[35] The system was rationalized in a way laid out in the famous despatch from the President of the Company's Board of Control in 1854 to the governor-general Dalhousie ('Wood's Education Despatch'), which provided for a dedicated Department for Education overseeing government schools and a system of grants-in-aid for private ones, established English as a medium of instruction in high schools, and ushered in universities on the 'London' model in the Presidency capitals in 1857.[36] The newly formed University of Bombay soon added both the Deccan and Elphinstone Colleges to its list of recognized institutions. In 1859 it was determined to shift *dakshina* to the Department of Education, transforming it into fellowships, tenable at the new institutions and open to all castes.[37] In effect the *dakshina* was cannibalized to the ascendant system of English education. By 1860, a few years before Tilak began institutionalized learning, the educative environment had thus been transformed. At the moment Tilak prepared to begin his schooling in Poona, the Director of Public Instruction Alexander Grant commented on the need for Europeans to continue to be employed at the higher pedagogical level, hoping that the whole educational milieu would be 'characterised by a literary and classical spirit, such as we find in the great public schools of England'.[38] Grant also instructed, it might be noted, that a minimum standard in the vernacular should be instituted as a requirement for those joining Anglo-vernacular schools. The government's perennial concern with the state of the vernaculars is a notable feature which survived the turn to Anglicized education—neither in approach nor outcome was its policy in fact monolithic.[39]

---

[34] A list of its illustrious principals is still lovingly displayed in the College's library building.
[35] *BC* 1873, 219 ff.
[36] Earlier administration of education had taken place in the so-called General Department; its files up to the year 1860 are still held with that department's files at the MSA.
[37] *Report DPI*, 1859–1860.
[38] *Report DPI*, 1865–1866, 12, 20.
[39] Ibid., 17.

In the area of Sanskrit studies, too, the new policy meant not a turn away, but a self-consciously new approach. Modes of Sanskrit scholarship refashioned in Europe were introduced to displace the approaches of the *pandits*, a turn indeed that in Madhav Deshpande's words involved the 'transformation' of some *pandits* to Professor, which title indeed some took.[40] This direction of Sanskrit scholarship was cemented by the appointment in 1859 of Martin Haug, previously of the University of Heidelberg, and collaborator with the celebrated Christian Bunsen, as the first European Professor of Sanskrit at the Poona College, thus bringing Poona into a cosmopolitan and transnational network of Orientalist, and specifically Sanskritic, scholarship.[41] In 1863 he was followed to western India by Georg Buhler, appointed Professor of Oriental Languages at Elphinstone College, through the influence of his friend Friedrich Max Muller, whom he knew from a period of study at Oxford.[42] The *Journal of the Royal Asiatic Society of Great Britain and Ireland* referred to this 'band of Sanskrit scholars' as the 'Bombay School'.[43] It should not surprise that Tilak's earliest foray into Vedic scholarship, *Orion*, cites the work of Haug, a past luminary of his own College, and his European colleagues like Muller. By the time Tilak started school, Alexander Grant was enthusing that 'soon every High School in this department will be a school for Sanskrit scholarship'.[44] Considerable efforts were to be made in this direction, just as with vernacular education, again in part because the government in fact feared that 'the minds of all [were] being turned to English'.[45]

It was Sanskrit scholarship 'according to the European method' of which Grant spoke, and which Tilak would be schooled in. This Europeanized milieu of Sanskrit study differed in some fundamental respects from the precolonial practice of Sanskrit *pandits*, introducing

[40] Madhav M. Deshpande, 'Pandit and Professor: Transformations in the 19th Century Maharashtra', in Axel Michaels, ed., *The Pandit: Traditional Scholarship in India* (New Delhi: Manohar, 2001) (Michaels' volume hereafter, Michaels, ed., *Pandit*), 10–11.

[41] Haug was also a prominent Zend scholar: see in particular his *Sacred Writings Language and Religion of the Parsees*. Biographical information is taken from the fourth edition, ed. E. W. West (London, 1907), xvii ff.

[42] Ramaswami Iyengar, 'Dr. Buhler', in *Eminent Orientalists*, 129–146.

[43] E. J. Rapson, 'Obituary Notice: Peter Peterson', in 'Notes on the Quarter (July, August, September 1899)', *Journal of the Royal Asiatic Society of Great Britain and Ireland* (October 1899), 915–919, 921–923.

[44] *Report DPI*, 1865–1866, 29.

[45] *Report DPI*, 1867–1868, 50.

European modes of critical scholarship significantly divergent from their approaches to texts; more importantly, it sought avenues into understanding India's temporal history with which the *pandit* approach, if it might be so called, was either unconcerned, or would consider improperly heterodox.[46] An early, notable example of this is Haug's edition, at the behest of the Director of Public Instruction, of the *Aitareya Brahmana* of the Rigveda—one of two Brahmanas forming the speculative and explicatory counterpart to the Rigveda's mantras.[47] His account of the Vedas in his introductory essay is ostensibly from 'the literary point of view', and is both historical and comparative.[48] He accounts for mantras in terms of their age, commenting for instance that the 'unpolished style' and 'poor imagery' of RV 1, 162—the hymn accompanying the horse sacrifice—suggest that it relates to the period of the most primitive Vedic literature.[49] It is, moreover, by analogy with the history and literature of 'other nations' that Haug is assisted in developing his own chronology. Haug is sceptical that the earliest writings of the Vedic poets could be those of the Samhita of the Rigveda, which contains the mantras. 'Generations of poets', just as in the case of 'the art of the bards and scalds with the Celtic and Scandinavian nations, must have preceded that period to which we owe the present collection'.[50] He endeavours to find traces of the earliest outpourings, surviving in the Vedic corpus, and finds them in the simpler sacrificial formulae that must have been necessary for the rituals of the earliest times. *Nivids*—invocations of the deity—and other *yajus* used in the sacrifice are preserved in the Brahmanas, according to Haug, and have the same relation to the Vedic Samhitas as Mosaic sacrificial ritual contained in Leviticus has to the later psalms of David.[51] For good measure, he adds an extended comparison with the Chinese *Shi King*, or

---

[46] A sense of the milieu of Sanskrit scholarship before the advent of the colonial educational milieu in India is offered in Sheldon Pollock, 'New Intellectuals in Seventeenth-Century India', *The Indian Economic & Social History Review*, 38/1 (2001) 3–31; and Johannes Bronkhorst, 'Traditional and Modern Sanskrit Scholarship: How Do They Relate to Each Other?', in Michaels, ed., *Pandit*.

[47] The Vedic Brahmanas are speculations on the meaning of the mantras of the Vedas, and the ritual contained therein.

[48] Martin Haug (trans. and ed.), *The Aitareya Brahmanam of the Rigveda*, 2 vols (Bombay, 1863), i. 2 (hereafter, Haug, *Aitareya Brahmanam*).

[49] Ibid., 11, 13.

[50] Ibid., 29–30.

[51] Ibid., 32, 39.

Book of Odes.[52] More significantly, the very composition of the Vedas themselves is related to the history of other peoples, particularly the people of the Zend Avesta, the Zoroastrians, who for instance share with the Vedic people the word 'mantra'.[53] It was assumed, as we shall see, that this betokened a common origin for the Zoroastrians and their 'Aryan' cousins, the Vedic Brahmins. Haug also suggests that Brahmanas record the conflict that occasioned their separation, the Devas representing the Vedic Aryans, the Asuras the Zoroastrians.[54]

This particular work would be an important starting point for Tilak's own research thirty years later. Haug furnishes evidence from the Brahmana of the position of celestial bodies to corroborate his dating, a technique followed by Tilak in *Orion*; Haug's chronology of 2400 BC for the commencement of Vedic literature is the most expansive of those Tilak cites in researching the Vedas' antiquity.[55] For Haug, commonalities between Avestic and Vedic passages suggest the composition of some of the Vedas before the Vedic Aryans and Zoroastrians split; Tilak would argue similarly.[56] And the search for textual traces that betray an earlier historical origin for the Vedas than that moment they achieved their final form is the central object of *The Arctic Home in the Vedas*. This and other debts to Haug's work will be discussed in the next chapter.

The foremost Indian Sanskritist trained on the European pattern in the newly reformed institutions of the Bombay Presidency was Tilak's senior contemporary Ramakrishna Gopal Bhandarkar (1837–1925), an important figure in Tilak's own career. As we shall see in later chapters, Bhandarkar was both Tilak's scholarly colleague in the preparation of his two books on Vedic history, and his opponent in reformist controversy. He was educated at the Elphinstone Institution (high school and then college); then appointed Dakshina fellow in 1859 for five years at Elphinstone College and then at Poona (later, Deccan) College, teaching English, logic, philosophy, and also Sanskrit when Haug was on leave in 1864.[57] Thereafter he was a School Master in Ratnagiri between 1864 and

[52] Ibid., 41 ff.
[53] Ibid., 2.
[54] Ibid., 18.
[55] Ibid., 42, 48.
[56] Ibid., 18.
[57] R. N. Dandekar (ed.), *Ramakrishna Gopal Bhandarkar as an Indologist: A Symposium* (Poona: Bhandarkar Oriental Research Institute, 1976), 10; H. A. Phadke, *R. G. Bhandarkar* (New Delhi: National Book Trust, India, 1968) (hereafter, Phadke, *Bhandarkar*), 11.

1868, during which time he was a family friend of the young Tilak, being as we shall see close to Tilak's father, a colleague in the education department.[58] It was during this period that he produced his Sanskrit grammar for use in preparing for the BA examination, the *First Book of Sanskrit*, which Tilak himself would have used at Deccan College.[59] Bhandarkar's reputation as a Sanskritist was considerable. In 1874 he became a Fellow of the Royal Asiatic Society, and he also had the honour of giving the inaugural Wilson Philological Lectures at the University of Bombay in 1877.

The close association of Bhandarkar and Haug at the Deccan College is reflected in some of Bhandarkar's assumptions and approaches. In his philological lectures Bhandarkar is explicit regarding his debt to the European development of modern philology, 'the science of language', singling out the German philological tradition in particular to praise its 'marvellous' progress.[60] He was as adamant as others of the 'Bombay school' that the Europeanized approach differed fundamentally from earlier Indian understandings of text, in the introduction to his Sanskrit grammar crediting the historical role of the Presidency Government in effecting change. What he referred to as 'the modern critical and progressive spirit' was not present in the Poona Sanskrit College: 'the old Shastris were allowed to carry all things in their own way'; only latterly had the Government displayed a 'more enlightened zeal in favour of Sanskrit'.[61] Bhandarkar's understanding of precolonial Indian critical textual practices may, in fact, have borne the taint of European scholars' scepticism towards them; but his perception is significant, and is one, as we shall see, that Tilak shared. His Wilson Lectures demonstrate his assumption of the development of Sanskrit from the other Indo-European languages, and, conjointly, his historicization of the Vedas. The 'most ancient' variety of Sanskrit, his lectures declared, 'is found in the hymns of the Rig Veda Samhita. These were composed at different times and by different Rishis', the style of

[58] Phadke, *Bhandarkar*, 12.
[59] Second edition (November 1866, Ratnagiri). Tilak would also have used the Sanskrit grammar of his own tutor there, Franz Kielhorn.
[60] R. G. Bhandarkar, *Wilson Philological Lectures on Sanskrit and the Derived Languages Delivered in 1877* (Bombay, 1914) (hereafter, Bhandarkar, *Wilson Lectures*), 5.
[61] R. G. Bhandarkar, *First Book of Sanskrit*, 8th ed. (Bombay, 1883) (Preface to 1st ed.), v–vi.

some being 'so antiquated that they defy all attempts at interpretation', even by the Rsis of the next period.[62] His description of the reasons for the 'unintelligible' words of the hymns, even by ancient times, is philological, though for that necessarily also historical. As we shall see, the quest for historical reasons for the obscurity of the meaning of the oldest of the Vedic corpus is a central impulse behind Tilak's *Arctic Home*.

Bhandarkar's assumption of European scholarly norms coexisted, however, with a resilient and at times defensive pride in Sanskrit literature, something to which Tilak might also be related. Responding to correspondence in the pages of the *Journal of the Bombay Branch of the Royal Asiatic Society* that claimed the Mahabharata could be dated to 1521 CE, he was compelled to counter this tendency of 'most European scholars and antiquarians to modernize everything Hindu' by sketching testimonies of its existence from the time of Panini.[63] In his criticism of Haug's *Aitareya Brahmana* edition, Bhandarkar commented that 'a European, for whom the sacrificial ritual of the Brahmins can have no more than a passing interest, may be satisfied in the verbal statements of a priest and believe in them', contrasting this with textual insights generated by a more thoroughgoing engagement born of a Brahmin's deep, atavistic connection; this was echoed in his later Wilson lectures where he refers to the 'peculiar advantages' which enable him to compete with his European brother'.[64] As shall be argued in the next chapter, Tilak's own researches may have been compelled by a related notion that it was the métier of Indian scholars to lead in the construction of their own history. Bhandarkar also saw a special role for Brahmins as pioneers of scientific philology, which in his view went back to the Samhita of the Black Yajurveda, and as transmitters of Vedic texts with utmost fidelity 'even to a syllable or an accent', something again we will find reflected in Tilak's work.[65]

---

[62] Bhandarkar, *Wilson Lectures*, 16.
[63] Narayana Bapuji Utgikar and Vasudev Gopal Paranjpe (eds), *Collected Works of Sir R. G. Bhandarkar*, 4 vols (Poona, 1927–1933) (hereafter, CWRGB), vol i 80–81, ('Consideration of the Date of the Mahabharata').
[64] Ibid., 494, ('A Review of Martin Haug's Aitareya Brahmana'); Bhandarkar, *Wilson Lectures*, 2.
[65] CWRGB i, 230, ('The Veda in India').

The 'Aryan Theory': Bombay origins and impact

A major intellectual framework being propagated within this rapidly changing intellectual and educational milieu related to the idea, which we have already encountered, of the racial commonality as 'Aryans' of the peoples speaking Indo-European languages. It is one that Tilak would inherit and be preoccupied with, particularly in the earlier part of his career. As in contemporary Europe, Aryanism had a profound impact on the construction of identities in Maharashtra from the mid-century, earlier than many accounts suggest. This section will make a significant intervention in the current literature on the development of ideas concerning the 'Aryan race', by highlighting the importance of Bombay missionary-scholars in formulating and propagating the idea that an invasion of India by Aryans from the northwest in ancient times, involving a clash with the indigenous population, gave rise to the social stratifications of varna. We shall then examine the diverse polemical uses and interpretations of the notion within mid-century Maharashtra, and how these imbricated with pre-existing cultural understandings. These set the scene for Tilak's interventions in Aryan history described in the next chapter.

The language family traceable to the common ancestor of Sanskrit, Greek, Latin, Celtic, Gothic, and Persian—an ancestor conjectured by the family's discoverer, Sir William Jones, in 1786—became known as Aryan through the 1840s, a development sometimes attributed, erroneously, to Friedrich Max Muller.[66] The term *Arya* is used in the Rigveda, the oldest Vedic text, as a self-designation, contrasting the Vedic people to those with whom they differed, and similarly in the Persian Avesta; in the early nineteenth century European philologists therefore applied the term to either or both of the Sanskrit and Persian branches of the linguistic family. But by 1847 it was used to describe the whole language family, thanks to its assumed currency as the original self-designation of speakers of these other languages, otherwise known as 'Indo-Germanic' or 'Indo-European'.[67] From its inception, the 'Indo-European' or Aryan

---

[66] See William Jones, *Discourses Delivered at the Asiatick Society, 1785–1792* (originally published Calcutta 1824; London 1993), 34; Thomas Trautmann, *Aryans and British India* (Berkeley, 1997) (hereafter, Trautmann, *Aryans*), 13.

[67] See Friedrich Rosen's classification, reproduced in G. Long (ed.), *Penny Cyclopaedia of the Society for the Diffusion of Useful Knowledge*, vol. 13 (1839; London, 1833–1858), 308–309. Here it is used to connote the Persian branch in distinction to the Sanskrit one; see J. C. Prichard, 'On

language concept also assumed a racial commonality of the modern speakers of Indo-European languages; the influential ethnologist J. C. Prichard's popularizing tract *The Natural History of Man* (first published in 1843) underlined the already current sense of racial commonality, and used the infant 'race sciences' of physical archaeology and craniology to buttress rather than undermine it, referring to the 'Aryan race' in such terms apparently (and apparently unnotedly) for the first time: the 'collective body of the European nations', he says, are 'a colony, or a series of colonies, of the Arian or Indo-European race'.[68]

And it seems that it was in Bombay that the notion that a branch of this 'Aryan race' invaded India in ancient times and subjugated its indigenous population through the creation of varna—a crucial element to 'Aryan race theory'—was first developed. The idea derived ultimately from the discovery of a separate and unitary Dravidian language family in the south of India, something in which the Marathi researches of the Bombay-based Scottish missionary and member of the Bombay branch of the Royal Asiatic Society John Stevenson were pivotal.[69] And it was Stevenson—as Thomas Trautmann notes—who posited an archetypical 'two race' theory of Indian civilization as early as 1849, with the invasion and subordination by the forebears of the Brahmins of the 'rude', Dravidian-speaking aboriginals, who became the Shudras.[70] Much

the Various Methods of Research which Contribute to the Advancement of Ethnology and of the Relations of that Science to Other Branches of Knowledge', in *Report of the Seventeenth Meeting of the British Association for the Advancement of Science: Held at Oxford in June 1847* (London, 1848), 241, in which it refers to the whole language family.

[68] See the highly enlightening study in Trautmann, *Aryans*, Ch. 2, on Jones' own efforts to trace this family to one of the sons of the Biblical Noah; J. C. Prichard, *The Natural History of Man: Comprising Inquiries into the Modifying Influence of Physical and Moral Agencies on the Different Tribes of the Human Family* (London, 1843) (hereafter, Prichard, *Natural History*), 180; on first use, cf. Trautmann, *Aryans*, 172, attributing it once more to Muller. Its first use is also misrecorded in the *Oxford English Dictionary* (*OED*): the 'quotation paragraph' in the *OED* for meaning 1. b. of 'Aryan', 'Of or pertaining to the ancient Aryan people', overlooks Prichard's contribution, despite that fact that the earliest authority it does cite, Daniel Wilson's *The Archaeology and Prehistoric Annals of Scotland* (Edinburgh, 1851), itself quotes Prichard (see 161 ff and 344). 'Aryan | Arian, adj. and n.', *OED* Online, December 2012, http://www.oed.com/view/Entry/11296?redirectedFrom=aryan&, accessed 5 January 2012.

[69] John Stevenson, 'Observations on the Marathi Language', *Journal of the Royal Asiatic Society of Great Britain and Ireland*, 7/I (1843), 84–91. (Trautmann, *Aryans*, 156, ascribes quotations from it in error to a work of Stevenson entitled 'An Essay on the Vernacular Literature of the Marathas').

[70] Trautmann, *Aryans*, 157–158, citing Stevenson's articles in the Bombay branch's *Journal* between 1849 and 1851; and 197, referring to this as the 'Big Bang' theory of Indian history.

existing literature is curiously lax or unconvincing in its tracing of the 'transmission' of this idea, despite enormous general scholarly interest in the means and control of knowledge propagation in colonial India; classic and modern studies, of great sophistication, in following this interest posit an Indian readership of Muller, or simply a response to 'his' theories, and generally engage with Indian responses only later in the century.[71] Muller's capacious and celebrated scholarship, and capacity to popularize the idea within Britain itself—and later his remarkable fame within India—notwithstanding, his earlier works especially would be a curious choice to suppose a large Indian audience for; and indeed some of his earliest papers on the subject draw from and cite the work, from 1852 in the *Journal* of the Royal Asiatic Society's Bombay branch, of Stevenson—a missionary proselytizer currently active in India—describing the consequences of the ancient clash of races visible in the 'high forehead, the stout build, and the light copper colour of the Brahmans and other castes allied to them' and their 'strong contrast with the somewhat low and wide heads, slight make, and dark bronze' of the lowest.[72]

From this perspective, the dissemination of the idea of European philologists *to* India is a misleading notion, for its development and transnational conveyance did not represent distinct stages. It was developed there in its classic mid-nineteenth-century form—incorporating the 'Aryan invasion'—by missionary scholars with a keen eye for its use in anti-Brahmin, and more broadly Hindu, polemic (notwithstanding the condescending tone adopted towards the 'lower castes' in such passages of scholarship as above). This, naturally, had important implications for how ideas of Aryan race would be consumed, assimilated, and employed in India. Stevenson's own editor was John Wilson, a fellow Church of Scotland missionary, and founding deacon of the Faculty of Arts at the University of Bombay in 1857 (and for whom the Wilson Lectures were

[71] Romila Thapar, 'The Theory of Aryan Race and India: History and Politics', *Social Scientist*, 24/1–3 (January–March, 1996) (hereafter, Thapar, 'Aryan Race'), 7; Joan Leopold, 'The Aryan Theory of Race', *Indian Economic & Social History Review*, 7 (1970), 272 (hereafter, Leopold, 'Aryan Theory'); Tony Ballantyne, *Orientalism and Race: Aryanism in the British Empire* (Basingstoke, 2001) (hereafter, Ballantyne, *Orientalism*), surprising in an otherwise penetrating study of knowledge transmission and adaptation.

[72] Cited by F. Max Muller, 'The Last Results of the Researches Respecting the non-Iranian and non-Semitic Languages of Asia and Europe', in Christian Bunsen, ed., *Outlines of the Philosophy of Universal History, Applied to Language and Religion*, 2 vols (London, 1854) (hereafter, Muller, 'Last Results'), i. 342.

named). We have direct evidence in the writing of the circle of the low-caste protester Jotirao Phule (the first major Indian polemicist to employ the theme) from the 1860s that Wilson influenced his conception of the alien origin of the tyrannical Brahmins, which we will see below. Wilson outlined this in his popularizing work *India Three Thousand Years Ago* (1858): the primary object of this booklet, an extension of a lecture delivered in Bombay, was, in Wilson's words, to 'produce a work which may assist the researches of those Hindus who wish to investigate critically the origin and history of their nation'; criticizing contemporary social customs, especially caste, he describes the 'extension of the name *Shudra* to the enslaved and servile classes of the country conquered by the Aryans'.[73] Within Maharashtra, apart from through direct missionary propagation, this Aryan idea was also spread through the succeeding Sanskritists of the 'Bombay school', like Buhler and Haug, in the new educational establishments described above: the importance of this educational nexus is emphasized by considering the religious reformist societies that owed as much to it as to missionaries, like the Prarthana Samaj, and its predecessor the Paramhansa Mandali; the Mandali situated its anti-caste reformism in an 'Aryan' framework.[74]

A consequence of this immediate dissemination from within India was how immediate the impact of this notion of the Aryan race was in discussions of social relations within Indian society, from the 1860s onwards; and in particular the primacy of the Bombay missionary-scholars in developing the theory meant that its use in Maharashtra was notably early, as alluded to with Phule. The new concept spoke to existing ideas; of course, drawing so heavily on Sanskritic materials, it could scarcely not. But it must be emphasized that though *Arya* had an important set of pre-existing connotations in Marathi as in other Indo-Aryan languages, the term 'Arya' was in fact little used in Marathi before the 1840s. Borrowed from Sanskrit, in which it had come to mean 'a respectable or honourable or faithful man' (M. Monier-Williams, 1888), or one of the three higher

---

[73] (Bombay, 1858), 56.

[74] The Mandali and Samaj are discussed in Kenneth Jones, *Socio-Religious Reform Movements in British India* (Cambridge, 1990) (hereafter, Jones, *Reform Movements*), 139–141. The work of the Mandali's leading light Dadoba Pandurang, *Dharma Vivechan* ('A Discussion of Religion'), was subtitled 'A few discriminating thoughts on religion and social institutions, chiefly of the Indian Aryas, by a cosmopolitan Arya' (Bombay, 1868).

varnas, Molesworth's Marathi-English Dictionary, noting its Sanskrit origin, defined it as meaning 'Of a good family, noble, genteel, respectable', or 'Proper, suitable, becoming'.[75] This dictionary, whose second edition appeared in 1857, was the first full-scale map of the language. Surprisingly, earlier efforts in this direction, such as William Carey's *A Dictionary of the Mahratta Language* (1810) and Vans Kennedy's work of the same name, contain no reference to the word, the more surprisingly as Kennedy criticizes Carey in his preface for overloading his dictionary with superfluous Sanskrit words only intelligible to the literary.[76] Its increasingly prolific use from the 1860s in Maharashtra was demonstrably a new departure in the region's social understanding.

The connotations of *'Arya'* in early modern India are often badly misunderstood; this is a problem because it hinders our understanding of the reasons and modes for the use of 'Aryan' from the nineteenth century. One notable and far-reaching account asserts that 'it was still used mainly as a descriptive term for the descendants of the Aryas who invaded India and dominated the plains of Hindustan' before the nineteenth century, a definition derived rather from a post-mid-nineteenth-century understanding of ancient Indian history.[77] Rather than connoting the descendants of invaders, its connotation before that as referring to the Brahmin, Kshatriya, and Vaishya Varnas helped see to it that caste was read as race by Muller, Wilson, and others, in passages we have seen. This same 'traditional' sense naturally conditioned the uptake of ideas of Aryan race in India. However, it also emerged in western India into a society in which there was a Brahminic belief—or at least assertion—that only Brahmins and Shudras remained in existence on the earth during the *Kaliyuga*, current and last in the succession of yugas or ages of cosmic time. This belief played an important part in underpinning Brahmin solidarity in the face

[75] M. Monier-Williams, *A Sanskrit-English Dictionary* (Oxford, 1888); Molesworth, James, *A Dictionary, Marathi and English*, 2nd ed. (Bombay, 1857) (hereafter, Molesworth), 74.

[76] William Carey, *A Dictionary of the Mahratta Language* (Serampore, 1810); Vans Kennedy, *A Dictionary of the Maratha Language* (1824, Bombay).

[77] Ballantyne, *Orientalism*, 172. Earlier in this chapter Ballantyne cites Arthur A. Macdonell, *A Sanskrit-English Dictionary* (London, 1893), (cited at 171), a dictionary that seems to suggest its familiarity with this more modern sense in its anachronistic-seeming definition of *Aryadesh* as 'district inhabited by Aryans' (28); the only other authority Ballantyne cites in support of his description of its use in medieval and early modern India is an uncertain reference to *Hobson-Jobson: A Glossary of Anglo-Indian Words and Phrases, and of Kindred Terms [and c.]* (London 1886), 352–354 (its entry for 'Aryan' at 27 containing no corroboration in any of the pre-nineteenth-century authorities it cites).

of elite Maratha, Sonar, and Prabhu claims to Kshatriya status and Vedic rites, alluded to earlier in the case of Chitpavans. It fed off an account in the *Skandapurana* of Parashuram, an avatar of Vishnu, who in a rage destroyed all Kshatriyas in the world twenty-two times. The Brahminic notion that the varna had ceased to exist is exploited in Phule's brilliant polemical account of the origins of Indian society, inverting Brahminic 'Arya' self-identity, exclusively identifying Brahmins with invading Aryans to decry the subsequent and enduring enslavement of the noble indigenous 'Kshatriyas' as Shudras—even Parashuram is given a guise as a rapacious Aryan invader.[78]

This imposition of the new ideas of Aryan race and invasion on the older binary vision of society is visible in the writings of the Maharashtrian Brahmin M. M. Kunte, for a time, as we shall see, Tilak's headmaster. His work *The Vicissitudes of Aryan Civilisation in India* (1880) suggests that the two ideas could reinforce one another. He gives a classic account of the theory of Aryan race as it applied to India, detailing the civilizational prowess of the Aryans, their fulfilment of 'grand schemes of the invasion and occupation of India' against the primitive and hopelessly disorganized 'aborigines' (Dasyus).[79] The origin of caste is explained through the incorporation of the conquered from the Aryans' initial colonizations in the Punjab, with the 'first three classes' forming the 'essential parts of the Aryan society as a whole'.[80] But, says Kunte, 'it is distinctly asserted that the internal division of the Aryas has become obsolete'—though this distinct assertion of Kunte's appears utterly unsubstantiated.[81] Earlier in his work, he does refer to the Parashurama myth, seeing in it a historical record of a war between the Kshatriyas and Brahmins, as the former were increasingly disgruntled at Brahmin power overshadowing that of the Kshatriya rajas: but there is no reference to the expunging of the Kshatriyas from the earth; the historical reasons for the binary state of modern Indian society are not discussed.[82] One inference of this is that such a state of affairs is so elementary as to not warrant explication; the

---

[78] This work is discussed in O'Hanlon, *Caste*, 137 ff.
[79] M. M. Kunte, *The Vicissitudes of Aryan Civilization in India* (Bombay, 1880) (hereafter, *Vicissitudes*), 7.
[80] Ibid., 363.
[81] Ibid., 509.
[82] Ibid., 250.

import of what he says, in any case, is that this dichotomous map of society is given greater delineation by the theory of the Aryan invasion, giving a separate origin and racial identity to the Brahmins than to the rest of society: in this sense the theory supplies the map its key. At the same time, it is obvious that it does so only by obscuring or ignoring much of the theory's classic content. The older Brahmin assertion and the new theory are superimposed on one another here somewhat clumsily; but it is nonetheless frankly and explicitly done.

There were other contemporary features of Maharashtra's intellectual milieu from around 1850 that gave 'Aryanism' prominence. Though the Aryan theory may have been a tool of missionary attack, it thus simultaneously also offered an ideology to defend pristine Hinduism; its very use by missionaries encouraged its use to recapture a positive Aryan ideology from the hostile and racialized missionary critique of caste. Hence it was used by groups like the Arya Samaj—founded in Bombay in 1875, albeit historically more prominent in north India—and Paramhansa Mandali that sought to supersede a system of hereditary caste.[83] In the area of social reform, Aryan race ideas also fed into existing patterns of criticism of contemporary Hindu society. Increasingly such criticisms as Lokahitawade's could be viewed in the context of the new theory, and Phule would for instance implicate the 'Aryan *shastra* makers' for 'the burden of our customs and manners'—while others, like Dayananda Saraswati, the Arya Samaj's founder, blamed, conversely, a descent from Aryan values. In this sense it gave succour in its vision of the past and an explanation for India's 'descent'. For such writers propounding the idea of a 'Vedic golden age', it gave a historical reification of pre-existing notions of decline, specifically the notion of the *Kaliyuga*; and its reification rested on enumerated historical racial communities, the Aryans and their antagonists. There was also succour in membership of a prestigious club, and an offer that status could be regained, perhaps through cooperation with the British Aryans. This in particular seems to have been a response of members of the collaborative elite like Kunte. The opening motto of Kunte's work proclaims that

---

[83] A classic account of the Samaj is given in Kenneth W. Jones, *Arya Dharm: Hindu Consciousness in 19th-Century Punjab* (University of California Press, Berkeley, 1976).

There is a glorious future before the Aryas in India, now that their activities, dormant for centuries and threatening to become petrified, are
likely to be revived and quickened by the ennobling and elevating many-
sided civilization which the Western Aryas have developed, and which is
brought to bear upon them.[84]

For the Indian authors responding to the idea from the mid-nineteenth
century onwards, it was not the novelty of the idea per se that provided its
fascination and its challenge, but how its language and source materials res-
onated with their existing cultural understandings, and how this newly imagined past provided a new lens through which to view pressing issues of
the present. Its use in western India's intellectual culture after 1880 would
continue to be complex and unpredictable, however, as it retained a hold
on the imaginations of many intellectuals into the opening decades of the
twentieth century, none more so than Tilak himself, for whom it was a major
concern throughout his intellectual career.

Tilak's early life and education

Tilak was born in Ratnagiri on 23 July 1856, the last of the four children
and only son of Gangadhar Tilak and his wife Parvitabai.[85] Gangadhar's
own father Ramachandra's duties in the survey department, and consequent absences from home, devolved some of the responsibility for
raising his children upon his father; thus Gangadhar was close to his
grandfather Keshavrao.[86] Tilak's father in his turn had a directly discernible and strong influence upon Tilak's intellectual trajectory. Gangadhar
entered into Marathi school at Dabhol, and thereafter, to further his own
education, and independent of family support, he went to Poona to continue schooling.[87] His father Ramachandra seems, however, to have become apathetic after the death of his wife, Gangadhar's mother, and left
his family first for Chitrakut, and ultimately to Benares where he formally

---

[84] Kunte, *Vicissitudes*, i.
[85] Early biographical information is taken from Kelkar, *Tilak*.
[86] Ibid., 11.
[87] Ibid., 12.

renounced as a sannyasi.[88] Thus in 1837 Gangadhar had to curtail his education, and provide for his family, taking service in the education department, and returning to the Konkan to teach.[89] Tilak's father appears to have been a well-respected teacher and schoolmaster, though his career prospects would have been limited by his lack of knowledge of English. He wrote textbooks on grammar and mathematics, and his Sanskrit study was apparently advanced enough for him to go by the appellation of 'Gangadhar Shastri'.[90] He also forged a close friendship while teaching at Ratnagiri with R. G. Bhandarkar, then a teacher at Ratnagiri High School, whose testimony (via N. C. Kelkar) we have of his intellectual stature.[91] At Gangadhar's transfer from Ratnagiri to Poona to take up the role of Deputy Assistant Inspector of the subdivision in 1865, Bhandarkar referred to him as 'a repository of grammar, a store-house of the Marathi language, an exemplar of the devotion between a preceptor and his pupils'.[92] The Divisional Inspector commented approvingly in his report on the appointment of 'an old and experienced schoolmaster'.[93] Bal Gangadhar Tilak was in fact home-schooled by his father, as well as being sent to Marathi school from 1861.[94]

Tilak too was then sent to Poona, to the newly established Anglo-vernacular Poona City School, where he took his first formal steps in learning English.[95] Though according to the inspectorate English was not well taught in these 'miserably endowed' schools, there were apparently great hopes for this one.[96] A satisfactory showing in middle school was, by order of the Director of Public Instruction, in any case required for entry to government high schools like Poona High School, where Tilak studied from 1869 to 1872.[97] The opening epigram to the report of the Director of Public Instruction for the year Tilak began his high school

[88] Ibid., 12, 15.
[89] Ibid., 13.
[90] Ibid., 14.
[91] Report DPI, 1865–1866, 2, records him newly appointed Headmaster of Ratnagiri High School.
[92] Kelkar, Tilak, 27. Kelkar (38) reports that Tilak was 10 at the time; in fact, the Report DPI shows that Gangadhar took up his appointment in June 1865, when Tilak was 8 (Appendix A, 4).
[93] Report DPI, 1865–1866, Appendix A, 4.
[94] Kelkar, Tilak, 34.
[95] Ibid., 38. Poona City School opened in January 1866 (Report DPI, 1865–1866, Appendix A, 10).
[96] Report DPI, 1865–1866, Appendix A, 10.
[97] Kelkar, Tilak, 38–39. Report DPI, 1865–1866, 16.

education emphasized the duty of government to bestow 'upon the natives of India those vast moral and material blessings which flow from
the general diffusion of useful knowledge'.[98] And the high schools were
certainly taken seriously, as feeders to the University of Bombay, and
the crucible for the next generation of educated Indians. The school was
under the charge of one H. P. Jacob, whom Kelkar records as a stolid dis-
ciplinarian.[99] In 1872 it had 448 students, 391 of whom were Hindus,
37 Parsees, and 20 'others'; there were no Muslim students. All studied
English, and 271 studied Sanskrit, a notable proclivity outstripping that
at Elphinstone High School.[100] The following year it was, notably, simply
described by the Director of Public Instruction as a 'Bramin [sic] school',
in a context in which government high schools on aggregate took twice as
many Brahmins as 'other Hindoos'.[101]

The Director of Public Instruction said of the high schools of the
Presidency that

the subjects prescribed for study are easy if compared with those taught
in the higher classes of an English public school, but difficult for an
Indian High School with mixed classes and with a foreign language as
the medium of instruction.[102]

The tenor of high school education is best gauged by the University
Matriculation examination, which it was their task to prepare boys for,
and upon which they were judged.[103] Candidates were examined in languages, mathematics, and general knowledge (incorporating various
branches of the arts and sciences).[104] The paper that Tilak sat on 'English

[98] *Report DPI*, 1869-1870, quoting the despatch of the Court of Directors of the East India
Company, dated 19 July 1854.
[99] Kelkar, *Tilak*, 40. *Report DPI*, 1866–1867 notes he was a graduate of Worcester College,
Oxford.
[100] *Report DPI*, 1871–1872, Appendix H, 3.
[101] *Report DPI*, 1872–1873, 53; *Report DPI*, 1869–1870, Appendix A, 84 (at government high
schools: 810 'Brahmins'; 2 'Cultivators'; 393 'other Hindoos'; 25 'Mohammedans'; 405 'Parsees'.
There was a 'very small' number of lower-caste children among the 'other Hindoos'). There was
also in the *Report DPI* for 1871–1872 information on the social position of the Poona High
School boys' parents: 'persons of property: 171; professional persons: 16; government officials: 37; private clerks: 144' (68).
[102] *Report DPI*, 1872–1873, 54.
[103] See comments in *Report DPI*, 1865–1866, 16.
[104] *BC*, 1873, 44.

Grammar, Idiom and Etymology' in November 1872—for which one of the examiners was William Wordsworth—required considerable facility, not to mention a certain Anglicized cultural familiarity.[105] Unseen passages for paraphrase were taken from William Cowper's 'On the Receipt of his Mother's Picture' and Thomas Campbell's 'The Soldier's Dream'; Tilak then had to, among other things, 'quote and illustrate the law of the sequence of tenses' and compose on a choice of topics, before giving the etymology of a series of words that included—perhaps appropriately—'viceroy', 'tribulation', 'retaliate', and 'emancipate'. In Elementary History and Geography, Tilak similarly was encouraged to display a historical consciousness allocating a prominent place to the great events of Western history.[106] A short account was required of two historical lives, from Pompey, Wolsey, the Duke of Marlborough, Themistocles, and Mahmood of Ghuznee, and a sketch 'of the reign of one of the sovereigns who ruled in England between the "Union of the Roses" and "Union of the Crowns"'. The history of colonialism itself, was, of course, not neglected: 'Under the rule of what Governor General before 1840', asked the next question, 'were the limits of British power in India most extended?' A list of the districts brought under British Government by the governor-general selected was required, 'and some account of the grounds of annexation'. The tendency to rote learning was underlined by the requirement for map-drawing, with mountains, rivers, and chief towns, of Australia, The Madras Presidency, or Ireland (a list that is also revealingly exclusively imperial), and to fashion a list of the 'principal cotton-producing countries of the world'. In Natural Science, Tilak had for example to name the 'three chief forces of nature', and the differences between them, and to name the essential constituents of the earth's atmosphere, with their relative proportions by volume.[107] Even at this stage, Tilak must also have demonstrated some knowledge of celestial phenomena, important in his later output: he was required to state the distances, in millions of miles, of the several planets from the sun, and to explain the 'general form of the Orbits of the planets' and the cause of the 'appearances termed eclipses'.[108]

---

[105] Ibid., Examination Papers appendix, v–vi.
[106] Ibid., vii–viii.
[107] Ibid., lix.
[108] Ibid., lx.

Tilak himself is recorded by his biographers to have been a head-strong and obstinate school student, with little patience for the formalities of classroom learning, or exam preparation.[109] Indeed, Tilak left the school for a short time on account of differences with Jacob, returning when it was taken over by M. M. Kunte, whose views on Aryan history discussed above may well have been present in embryo during this period.[110] Nonetheless, he was one of twenty-five boys from the school who passed the University of Bombay's matriculation examination, just four months after the death of his father, going on to attend the affiliated Deccan College for his undergraduate studies, reading for the BA degree between 1873 and 1876.[111]

Tilak was one of forty-nine new young men at the Deccan College in 1873. There were in all 110 students at the College: 96 Brahmins, 7 lower-caste Hindus, 6 Parsees, and 1 European student; there were again no Muslim students listed. Most of the students were apparently 'sons of Government officials or of clerks of Native States'.[112] The acting Principal Franz Kielhorn expressed himself, in a blistering report for the following year, unhappy generally about the state of the College and higher education in the Presidency. The standard of English was one complaint; further, the 'teaching staff of the college is not in every respect as complete or as perfect as it might be'; and too many were failing at exams, 'the real cause' of which was that

> the colleges in this country are too crowded with a number of students who in no other country would aim at, and who certainly are no way fitted to receive a University education

and who should rather be content with an education without such 'sounding titles', instead of leaving useless yet 'full of their own importance' if they were 'by chance successful' in obtaining a degree.[113] The existing structure of the university board and affiliated colleges 'should

---

[109] See, for instance, D. V. Athalye, *The Life of Lokamanya Tilak* (Poona, 1921) (hereafter, Athalye, *Tilak*), 5.
[110] Kelkar, *Tilak*, 40. *Report DPI*, 1871–1872, Appendix A, 64: from October 1871 it was under Kunte's direction, after Jacob left through sickness in September.
[111] *Report DPI*, 1872–1873, Appendix A, 21. Kelkar, *Tilak*, 42.
[112] *BC*, 1873, 41–42.
[113] *Report DPI*, 1874–1875, Appendix A, Kielhorn's report (extracts), 140–141.

be done away with', and there should be 'in this Presidency, a University' which should be 'in reality, what at present we have only in name, a seat of learning'.[114] It is hard to gauge the judiciousness of Kilehorn's remarks regarding the still young institution. One interesting insight comes from a petition of '144 students at Deccan College representing the need of a better staff of Professor' there in March 1876, as Tilak was finishing his degree.[115] The students complained that the Elphinstone Institution, as well as having better-off students, had all advantages in quality of academic staff; a British 'civilian' (referring to career government employees) with an 'indistinct voice' was singled out for failing to properly teach them Wordsworth's 'Prelude'. Tilak's name does not appear among the sixty-six students who signed it, unlike his future colleague V. S. Apte and his great (though disputatious) friend and colleague Gopal Ganesh Agarkar. Student dissatisfaction, then as now, was more reasonable at some times than others; the College handed down rustications leading to a craven student apology. The Director of Public Instruction wrote to the Education Department scorning the students as 'absurd', and suggesting that the poor results of recent examinations reflected more upon them than the staff: the very wording of the petition demonstrated that 'their knowledge of English was so slight that they could not understand the language of an educated English gentleman'.[116] He gave a roll call of the staff's qualities, noting among others that Chhatre was a 'teacher of great experience', and that Kielhorn had a 'European reputation': these two we shall shortly meet as Tilak's own tutors.[117] The College was not loved by the Director, who complained in any case that it was maintained by the government at great cost 'almost solely for the convenience of Deccan Brahmins' (and marginalia added that no Parsees or Christians signed the petition): a good economy could be effected by closing it and diverting the resources to 'institutions of a more generally useful character'.[118] What can be said about this spat is that the 'European' staff certainly struggled to maintain the respect of the students, and that this was reciprocated; but neither

[114] Ibid., 141.
[115] MSA ED 1876, vol. 7. The petition was sent on 18 March 1876, apparently improperly, directly to the Government of Bombay. The students forgot to date it and sent a note of 19 March to this effect to the Educational Secretary.
[116] Ibid., Chatfield to Gonne, 28 April 1876.
[117] Ibid.
[118] Ibid.

typical student grievances nor the bureaucracy's haughty response fairly reflected on the quality of the educational environment. Tilak himself, though, remained not an ideal student: his biographers note that he had more interest in swimming and gymnastics in his first year than studying, and, indeed, he is listed as not having passed the First Examination for his degree at the end of the year; he eventually did so in 1875.[119] Nonetheless, Tilak achieved first class results in his final examinations, in his chosen subjects of Sanskrit, Dynamics and Hydrostatics, Analytical Geometry, and Differential and Integral Calculus, his degree being conferred during the academic year 1876–1877.[120]

In terms of the milieu of Sanskrit studies Tilak encountered at the College, ostensibly the most important was the Superintendent of Sanskrit studies, who was also Acting Principal for Tilak's entire time there, Franz Kielhorn, a noted Sanskritist whose contribution was eventually recognized in his being decorated a Companion of the Indian Empire (C.I.E.).[121] Kielhorn was a product of the University of Leipzig, where he took his PhD at the age of just twenty-one, before assisting Monier Monier-Williams at Oxford in the preparation of his Sanskrit-English Dictionary.[122] Kielhorn arrived in India to work for the Education Department in 1866, just seven years after Haug had arrived in Poona, and stayed in the Presidency until 1881; *The Mahratta* declared warmly upon his leaving for Gottingen that the Deccan College would miss him.[123] In conjunction with Buhler at Elphinstone, he founded, soon after his arrival in India, the Bombay Sanskrit Series, and cooperated in the search for and collection of Sanskrit manuscripts in western India.[124] His Sanskrit grammar, first published in 1870 and intended for students of the BA course, ran through four editions, and in fact became along with Bhandarkar's a 'standard guide for those who seek an introduction to the language according to the usual Western method'.[125]

---

[119] Athalye, *Tilak*, 9. *BC*, 1874, 186, 249; *BC*, 1876, 195.

[120] *BC*, 1877, 191, 314.

[121] J. F. Fleet, '[Obituary Notices:] Franz Kielhorn, C.I.E.', *Journal of the Royal Asiatic Society of Great Britain and Ireland* (July 1908), 159–163 (hereafter, 'Kielhorn Obituary').

[122] Ibid.

[123] *Mahratta*, 9 October 1881.

[124] Kielhorn's communication to the DPI suggesting the series is reproduced in *Report DPI*, 1856–1866, Appendix H.

[125] Kielhorn 'Obituary'; Franz Kielhorn, *A Grammar of the Sanskrit Language*, 3rd ed. (Bombay, 1888), vii (Preface to 1st ed., 1870).

His first efforts in the study of such *vyakarana* (grammar) culminated in an edition with translation, in the Sanskrit Series, of Nagojibhatta's *Paribhashandusekhara* (1868–1874), a work whose preface reiterated the decline of 'that traditional learning which we can so ill dispense with in the interpretation of the enigmatic works of Hindu antiquity'.[126] For all this, though, Kielhorn could also be dismissive of what he saw as the ahistoricism of the 'traditional' pandit approach to textual analysis. The significance of his views would have been to have put the 'laws of the critical art' at the forefront of the minds of his students, with its emphasis on the historical construction of texts.[127]

Another significant figure was Keru Laxuman Chhatre, Professor of Mathematics and Natural Philosophy. Apart from stimulating Tilak's mathematical interests, Chhatre had a strong interest in astronomy; previous to taking the post, he had been employed at Coloba Observatory from 1851, and brought out a Marathi handbook on *Siddhanta* called the *Graha-sadhanachi-koshtake*.[128] Astronomy was a subject that Tilak would return to again and again, most obviously in his attempt to calculate the date of the Vedas from astronomical references within them in his *Orion*, upon which, as we shall see in the next chapter, Chhatre had a direct influence. Tilak also turned to astronomical calculations in *The Arctic Home* in an attempt to calculate geological time; and he reprised some of the concerns of *Orion* with a full-blown study, unpublished at his death, of the *Vedanga Jyotisha*. A few years previous to *Orion*'s publication, Tilak was on the board of management of the observatory that the Chhatre memorial committee resolved to put up in his memory.[129] Chhatre appears to have been well esteemed, being given the honour of Rao Bahadur in 1877. *The Mahratta* under Tilak's editorship in its first months published Chhatre's research on rainfall.[130] N. C. Kelkar, Tilak's long-serving lieutenant, referred to Chhatre as Tilak's 'guru'.[131]

---

[126] F. Kielhorn (ed.), *Paribhashandusekhara of Nagojibhatta*, 2 vols, (Bombay 1868–1874), i, xxiv–xxv.

[127] A. Grant Bart, *Catalogue of Native Publications in the Bombay Presidency Up to 31st December 1864*, 2nd ed (Bombay, Byculla, 1867), 25.

[128] Rajesh Kochhar and Jayant Narlikar, *Astronomy in India: A Perspective* (New Delhi, 1995).

[129] *TOI*, 13 June 1887.

[130] 8 May 1881.

[131] See 'Character Sketch' of Tilak by Kelkar contained in N. C. Kelkar (ed.), *Full and Authentic Report of the Tilak Trial (1908)* (Bombay, 1908) (hereafter, Kelkar (ed.), *Trial (1908)*), 3; the *Journal of the Poona Sarvajanik Sabha* published his work on sun-spots and the rain (Kelkar, *Tilak*, 54).

What we can say from the evidence of these figures, forming the central element of Tilak's pedagogical milieu in the Deccan College, is that important features of his published output, discussed in the next chapter, can be traced back to them. The critical and self-consciously historical approach exemplified by Kielhorn in particular marked Tilak's own Sanskritic researches, and gave him an appreciation of the labours of European philologers and Sanskritists. Other figures that filled the Deccan College would have made for a stimulating intellectual atmosphere. William Wordsworth, a graduate of Balliol College, Oxford, was its Principal upon Tilak's arrival (though he was Acting Principal of Elphinstone College). H. Batty, BA, CS, educated at Christ's College Cambridge and at Lincoln's Inn, was Acting Professor of History and Philosophy, having served in Bombay as an assistant collector and magistrate.[132] From among its Fellows, Edward Hamilton Aitken, Latin reader, the son of a Free Church of Scotland missionary, would become a prominent naturalist and Anglo-Indian commentator. In terms of Tilak's contemporaries there, his closest friendship is said by his biographers to have been with G. G. Agarkar, who joined him in founding the New English School, *Kesari* and *The Mahratta*, and the Deccan Education Society, before parting ways with Tilak in the late 1880s on account of an unbridgeable attitude to reform, Tilak resisting the social change that Agarkar would advocate.[133] Agarkar only passed matriculation in 1875, and attended from 1876, at the same time Tilak enrolled in law school in Bombay, though they lived together at Deccan College later while Tilak was still studying for the LLB.[134] It appears that Vishnushastri Chiplunkar, another collaborator in the School and the newspapers from 1880 was a major influence. Chiplunkar was a graduate student when Tilak arrived.[135] The son of Krishnashastri, Assistant Professor of Marathi in Poona College, Vishnushastri started the Marathi monthly *Nibandhamala* ('garland of essays'), in 1874. Chiplunkar's contribution is such that it is held that his writing heralded 'a new era in … the intellectual life of Maharashtra generally', transforming Marathi prose into

---

[132] *The India List and India Office List* (1905) (London, 1905).
[133] Athalye, *Tilak*, 18–19. And see the 'discussion' reprinted between them in Kelkar, *Tilak*, Appendix I.
[134] *BC*, 1876, 234; Kelkar, *Tilak*, 56.
[135] *BC*, 1873, 228.

a vehicle of political and literary expression, and pioneering the essay form in Marathi in the process.[136] Tilak was likely in his shadow at the beginning of his career. S. G. Jinsiwale, a Fellow during Tilak's time there, would go on to have an important role as an 'orthodox' ally in Tilak's politics in the 1890s, and assist Tilak in preparing both *Orion* and *The Arctic Home in the Vedas*.[137] He too was encouraged by K. L. Chhatre, who had awarded him essay prizes while at school in Ahmednagar, and shared Tilak's enthusiasm for mathematics.[138] Moreover, he like Tilak would go on to publicly argue heterodox points like the '*paurushey*', or human, origins of the Vedas; he and Tilak were both figures whose ostensible orthodoxy—contrasting with, for example, Bhandarkar—coexisted with the acceptance of temporal accounts of Vedic history.[139]

In 1876 Tilak enrolled at the Government Law School, also an affiliated College of the University of Bombay, reading for the Bachelor of Laws (LLB) degree.[140] The School had been founded by a subscription raised by the inhabitants of Bombay in November 1852, and the government contributed 700 Rs. per mensem to it, *inter alia* to maintain its Professorships. It was a legal training school, and Tilak's LLB (Second Class) would of course have enabled him to practise. Tuition was provided in Jurisprudence and the Roman Civil Law; Personal Rights and Status and the Law of Succession; the Law of Property, Contracts, and Torts; and the Law of Evidence, of Crimes, and of Procedure, Civil and Criminal. Of interest here is the set text on Hindu law, by Thomas Strange, former Chief Justice of Madras: *Hindu Law, Principally with Reference to Such Portions of It as Concern the Administration of Justice, in the King's Courts, in India* (1830).[141] Its dedication, to King George IV, described Indians as

---

[136] Kusumawati Deshpande and M. V. Rajadhyaksha, *A History of Marathi Literature* (New Delhi, 1988), 64.

[137] See Chapter 5 for his association with Tilak in the Shivaji memorialization; and Cashman, *Myth*, for his role in the Ganapati festival. His relation to Tilak's texts is also discussed in Chapter 2. It is not clear what Jinsiwale's teaching responsibilities were, but Kelkar notes that Sanskrit was among them. Kelkar, *Tilak*, 44–46.

[138] Narayan Krishna Gadre, *Pro. Shridhar Ganesh Jinsiwale Yanche Trotak Charitra* (Poona, 1903) (Biographical sketch of Prof. S. G. Jinsiwale), 6–7.

[139] Ibid., 24–25.

[140] *BC*, 1876 listed Tilak as being at the Government Law School as a candidate law student. In *BC*, 1877 and *BC*, 1878, he was listed as a senior law student.

[141] *BC*, 1876, 33.

by nature a gentle, and historically an interesting race, gratefully acknowledging your mild rule; and, in return for attachment, suppli-
cating only, together with protection, the preservation to them of their
Institutions, (however superstitiously deduced,)—subject to as little
change, as may be consistent with its stability.[142]

The work covered the areas of Hindu law with which the Company had
been preoccupied. The area of principle interest in terms of Tilak's future
public statements on 'Hindu law' is that concerning marriage. Strange's
account of this is not only significant background to those statements,
but is revealing of the whole work's conception of Hindu law. 'By no
people is greater importance attached to marriage, than by the Hindus',
it declared.[143] As to 'the proper time' for this, on the authority of Culluca
Bhatta, this 'precedes puberty', Manu having enjoined marriage by the
age of 8 for girls for the betrothment, after which she should stay in the
care of her family 'till her maturity admits of her husband claiming her;
of which it is the province of the mother to give notice'.[144] Strange goes on
to say how 'revolting' is 'the idea of an engagement of this nature being
finally contracted thus early'.[145] A promise of betrothment, meanwhile,
can be broken only with good reason: 'according to Hindu supersti-
tion', the presence of unfavourable auspices when trying to find a 'prosperous hour for the wedding', such as a 'flight of birds, or the chirping of
a lizard', would constitute such. 'Such is the law', Strange declares, citing
H. T. Colebrooke's digest of the opinions of *pandits*; 'but so obsolete is it
in practice, that it may be considered as a dead letter, upon which no pro-
ceeding could be instituted at the present day, with any hope of success'.[146]

In its citation of the ultimate authority of Manu, the supposed fount of
Hindu law, and the informant of Hinduism's true and original customs,
this is a classic account of Anglo-Indian jurisprudence (though it com-
bines this with a tacit and pragmatic acknowledgement of the importance of custom in defining the structure of legality). The text-anchored

---

[142] First published as Sir Thomas Strange, *Elements of Hindu Law Referable to British Judicature in India* (London 1825), frontmatter.
[143] Ibid., 34.
[144] Ibid., 35–36.
[145] Ibid., 36.
[146] Ibid., 36–37.

and concrete colonial notion of Hindu law is well documented. Though the condescension and superficiality of Strange's account makes it hard to believe Tilak was greatly influenced by his reading, the fundaments of this work, an accepted reading of the Indic legal tradition by European Sanskritists, formed an important reference point, and an observable anchor of legal culture in late colonial India. As for Tilak, he was in the course of his career not only an instructor on Hindu law (a useful augmentation of his income), but a prominent voice on Hindu law as it related to the reform of Hindu society, principally through his part in the age of consent controversy.

Tilak passed the LLB in 1879, and would soon embark on his career with the Deccan Education Society, and work on the newspapers *Kesari* and *The Mahratta*, the latter as editor.[147] It is to these, along with the rest of his written output, we shall now turn, to offer an overview of it.

---

[147] *BC*, 1880, 240.

2

Tilak as a Writer

Tilak's writing career lasted from 1881, when he became the first editor of the newly founded weekly English-language *Mahratta* newspaper and a contributor to its twin, the weekly Marathi-language *Kesari*, through to the final six months of his life in 1920, when he was still contributing to them both. He also wrote three full-scale scholarly works published during his lifetime, two in English (*The Orion: Or Researches into the Antiquity of the Vedas* and *The Arctic Home in the Vedas*) and one in Marathi (*Srimad-Bhagavadgita-Rahasya*, or 'Secret Import of the Bhagavad Gita'), and a number of other projects in draft, all apparent ones being published posthumously. His collected works come to eight volumes, published between 1974 and 1995: in addition to his three major works, they contain over a thousand articles and statements directly attributed to him.[1] Tilak was also editor of *The Mahratta* for six years, and *Kesari* for nineteen. Tilak's own written interventions during these years show the individuality of his voice; but the papers' general content over the period cannot of course be isolated from them. This chapter will give an overview of Tilak's entire written output and editorial career. It will take *Mahratta* first, describing its rationale and agenda in January 1881 and how this was realized in its first eighteen months, and again between 1891 and 1896, under Tilak. It will look at the general tone, policy, and coverage of the paper, with an eye to Tilak's priorities and stances on major contemporary controversies. It will also survey his entire (relatively small) attributed personal output in *Mahratta* during, between, and after his stints as editor.[2] Turning to

---

[1] The eighth volume is rare, most libraries outside India stocking the series merely holding the first seven volumes published between 1974 and 1976.

[2] This work, specifically, will assume all editorials during his editorships, at the least, express his broad views on specific questions, even if we cannot assert direct authorship (though he is recorded by many, including Kelkar, as habitually dictating *Kesari*'s editorials from the veranda of his Poona wada). Beyond this, attribution is difficult, as will be discussed further below, in relation to *Kesari* specifically. The stylistic and topical criteria outlined by Y. S. Kanitkar, SLT 8 Preface, in selecting Tilak-authored *Mahratta* articles for inclusion in that volume is insufficient

The Thought of Bal Gangadhar Tilak. Robert E. Upton, Oxford University Press. © Robert E. Upton 2024.
DOI: 10.1093/oso/9780198900658.003.0003

Kesari, in which his directly attributable writings were more numerous, this can more fully attest to Tilak's thought throughout his career, although original issues have been consulted, where possible, in order to form a view on *Kesari*'s more general approach during his editorship (as will also be apparent through citations in other chapters).[3]

The chapter will then give an account of Tilak's three main published Indological works, the grandest of his intellectual outputs: *The Orion, The Arctic Home,* and *Gita Rahasya*.[4] It will sketch out their content, and investigate Tilak's aims with reference to his contexts. These comprise his intellectual context, including his influences and authorities from within his circle; and, more broadly, his social and political context (including the development of his own career). We have evidence that Tilak was engaged in preparing materials for scholarly publications from 1889 through to the year before his death.[5] We are therefore concerned with a period that spans Tilak's entire career apart from its first eight years; scholarly investigation is something that Tilak graduated onto after establishing his reputation within Maharashtra, and something that he never again forsook. The consideration of the major works side by side with Tilak's journalism is useful. It assists in answering a central question regarding the relevance of the former to his political career; whether

to account for all, but I judge it unlikely in those instances to have incurred false positives. They can therefore be discussed here fairly safely.

[3] The poor state of preservation of the original surviving *Kesari* hard copies from Tilak's lifetime, and the microfilms of them, renders the use of the SLT's 1970s reprints of the attributed articles preferable in any case; where possible, comparison has been made with originals held at the Centre of South Asian Studies, Cambridge. SLT 3, 4, and 5 contain what is reckoned by the editors 'beyond doubt' to have been Tilak's, based on Kelkar's collection, and articles indicated by Kelkar and others to be by Tilak's hand (see description in SLT 8, Preface). There is no reason to doubt these inclusions; indeed the greater danger is inattentiveness to other articles from his editorship not included therein, hence the scrutiny of the original *Kesari* issues. In SLT, *Kesari* articles are divided into 'political' (vol. 3), those on the 'New Leadership' of Tilak (vol. 4), and those on social, cultural, and historical themes (vol. 5). These are somewhat crude divisions, and they have not been used to structure this work.

[4] There are some other incomplete or posthumously published projects of Tilak's which are of less importance to us here. While imprisoned in Mandalay Tilak worked on three texts besides the *Gita Rahasya*: a fully-fledged periodization of Vedic literature in his 'Vedic Chronology' of which only the first two chapters were completed, and an essay on the 'Vedanga Jyotisha', the 'small tract on astronomy appended to the Vedas', were published posthumously as *Vedic Chronology and Vedanga Jyotisha* (Poona, 1925) (hereafter, '*Vedic Chronology*'). Also reprinted in the same volume is his essay of 1917 on 'Chaldean and Indian Vedas'. He also while in Mandalay composed a Sanskrit commentary on the Brahmasutra, *Brahmasutra vriti* (Pune, 1947).

[5] *Orion* iii; his final publication was a small paper published in 1917: see his *Vedic Chronology*, 123 ff. Correspondence on this paper carried on until 1919.

they were in effect politics carried on by other means, or were recondite contemplations from outside the political fray. They are indeed often considered the product of his retreat to apolitical contemplation, twice enforced through imprisonment.[6] This only encourages their discussion in an afterword to treatments of his career.[7] Yet Stanley Wolpert's classic account still suggests that all three works, despite appearing to be 'devoid of political content or implications', were 'more significant contributions to the literature of Indian nationalism than to Indology'.[8] The view of these works as apolitical cannot stand; yet they are both practical and scholarly statements, and a narrowly instrumentalist interpretation of Tilak's scholarship does not account for it well. Equally, our understanding of Tilak as a political thinker would remain unfortunately narrow through maintaining a dichotomy between more explicitly political statements and his reflections on ancient history and Hindu dharma.

Before embarking on a study of the newspapers, it should be emphasized that this chapter provides a corrective to the standard assumption that both were essentially 'Tilak's newspapers' all through his career, something which betrays a lack of understanding of the circle Tilak emerged from and worked within in Poona, but also shows the effect of his historical celebrity in hindering a nuanced picture of authorship and historical agency.[9] *Mahratta* in particular has been assumed to bear his stamp even when its editorship was out of his hands and acting divergently to his wishes.[10] This is doubly unfortunate because, as we shall see, Tilak's Marathi journalism exhibits differences in outlook and object than that in English, something occluded by this approach. N. C. Kelkar, as is well known, undertook the editorship of *Mahratta* in March 1896, after which Tilak never edited it again.[11] And Kelkar himself points out that his namesake, Professor Vasudevrao Kelkar, had edited it from Tilak's first imprisonment (for libel) in 1882 until Tilak finally took over full financial and editorial control of both newspapers on 3 September 1891.[12]

---

[6] Radhakrishnan's account in *Eminent Orientalists* provides the classic statement of this.
[7] Masselos, 'Tilak', is a very clear example.
[8] Wolpert, *Tilak and Gokhale*, 63.
[9] This question will be examined further in Chapter 6.
[10] Rao, *Foundations*, seriously errs in studying Tilak's whole career almost solely from *The Mahratta*.
[11] (17 March). Gole, *Kelkar*, 12.
[12] Kelkar, *Tilak*, 114, 184; see also *100 Years of the Kesari* ([1981?] [s.l./Pune?]: [s.n./Kesari-Mahratta Trust?]).

Before this time, *Kesari* under Tilak and *Mahratta* under Vasudevrao Kelkar were described as 'two yokehorses breaking loose and attacking each other'.[13] Tilak of course as proprietor, and as a born political propagandist, would always have maintained an influence over his staff after September 1891. Yet even the threat to sack N. C. Kelkar, and Kelkar's own resignation in the face of working difficulties at *Mahratta*, are as much an emblem of tensions and divergences as they are of vice-like control.[14] It should be noted that *Mahratta* was only under Tilak's direct editorship from January 1881 to July 1882, and September 1891 to March 1896, a total of six years over his forty-year career. He was editor of *Kesari* meanwhile from October 1887 (when he took over joint financial control of that paper) to June 1897, the time of his second imprisonment, this time for seditious writings in that paper; and from July 1899 to June 1908, the date of his final sedition conviction and exile.[15] Upon his return, he edited neither again.

Mahratta

Together with *Kesari*, *Mahratta* was conceived amongst a graduate collective in Poona in 1880. Tilak had joined hands soon after the completion of his LLB with his friend G. G. Agarkar and their slightly senior contemporary Vishnushastri Chiplunkar in founding the New English School in 1880, very likely a dream of Tilak and Agarkar during their college days. Soon after, they were joined by M. B. Namjoshi and V. S. Apte, another friend from the Deccan College. The school was independent of government, and an ethos of cultural self-renewal was an important part of its objective. In furtherance of this, the colleagues soon decided to start two weekly newspapers in addition, one in Marathi and one in English, printed at an independent press they would establish themselves (Tilak recalled how he carried the type-cases on his shoulders to their new home in Budhwar Peth in Poona).[16] *Mahratta* began on Sunday 2

---

[13] Kelkar, *Tilak*, 184

[14] Rao, *Foundations*, 39. See also Tilak to Kelkar, November [?] 1907, SLT 7, 679.

[15] Kelkar, *Tilak*, 109, 184; *100 Years* [unpaginated]. Tilak took over on 25 October 1887 and stopped editing upon his arrest in 1897; he began again on 4 July 1899, as is clear from the editorial of that date. He finally ceased editing upon his 1908 arrest.

[16] Kelkar, *Tilak*, 105–106.

January 1881, with Tilak as its acknowledged editor, although it did not proclaim its editorship, simply anonymously stating that it was produced 'for the proprietors at the Arya-Bhushan Press'.[17] It should not be imagined that Tilak was at this point foremost among this group as a writer: Chiplunkar, as we have seen, was already among the most noted men of letters in Maharashtra, through his periodical *Nibandhmala*; Namjoshi was an established editor, of the *Deccan Star*, thenceforth incorporated into *Mahratta*. Reflecting on *Mahratta*'s output in the 1920s, N. C. Kelkar claimed that 'forbearance, coolness of temper, liberalism in outlook and chivalry in manners' was its style; its English medium was its 'surety for good behaviour and gentle comment'.[18] This is doubtful. One of its main purposes was to represent the opinion of its proprietors directly to government, rather than them relying on their translation of the Marathi *Kesari*, and government from time to time disagreed strongly with Kelkar's benign reading, as we shall see.[19] But *Mahratta* never engaged government's ire as much as *Kesari* (and specifically never led to sedition convictions for Tilak, unlike the latter). It was also intended to inform opinion and raise political awareness among the educated classes, and its very first issue chided its 'dry and insipid' local contemporaries like *Native Opinion*. Less provincial and vernacular in content than *Kesari*, *Mahratta*'s coverage was broad and international.[20] Its first issues had a circulation of 850 copies, with 6 rupees 6 annas annual subscription in town, 8 rupees in moffusil compared to the flat 1 rupee with 10 annas postal charge for *Kesari*.[21] The opening editorial served as its prospectus.[22] The 'inevitable tendency of progress' observable in 'all countries communities and ages' it grandly declared, meant people were ready for a new response to their writers: clearly, it conceived a significant position for its efforts. It also noted, though, how it echoed the patriotic cooperation of contemporaries in Madras, Bengal, and the Punjab and the Northwest Frontier, thus filling a 'Deccan gap'. The dangers it

---

[17] Ibid., 111; *Mahratta*, 2 January 1881.
[18] Kelkar, *Tilak*, 111.
[19] The Bombay government required information about all periodical publications of the 'native press' and examined copies of them, with excerpts translated as necessary and compiled in the Reports on the Native Press in the Bombay Presidency (hereafter RNPB), held at IOR/L/R/5.
[20] Kelkar, *Tilak*, 111.
[21] RNPB 15 January 1881 (its first mention).
[22] 'Ourselves', *Mahratta*, 2 January 1881, 1.

sought to meet were that 'stubborn and thoughtless governors' had for a time 'weakened and disgraced' the good government of Queen Victoria; its concerns were all points that involved the 'longevity of the benign British rule'. The historical connotations of its name did not betoken unthinking reaction. Neither, despite being 'in the hands of a few educated Brahmins of Poona', was it to be a 'sectarian journal', although it clumsily underlined the point by protesting that it would extend its sphere to 'alien communities' from time to time. Its duties were interpretation and petition, instruction and advocacy. Communication with government was central: 'foreigners are not likely to know exactly what the wants and wishes of the ruled are', therefore *Mahratta* would endeavour to point out how the yoke can press 'as little as possible'. The 'multifarious evils' to be combatted included: the *ryotwari* land tenure system, which beggared agriculturalists and had 'ruined Madras'; heavy transit duties, which had broken Indian manufacturers; the destruction of municipal institutions which had given continuity to public life; the burdensomeness of new ones, and of 'grinding taxations'; the destruction of the 'native aristocracy', those patrons of agricultural improvements and consumers of goods; the 'exotic system of English law', which had 'most painfully checked the growth of native society'; and, ultimately the paper's most controversial cause during Tilak's time as editor, the destruction of native states: it concluded here that 'the decline in a native state commences from the moment the English come into close contact with it'. Trouble might have been predicted, *pace* Kelkar: the motto from its earliest days was 'Malo mori quam demorari'—'Rather death than delay', or 'holding back': the note is of youthful pride and impetuousness.

The paper was fairly faithful to this prospectus in its criticisms of government over its first eighteen months. But an extra notable feature was its broader imperial and indeed global outlook: during its first six months it covered, in addition to a regular Westminster Parliamentary summary, the Greco-Turkish question; constitutional freedom in Russia; the present state of China (*Mahratta* thought it wealthy because it was self-governed); similarly, praise for 'that favoured spot', Japan, a would-be 'model'; and with more pointed hostility to British imperialism, it celebrated the 'pluck' of the South African 'Boers' and the Afghans.[23] The

---

[23] The summary began 30 January; 23 January and 27 February; 3 July; 23 January ('The present state of China: a warning to the British Indian administration'); 6 February; 6 March.

Second Afghan War itself was 'the most monstrously iniquitous of all wars', and the retention of Kandahar was deplored repeatedly; its prosecution and expense were of course a domestic issue, bearing on the Indian tax-payer.[24] Above all, though, *Mahratta*'s wider gaze was turned to Ireland. Its hostility to the Coercion Bill was sustained; Parnell was praised for risking his life for his nation; ten centuries had shown that England could not govern Ireland to benefit the Irish, therefore Home Rule was necessary.[25] Not that its Indian policy was so 'advanced': though it griped at the octroi and salt tax and sundry injustices of the administration, and advocated replacing the British machinery of government with Indian, it did so relentingly; it even printed correspondence from a 'warm sympathiser' of British rule.[26] The paper underlined explicitly the need to build political awareness first: '"Slow but steady wins the race" is our motto', it declared; but 'in time not only Ireland but dumb India will come to the front'.[27] Indeed, from the first issue it had been positive about the efforts of the Liberal Viceroy, Lord Ripon. Even so early in his career, though, Tilak looked forwards to his famous 'seditious' stance of 1908: in India as in Ireland, anti-government agitations merely reflected how 'a thoughtless mother does not respect her children'; and asking the question 'British rule in India: is it permanent?', the paper noted, in a variation on a favoured metaphor, 'the shoe pinches'; a fortnight later *Mahratta* said outright that it would not last because it was despotic, hence unstable.[28]

But it was other kinds of machinery, rather than the machinery of government, that was often foremost on *Mahratta*'s mind. In its first month it urged that natives must accumulate capital and 'begin new industries', and bemoaned the lack of Indian capital in railways and the political conditions that strangled it; six months later it more emphatically declared India must 'seek civilization from the development of material industries', and called for investment in specific schemes.[29] There was also a pioneering call for boycott and *swadeshi*, a full twenty-five years before the famous movement centred on Bengal: in March 1881 the passing of

---

[24] 20 February 1881 (though the Afghan War was discussed from the first issue); on the expenses see 13 February 1881, page 1 in particular.
[25] For example, 27 February 1881; 30 January 1881; 28 August 1881.
[26] For example, 6 February 1881; 27 February 1881.
[27] 27 February 1881.
[28] 23 January 1881; 27 February 1881; 13 March 1881.
[29] 23 January, 30 January, 5 June 1881.

the Factory Act, which restricted factories' working practices, was met with: 'let us unite and resolve that no Manchester cloth will be worne! [sic]'.[30] The hope that people would boycott foreign products and aid ailing Indian industry was recurrent, but in June 1882 *Mahratta* reflected that 'the people are not yet civilised enough to take a little loss suffered for the sake of the country'.[31] *Mahratta* had a lively interest in technology, and enthused for instance over the storage of electricity in the new Siemens machine.[32] It also called for applied scientific education in India: scientific agriculture; not just steam locomotives, but how to work them.[33] Traces of a broader philosophy of education are also evident, particularly its political aspect. Indeed political education would be a prerequisite of greater self-rule for Indians: the British had, through education, made Indians despise their own 'barbarous despotisms', said *Mahratta*, and they 'naturally cling' to their British tutor.[34] Slightly vaguely, the system of education was also seen to have 'demartialised' India, an unusual term used twice in this connection in *Mahratta*'s first months.[35] And there was a more general sense of civilizational antagonism between Britain and India. Celebrating the growth of Freethought in Britain, *Mahratta* noted that Christianity was the 'worst enemy of liberty', something that it repeated six months later.[36] *Mahratta* also carried a tally of alcohol-related misadventures, reported in the 'Poona local'. The evil was associated with British rule and a symbol of its insalubriousness: it was to India what opium was to China.[37] But *Mahratta* also entertained severe criticisms of Hindu society: most startlingly, caste was described as an 'incubus on the Hindu race', although the words seem divorced from much concrete policy.[38] It also inveigled against the 'evils of child marriage', and encouraged widow remarriage, albeit reassuring readers that it did not have 'old hags' in mind.[39]

---

[30] 13 March 1881.
[31] 11 June 1882.
[32] 3 July 1881.
[33] 23 January 1881; 13 February 1881.
[34] 6 February 1881.
[35] Ibid., and 13 March 1881.
[36] 19 June 1881; 22 January 1882.
[37] For example, 13 February; 24 April 1881.
[38] 10 July 1881.
[39] 22 and 29 May 1881; 16 April 1882.

In sheer volume and repetition, though, two issues dominated. The first was that of the 'native aristocracy'. *Mahratta* took up the issue of the suffering of the *inamdar* (landlords whose landholding originated in a feudal grant or *inam*), 'at the mercy of the tenant'; how they were affected by the land revenue code was a particular concern.[40] Some of the paper's most intense attention was paid to the Deccan Agriculturalists' Relief Act which had come into effect the previous year, aiming to reduce the indebtedness of farmers and restrict land transfer to their creditors.[41] The second issue was that of the native princes. Early on, *Mahratta* bemoaned that they were 'soft and given to pleasure', but their rights and good rule were a repeated concern.[42] It was agitated over the restitution of Mysore, and feared that the British coveted Cashmere; it repeatedly criticized the Government's policy towards Baroda; constructively, *Mahratta* publicized a mooted constitution for native rajas.[43] Tilak's stint as editor ended with an imprisonment for defamation concerning a well-documented controversy over the mental health of the minor Raja of Kolhapur, Tilak, along with the *Kesari* under Agarkar accusing Mahadeo Barve, the state *Karbharee* (administrator), of maltreating the Raja and fabricating his insanity for political ends, in cooperation with the British authorities.[44] Tilak's use of the press to publicize the trial from February 1882 (it came to utterly dominate the paper's coverage) looks forwards to his use of the courtroom as a political platform in 1908. Although forced into a grovelling apology when evidence emerged that he had published faked correspondence, Tilak had always wished in the trial to appear as representative of the press and its freedom.[45] Beyond this, the newspaper had always used its power of (sometimes strident) advocacy through these eighteen months. It was a function that the paper made explicit: they must act the advocate, for Indian conditions being as they were, it was 'impracticable for newspaperwallahs to perform the functions of a judge'.[46]

---

[40] 16 January 1881; 30 January and 9 October 1881.
[41] 3 April 1881 (and then spring and summer *passim*, with a ten-part series up to 21 August).
[42] 16 January 1881.
[43] 27 February 1881; 22 May 1881; 24 July ff; 11 September 1881; (August–October 1881 *passim*).
[44] On 16 July 1882, Tilak was sentenced to four months imprisonment along with Agarkar, but was released early on 26 October.
[45] 16 July 1882, Editorial Notes, carries Tilak and Agarkar's apology letter.
[46] 2 October 1881.

Tilak took up *Mahartta*'s reins again in 1891 under very different circumstances. He had been *Kesari* editor since 1887, but had fallen out in
1890 with his then colleagues in the New English School and the Deccan
Education Society he had coestablished in 1884. He had quickly established an India-wide reputation as the leading voice of the anti-reformist
faction in Poona over the age of consent controversy earlier in 1891.
For the first time, therefore, Tilak had a personal, defined political constituency and control over both newspapers to further an autonomous
agenda. Its reputation continued, according to one government report, as
a 'well conducted journal, much given to writing on political subjects'.[47]
The most significant point for our purposes is where it demonstrated a
distinct message from *Kesari*'s. This emerged mainly over its role as representing the Tilakite view to government, nowhere more so than over
the communal riots in western India in 1893–1894. 'Muslims may attack
the Hindus unprovoked at any time', *Mahratta* said in their immediate
aftermath, 'and it seems to us that this tendency cannot be checked unless Government takes a firm attitude in such matters and inflicts exemplary punishments upon the aggressors'; it immediately suggested
police restrictions on 'so-called religious meetings' (even while inno-
cently claiming it was 'too soon to express an opinion').[48] The cow protection movement had been roundly blamed; Tilak defended it to the
Government (but does not appear to have been active within it, despite
common assumptions): *Mahratta* spelled out, with italics, for the benefit
of the Government, that the 'cow protection movement is not of recent
origin', nor has anything been done recently to interfere with the '*just
and legal* rights' of the Bombay Muslims.[49] The Government of India was
warned not to 'support the Muslims against the Hindus in the same way
as Lord Salisbury has been supporting the Protestant population of Ulster
against the Irishmen generally'.[50] This culminated in a sustained campaign through 1893–1894 to vindicate the Hindu right to play music in
front of mosques.[51]

[47] MSA Political Dept 1893, no. 176, Appendix F (report by G. M. Sathe, reporter on native
press).
[48] 13 August 1893, 5.
[49] 20 August 1893, 3.
[50] Ibid.
[51] 22 October, Editorial., 3, 'Hindu Mahomedan Riots at Yewala in the Nasik District', contains
an early notable iteration of this.

Aside from these periods of editing, Tilak wrote regularly for *Mahratta*. The most distinct of these included a sequence, at the height of the 1885 'native volunteering movement' occasioned by the apparent Russian threat, demanding that natives be allowed to volunteer for military service, and satirizing the notion that it represented a danger, as if the native princes, with their armies, were a danger themselves.[52] His concern here for the revitalizing aspects of military service, and his estimation of current weakness, was recurrent through his career, as we shall see in the chapter on 'Reforming Hindu Society'. Tilak also contributed a pair of notable exegetical articles on the constitutionalism of Indian agitation, at the height of the Swadeshi agitation in February–March 1907, and a larger series on the freedom of the press in June–July 1907 after the deportation of Lala Lajpat Rai. More broadly, education and history, as often in *Kesari*, were topics to which he turned his pen. His writing seems fairly sparse in the latter years of his career. His decisions to do so perhaps, then, carry more weight: it is interesting that his last significant piece was on the lessons to be learned from a month-long mill-strike in Bombay.[53] Arguing that the strike was a matter of courageous millmen forced by 'the prompting of the belly', it reflected Tilak's apparent increased sympathy for the cause of labour against capital (perhaps influenced by the close relations he had developed with Labour Party officials in Britain during his stay in 1918–1919); his solutions fell short of the programmatic, however, merely being an exhortation to the mill-owners in 'this religious land' (unlike the West, with its 'individualistic materialism') that they remember that 'We believe in God', who ordains 'that every being must get sufficient food to live'.

It is worth emphasizing that, as Kelkar notes, *Mahratta* was always a losing concern, sponging off its ultimately profitable sister paper all through Tilak's life.[54] It never enjoyed a mass readership—never apparently much exceeding its initial circulation figures. It is significant, of course, that the paper would have continued to have been run at a loss over a sustained period. Those relatively few readers were precious to the proprietors, ultimately Tilak personally. Aside from the ear of the

---

[52] SLT 8, 9–11, 13.
[53] Ibid., 157 (8 February 1920).
[54] Kelkar, *Tilak*, 109.

Government, the paper, of course, could gain notice throughout India outside Maharashtra, and could be readily quoted and reprinted. It is tes¬ tament to Tilak's and his colleagues' faith in an all-Indian readership of the English-educated, and their common investment in the development of an all-Indian political community, right from its outset in January 1881, that the paper was conducted.

Kesari

Kesari's prospectus, appearing in Chiplunkar's *Nibandhmala*, was functional and innocuous.[55] It offered a new Marathi paper with 'comparatively low' subscription rates. This seems to have been a bold bid for readership, and its 1800-copy initial circulation was twice that of *Mahratta*: during the Kolhapur case, it rose to 3,500, and then in 1884–1885 to 4,500.[56] It finally became profitable in 1888.[57] It is clear that Tilak, Agarkar, and Chiplunkar were central to *Kesari*, as to the whole press enterprise. Although articles were not accredited, there is evidence from several sources (including Kelkar himself) indicating Tilak's specific output, and his strong preference for the subjects of religion and law.[58] Chiplunkar's output, as in *Nibandhmala*, was heavily literary, while Agarkar ranged over historical, economic, and social fields.[59] That said, the literary eminence of Agarkar and Chiplunkar does seem to have overshadowed Tilak's output at first, and under the years of Agarkar's editorship, he appears to have written little: a mere nineteen of the almost 600 mostly *Kesari* Marathi articles attributed to him in SLT 3–5 are from this period. They cover those topics of Tilak's interest referred to: the relations of the region's three Brahmin subcastes, Konkanastha, Deshashtha, and Karhade (SLT 5, 1–2, 1881); the socio-religious issues of the early marriage of girls and the necessity of adoption (ibid., 5–15, 1883–1884); there is also a classic consideration of the priority of political over social reform in contemporary India ('What's First: Social or Political?', ibid.,

---

[55] Reprinted SLT 6, 1.
[56] Kelkar, *Tilak*, 108.
[57] Ibid., 184.
[58] Ibid., and SLT 8, Preface.
[59] Kelkar, *Tilak*, 107–108.

16–17, 1886). Towards the end there was a series on the curriculum of the Poona female high school (though supporting the school, he felt the curriculum should not involve English and should be focused towards domestic duties: 'If we don't take into account the duties and functions of women in the current society and force them to take the same education as that of men, it would be detrimental for the community', ibid., 44–47, September–October, 1887).

Tilak took over the editing of *Kesari* on 22 October 1887 after Agarkar left in order to set up his own reformist paper, *Sudharak* ('reformer'), feeling, in addition to personal frictions, that his priorities were not echoed by others connected to the papers. Reformist controversies, indeed, were a familiar issue of Tilak's first *Kesari* editorship period. The largest of them related to the bill moved in January 1891 to raise the age of consent for married and unmarried girls to 12. Tilak came out as strongly opposed to it (SLT 5, 51–53, 1890), in a significant step which announced him as the leading Poona anti-reformist voice, a shift from his editorial line in *Mahratta* a decade previously. Tilak's position will be discussed a little more in Chapter 4. It is sufficient to note that the intervention of the colonial state was critical in shifting Tilak's attitude: Tilak satirized reformers as sending application forms to the foreign government requesting new laws: 'these same people now hold our nation guilty because of a few cases of rapes on minor girls and want the government to amend the laws. How devoid of self-respect can one be?' (SLT 5, 51). But his resistance also turned into an absolute hostility to all reform on the issue. In the ensuing years a somewhat hardened position was visible on the question of remarriage (SLT 5, 55–57). Tilak continued in his writing on *gramanyas* the Chitpavan tradition of restricting Vedic rites to Brahmins, foreshadowing his stance, as we shall see, in the Kolhapur 'Vedokta' affair a decade later (SLT 5, 21–22, 1892).[60] On educational questions, Tilak pondered on the early death of graduates (SLT 5, 25–27, 1894), which he was inclined to blame on English-medium schooling straining their mental fibres. He also showed concern for the promotion of vernacular languages, particularly the role of the universities in it (SLT 3, 22–24, 1894).

---

[60] On *gramanyas* in the 1820s and 1830s, see 'Maharashtra in the mid-nineteenth century' in Chapter 1.

In terms of 'communal' issues, Tilak of course wrote much on the riots of 1893–1894 and the proper response to them; *Kesari* was useful in advertising his efforts to cohere Hindu society (SLT 5, 70–101). *Kesari* in particular welcomed the enhanced Ganapati festivities in this light in September 1893; they gained no mention in *Mahratta*. Tilak popularized and explicated the new festivities in *Kesari* from 1894; in particular he outlined and discussed their political aspect, as 'mass rallies', in the paper in 1896 (SLT 4, 3–5). Similarly, the restoration of Shivaji's memorial monument and his broader commemoration was trumpeted by *Kesari* from 1895 (SLT 4, 6–7, 1895–1896)—though it should be noted here that it was not the first publication to advocate either 'festival' (his involvement being discussed further in Chapter 3). Tilak underlined his support for the Shivaji commemoration by urging the national importance of worshipping historical heroes (SLT 4, 2, 1896). On cultural and philosophical matters Tilak commented for his readership on the Vedanta lectures of F. Max Muller (SLT 5, 107, 1894), and the 'Brahma Mimansa' (exploration of knowledge of the supreme Brahma) of the prominent jurist and Hindu reformer M. G. Ranade, with whom Tilak was often in conflict (SLT 5, 108–110, 1896); he also wrote on the rejuvenation of 'Aryan medicine' (SLT 5, 174, 1896). Tilak also put some thought into rituals of repentance (*prayaschitta*) (SLT 8, 23–25, 1892). Indeed this was an extension of Tilak's self-vindication after the so-called Pancha Haud Tea Episode, concerning the taking of tea at a Christian missionary function in Poona by Tilak and others who had been anti-reform during the controversy over the age of consent in 1890: although the fact had been revealed, and the anti-reformists charged with hypocrisy, in March 1891, Tilak was still responding to this in December 1892 (SLT 8, 31–32, 34–37, November–December 1892).[61] Giving a social application to his interest in scientific knowledge, Tilak wrote on drought, its reasons and prevention (SLT 3, 85–86, 88–89, 1896–1897), and famine (SLT 8, 76–79, October 1896). And he memorably broached economic matters, endorsing Dadabhai Naoroji's

[61] On the incident see Aravind Ganachari, *Nationalism and Social Reform in the Colonial Situation* (Delhi: Kalpaz Publications, 2005), Ch. 11, 225 ff.

'drain' theory, which also helped to explicate bimetallism (SLT 3, 107–112, 1892).[62]

On more firmly political ground, Tilak made regular comments on sessions of the Indian National Congress, which he first attended in 1889, and other political conferences (SLT 4, 30ff), and engaged in a conflict, which grew through the 1890s, with *mawal* or 'moderates', favouring a less pugnacious approach to Congress's demands of the British. His focus was on his regional rivals like Ranade (SLT 4, 71, 1893), or more spectacularly G. K. Gokhale (SLT 4, 74–75, 1895), Tilak abusing the latter while successfully demanding in 1895 that the 'Social Conference' (dedicated to reform questions) be severed from the Congress (that year taking place in Poona), and not take place in its pandal as previously. He showed sustained hostility towards Lord Harris, the Governor of Bombay between 1890 and 1895, whose tenure was marked by a hostility to the early agenda of the Congress to increase Indian representation in the administration (SLT 3, 155–157, 1895, and the earlier Indian Councils Act articles of 1892 [SLT 4, 154–155]). He offered a pointed defence of trial by jury after its suspension in Bengal (SLT 4, 160–163, 1892–1893), a matter of crucial intellectual as well as practical importance to Tilak in his later career. Tilak was also outspoken on the costs of government (SLT 3, 114, 1892), specifically on agricultural taxes (SLT 3, 52–57, 1892), and employed *Kesari* to unveil further thoughts on *swadeshi* and boycott (SLT 4, 94, 1896). This was blended with a deeper analysis of the political conditions of colonialism ('How have we gained during the British Raj?', SLT 3, 1, 1892, and 3–5, 1893–1894). These culminated in his ironic, yet more than merely caustic, 'Praise of the Empress' series in June 1897 (SLT 3, 7–9), adduced at his trial shortly after for sedition. That trial, which ended this period of editorship, centred on two articles in *Kesari* on 15 June reporting and reflecting on the Shivaji commemorations of June that year, at which Tilak spoke. The broader tone of *Kesari* had been increasingly strident as plague ravaged Poona and the government's heavy-handed response was criticized: plague remedies and their criticism were themselves much featured over these months (SLT 4, 121–126, 1896–1897).

---

[62] T. V. Parvate, *Tilak, the Economist* (Bombay: Maharashtra State Board for Literature and Culture, 1985).

Even after the murders of the British plague commissioner W. C. Rand and his escort Lt. Ayerst in late June, Tilak wrote the editorial 'Has the government lost its mind?' (SLT 4, 109, 6 July 1897), in criticism of plague measures: it remains a much-remembered expression of anti-British dissent in Maharashtra.[63]

After early release from an eighteen-month imprisonment sentence, and a period of convalescence, Tilak began editing again in July 1899 (SLT 4, 110). Prison had not dampened his enthusiasm for writing on the plague, but he now wrote from a more scientific perspective (SLT 4, 127–134, 1899–1900). This was the beginning of a near-decade of editorship, lasting until his second and final sedition imprisonment in 1908; but it should not be imagined that Tilak was an active figure of bourgeoning prominence for all of it. Whether through caution, or because of the draw upon his energies of the protracted 'Tai Maharaj case' (centring around the adoption of a son by Tai Maharaj, widow of Baba Maharaj, of whose estate Tilak was a trustee), there appears to have been a relative lull in his output before the breaking of the storm in 1905, with Lord Curzon's announcement of the partition of Bengal. During this period he showed further significant interest in educational questions (SLT 3, 26–43, 1899–1904). He was also drawn into the 'Vedokta' affair of Kolhapur, over the right of the Maharaja to receive Vedic rites as a Kshatriya (the same principle at issue in the *gramanyas* noted earlier). This had been rumbling on for months by the time of Tilak's own statement, that the Maharaja could be given them as a *rajan* or ruler, rather than by dint of hereditary varna (SLT 5, 31–32, 1901), a position which suggested, quite deliberately, that the mass of self-professed Kshatriyas in the region, who supported the Maharaja in his stance, had no such claim to Kshatriya status. There was a stream of articles on religious questions in 1904 (SLT 5, 62–67), including on the notion of Hindutva (not, indeed, as has been often claimed, V. D. Savarkar's coinage; Tilak's use of the term is something we shall return to). Tilak's turn was scholarly at this point, as he wrote heavily at the same time on Marathi linguistics (SLT 5, 119–126, 1904) and research into the

---

[63] Both were shot on 22 June 1897, on Queen Victoria's Diamond Jubilee; Ayerst died on the spot, Rand on 3 July from his wounds. Tilak's resistance was also expressed in SLT 4, 112, 'Ruling does not mean indulging in reprisals'.

Hindu calendar (SLT 5, 167–170, 1900, 1905); this was capped off by an eight-article sequence on the Mahabharata in 1905 (SLT 5, 147–154). True to his earlier preoccupation in *Mahratta*, Tilak wrote six articles in three months defending landowners' rights in 1899 (SLT 3, 78–83); similar concerns underpinned his response to the Bombay Land and Revenue Bill of July–August 1901 (SLT 3, 61–70), on which Tilak wrote at least ten articles in two months, a frequency barely equalled anywhere in his output. Tilak's response was, in fact, reflected by other Congress politicians, horrified at the proposed scale of the state's takeover of unassessed or forfeited land.[64] Tilak's interest in drought dovetailed with this concern in a series on the land tax and drought (SLT 3, 96–98, 101–104, 1900–1901). There was also a flowering of Tilak's interest in industrial progress, questioning 'How did our industries die' and urging a reversal (SLT 3, 134–137 1902–1905). Tilak's eyes were only sometimes here set further afield, and there are glimpses of pan-Asianism in Tilak's thoughts (SLT 4, 183, 1903, 'Unanimity in thoughts of Eastern nations), and a fascination with Japan even before, unsurprisingly, Tilak heralded the 'disconcertment of Russia' through Japan's victory in the Russo-Japanese war in 1905 (185–86, 1904–1905).

The Viceroy from 1899, Lord Curzon, had already personally whetted Tilak's commentarial appetite by displaying his own talent for outspokenness (for instance addressing University of Bombay students to the effect that truth was a 'western concept', responded to in SLT 3, 169–170, February 1905). The effect of Curzon's announcement of the Bengal partition in July 1905 led to a much more virulent attack on the British administration from Tilak, not to mention a much fuller set of statements on political agitation and on Indian public life. Indeed it seems to have focused and galvanized his journalistic efforts, as it gave a new impetus to agitation in India in general. Ironically it was his split with his own Congress colleagues at Surat in December 1907 that occasioned the most intense writing on Congress politics (SLT 4, 58–66, January–March 1908; also SLT 8, 173–175, December 1907). But *Kesari* was the mouthpiece for Tilak's advocacy of *swadeshi* and boycott (for example SLT 4, 95–96 1905), and, significantly, the broader political boycott, which formed part

[64] I. J. Catanach, *Rural Credit in Western India, 1875–1930* (Berkeley; London: University of California Press, 1970), 39 ff.

of his approach to passive resistance described in Chapter 5 (SLT 4, 100–102 1905, esp. 100, 'National Boycott'). The months leading up to Tilak's sedition conviction also saw an increase in his writing on the allied issue of liquor prohibition, which apart from alleged social good would deplete government revenues (SLT 4, 103–105, 1908). These controversies, on top of Tilak's own post-1897 celebrity, saw *Kesari*'s readership grow from 4,300, the second largest of any Marathi newspaper, in June 1893, to 20,000 by April 1908 (its nearest rival numerically by this stage, *Kal*, sold only 7,000); by comparison *Mahratta* still sold only 1,000 copies.[65] It was ultimately its outspokenness after the Muzaffarpur bomb blast aimed at the life of Presidency Magistrate Douglas Kingsford that led to Tilak's trial and conviction for sedition: his articles of 'praise to the bomb' as a safeguard against autocracy in May 1908 are discussed in Chapter 5.

After Tilak's release in 1914, the editorship stayed in the hands of N. C. Kelkar. Tilak cultivated non-journalistic sources of political influence, with the press being run by Kelkar and other trusted lieutenants like K. P. Khadilkar. These channels included formal institutions such as the Home Rule League he set up in Maharashtra in 1916 (discussed in the next chapter), for which he undertook extensive speaking tours, taking him physically away from the *Kesari*'s Poona office much of the time. Nonetheless, he took the trouble of writing in *Kesari* himself in furtherance of his Home Rule agitation from 1916. One of the most insistent calls in *Kesari* in 1917 and 1918 was for Indians to join the King-Emperor's armies in the war against the Central Powers (SLT 4, 20, 24, 25, 1917–1918). Though Tilak appeared to set conditions—the granting of political rights—in exchange for supporting enlistment, he in fact retreated from this position; physical strengthening and recovering lost martiality among Hindus were vital, and Home Rule without them was useless. He therefore even urged enlistment absent substantive political change.[66]

Nonetheless dissatisfied with the Government's stance regarding the connection between Home Rule and military service, he came out in *Kesari* to attack the Delhi and Bombay War Conferences (the latter of which he had stormed out of) (SLT 3, 179–180, May–June 1918). The proposed 'Montagu-Chelmsford' reforms announced in July 1918, a

---

[65] RNPB, 27 May 1893, IOR/L/R/5/148; and 1 April 1908, IOR/L/5/163.
[66] Discussed further in Chapter 4.

sequel to the Montagu Declaration of the previous year promising ultimate full self-government within the Empire for India, caused conster-
nation among many for their timidity: Tilak once more took to *Kesari* to
denounce the 'sunless morning' which had arisen (SLT 4, 26, 27, 1918).
He subsequently defended his policy of 'Responsive Cooperation'—a
significant break from his previous policy of 'passive resistance'—in response to the enacted reforms of 1919 (SLT 4, 28, 1920) and the Congress
Democratic Party which he instituted to push for it (SLT 4, 69). This final
period of Tilak's output was not entirely given over to military recruitment and constitutional reform, however, as Tilak used *Kesari* to make
clear his personal opposition to inter-caste marriage (SLT 5, 40, 1918).

Tilak's output in *Kesari* was at the heart of his political impact, and his
reputation and influence. It made him by the 1900s the most influential
man of letters in western India, and established his voice as a chastiser of
government and an advocate of expeditiousness (not to say extremism) in
the way of gaining political rights for Indians, and his reputation as a defender of Hindu cultural authenticity, or, more ungenerously, as a stubborn
resister of social reform measures. Its language was frequently colloquial
and employed colourful metaphor, though also (as was demonstrated vividly at his trial in 1908) showed Tilak an innovator of Marathi as a language
of political discussion—and showed him a deft exponent of the modern
arts of the wide circulation vernacular press and mass communication.
Today in Pune Tilak's name is still overwhelmingly associated with *Kesari*,
a newspaper that is still published, bearing his image on its masthead.[67]

The Orion

The Orion: Or Researches into the Antiquity of the Vedas, published in
1893, is the most overlooked text among his three main works; this is
mainly because its most important themes are reprised and developed in
his later work, *The Arctic Home*. Nonetheless, not only do ten years separate the publication of these works, in aims and methods they are quite
distinct, and it was probably conceived as a solitary work.[68] This section

---

[67] http://www.dailykesari.com/.
[68] See Tilak's comment that he did not foresee returning to the issue, *Orion*, vii.

thus adds something by offering a discrete treatment of it. Wolpert's comments on *Orion* form the standard scholarly viewpoint by default: that
the text was developed 'for the intellectual arsenal of Hindu nationalism'.[69] This is not the most useful framework. But the appeal to Hindu
and Brahminic chauvinism within the work nonetheless had its political
uses to Tilak. He was, indeed, at a low political ebb in 1893 as he prepared
the manuscript for publication. The agitation of the Age of Consent Bill
in 1891 having subsided, the leadership he had established of the largely
Brahminic anti-reform constituency in Maharashtra could not easily be
sustained.

In *Orion*, Tilak argues that the date of the earliest of the Vedic texts,
the oldest Sanskrit texts in existence, can be no later than 4000 BC (when
the Vernal equinox was in Orion). His argument is based almost entirely
on astrochronology, specifically dating the Vedas from references within
them to positions of celestial bodies. As Tilak states, this question is essentially one rather for 'Sanskrit scholars than astronomers to decide', and
it is a work of Sanskrit exegesis, not astronomy.[70] These references are,
Tilak finds, corroborated by 'other sections' of the Aryan race: the Vedas
recorded a time when the Indian, Greek, and Iranians sections 'lived
together'.[71] Tilak presents this argument over six main chapters, each
dealing with traditions recorded in the Vedas that are thus explicable.

This section will make no attempt to scrutinize the veracity of Tilak's
claims, instead observing Tilak's positionality within his milieu in
making them. Tilak's study engaged with fields that were both well established and still very open. The field of dating the Vedas was a controversial
one among American and European Sanskritists in the 1880s. The Vedas
had a particularly important status as arguably the oldest Aryan text.
Therefore, in the words of Muller, there was 'nothing in the world equal
in importance' to them in the study of the Aryan race, or even—showing
the dominant position of the Aryan race in the minds of this generation
of Sanskrit scholars—the study of man as a whole.[72] An attempt had been

---

[69] Wolpert, *Tilak and Gokhale*, 124.
[70] *Orion*, v.
[71] Ibid., 198–199.
[72] F. Max Muller, *India: What Can It Teach Us? A Course of Lectures Delivered before the
University of Cambridge* (London, 1892). This is cited in *Orion*, 1.

made by Muller in his seminal *History of Ancient Sanskrit Literature* to establish a rough chronology for Vedic composition. It used the division of ancient Sanskrit literature into four successive chronological periods, the *Chhandas*, *Mantra*, *Brahmana*, and *Sutra*.[73] Working back from the date of termination of the final period provided by the spread and political ascendancy of Buddhism in the 4th century BC, it allocated 200 years for the development of each, and thus posited a date of 1200 BC at the latest for the date of the composition of the Rigveda. This dating achieved something of the character of an established orthodoxy to some philologists, despite Muller's own reservations.[74] Nonetheless, a prominent early critic of Muller's dating was Oxford's Professor of Sanskrit H. H. Wilson, commenting that 200 years is 'much too brief for the establishment of an elaborate ritual' in the *Brahmana*.[75] Martin Haug, Professor of Oriental Languages at Elphinstone College, in his Introduction to the *Aitareya Brahmana* discussed in the previous chapter, agreed, supposing 500 years for each of the periods, and positing a date of 2400–2000 BC for the Rigveda.[76] The American William Dwight Whitney similarly suggested a date of 2000 BC.[77] That this controversy was carried out largely between European and American scholars should not surprise. The historicity of this scholarship diverged from the orthodox conviction that the Vedas were beyond historical time, *anadi* (beginningless). But this modern globalized milieu of Sanskrit scholarship did, of course, incorporate Indians, like R. G. Bhandarkar, through their education at institutions like the Elphinstone and Deccan Colleges, from the 1860s, as we have seen. Their historicization of the Vedas is the context in which Tilak very consciously sets his work.[78]

---

[73] F. Max Muller, *A History of Ancient Sanskrit Literature So Far As It Illustrates the Primitive Religion of the Brahmans*, 2nd ed. (London, 1860).

[74] See Edwin Bryant, *The Quest for the Origins of Vedic Culture* (New York and Oxford, 2001), 245.

[75] H. H. Wilson, 'Max Müller's Ancient Sanskrit Literature', *Edinburgh Review*, 112 (1860), 361–385.

[76] Haug, *Aitareya Brahmanam*.

[77] W. D. Whitney, *Oriental and Linguistic Studies* (New York, 1873).

[78] *Orion*, 4, cites the work of H. H. Dhruva 'submitted to the Ninth Oriental Congress', attempting to ascertain Vedic chronology. This is an obscure citation; Dhruva's work does not appear in its proceedings. Tilak may have had sight of Dhruva's manuscript.

Tilak notes that his preferred astrochronological technique, favoured by late eighteenth-century Sanskritists, had more recently been dismissed as 'inaccurate and conjectural'.[79] But the technique was in fact more current than he knew. The remarkable and exactly contemporary work of Hermann Jacobi demonstrates this. Exactly like Tilak searching to secure an earlier date for the Vedas than that commonly accepted by what Tilak calls the 'literary' method, Jacobi independently published his work, unknown to Tilak. In his brief article, Jacobi argued from references to the position of the sun at the start of the year in two Vedic hymns that they must have been composed between 2500 and 4500 BC.[80] The astrochronological technique was also employed by Indians: another Chitpavan, Krishna Sastri Godbole, published in the *Theosophist*, used the same technique to assert an early date for the Vedas. Godbole too was concerned with the traditional date of the *Kaliyuga*. Tilak was unconcerned with this in *Orion*, and is actually dismissive elsewhere of the chronology that Godbole defended, though he nonetheless here acknowledges Godbole's cognate scholarship as 'suggestive and valuable'.[81] Within Tilak's own circle, it was a topic engaged with in a history of astronomy in Marathi, soon to be published as a widely influential textbook, by Tilak's friend Shankara Balkrishna Dikshit (1853–1898), a mathematics teacher and the principal of the Teachers Training College in Poona.[82] Tilak had sight of Dikshit's manuscript and discussed his theories with him, as he did with his old tutor K. L. Chhatre, whom Tilak informs us held similar views, though he did not publish them.[83]

From *Orion*'s content we can infer several distinct aims on Tilak's part. Characteristically, Tilak is alive to political possibility, though it would be a mistake, as we shall see, to reduce the text to an essentially political statement. The features of the text that have political relevancies are

---

[79] Ibid., 6, citing Albrecht Weber's *History of Indian Literature*, 3rd ed. (London, 1892). But see Haug, *Aitareya Brahmanam*, 42 ff.

[80] *Orion*, 3. H. Jacobi, 'Beitrage zur Kenntnis der Vedischen Chronologie', ('Contributions to the knowledge of Vedic Chronology'), *Nachrichten von der Königl Gesellschaft der Wissenschaften* (1894), 105–115. Jacobi also discusses his views in 'On the Antiquity of Vedic Culture', *Journal of the Royal Asiatic Society of Great Britain and Ireland* (1909), 721–726.

[81] *Orion*, 8. He says nothing on the *Kaliyuga* in *Orion*, but criticizes the chronology as resting on Puranic 'artifices and devices' later in *Arctic Home*. (In Bryant, *Quest*, he is mistakenly referred to as Godgole.)

[82] S. B. Dixit, *Bharateeya Jyotishashastra*, trans. R. V. Vaidya (Delhi, 1969).

[83] *Orion*, 8.

those, broadly speaking, that inspire pride in the hereditary culture of the Indian Aryans and its antiquity. That writing on astronomy should carry political implications is not surprising; in a sense, it could hardly not. As C. A. Bayly notes, astronomy had always been a political science in India, determining auspicious dates for the polity; Tilak's asserting the value of the Brahminic tradition of astronomy and making his own positive astronomical contribution to determine Vedic dating were within that tradition in sounding political overtones.[84] Beyond this, claims about the stature of Indo-Aryan civilization were being made to a global audience. As Tilak notes, the 'high antiquity' of Egyptian civilization was at the time 'generally admitted', but 'scholars still hesitate' to set the commencement of Vedic civilization earlier than 2400 BC.[85] His dating asserts the venerability of 'Aryan civilisation' over non-Aryan, therefore; but specifically it does so by extolling the antiquity of the Indo-Aryans, whose most sacred books were the Aryans' 'oldest records in the world'.[86] This point about the venerability of the Indo-Aryans' achievement is underscored in his conclusion. Commenting on the suggested renaming of the constellation after Napoleon or Nelson, Tilak states that his discovery 'preserves for us the memory of far more important and sacred times in the history of the Aryan race'. Regardless of the political-military imperium enjoyed by Europeans in his day, the foundational period of Aryan civilization, that of the composition of the Vedas, naturally dwarfed it.[87]

This is the case, indeed, despite the explicit commonalities of the Indo-Aryan branch with Greek and Persian in Tilak's text. The Vedas recorded a period in which 'the Hellenic, the Iranian and the Indian Aryans lived together'; the other two sections share the distinction of their presence during the sacred period, their texts recording it too in the form of shared mythology.[88] Tilak is here imbibed of the understanding of the Aryan race family developed earlier in the nineteenth century, and which was examined in the last chapter. This posited a unity of race between the speakers of the Indo-European languages and their ultimate descent

---

[84] C. A. Bayly, *Empire and Information: Intelligence Gathering and Social Communication in India, 1780–1870* (Cambridge, 1997), 247.
[85] *Orion*, iii.
[86] Ibid., vii.
[87] Ibid., 220.
[88] Ibid., 198.

from a common ancestral 'Aryan' race with a common habitation. What is remarkable in the statement above is the conservatism of Tilak's notion of the race family. This idea of racial affinity, drawing on philological study, had been assailed from the mid-nineteenth century, in many cases by exponents of the new techniques of race science, claiming Aryan identity, usually, for only some of the peoples of contemporary Europe. We saw in the last chapter that it is easy to exaggerate the ascendancy of race science, and its dismissal of the notion of Aryan racial commonality between contemporary Europe and India. Such a notion survived in the writings of many proponents of 'race science'. And, though their sense of the competence of their disciplines to speak upon it was shaken, it remained a fundamental conviction of philologers and Sanskritists like Muller. The inscription composed by the Professor of Sanskrit at Oxford University, M. Monier-Williams, composed in 1883 for the university's new Indian Institute, demonstrates this older sense in full bloom. 'This building was erected for the use of Aryans (Indians and Englishmen)' the official translation of the transcription reads, the parenthesis making the commonality explicit; a mere decade before *Orion*'s publication.[89] Tilak, in his framework and references, is fully imbued of this sense.

Yet though Tilak maintains this sense of pan-Aryan commonality, ultimately it is the Indo-Aryans who are venerated. Tilak speaks of the 'sections of the Aryan race' as separate peoples living in the same location, a perfectly conventional formulation; he still assumes an essential differentiation even at this stage of antiquity, and the 'sections' are also referred to as 'nations', revealing a Romantic conception of nationhood as timeless and immutable.[90] But as we shall see, there is a suggestion that Vedic culture was a common Aryan culture up to the late Orion period. The other branches, though, did not inherit this tradition. It was the 'cultivated memory' of the Indian Aryans that preserved this Vedic culture.[91] It is for this reason that the other sections of the Aryan race did not record any astronomical evidence of this period of common living,

[89] The inscription, still present in the portico of the old Indian Institute in Oxford, is discussed in Trautmann, *Aryans*, 13.

[90] *Orion*, 92, 119. Tilak refers to 'Aryan races', but more usually to 'race' singular. It should be noted that Tilak does not, as we shall see in 'The Nature of the Indian Polity', see the Indian nation as coterminous with the Indo-Aryans.

[91] Ibid., 199.

as it was contained within the Vedas themselves. For Tilak posits a lapse of time between composition of the Vedas and their codification, conceding that the period of the tradition they refer to may predate that of their writing by some time. The traditions of *Orion* were incorporated into Vedic hymns, and these hymns were transmitted 'mouth to mouth' before being reproduced 'in the form in which we now possess them'. It is thus that he dismisses the antiquity of the other branches' achievement—they did not *remember* the Vedas.

The maintenance of Vedic civilization also conferred enormous prestige upon its carriers, the Brahmins. Thus it was not just that these most sacred books conferred upon the Indo-Aryan branch a higher status; the Brahmins themselves had an elevated status on account of them. For 'a super-religious fidelity and scrupulousness' saw to it that the traditions were memorized and maintained.[92] This scrupulousness connoted a vital ritual of recitation and transmission among the Indian Aryans, which kept the Vedas themselves alive. Vedic civilization continued, in an important sense, utterly unbroken, through the Brahmins; their métier in Tilak's time, as ever it was, was to be the guardians of the Vedas, a role they inherited through direct descent. Asserting the ritual significance of Brahmins in fact contributes to Tilak's assertion of the elevated position of the Vedas in this work: the two were mutually constitutive. Tilak observes that 'native writers' have tried to ascertain the date of the Ramayana and Mahabharata through the same method. But, he says, we cannot be sure we even possess these works in the form originally written, while of the Vedas there 'can be no doubt'.[93] Tilak here obliquely refers to the diversity of the narrative tradition of the epics, and their appropriation by diverse communities.[94] His conviction of the Vedas' textual reliability rests already on a notion of utmost fidelity in their Brahminic transmission.

Simultaneously, Tilak thus venerates the medium of Brahminic textual transmission, Sanskrit. For Tilak's account implies, albeit obliquely, that these different branches of the Aryan race had some of these hymns in common, effectively sharing a common Vedic culture. Tilak refers, citing Muller, to the existence of

[92] Ibid., 206.
[93] Ibid., vi.
[94] See Paula Richman (ed.), *Many Rāmāyanas: The Diversity of a Narrative Tradition in South Asia* (Delhi, 1992).

mythological names which may be shewn to be common to Greek and Sanskrit. If so many mythological names can be shewn to be phonetically identical, it is impossible to suppose that no songs, celebrating the deeds of these deities, existed in the Indo-Germanic [i.e. Indo-European] period.

As Tilak pithily footnotes, 'If all these deities existed in the Indo-Germanic period why not their hymns?'.[95] Tilak has made it clear that the Vedic hymns might have been 'somewhat modified *in form* in passing from mouth to mouth' before they came into their final form, but Tilak's italics here point to the fact that he rejects the notion of substantive change.[96] Therefore the common language of the branches who sung the hymns was Sanskrit, and they were transmitted in Sanskrit with little change by the Indian Aryans until they were written, while the other branches diverged from them. Only that branch that remembered the Vedic hymns retained the character and title of Vedic Aryans. This account makes Sanskrit once more the mother of Greek and Persian, effectively placing it at the root of the Indo-European languages. This is a remarkable reformulation of an older Brahminic idea, of the eternal unchanging Sanskrit from which all other languages are derived. Tilak salvages this idea from the modern notion of the Aryan race, which had at its root the notion pioneered by William Jones of all the existing Indo-European languages being ultimately offshoots of one common lost language, proto-Indo-European. His reformulation places Sanskrit in a position not commonly afforded to it by philologists since the work of K. W. F. Schlegel on the Sanskrit *ursprache*. For Tilak, through the process of transmitting the Vedas, the *ursprache* survived.[97]

For all its appeal to Indo-Aryan/Brahmin chauvinism, including its celebration of the antiquity and quality of Brahmin astral science, the text must not be reduced to being essentially political in intent. It was also a conscious contribution to a scholarly debate on the dating of the earliest periods of Sanskrit literature, and also that on Brahminic astral science; indeed it is a stretch to say that an 'orthodox' constituency of Poona

---

[95] *Orion*, 210 and n., citing F. Max Muller's *Biographies of Words*.
[96] Ibid., 209.
[97] Schlegel is discussed in Trautmann, *Aryans*.

Brahmins was the natural constituency for the historicizing method Tilak employs. Tilak's first audience, was, in fact, the Ninth International Congress of Orientalists, which met in London in September 1892, among whose delegates printed copies of Tilak's own summary were distributed, at his expense, before its inclusion in the Congress's transactions.[98] As well as seeking scholarly collaboration, he also clearly watched for scholarly reaction.[99] In the text he describes his research as complementary to that in other disciplines in the milieu: his conclusions are already supported, he says, on 'geographical and historical grounds', and are also consistent with recent researches in comparative philology.[100] His contribution was in a sense modest, in keeping with an established though unfashionable scholarly method, and attuned to current concerns and controversies. There is, though, a sense in which Tilak enters these fields in order to speak for India in them. He not only enters a Western-initiated field, that of Vedic dating, to urge a more venerable age for Vedic culture than any Western authority; he adopts what appears to have been a Western method to do so. Tilak thus appropriates Western scholarly techniques to demonstrate Indian antiquity and precocity. Though indebted by his own account to scholars like Haug and Muller, there is surely a sense in which Tilak feels their field should be led by India.[101] The scholarly impulse coexisted with an aim to intervene in cultural politics in India, and imperial and global cultural politics, Tilak's claims for Indian civilization capable in some measure of shaping perceptions of India's place in the world of the late nineteenth century. These conscious implications of the text do not render it ultimately or fundamentally political, any more than his scholarly agenda makes it apolitical.

---

[98] The summary is reproduced in E. D. Morgan (ed.), *Transactions of the Ninth International Congress of Orientalists*, 2 vols (London, 1893) (hereafter, Morgan (ed.), *Transactions*), i. 376–383.

[99] He records this in his Preface to *Arctic Home*; and considerably later in Mandalay jail he would draw up a list of responses to refer to in a second edition (see Tilak, 'Vedic Chronology', 167).

[100] *Orion*, 217, 210.

[101] His approach is perhaps a complement to that which dismissed the Western Orientalist scholarly method as described by Michael S. Dodson, 'Contesting Translations: Orientalism and the Interpretation of the Vedas', *Modern Intellectual History*, 4/1 (2007), 43–59.

The Arctic Home in the Vedas

Tilak's preface to *The Arctic Home in the Vedas* remarks that it is the sequel to *Orion*, which it is vastly bigger than in scale and scope. But, he says, drawing corroboration from the comments of the distinguished philologist Maurice Bloomfield, the language of the Vedas is 'not so primitive as to place with it the beginnings of Aryan life', which probably 'reaches back several thousand years more'.[102] Thus Tilak set out to find traces of its '*Ultima Thule*'. His line of search differs from the astrochronology of *Orion*. Rather, he searches for traces within the Vedas that the ancestors of the Vedic rishis 'lived in an Arctic home in inter-Glacial times'.[103] He finds them in the 'Polar attributes of the Vedic deities, or the traces of an ancient Arctic calendar'. The latest research in geology and archaeology of 'the primitive history of the human race and the planet it inhabits' renders this conclusion plausible: using this key, he even describes many of the Vedic passages 'hitherto looked upon as obscure and unintelligible' as 'plain and simple' when interpreted 'in the light of recent scientific researches'.[104] Tilak also refers to the *Zend Avesta*'s explicit account of an Aryan Paradise, located in a region where the sun shone once a year, and destroyed by invading snow and ice.

Tilak had, he tells us, continued his research on Vedic origins in the aftermath of *Orion*'s publication. But it was his imprisonment in 1897 that provided impetus to this, giving him the necessary leisure to pursue research.[105] Allowed to study at night by candlelight, Tilak busied himself with Vedic exegesis, working *inter alia* from a copy of Muller's second edition of the Rigveda sent to him by the editor.[106] In prison Tilak worked on a hypothesis of Aryan origins formed by new scientific discoveries on prehistory noted above: his first letter after release, to Muller, details his conclusions as to the Arctic home.[107] Nonetheless, the significant delay in publication after his early release in 1898 was, he informs us, in part due to his diffidence relating to his understanding of these fields, and his

---

[102] *AH*, ii.
[103] Ibid., iii.
[104] Ibid., vi.
[105] Ibid., xii.
[106] Ibid., iii.
[107] Ibid., vii.

need to consolidate his knowledge of them. Tilak is clear that he worked under considerable disadvantages in terms of the availability of scholarly resources.[108]

In the work, Tilak sets out, in thirteen chapters and over 500 pages, to demonstrate this Arctic home. His first three chapters specify the outcomes of scientific research positing the antiquity of man, the viability of the Arctic regions for habitation before the last Ice Age, and the characteristics of such an Arctic home; chapters IV–VIII, the bulk of the work, examine the Vedic evidence (with some digressions) that reflects these characteristics; his following two chapters deal specifically with certain Vedic myths that also seem to refer to Arctic conditions. Chapter X then showcases the independent Avestic evidence shedding light on the destruction of the Arctic home, while chapter XI describes various European traditions that reflect a common habitation there. His final chapter summarizes the import of his findings on Aryan culture and religion. His conclusion is that the fragments relating to the arctic home are remembered and incorporated into hymns in the Orion period, harmonizing it, with some amendments, with his earlier chronology.

An analysis of Tilak's references quickly reveals his cognizance of modern global scientific advances and scholarly debates. His first two chapters engage with a range of fields relating to prehistory in which the later nineteenth century had witnessed enormous change. Beginning with the archaeological classifications of the Stone (Palaeolithic and Neolithic), Bronze, and Iron ages, before switching fields and delving deeper, to the five geological classes of stratified rock, he fixes on the most recent Quaternary era, and its division into the Glacial period, containing the Palaeolithic period, and the Post-Glacial period, which gives way to the Neolithic period—the last 'Glacial epoch', or Ice Age, being described as the division between the two.[109] Tilak also invokes recent discoveries pointing to the existence of man as early as the Tertiary era, and certainly not merely the Post-Glacial period. He acknowledges a debt in particular to the summary work of Samuel Laing in his recent *Human Origins* (1892), and refers specifically to John Lubbock's *Prehistoric Times*

---

[108] Ibid., x.
[109] Ibid., 7–12.

(1890 ed.).[110] Tilak is critical rather than passive in this engagement, tentatively embracing for instance the estimates of American geologists like G. K. Gilbert of the Post-Glacial period's commencement around 10,000 years ago, against Geikie's estimates of 50,000–60,000 years, on the basis of erosion, for example.[111] In his second chapter, mostly concerned with the climate of the Arctic during the Inter-Glacial period, Tilak again cites Geikie to note its 'clement winters and cool summers' and its tropical flora and fauna.[112] Tilak also sifts the contentious evidence as to the reasons for the glacial epochs, critically, and very technically, evaluating James Croll's explanation concerning the precession of the equinoxes and the nature of the earth's orbit, before settling on Charles Lyell's geological theory. In short, Tilak is at pains to argue an informed and cohesive account of prehistory to situate his Vedic reinterpretations—and his notion that his thesis is a consequence of recent 'advances in knowledge' is in one sense correct.[113]

Tilak also follows current theories on Aryan origins. As he notes, it is because of the discovery of Aryan skulls found at the very beginning of the Neolithic period in Europe that scholars must 'give up the theory of successive migrations into Europe from a common home of the Aryan race in central Asia', and that the 'time telescope' for the origins of the Aryans must 'be adjusted to a wider range'.[114] In this conviction he reflects the work of the ethnographer and Anglican canon Isaac Taylor. With the discovery of these skulls, said Taylor, 'the earliest existing documents for the history of mankind come not from Asia, but from Western Europe'.[115] Tilak comments that a 'rude shock' had been given to the assumptions of philologers and Sanskritists on account of the scholarship

[110] S. Laing, *Human Origins* (London, 1893); J. Lubbock, *Prehistoric Times* (London, 1865).

[111] James Geikie, *The Great Ice Age and its Relation to the Antiquity of Man*, 1st ed. (London, 1874); James Geikie, *Fragments of Earth Lore: Sketches and Addresses, Geological and Geographical* (Edinburgh; London, 1893); Tilak takes Gilbert's views from T. G. Bonney, *The Story of Our Planet* (New York, 1893).

[112] *AH*, 15–18.

[113] Ibid., v, 20, 25–34. This is not the place to undertake an assessment of the fullness or accuracy of Tilak's understanding of these researches; it may of course be that Tilak, despite his attraction to the explanatory power of the astronomical thesis, nonetheless accepts the later date for the commencement of the post-Glacial epoch according to the geological one, so that his own thesis of a remembrance of Vedic passages is not vitiated.

[114] Ibid.

[115] Isaac Taylor, *The Origin of the Aryans: An Account of the Prehistoric Ethnology and Civilisation of Europe*, 3rd ed. (London, 1908) (hereafter, Taylor, *Origin*), 18.

Taylor summarizes, and that it is 'generally recognised' that a Central Asian homeland was no longer a tenable theory. Indeed, it was increasingly abjured; and it may appear that Tilak simply accepts the weight of near-consensus.[116] But it should be noted that his reading of this milieu does in fact involve certain interpretive decisions. He states that, as pre-Neolithic Europeans were decided to be so primitive as to be non-Aryan, the Aryans represented by the skulls must have come from 'somewhere else'; there seems no reason to deny that Aryans were autochthonous to Europe, as indeed many had argued, beyond, perhaps, a desire to deny Europeans the prestige they wished to accrue through such an argument. That said, Tilak's following of the milieu is perhaps surprisingly close. In positing an arctic home, he was, he readily acknowledges, anticipated by the 'learned and suggestive' work of William F. Warren, the first president of Boston University, who posited a *Cradle of the Human Race at the North Pole* in his 1885 work.[117] Tilak saw himself as clearly following a scholarly agenda, quoting Muller's view that a full translation of the hitherto unintelligible parts of the Vedas would be a task for the twentieth century.[118]

Not merely does Tilak follow in fashionable scholarly modes, he is rather modest, in a sense, in the claims he makes for the Indian Aryans. For Warren had rested his work largely on the accounts in the Zoroastrian text the *Zend Avesta* of the 'Aryan Paradise', or *Airyana Vaejo*, and its destruction by snow and ice, as well as the traditions of 'other nations'.[119] And Tilak does not at all dissent from Warren, but rather explicitly endorses his account of the Avestic evidence in his eleventh chapter. 'Our inquiry of the original Aryan home', says Tilak, 'is, therefore, not only not inconsistent with the general theory about the cradle of the human race at the North Pole, but a necessary complement to it'.[120] Tilak similarly aligns with the work of the Professor of Celtic at Oxford University, John Rhys, whose lectures of 1886, *On the Origin and Growth of Religion as Illustrated by Celtic Heathendom*, charts the reminiscence of an ancient Arctic home

---

[116] *AH*, 4.
[117] William F. Warren, *Paradise Found: The Cradle of the Human Race at the North Pole*, 10th ed. (Boston, 1893) (hereafter, Warren, *Cradle*). This is the edition Tilak cites.
[118] *AH*, vi–vii.
[119] Warren, *Cradle*, 9.
[120] *AH*, 350.

in the traditional literature of the Greek, Roman, Celtic, Teutonic, and Slavonic branches of the Aryan race. Tilak gives his twelfth chapter over to considering the evidence offered by comparative mythology, and this is essentially a paraphrase of Rhys' work. Rhys suggests a common Aryan homeland at 'some spot within the Arctic circle'; Tilak merely goes 'a step further', in showing how this is borne out by the Vedas and Avesta. The inclusiveness of Tilak's *Arctic Home* is explicit: 'My object', he says, 'is to trace from positive evidence contained in the Vedic literature the home of the Vedic and, therefore, also of the other Aryan races'. It is worth pausing to reflect for a moment on this unremarked inclusivity: Damodar Hari Chapekar, found guilty for the murder of the Poona plague officials Rand and Ayhurst in 1897 (which led on to Tilak's own imprisonment for the *Kesari* articles that had apparently inspired it, and hence these Vedic researches), gave testimony after his conviction that he and his brothers had earlier disfigured Queen Victoria's statue in Bombay by covering it with tar 'in order to rejoice their Aryan brethren [and fill] the English with sorrow'. Such was the note of exclusiveness and confrontation that 'Aryan' could sound in the politics of those associated with Tilak.[121]

And in fact Tilak diverges from Taylor crucially upon this point. Taylor's work, though Tilak does not acknowledge it, is an emphatic dismissal of the idea that the Aryan peoples had a common origin 'under one roof', as found in the classic mid-nineteenth-century formulation of Muller.[122] 'The assumption of the common ancestry of the speakers of Aryan languages is a mere figment', asserted Taylor; the 'old assumption of the philologists, that the relationship of language implies a relationship of race, has been decisively disproved and rejected by the anthropologists'.[123] In this scheme, populations were assumed to have acquired Aryan speech by acculturation, but the question of the degree of their ethnic affinities was open.[124] Indeed, it is, specifically, the 'southern and eastern extensions of Aryan speech' that are assumed not to betoken racial descent.[125] Tilak's maintenance of the ideas of the unity of Aryan race and origin, while in fact using Taylor's work

---

[121] *Sedition Committee 1918 Report* (Calcutta, 1918) (hereafter, *Sedition Committee Report*), 4.
[122] Taylor, *Origin*, 10.
[123] Ibid., 4–5.
[124] Ibid., 7.
[125] Ibid., 32.

as an authority in the *Arctic Home*, though, is remarkable. The 'hasty philological deductions' regarding a common Central Asian homeland, Tilak approvingly quotes him as saying, 'must be abjured in favour of those of 'prehistoric archaeology, craniology, anthropology, geology and common sense'.[126] Tilak even accepts the new racial indices: discussing the identity of the races represented by the Neolithic remains in Europe, Tilak points out that 'no inference can be drawn as to the language used by the ancient man'; he asserts instead that the 'shape and the size of the skull' may be 'taken as the chief distinguishing marks' to classify one as Aryan.[127] Ultimately, in this milieu of scientific racism, Tilak asserts through the remembrance of the Arctic Home a linguistic, even textual definition of race, showing Brahmins to be the descendants of Vedic Aryans in the Arctic Home through the fact of their remembrance of the Vedas. Indeed, it is worth noting that this necessary link between Brahminhood and Aryanness was fundamentally broken in mainstream ethnography by the time Tilak finalized *Arctic Home*: the Census Commissioner for India from 1899, H. H. Risley, developed his noted indices of nasal size and shape to determine the racial 'Aryanness' of different castes, still supposed in his analysis to bear the racial trace of the 'Aryan invasion'. But the progressive restriction of this Aryanness is visible in his Census of India of 1901, showing the culmination of a trend of thought building for at least twenty years previously: the only locus of the Aryan race in India was the northwest: the largest part of the Bombay Presidency, his ethnographic map graphically showed, bore no Aryan stamp, but was 'Scytho-Dravidian' (Figure 2.1). As we shall see in 'Reforming Hindu Society', the new assumptions regarding the low prevalence of the Aryan race in modern India tended to freeze the people of western India not only out of prestigious Aryanness, but specifically out of presumed membership of India's 'martial races', in favour especially of those from the 'Aryan' Punjab: Tilak's emphasis on Brahmin Aryanness in *The Arctic Home* should also be read in the light of its associations with martial vigour.

The Indo-Aryan branch alone, in fact, had the precocity *après le déluge* to maintain the civilization of the Arctic Home, while the European

---

[126] *AH*, 17.
[127] *AH*, 7.

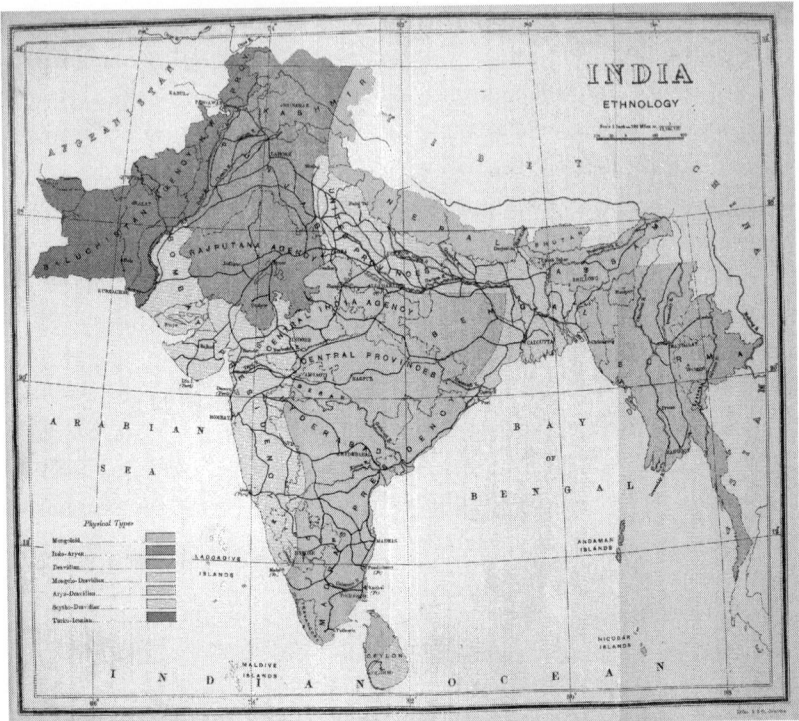

Figure 2.1 The ethnological map of India from the report on the 1901 census. Note the restriction of the 'Indo Aryan' type far to the north, excluding even Maharashtrian Brahmin communities. © The British Library Board (Asia, Pacific & Africa 0 W 7876/4, 59).

The map presented here holds historical significance. Therefore the map above does not claim to depict the present political boundaries of post-Independence India or its international borders. For accurate and up-to-date information on India's current internal and international boundaries, please refer to the Political map of India issued by the Survey of India.

Neolithics lapsed into a (pardonable) barbarism.[128] The position of the Vedas at the dawn of history, and that of Sanskrit as the mother language, are both secured; in fact they mutually substantiate each other, portions of the Vedas being, uniquely, propagated from prehistoric times through the unchanging medium of Sanskrit. In asserting that the Vedas' beginning is 'lost in geological antiquity', Tilak gives an historicizing reconstruction of the idea of their beginninglessness.[129] This does not quite

---

[128] *AH*, Ch. 13.
[129] Ibid., 451.

लोकमान्य टिळक यांचे आगमन.

Figure 2.2 'Arrival of Lokmanya Tilak' to his Pune home after release from imprisonment, as publicized by *Kesari*, 23 June 1914. Image courtesy of the Cambridge South Asian Archive.

salvage the orthodox belief from the jaws of modern science: Tilak offers in chapter XIII an extended comparison of the 'theological' and 'scientific' views, once more attempting to explain the essential validity of orthodox belief with reference to their scientifically provable extreme age, yet ultimately acknowledging that the two modes of explanation must 'stand apart'. Yet if modern historicism had undermined the orthodox view for Tilak, he could nevertheless offer a reformulation that restored the Vedas' mystique and secured them as the bedrock of Aryan civilization. And the prestige of Brahmins as carriers, as in *Orion*, is assured along with this: the 'accent for accent' transmission of the Vedas is emblematic of the resilience of Indo-Aryan civilization; it was accomplished by 'the class of priests', who, Tilak notes, it has been the fashion to 'cry down'. Tilak's is in fact a vindication of the role of priests in an age of science.

Tilak's lack of explicit engagement on the topic of caste—especially given his Maharashtrian background, with the heavy inheritance of Jotirao Phule's polemic (as we saw in the last chapter) undermining Brahminic so-cial authority—is remarkable; as too is his broader lack of engagement with India's civilizational 'descent'. Other prominent Maharashtrian Brahmins like M. G. Ranade were clear in elaborating how the Vedic 'Golden Age' was ruined by the assertion 'of a lower type of character and morality' by 'the down-trodden races, which had been driven to the hills', by the invading Aryans, before issuing from their haunts; at times he even pro-vided a litany of non-Aryan vitiators of Indian civilization, culminating with the 'lower ideal' of 'respect for the female sex' of its Mohammedan conquerors.[130] Conversely, as has been noted, in his associate Dayananda's innovative historical formulation, the Aryas quarrelling and splitting from the Dasyus in humanity's common home of Tibet then entered an unin-habited Aryavarta, thus obviating any prehistoric conflict with aborigines which resulted in varna.[131] The argument that Indian Muslims were Aryan in race was put forwards, for instance, by Tilak's future Congress collabor-ator, Lala Rajpat Rai.[132] That Tilak, even in his discussion of the post-Arctic history of the Aryan peoples in his thirteenth chapter, discusses none of the implications for caste or community in this context is remarkable. From his description of the Aryans overcoming non-Aryan tribes south of the arctic, it is clear that Tilak has as firm a belief as any in the superior power of the Aryan peoples; the strong implication of his work is Brahminic chauvinism vis-à-vis other castes, though he assumes an aloofness from explicit debates on the issue. Similarly, he does not broach at all the idea of the decline of

---

[130] Ranade's essay 'State Legislation on Social Matters', in M. B. Kolasker, ed., *Religious and Social Reform: A Collection of Essays and Speeches by Mahadeva Govind Ranade* (Bombay, 1902), 98; 'The Age of Hindu Marriage', in ibid., 29–32. Ranade's moderation of his message in ad-dressing different groups, noted by Deshpande, for instance at the Eighth Social Conference in Madras in 1894, emphasizes the obvious political content of his pronouncements on the issue.

[131] Ballantyne, *Orientalism*, 177–179.

[132] Lala Lajpat Rai, *Writings and Speeches*, ed. V. C. Joshi, 2 vols (Delhi, 1966), i. li, 186; ii. 190.

Aryan civilization in India, though the implication of his whole work is the Indo-Aryans' unerring capacity to propagate Aryan culture. On both issues, his silence itself is political—though only because of the political import of his implications.

This consideration of Tilak's contribution and those of some of his contemporaries to the historiography of the early Aryans suggests problems with our understanding of its development in late nineteenth-century India. One problem is the assumption in the literature that the use of the Aryan theory, and the notion of a golden age of Aryan civilization that is usually associated with it, inexorably led to new forms of Hindu nationalist consciousness. Some of the historiography on Aryanism is in fact explicitly preoccupied with its later formulations, which form part of the Hindutva agenda, leaving nineteenth-century writers to be viewed simply in relation to this tradition.[133] Yet Tilak's account of exogenous origins was actually antithetical to the 'Hindutva' interpretation of Aryan origins, which was nascent in Tilak's own time; early Hindutva ideologues insisted upon endogeneity, rubbishing the notion of an Aryan invasion: M. S. Golwalkar had to carefully revise Tilak's conclusions, placing the North Pole in Bihar.[134] Further, the very 'degenerationist vision' of Hindutva, emphasizing 'the corrupting influence of Islam', cannot be seen as a function of the Aryan theory: it is contestable that the 'essential structure' of the Vedic golden age followed by decline was as constant as has been suggested; the invocation of the 'Aryan' name and concept could as well suggest the Dravidian as historical villain, and the pernicious influence of Buddhism is one that Ranade for instance emphasizes.[135] This reasoning should only be pushed so far: clearly, non-Aryan peoples, be they Dravidian, Shudra, or Muslim, were placed at some distance from the glories of Aryan civilization, something hardly incompatible with later Hindutva formulations; and the ill-influence of Muslims is often stated. Yet Tilak's own statements

---

[133] See Romila Thapar, 'The Historiography of the Concept of "Aryan"', in Romila Thapar [et al.], *India: Historical Beginnings and the Concept of the Aryan* (New Delhi, 2006); also Thapar, 'Aryan Race', 8.

[134] Golwalkar's polar swerve is discussed in Chapter 6; the 'Indigenous Aryans' thesis was put forwards by another Chitpavan, N. B. Pavgee, in Bharatiya samrajya ['The Indian Empire'] (11 vols [Poona?, 1893–1901]); Deshpande, 'Arguments', 101, discusses this, though his reading appears teleological.

[135] Ballantyne, *Orientalism*, 184–185. Ballantyne cites Partha Chatterjee, 'History and the Nationalization of Hinduism', in Vasudha Dalmia and Heinrich von Stietencron, eds, *Representing Hinduism* (Delhi, 1995), 103–28, 117.

on Aryan history in these texts and the *Gita Rahasya*, where he emphasizes too the influence of Jains and Buddhists in vitiating Hindu dharma,
tell against a universal tendency to construct essentially anti-Muslim narratives from these historical materials.[136] Perhaps more importantly, the
association of the Aryan theory with the Vedic golden age itself is problematic. The above implies a 'refashioning' of Hindu history of this nature
through Aryan theories; yet the older, Hindu degenerationist tradition,
going back to the *Smritis* and epics, of the successively deteriorating ages—
the yugas—which we saw in the previous chapter, had actually provided
material for the construction of the Aryan idea. Descriptions of the culminating *Kaliyuga* in the *dharmashastra* even emphasized the existence of
mleccha or foreign rule over India.[137] The Aryan theory did re-emphasize
the glories of India's past, and this sense of loss, but in doing so it gave another layer to indigenous visions. In no way did these notions determinis-
tically give rise to new forms of communal consciousness. The notion that
divergent interpretations, Tilak's among them, could have no effect but to
unwittingly give grist to the mill of Hindutva politics, mechanically produ-
cing anti-Muslim sentiment, rests on a distorting teleology.

Tilak's treatment of the Aryan theme in *The Arctic Home* can also help
us understand better some of the broader, extraordinary popularity of the
use of the term 'Aryan' in India in the late nineteenth century that we have
encountered over the last two chapters. The range of Indian responses, it
should be said, is so remarkable that it might be suggested that the term
'Aryan', a near universal rallying cry, with different meanings for different
groups, but with little stability, is better understood not as an idea, but as
a locution, connoting a spectrum of ideas.[138] Part of the reason for the
deployment of the term was of course its very modernity and currency;
it was a natural response to canalize it. But as we have seen, it spoke to
pre-existing cultural and historical ideas. And therefore the language of
the 'appropriations' of the concept, or its being 'coopted', is misleading.[139]

[136] This aspect of the *Gita Rahasya* is discussed in Chapter 4.

[137] P. V. Kane, *History of Dharmashastra: (Ancient and Mediaeval Religious and Civil Law)*, 5
vols (Poona, 1930–1962), v, 828.

[138] Cf. Trautmann, *Aryans*, 2, where he states that the concept has 'formal qualities which are
stable', along with different perspectival aspects, but this is surely belied by Dayananda's seminal
use, which rejects practically all of them; indeed Trautmann remarks on the 'slippage' of the apparently stable idea (218).

[139] For instance, Romila Thapar, 'Some Appropriations of the Theory of Aryan Race Relating
to the Beginnings of Indian History', in Daud Ali, ed., *Invoking the Past: The Uses of History
in South Asia* (1999); Michael Bergunder, 'Contested past: Anti-Brahmanical and Hindu

Aryan ideas current in nineteenth-century India, such as Tilak's, represented rather a kind of continuous dialogical construction; as British 'new
Orientalism', from which sprung the Aryan theory, was constructed with
Indian input, but with control of its outcome resting with 'Europeans',
so Indians' reworking of this idea to fashion new outcomes is a symmet-
rical phenomenon, a dialogic response, drawing often on earlier Indian
understandings of the term *Arya*.[140] And it is important to note that this
dialogue was continuous; this was not a process of the 'construction' of
this knowledge and its subsequent 'discussion'.[141] The Aryan theory in
Europe never stopped being constructed through the nineteenth century,
for instance through the shifting indices of language and race, and the
changing notions of Indian-European unity, and of which communities
in India might be described as Aryan. Indian responses contesting this
were often contemporaneous, as was Tilak's to Risley's ethnographical
census data. The Aryan theory as it pertained to India was thus continu-
ally dialogically constructed. For Tilak, this involved most prominently
the reassertion of the position of the Vedas as in a sense prehistorical,
emanating in his scheme at the beginning of humanity's journey, rather
than at a later historical stage.

Gita Rahasya

Tilak's magnum opus is more purely a work of prison literature than his
previous works. Sentenced to six years transportation to Mandalay for
sedition for *Kesari* articles in 1908, Tilak produced an exegesis on the
Bhagavad Gita, the dialogue between Krishna and Arjuna on whether
or not Arjuna should fight in the epic Mahabharata. The *Srimad-
Bhagavadgita-Rahasya: Or Karma-Yoga-Shastra* (*Gita Rahasya* in its
short form, or 'Secret Import of the Gita') was written in an extraordin-
arily short period of time from November 1910 to March 1911, Tilak

nationalist reconstructions of Indian prehistory', *Historiographia Linguistica* 31.1 (2004): 59–
104; Bryant, *Quest*, 56; Deshpande 'Arguments'.

[140] Eugene Irshick, *Dialogue and History: Constructing South India, 1795–1895* (Berkeley,
1994), 8.
[141] Trautmann, *Aryans*; Ballantyne, *Orientalism*, 172–3.

having been granted access to books by the prison authorities.[142] Tilak apparently always intended the work for publication, which it achieved, ostensibly little altered, one year after his release.[143] Its context was one of victimization and failure, which his political achievements after release should not blind us to. It was a Tilak whose career—and, indeed, life—seemed to be drawing to its close, in exile first to the hinterlands of politics and then the hinterlands of British India, who set himself to the *Gita Rahasya*. The works seems valedictory. Tilak's preface states that 'my physical condition is now becoming weak ... and my contemporaries in life have passed on': he had decided to 'place before the public the information which I have gathered' while he was still able to do so.[144] His state of health does seem by this stage to have been poor; 52 at the time of his transportation, he had even by the time of his trial been suffering from diabetes for 'some time'.[145] The text thus stands as a sort of testament. Yet though scholarly, arcane, and at 1,200 pages extremely broad in scope, its theme of legitimizing enmity and violence ties it to Tilak's activity immediately before arrest.

The *Gita Rahasya* was composed in Marathi, first and foremost for a Maharashtrian readership. Although it went through Hindi, Kanarese, Telegu, and Guajarati translations in Tilak's lifetime, and according to his son he intended an English translation, its language of composition, unique among his major works, and its content mark it out for this audience.[146] This Marathi readership must necessarily have been largely highly educated; its audience was likely mainly those educated Maharashtrian Brahmins who were familiar with the otherwise abstruse Hindu philosophical concepts that he used (as well as authors as varied as Epicurus, Comte, Spencer, and Kant). He chose a Marathi treatise, not a Sanskrit one, however, and was at pains to explicate Sanskrit terminology, something which at least suggests a broader literate readership. The *Gita Rahasya* also abounds in references to Maharashtrian social and intellectual culture; Tilak thus hits home with a vernacular appeal quite

---

[142] See interview in *Mahratta*, 28 June 1914, reprinted SLT 7, 387–391. Information on the manuscript is given in *GR*, i. xxviii.
[143] Ibid.
[144] Ibid., xlv.
[145] See his bail application, Kelkar (ed.), *Trial (1908)*, 12.
[146] For publication information see *GR*, i. xi.

different to those authors on the Gita in the same period who wrote in English. One of his aims may well, indeed, have been the development of Marathi as a language of philosophy; and Tilak was conscious of the example of Jnaneshwar, whose verse commentary on the Gita had established Marathi as a literary vernacular six centuries earlier.[147]

Tilak's main aims are not obscure. Tilak urged his Hindu readership that their most venerated text enjoins active participation in the world: the Gita is a guide to proper action (*karmayoga*). This is so often repeated as to be the text's primary and unavoidable import. His text would inspire a more energetic, less apathetic Hindu population. In support of this aim, his conclusion makes much of 'active' Kshatriya virtues, and bemoans their falling away in modern India; Brahmins, specifically, are exhorted to emulate them rather than retreat into inactive contemplation. Tilak does attribute the downfall of India to the way Hindus had become:

it need not be said in so many words, that when this ancient religion, which is beneficial in this life and in the next, lost following in our country, it (our country) reached its present fallen state.[148]

He is equally clear that when the Vedic religion was observed according to its original precepts, India's 'prosperity' was at its greatest height; it had, indeed, a golden age.[149] The suggestion that Hindu religion had become renunciatory, and that this ill-equipped it for the modern age, was common to many expositing views of Hinduism in Tilak's time, many of them like Sarvepalli Radhakrishnan and Bankim Chatterjee commonly identified, somewhat problematically, as 'Neo-Hindus'.[150] Specifically, this comprehensive worldly engagement among Hindus

[147] Jnanedeva, *The Jnaneswari*, trans. Ranganath Shamachary Lokapur, 3 vols (Belgaum 1995–1999). Tilak comments on the beauty of Jnaneshwar's descriptions, *GR*, i. 26.

[148] *GR*, ii. 713.

[149] Ibid.

[150] See Paul Hacker, 'Aspects of Neo-Hinduism as Contrasted with Surviving Traditional Hinduism', in Wilhelm Halbfass, ed., *Philology and Confrontation: Paul Hacker on Traditional and Modern Vedānta* (Albany, 1995) The term implies a deviation from a timeless norm, and is thus criticized by, for example, Brian K. Smith in 'Questioning Authority: Constructions and Deconstructions of Hinduism', *International Journal of Hindu Studies*, 2/3 (1998), 313–339 (hereafter, Smith, 'Questioning Authority'). Though we shall investigate Tilak's relationship to 'Classical' *dharmashastra* and Vedanta, the framework of neo-Hinduism is not one that shall be employed.

that Tilak enjoins extends to undertaking 'even the most horrible war-fare'.[151] Both the general exhortation to action and its specific extension to action's darker modes have political implications; though, contrary to the preoccupations of most accounts of Tilak's writing, dwelling on these implications is scarcely a feature of the text. It should be noted, though, that this is a vision of politics in which all castes can participate. Tilak's dismissal of Krishna's notion of *varnashrama dharma* as not relevant to the modern age in the *Gita Rahasya*'s conclusion is remarkable, and over-looked.[152] Tilak ultimately gives a casteless vision in which all varnas have the same, somewhat Kshatriya-redolent dharma, and are able to choose duties regardless of their varna.[153] This sits askance many of Tilak's other statements on *varnashrama dharma*, particularly his stance on lower-caste political participation; although a particular preoccupation with Brahmin performance of Kshatriya attributes is likely Tilak's focus here.

Tilak's crystallization of the Gita's import is also an attempt to define Hinduism—even though the Indian Supreme Court's citation of the *Gita Rahasya* in 1966 as a 'working formula which may be regarded as fairly adequate and satisfactory' is in fact in error.[154] The claims he makes for the Gita are extraordinary: it is, he says in one of his speeches popular-izing his work, 'universally acknowledged to be a book containing all the principles and philosophy of the Hindu Religion'; his preface states it ex-pounds the 'root principles of the present Vedic Religion, as also its final aspect'.[155] Such examples could be repeated. Tilak thus locates Hinduism in this text and divines its true meaning. Tilak defines Hinduism ac-cording to *advaita* Vedanta, the non-dualist conception of the universe associated with the eighth-century Hindu thinker Adi Shankara. *Advaita* Vedanta, with its assertion of fundamental unity, seems to have lent itself to the project of giving a philosophical core to a united Hinduism in this period.[156] Indeed this appears to have emerged within Hindu philosophy over the longue durée, as Andrew Nicholson has observed considering those primarily Vedantin philosophers and doxologers who propounded

---

[151] *GR*, i, 550.
[152] Cf. Rao, *Foundations*, 303–304, 'the Gita being an orthodox text supported Manu's and thereby Tilak's view of caste'.
[153] Ibid., 305; Rao's account does not comprehend Tilak's statements in his concluding chapter.
[154] This will be discussed in Chapter 6.
[155] *GR*, i. xxiv, lii.
[156] Smith, 'Questioning Authority', 326.

the unity of the *astika* philosophical 'schools' as early as the twelfth century.[157] Tilak, in one of a number of manoeuvres in his career aimed at attaining Hindu unity, here rallies Hindus around the Gita. The sudden dismissal of *varnashrama dharma* in his concluding passage is consistent, at least, with a socially transcending and unifying vision. It parallels the public assertion of the unity of Hinduism at the World Council of Religions by the *advaitin* Swami Vivekananda—indeed, an influential figure in Tilak's thought on dharma—in Chicago in 1893. Tilak appears to have put particular effort into defining Vaishnavism—a group of traditions venerating Vishnu as the Supreme Being—as being consistent with this vision of Hindu dharma; and in this reflects others of the broader period, such as Bankim, who asserted a militant Vaishnavism.[158] Indeed this definition and consolidation of Hindu dharma and Hindu community does not imply an attempt to define the Indian nation in those terms: in fact Tilak's *advaitin* understanding is explicit that the nation is at the apex of a hierarchy of identification (barring the highest, identification with all created things). All forms of communal identity were below: 'pride of one's family, pride of one's religion, and pride of one's country are the ascending steps which lead to that highest of all states'.[159]

Tilak also aimed to inspire confidence in Hindus in their philosophical traditions, specifically Hindu ethics. On the authority of Paul Deussen, he takes it as accepted that 'the philosophy of the absolute self' in the Upanishads has not been surpassed.[160] And the ethics that derive from this all-embracing metaphysical view are therefore the highest that obtain, demonstrably superior to those of modern Western moral

---

[157] Andrew Nicholson, *Unifying Hinduism: Philosophy and Identity in Indian Intellectual History* (Colombia University Press, 2010).

[158] Tilak, unlike the Shaivite majority of Chitpavans, was himself a Vaishnavite, a fact generally not understood (see Rao, *Foundations*), despite the fact that Tilak had himself often been photographed displaying the characteristic Vaishnavite sandalwood paste markings on his forehead (see Figure 2.2). Tilak dedicated the *Gita Rahasya* to the 'Lord of Lakshmi' (that is, Vishnu), the 'highest Purusha' (*GR*, i. xlii). Tilak's efforts seem to be deliberately pan-sectarian and not merely self-apologetic, however. On Bankim's militant sannyasis in his novel *Anandamath* (1882), see Tanika Sarkar, *Hindu Wife, Hindu Nation Community, Religion, and Cultural Nationalism* (Dehli: Permanent Black, 2003) (hereafter, Sarkar, *Hindu Wife*), 178.

[159] *GR*, i, 556, 560. Tilak seems not to have totally decided on all aspects of this order: but that quoted above is the most explicit and hence definitive statement from him on the subject. Cf. Seth, 'Critique').

[160] *GR*, ii, 667. Tilak cites Paul Deussen, *Elements of Metaphysics, tr. by C.M. Duff. With an Appendix, Containing the Address on the Philosophy of the Vedanta in Its Relations to Occidental Metaphysics*, 2nd ed. (London, 1894).

philosophers, especially those of the 'materialistic school' (*adhibautika sukhavada*) 'which asks you to decide all questions of Morality by the sole external test of "the greatest good of the greatest number"', a 'one-sided and scientifically insufficient' criterion that he impugns elsewhere in his output.[161] Under this banner of Materialism, Tilak places a great number of ethical traditions: Mill and Spencer in essence agree with the assertion of Comte and the Positivist *adhibhautika* thinkers.[162] Tilak insists that they merely attend to external effects without considering the reason of the doer: yet a river is not excoriated as immoral for causing flooding; how then can external effects be a test of moral rectitude?[163] For Tilak, identification of the self with all created things, according to *Advaita Vedanta*, is instead the foundation of ethics, a notion surely evidencing the influence of Vivekananda (whom Tilak eulogized remarkably in *Kesari*).[164] And this sense undergirded his conception of the right of the individual to political rights, specifically the 'birthright' of Swaraj, discussed in the next chapter; Tilak can indeed be related to other Indian thinkers of the period who identified the divine in every self in order to do so, contesting colonial power in the process.[165]

Tilak, indeed, feels the need to assert that Hindu philosophy can convey ethics at all. Once more this need is a response to colonial critique. 'It is the common belief of many persons', he states, 'that our ancient writers, being steeped in the deep contemplation of Release, have forgotten to deal with the subject-matter of morality of ethics'.[166] This misconception arises from the works of Western Materialistic philosophers: they conceive of and therefore criticize ethics materialistically; therefore those influenced by them 'think that Morality or Ethics has not been dealt with in any work in Sanskrit literature'.[167] The entire colonial educational milieu is therefore Tilak's antagonist here. As Materialistic philosophers rather even than English metaphysicians like T. H. Green 'are principally taught

---

[161] Ibid., 676.
[162] Ibid., i, 87; though Tilak is sensitive at some points to differentiation, noting Spencer's divergences from Mill, ibid., 123.
[163] Ibid., ii, 668.
[164] 'There was the Shankaracharya, some 1000–1200 years ago, who believed that the Hindu religion is very rich and to spread it is our duty, and there was in our times Vivekananda'. Editorial, 8 July 1902. SLT 5, 190, 'Swami Vivekananda is no more!'
[165] See Banerjee, 'Sovereignty'.
[166] *GR*, ii, 666.
[167] Ibid.

in our colleges' (Tilak specifically notes that the English utilitarian Henry Sidgwick has prominence in the syllabus), the 'fundamental principles of *karmayoga* mentioned in the Gita, are not well understood even by learned persons among us, who have had an English education'.[168]

Not only this, but the Gita actually anticipates all subsequent developments in ethical thought. It systematically examines questions of right and wrong, long before Aristotle; indeed 'no moral doctrine has yet been evolved, which is different from the doctrines metaphysically expounded in the Gita'.[169] The corollary is that some Western authors are praised for the similarity of their insights to the Gita ethics. In particular, Tilak displays an admiration for Immanuel Kant and T. H. Green. For Tilak, Kant considers the question of ethics 'from the metaphysical point of view', as although he does not clearly expound on the unity of Brahman and Atman, he begins his disquisition with a consideration of 'Pure Reason' which Tilak translates as *vyavasayatmika buddhi*.[170] Green, for Tilak, simply refines Kant's metaphysics, to be more closely aligned with the philosophy of the Gita.[171] Tilak, indeed, explicitly defends his own account of the Gita's ethics by comparing them to Kant, noting that missionaries do not suggest that Kant's ethics allow the latitude for someone with pure reason to commit crimes, as they do of the Gita's.[172] 'When we realise', says Tilak, that 'even in the Western countries', the doctrines of Kant and others are

> very much akin to the doctrines of *Vedanta* philosophy, we cannot but feel a wonder about the supermanly mental powers of those persons, who laid down these doctrines of *Vedanta* by mere introspection, in an age when the Material sciences were not so advanced as they are in the present day; but we must not stop with feeling wonder about this matter—we must feel proud of it.'[173]

[168] Ibid., i, 93, 49.
[169] Ibid., i. l–li, in addition containing a list of the precepts anticipated.
[170] Ibid., 528–529, cf. Shruti Kapila, 'Self, Spencer, and Swaraj: Nationalist Thought and Critiques of Liberalism', *Modern Intellectual History*, 4/1 (2007) (hereafter, Kapila, 'Self'), 118, suggesting that Tilak rejected the claim of strong resemblances between his thought and Kantian metaphysics. This phrase may mislead: he was explicit on many areas of similarity, though not on Kantian dualism. Her view that he endorses 'only Nietzsche' in 'Violence', 446n, is inaccurate.
[171] *GR*, i, 310. Tilak does, though, sometimes slip into a tendency to dismiss all Western thinkers as materialistic, ibid., ii, 681.
[172] Ibid., i, 533.
[173] Ibid., 201.

In a revealing phrase, he describes his *Gita Rahasya*, in which Western philosophers are invoked to demonstrate the pristine brilliance of the Gita, as like the English recutting of the Kohinoor diamond in 1852—through which that everlasting stone shone with brighter lustre.[174] To establish the Gita's precocity, Tilak has to affirm its antiquity. His Appendix, containing a study of its 'external' features, gives an emphatically historicizing account of the Gita, making clear that Krishna promulgated the Gita on the morning of the battle at Kurukshetra, 1,400 years before Christ, there being therefore no influence of the Christian Gospels upon it.[175]

Tilak is quite insistent that he has 'put aside all criticisms and commentaries', and, 'getting out of the clutches of the commentators', simply let the Gita speak (or sing); indeed, despite its name *Rahasya*, there Tilak claims to unearth no hidden, inner meaning, other than that hidden in plain sight: to blame for the obscurity were previous commentators arguing that the Gita advocated the path of devotion (*bhakti*) or knowledge (*jnana*).[176] He insists Western authors had only looked at the text's 'external aspect'.[177] Tilak credits his own as the first commentary in favour of *karmayoga*, other than early, lost commentaries referred to in Shankara (a *jnana* supporter). Perhaps desiring to appear more venerable, Tilak does not credit the activist philosophy of Vivekananda, whose thinking on Vedanta, and use of the Gita as a core text, anticipates Tilak in many ways, and who Tilak was strongly influenced by.[178] But Tilak does draw on established concepts within Hindu *dharmashastra*. Particularly important is the *Kaliyuga*, the fourth and final age of the current cycle of cosmic time, which precedes the destruction of the universe in the dance of Shiva, and is a time of diminished dharma on earth.[179] As we have seen, Tilak was not inclined to

[174] Ibid., xlviii. The diamond in 1915 sat in the crown of the Empress consort of India, Mary, wife of King George V.

[175] Tilak has in his sights the comments of Franz Lorinser—(mistransliterated from the Marathi as Laurincer in the English edition)—in his German translation of the Gita, published in 1869.

[176] See Robert Minor (ed.), *Modern Indian Interpreters of the Bhagavadgita* (Albany, 1986), 224. Minor extends this to Tilak himself, surely wrongly.

[177] *GR*, i, liv.

[178] This will be discussed in Chapter 5.

[179] On the *Kaliyuga*, see especially Kane, *Dharmashastra*, iii, Ch. 34 and Heinrich Steitencron, *Hindu Myth, Hindu History; Religion Art and Politics* (Delhi, 2005) (hereafter, Steitencron, *Hindu Myth*).

defend its traditional dating in his works on Vedic history. But he asserts the historical reality of the yugas here.[180] In the *dharmashastra*, the *Kaliyuga* was associated with the abnegation of several other rules from older texts. Tilak's use of its implications is broader. In his twelfth chapter, on worldly affairs, Tilak uses it to justify wicked actions to the wicked, as an inevitable consequence of the age.[181] It is deployed significantly elsewhere in the work. The final words of the body of his text are a prayer that the devotees of renunciation (*sannyasa*) acknowledge that worldly action, 'preached by the Blessed Lord in the Gita, is the most proper path to be followed in the *kaliyuga*.'[182] There are other resonances of the *Kaliyuga* in the *dharmashastra* that Tilak may have been aiming to exploit by apparently superfluously invoking it at the close of his text, as the ultimate sanction for *karmayoga*. Although the *Kaliyuga* is a time of wickedness and avarice, it is also a divinely ordained period; and in it one can attain *moksha* (liberation) more easily, by simple fact of the greater prevalence of such *adharma*, and the commensurate increased value of dharmic acts.[183] The physical place that is afflicted by the *Kaliyuga* is, indeed, known in *dharmashastra* as *karmabhumi*—the land where acts can gain liberation.[184] Invoking such an age is a way for Tilak to underscore the imperativeness of the dharmic action he describes.

There is also a strong regional inflection to Tilak's interpretation of the Gita. In his concluding chapter, Tilak cites Maharashtrian authorities for his *karmayoga* interpretation, noting that the Marathi translations of the Mahabharata in the form of *bakhars* propagated something of its spirit in the eighteenth century. Above all, though, *karmayoga* is associated with Ramdas, whom he describes as guru to Shivaji, the seventeenth-century Maratha warrior-king.[185] His was the 'only exception' to prevalent interpretations in favour of renunciation over the preceding centuries: 'and anyone

---

[180] *GR*, i, 513.
[181] This chapter is discussed at length in Chapter 5.
[182] *GR*, ii, 663. He substantiates this (ibid., 701) to point out that *samnyasa* is *kalivarjya*—that is, one of the proscribed practices in the *Kaliyuga*. But this does appear superfluous given he has inferred the correct path directly from Krishna's words in the Gita, irrespective of the later yuga.
[183] Steitencorn, *Hindu Myth*, 152.
[184] Ibid., 161.
[185] On *bakhars* see Velcheru Narayana Rao, David Shulman, and Sanjay Subrahmanyam, *Textures of Time: Writing History in South India 1600–1800* (New York, 2003), Ch. 5, 'Tarikh, Caritra, Bakhar', 184–249.

who wishes to see, the true glory of the Path of Action, in pure and inspired Marathi language, must study [Ramdas'] *Dasbodh*.[186] Yet Ramdas is actually quoted sparingly in the text, and only in two of its chapters. It is perhaps, in his conclusion, more important for Tilak to evoke a memory of Ramdas, as a cultural authority, associated with a golden age in Maratha history (as well as a proponent of activist, *advaitin* Vaishnavism that Tilak aimed to inspire).[187] Certainly, in this period, Maharashtra's Brahmins increasingly asserted and celebrated Ramdas' role in Maratha history; the writings of V. D. Savarkar and V. K. Rajwade testify to this.[188] Tilak very consciously relates himself to a tradition of active Hindu patriotism in Maharashtra. Its particular articulation here was a function of the historical moment as much as of a unitary and unvarying regional philosophical tradition.

It is worth dwelling on the question as to why Tilak turned to the Gita at this moment in his career—having hitherto engaged most deeply with the Vedas—as so many in his period did; this throws further light on his aims in the text, and also briefly on the circumstances that produced the Gita's 'iconic status' today among Hindu texts, which one influential account indeed dates to 1880–1900.[189] The Gita indeed had always been one of the most important Hindu *Smriti* texts in the pre-modern period, and was prized by Vedantins as part of the three-fold canon (*prasthanatraya*) that formed the 'end', or culmination, of the Vedic corpus. It also had a special status in Maharashtra, on account of the historical and literary importance of the *Jnaneshwari*. Yet even so, Tilak turned to it only now for major exposition, his claim that over twenty-five centuries it had been as authoritative as the Vedas themselves an ironically revealing insistence.[190] It was, indeed, the only work that Tilak completed in prison, from a significant list of projected and initiated projects.[191] His was a change that reflected the times.

[186]   *GR*, ii, 706.

[187]   On Ramdas' *advaitin* conception, see, for example, Ch. 5, subchapter 6, of his *Dasbodh*. Ramdas, 'Explanation of Pure Knowledge', in *Dasbodh: Spiritual Instruction for the Servant*, trans. Shilpa Joshi and Shrikrishna Karve [s.l.] (2010), 111 ff.

[188]   See the discussion in 'Reforming Hindu Society'.

[189]   S. Kapila and F. Devji, 'The Bhagavad Gita and Modern Thought: Introduction', *Modern Intellectual History*, 7/2 (2010), 269–273; Eric J. Sharpe, *The Universal Gita: Western Images of the Bhagavatgita: A Bicentenary Survey* (London, 1985).

[190]   *GR*, i, 2.

[191]   Tilak, *Vedic Chronology*, 171.

We can assume he chose the text because it could readily bear out his *karmayogin* interpretation of Hindu dharma. The Gita became more relevant to Tilak as he felt more urgently the need to press for action over apathy, and the failure of the politics of the 'Extremists', the group's expulsion from Congress in 1907, and their repression by the state that had seen him ultimately imprisoned, offers a particular reason for this. More broadly, and despite this setback, the all-Indian political movement inaugurated by the Swadeshi campaign, incorporating new techniques of anti-state violence, rendered more relevant such a philosophy; and hence Tilak's 'activist' Gita, on which he had intermittently publicly expounded since 1897, as we shall see, came into its own. The Gita's ethics of action meant that it could indeed ground in the *dharmashastra* a fully-fledged theory of politics, something we shall further explore in Chapter 5. This was in large measure a legitimation of political violence. At one level, the Gita may have appealed in a colonial context as offering a justification of a victorious dharmic fight against the usurpation of political authority.[192] Yet there was more to it than this. As Sheldon Pollock remarks, historically, justifications of violence had not formed a significant part of political philosophy in India.[193] Theories justifying political violence were developed in early modern Europe in a context of coercive, 'absolutist' states; such autocratic government was not, in fact, characteristic in India in the same period, and thus such theories were not developed. Therefore Tilak and other writers of his generation were in a novel situation, and broached new ideological ground because of it. In furtherance of this, they turned to the Gita, for the sake of its theme of how apparently *adharmic* things—specifically, acts of violence—can be undertaken without incurring *adharma*. Indeed, Tilak had been imprisoned for arguing in *Kesari* that the state was behaving unprecedentedly autocratically over the partition of Bengal, and that violence was therefore justifiable against it—*the Gita Rahasya* was an implicit expression of the same.[194] Tilak was in fact inspired in his justifications of violence in *Kesari* and *Gita Rahasya* by the

---

[192] In the Mahabharata, Arjuna is one of the Pandavas who had been usurped of their kingship by their cousins the Kauravas.

[193] Pollock, *Ends*, citing J. J. L. Gommans, 'The Embarrassment of Political Violence', in Jan E. M. Houben and Karel R. Van Kooij, eds, *Violence Denied: Violence, Non-Violence and the Rationalisation of Violence in South Asian Cultural History* (Leiden, 1999).

[194] This is discussed most fully in 'The Conduct of Politics'.

actual existence of political violence in India: the bomb-blast of 1908 ushered in a new political reality, and Tilak's theory of violence, like so much
political theory, was reactive in rationalizing and justifying it.

This work will now proceed with thematic treatments of Tilak's responses to critical questions across his output.

3

The Nature of the Indian Polity

This chapter focuses on Tilak's views on the relationship between religious community, political authority, and national identity in India.
It will also consider Tilak's conception of the basis of legitimate political authority in representative government—which Tilak also came
to define according to religious community. A dominant conception
today, in both popular and academic circles, as the Introduction discussed, is that Tilak was either a 'nascent shape', or a fully-fledged early
exemplar, of a linear Hindu nationalist tradition in Indian politics that
emerged as a major distinct force soon after his death.[1] This chapter
will argue rather that Tilak's conception of the Indian polity was pluralistic, Indian society comprising distinct, unitary, and primordial Hindu
and Muslim communities, which were to be constituted politically; and
that his efforts to mobilize the Hindu community coexisted with efforts
to build up nationalist feelings. Thus was the Indian nation being constructed, paradoxically, from diverse historically constituted materials
under colonial conditions by Tilak and many of his fellow nationalist
thinkers. Indeed, in this, Tilak subscribed in a classic manner to what
Gyanendra Pandey describes as the 'composite body' idea of the Indian
nation, prominent among 'early' nationalists.[2] This work departs from
his view that this was characteristic of north Indian articulations of nationalism, a function in particular of such a prominent Indo-Muslim
court culture and shared quotidian social-cultural experiences; for they
mattered less for Tilak than the structural power of the colonial ethnographical 'knowledge', of India as a land of communities; and of course

---

[1] Jaffrelot, 'Reader'; Rao, *Foundations*, and Bhatt, *Hindu Nationalism* both reflect Tilak's full
articulation of such Hindutva from different perspectives.
[2] Gyanendra Pandey, *The Construction of Communalism in Colonial North India* (Oxford
University Press, 1990) (hereafter, Pandey, *Construction*), ix, 210.

The Thought of Bal Gangadhar Tilak. Robert E. Upton, Oxford University Press. © Robert E. Upton 2024.
DOI: 10.1093/oso/9780198900658.003.0004

the political structure which provided the imperative as well as the hermeneutic framework for plural communal mobilization for the winning of political rights.

This communitarian conception is visible in relation to the 1893 riots in Bombay, when Tilak organized to cohere the local Hindu community and to urge its rights to government, and also in his support for the revived Ganapati 'festival' in 1893–1894—misremembered as an emblem of his Hindu cultural nationalism (as indeed it is misremembered as Tilak's innovation at all)—as a related effort to consolidate a more discrete Hindu community regionally in this atmosphere of heightened intercommunity tension. It ultimately found political expression in the pact between the Congress and Muslim League, in which Tilak had a pivotal role, at Lucknow in 1916, guaranteeing separate Muslim representation in provincial councils. In his understanding of the nation, he differed not only from the dominant ideas of Hindutva that crystalized in the early-mid 1920s (and whose ideologues appropriated him at that moment to it, as we shall see in the final chapter); his political vision of communal political rights was in fact in direct opposition to Hindu Mahasabha politics during the last years of his life.

If Tilak's vision of the polity was in a kind of majoritarian mode of pluralism, in which the strengthened and consolidated Hindu community retained preponderance, it is perhaps unsurprising that his attempts to imagine a broader pan-communal India floundered because of his lack of imaginative resources and historical symbols, which drew disproportionately on the culture, and history, of the majority community. Partly this was a matter of his own cultural conditioning; but indeed the misremembrance of his 'instigation' of the enlarged Ganapati *utsav* is pertinent, as it implies a greater command of the deployment of cultural resources in the furtherance of his politics than he in fact possessed: Tilak as much as any other politician used materials of existing cultural currency, as in his use of the memory of Shivaji. Nonetheless, in this treatment in particular, Tilak contrasts markedly not only with modern but contemporary attempts to assert Shivaji's memory as a fighter for the Hindu *rashtra* against the Islamic Mughal state—or more broadly among nationalists of the period to denigrate the social and political culture of the 'Islamic' period in Indian history.

The conception of the polity expressed at Lucknow was one in which legitimacy was vested in the representation of India's communities. This conception of legitimacy was underlined in Tilak's contemporary speeches on the illegitimacy of the colonial state, and the necessity of achieving *Swarajya*, or 'Home Rule'—two broadly interchangeable terms for Tilak, but with significant and distinct provenance and historical connotations of political rights. Indeed Tilak's use of *Swarajya* carried knowing echoes of popular political rights commonly read into seventeenth-century Maratha history, implying the importance of this historical memory in forming Tilak's conceptions of political legitimacy; and Tilak's famous definition of 'Swaraj' as his 'birthright' in 1916–1917 derived from the seventeenth-century lexicon of English political rights, so influential to Tilak's own agitations against authority, the expression's vernacular equivalents (competing versions of which emerged) being freshly coined to express Tilak's political conceptions.[3]

'Two brother communities'

Tilak's conception, consistent through his career, was of India as a 'land of communities', and his statements on the rights of India's 'two principal' communities, Hindu and Muslim, from the years of tension and communal conflict in the Bombay Presidency in the early 1890s to the final months of his life in the shadow of the *Khilafat* movement can all be seen in relation to this. Tilak in fact in large measure reflects the phenomenon Pandey describes, a reproduction (once more for Tilak) of colonial knowledge, in terms of the 'communal' character of Indian society, the very term's special use in relation to India betraying an essentialized understanding of its distinctness. This informs Tilak's notion of communal rights within the Indian polity. Such a conception is markedly visible in Tilak's response to the Hindu-Muslim riots in Bombay in 1893, and his

---

[3] Disagreement abounds as to when Tilak first spoke this phrase, long since associated with him publicly. Cashman, *Myth*, 218, claims he said it in 1905 (but produces no citation); Ram Gopal, *Lokamanya Tilak: A Biography* (Bombay, Asia Publishing House, 1956) (hereafter Gopal, *Tilak*), 283, similarly suggests it is 1907; as we shall see in 'Remembering Tilak', the favoured date for its modern commemoration is 1916. I can find no verifiable trace of its use before January 1917, in the context of the Home Rule League speeches Tilak was making in the wake of the Lucknow Congress.

stance on the defining issue of cow protection, which this section will first describe. The succeeding section will demonstrate the rationale behind Tilak's promotion of the public celebration of the Ganapati festival, a regional Hindu communal consolidation conceived in a direct response to this conflict. This will provide the long-term framework to understand his part in the Lucknow Pact, discussed in the section following. The pact can be seen as expressing in structural terms the communal conception of the Indian nation he had enunciated from the 1890s. His dissension from the *Khilafat* movement, so strongly urged by Gandhi and coolly sidestepped by Tilak, provides an addendum; sceptical over its use as an all-Indian nationalist rallying point, Tilak conceived of it as a matter for separate Muslim deliberation and representation—mirroring the rationale behind his own encouragement of the Ganapati *utsav* in 1893–1894.

Though Tilak's hostile rhetoric towards Bombay's Muslims in the wake of the riots of 1893 has absorbed much attention, Tilak's substantive response to it has not, and is more telling. 'In connection with these riots', the Bombay Government recorded, and many have concurred, 'Tilak's personality asserted itself' and he stood forth as an opponent 'of the "Moderate" party of the community'.[4] The violence of that August was a seismic event in the city's history, and the Presidency's politics. *Mahratta*'s front page of 20 August likely spoke for many in stating that 'No body would have believed ... that Friday week was to be made notoriously immemorial [sic] in the history of peaceful and prosperous Bombay'. These riots remain the largest exception to the 'general rule that Hindu-Muslim riots in Bombay were rare before the 1920s', although the context of contemporary inter-community violence in northern India in the middle of 1893 is in fact vital to them.[5] On 11 August, after noon prayers at the Jama Masjid in Bombay, an unusually large group of worshippers left the mosque, and with cries of '*deen*' proceeded to attack the Hanuman Lane Hindu temple, reforming after being dispersed and spreading to neighbouring areas; that day and the following day groups of crudely armed Hindus, latterly reinforced by local mill-hands,

---

[4] *Source Material for a History of the Indian Freedom Movement in India*, 11 vols (Bombay, 1957–), ii. 201.

[5] Rajnarayan Chandavarkar, *Origins of Industrial Capitalism: Business Strategies and the Working Classes in Bombay, 1900–1940* (Cambridge, 1994) (hereafter, Chandavarkar, *Origins*), 421.

fought pitched battles with Muslim counterparts.[6] By the time the rioting subsided—though the worst was over by the following Monday, there would be many more days of it—at least eighty-one persons had been killed, 700 injured, and 1,550 arrested; sixty temples and thirty-three mosques were damaged or destroyed.

In the riots' immediate aftermath, the Bombay Government pinned blame on the provocative action of the Presidency's cow protection societies (*Gaurakshini Sabhas*)—a somewhat smaller phenomenon there than further north and east in India, where it had grown since its modern inception in the early 1880s.[7] The *Gaulapan Upadeshak Mandali*, in particular, founded by one Lakhmidas Khimjee, had allegedly distributed in Muslim neighbourhoods handbills against Muslim cow slaughter.[8] Tilak mounted a stout, though not uncritical, defence of the *Sabhas* and their rights as a facet of those of the local Hindu community vis-à-vis the Muslim. A *Mahratta* editorial immediately after the riots noted that the refusal of the Governor to meet with an 'influencial [sic] Hindu gentleman'—Khimjee—who had come to Poona to solicit a meeting had given 'indirect encouragement' to Bombay Muslims.[9] Further, it was 'indiscriminate cow-slaughter' that had in fact gotten out of hand.[10] Within a month, at a Hindu 'mass meeting' called 'for the purpose of placing before Government the Hindu view' of the riots and the 'means to restore harmony', Tilak tabled a motion stating that the '*due* protection of the cow *has not* led and *cannot* lead to any estrangement of feeling between Hindus and Mahomedans'.[11] Rather, the riots were down to 'the absence of any authoritative exposition of policy ... of Government officials', a want of 'record ... of existing religious and social rights and privileges', and 'mistaken notions' about the impartiality guaranteed by the Queen's Proclamation of 1858. More than anything for Tilak it was the historical

---

[6] Details on the riots are drawn from *The Bombay Riots of August 1893*, reprinted from *The Times of India* (Bombay, 1893); *The Mahomedan and Hindu Riots in Bombay, August 1893*, from *The Bombay Gazette* (Bombay, 1893).

[7] Gyanendra Pandey, 'Rallying Round the Cow: Sectarian Strife in the Bhojpuri Region, c.1888–1917', in Ranajit Guha, et al. eds, *Subaltern Studies: Writings on South Asian History and Society*, 10 vols (Delhi: Oxford, 1994–1999), ii. 124 (hereafter, Pandey, 'Rallying').

[8] Prashant Kidambi, *The Making of an Indian Metropolis: Colonial Governance and Public Culture in Bombay 1890–1920* (Ashgate, 2007), 178.

[9] *Mahratta*, 13 August, 3.

[10] *Mahratta*, 27 August, 4.

[11] *Mahratta*, 17 September, 3. The meeting was held on 10 September. Italics original.

relationship between the communities of Maharashtra that determined the appropriate limits of their rights vis-à-vis one another in the present day. As he had already made clear in *Mahratta* in defence of the *Sabhas*, a hundred years ago 'a Marathi *Sirdar* obtained a *Sanad* disallowing the slaughter of the cow in the territories under the Mahomedan rule'; therefore the notion that this novelty was unsettling was based on an historical misunderstanding of the strength of the Marathas, and gave 'direct encouragement to the Mahomedans', who now anew were 'led to believe they have an inherent right to kill a cow in Hindu quarters'. Lord Harris, the Presidency's Governor, would be 'sowing the seeds of future riots' if he failed to regard the 'traditions of Maharashtra'.[12]

But not, even in Maharashtra, did this mean for Tilak that Muslims had their own rights to their customs denied. At the Hindu mass meeting, he stated 'no Hindu has the right to gratuitously offend the feelings of his Mahomedan brother', warning his audience that 'you will not be justified if you go out of your way and snatch a cow from a butcher's hands'. There are 'limits to your movement', he stated; beyond this 'persuasion and friendly agreement is necessary'.[13] Interestingly, despite his defence of them at this juncture, Tilak selected his alleged 'foundation' of cow protection societies in the Deccan as one of six ways he had been defamed by the *Times* journalist Valentine Chirol, who labelled Tilak the 'Father of Indian unrest' in his 1910 work *Indian Unrest*.[14] There is a persistent assumption of Tilak's investment in cow protection: the Vishva Hindu Parishad (VHP), part of the 'Sangh Parivar' family of Hindutva organizations, still prominently claim Tilak as a precedent for their cow protection efforts.[15] There seems, indeed, to be no evidence of Tilak's membership of, still less instigation of, any movement for the protection of cows. Tilak's identification with the societies here was as part of his community, asserting, in his view, its just rights. Tilak rallied round the

---

[12] *Mahratta*, 20 August, 3 (editorial).
[13] SLT 5, 79, 'Mass Meeting of Hindus in Pune' (*Kesari*, 19 September 1893).
[14] *The Legal Proceedings in the Case of Tilak v. Chirol and Another: Before Mr. Justice Darling and a Special Jury, January 29th 1919–February 21st 1919* (London, 1920).
[15] The VHP's website states 'great leaders of the freedom movement like Lokmanya Tilak and Mahatma Gandhi declared that their first act after ousting the British ... [would be] making law totally prohibiting the slaughter of cow' (https://vhp.org/cow_protection/). Scholarly writing follows this assumption, recently, for instance, in Guha, *Makers*, 108.

Sabhas as the integral part of his defence of the Hindu community's position, with reference to its historical regional circumstances.

While concerned explicitly to conciliate the two warring communities of the Bombay Presidency, Tilak is clear that the whole of India, in its several provinces, is divided into 'two principal communities'.[16] It has been noted that violence between Hindus and Muslims 'acquired a new social meaning in the late nineteenth century'; having registered 'as neighbourhood conflicts and local rivalries, reflecting competition over trade, employment, housing or local power' by the 1920s in the Bombay Presidency, and in other areas earlier, they are 'perceived and explained' in purely communal terms.[17] Tilak's language here in fact indicates that they could be understood this way there an entire generation earlier. His response can be read at one level as a reflection of observable realities as far as Bombay city is concerned, as it witnessed in the mid-to-late nineteenth century a strong and well-documented coalescence of community identities, at both caste level and pan-Hindu and pan-Muslim levels.[18] Bombay was also increasingly part of broader pan-regional community networks, facilitated by improved communication, linking it to areas which had experienced violence earlier in the year, particularly that three weeks before the Bombay riots in Prabhas Patan in Kathiawad; Bombay city coreligionists of the victims, Hindu and Muslim, had organized in sympathy with them.[19]

But for Tilak, these communities were not new, or coalescing. His call was for an inquiry to set up machinery to settle, in this new period of more fraught communal competition, disputes between these two 'brother communities that could live without any such breach for several centuries'.[20] These communities were ancient, the expression of old, even primordial identities. This seems at one level to involve Tilak in reproducing, in Thomas Blom Hansen's terms, this 'orientalist mode of production of the people'.[21] For the fundamentally dichotomized view of Indian society is described by Thomas Metcalf as prefigured

[16] *Mahratta*, 20 August.
[17] Chandavarkar, *Origins*, 178.
[18] See Christine Dobbin, *Urban Leadership in Western India* (London, 1972), 217, 224–228.
[19] *Mahratta*, 20 August 1893 (4, editorial notices). Pandey, 'Rallying'.
[20] *Mahratta*, 17 September, 3.
[21] Hansen, *Saffron Wave*, 60.

in the earliest European travelogues of India, and the convictions of Company servants like Robert Orme in the mid-eighteenth century.[22] It was a vision that hardened due in part to administrative convenience, a simplifying, comprehending structure for Indian society and its administration, as expressed in the drive to codify bodies of 'Hindu' law and 'Muslim' Law; and, as we saw in Chapter 1, the overarching categories of 'Hindu' and 'Muslim' were crucial and arguably influential in comprehensive census production from as early as 1872 in western India (though caste and sect significantly cut across them). Tilak's communitarian vision therefore cannot simply be ascribed to economic rationality or political positioning, but is a matter of his historical consciousness in his time and place, not least in Tilak's comprehending of Maharashtrian historic specificities to this all-Indian 'communal' relationship, in the context of revived 'Maratha' patriotism (discussed further below). Indeed the impact of colonialist stereotypes of a hyper-unified and therefore threatening Muslim community (which would also stimulate different and new forms of Hindu mobilization in the 1920s) has also been well noted.[23] The political context was vital in a broader sense: as Tilak alludes to, the self-conscious neutrality of the post-1858 colonial state placed it in a sense, and unprecedently, 'above' society, as an adjudicator of 'Hindu'-'Muslim' disputes. As has been noted, this encouraged the hardening of communal identities, the better to assert such community rights within such a political framework.[24] This became more pronounced, naturally, the greater the political rights that were at stake through the late nineteenth century. But specifically in 1893 in the Bombay Presidency, the stance of the Governor, Lord Harris, provides an almost parodic exemplification of this political role: a cricket fanatic and former England captain, he conceived of his role specifically as that of umpire between communities, and in fact wholeheartedly supported Tilak's efforts at community 'conciliation' from the days after the riots in August 1893—for which he was, rather unusually, thanked by *Mahratta*.[25] And within this context, for

---

[22] Thomas R. Metcalf, *Ideologies of the Raj* (Cambridge, 1995) (hereafter, Metcalf, *Ideologies*), 133.

[23] Mushirul Hasan, 'The Myth of Unity: Colonial and National Narratives', in David Ludden, ed., *Making India Hindu* (Oxford, 2007), 185–208.

[24] See Pandey, *Construction*.

[25] Katherine Prior, 'Harris, George Robert Canning, Fourth Baron Harris (1851–1932), Cricketer and Administrator in India', *Oxford Dictionary of National Biography*, https://doi.org/10.1093/ref:odnb/33724; *Mahratta*, 27 August 1893, 2.

Tilak, measures to consolidate and strengthen Hindu community—while at the same time aiming, not always successfully, to transcend this in the fashioning of all-Indian identities—were vital.

Tilak and Ganapati

Tilak's role in the creation of a public Ganesh *utsav* or festival in Maharashtra—from the formerly private and devotional one—has been much distorted in the telling. It needs to be flatly stated that Tilak in no sense initiated the public *utsav*, as commonly stated in scholarly literature as much as in popular remembrance.[26] But his championing of it is nonetheless, of course, extremely significant, for the *utsav* itself and for our understanding of his career. It is frequently seen as an attempt to rally the populace for nationalist politics around a specifically Hindu symbol— and thus as a pillar of his Hindutva cultural nationalism.[27] But his concern was in fact narrower: it was a mobilization of the Hindu community of the region in the context (which we saw above) of the highly communally contested atmosphere there (as elsewhere) in 1893–1894, and the importance of demonstrating communal cohesiveness to the colonial authorities, who adjudicated a space of contest between the rights of recognized religious communities. Tilak's efforts to consolidate the Hindu community were fruitful enough that the definition he came to propose for Hindu dharma in connection with the festival is used as a legal definition of 'Hinduism' in India today.[28]

The public celebration of the festival seems to have grown from 1892, under the influence of one Bhau Lakshman Javale (aka Rangari) in Poona: this is attested in *Kesari* itself, which in September 1893, far from announcing a Tilakite innovation, welcomed Rangari's celebration

---

[26] See 'Remembering Tilak'. Even specialized works on Ganesh, such as Paul B. Courtright, *Ganesa, Lord of Obstacles, Lord of Beginnings* (Oxford, 1989), refer to 'Tilak's innovations' in the 1890s (see 234). Raminder Kaur, *Performative Politics and the Cultures of Hinduism: Public Uses of Religion in Western India* (London, 2005) (hereafter, Kaur, *Performative Politics*), has noted the importance of other forgotten actors, and this work reaffirms (for Tilak's authorship is still common currency) Kaur's view, through a study, crucially, of archival evidence, which Kaur erroneously identifies as attaching Tilak's name to the *utsav*.

[27] See Seth, 'Critique'.

[28] This is further discussed in 'Remembering Tilak'. The Supreme Court did not correctly identify its provenance, assuming instead it came from the *Gita Rahasya*.

of earlier that month.[29] But despite the notability of this expanded festival, the common dating of the *utsav* from 1893 (wrongly attached to Tilak's name) is also misleading, for despite these early efforts, the Bombay Government's archives show its registering—with some comprehensible unease—of a festival totally new in scale in 1894, with other regional newspapers also greeting the 1894 celebration as a novelty.[30] We can safely assert Tilak's role as a champion and publicist, not for the last time, of the efforts of others, given Rangari's celebrations appear barely noted before Tilak.[31] The fact that it did swiftly become associated with Tilak demonstrates the influence of his publicity, specifically through *Kesari*; but Tilak is most accurately seen as one of a number of organizers and publicists of the enhanced 1894 *utsav*, and not necessarily the most prominent. The pre-distributed handbills (attached to the doors of temples) collected by the Government in July–August 1894 indicate a number of publicists and presses responsible: the Shri Shivaji Press was responsible for one, informing people of the 'good proposal' to have 'processions on the Ganesh chaturthi day this year in honour of Shri Ganpati' and noting that 'excellent songs have been prepared for the occasion.'[32] The songbooks that contained them, collected at the same time by the Bombay Government, bore the names of other Poona figures such as Jagannath Ganesh Badekar, and presses such as the Shree Vithal and Shri Samarth.[33] A petition to the Government of 371 inhabitants of Poona headed by one Abdullah Khan Ali Khan Mokasi complained of the arrogance of the local Brahmins in general and their building a union among themselves and the Marathas and testing it 'against the Muhammadans.'[34] Thus it is not surprising that for the Government of Bombay (which charted the influence of *Kesari* along with the rest of the 'native press' assiduously) figures such as Tilak's old associate Mahadev Ballal Namjoshi

---

[29] 26 September 1893.

[30] The festival is most commonly dated to 1893 in popular remembrance (see 'Remembering Tilak'), and scholarly treatments commonly, though not universally, follow (see V. Barnouw, 'The Changing Character of a Hindu Festival', *American Anthropologist*, 56/1 [February 1954], 74–86). The annual Press Report for 1894 referred to the 'Ganapati procession of Poona' as a unique celebration of the year under report. MSA PD 1894, 157, 'Native Press', f. 141.

[31] Extant newspapers are, as we have seen, sadly rare for the 1890s in western India. The RNPB for 1893 records no mention of Ganesh celebrations at all.

[32] MSA JD 1894, 287, enc. to District Superintendent of Police to District Magistrate Poona, 10 August 1894.

[33] Ibid., f., 263 ff.

[34] 31 July 1894. Ibid., f. 317–326.

were considered equally important in bringing the 1894 *utsav* about, with Tilak, if mentioned, being for instance a mere member of a 'reactionary party' of Chitpavans.[35]

Thus the assumption of Tilak's progeniture of the Ganesh festival is not 'testament to the power of the printed word in archives', for the most relevant contemporary ones contain none such.[36] It was in the years that followed, it seems, that the prevalence and energy of his public speaking, and its propagation by *Kesari*, secured his reputation as the pre-eminent figure in this regional festival; his name attached to it thus throughout India, not least through the celebration of his biography at the time of his sedition convictions.[37] And this is important, rather than pedantic, for our estimation of Tilak's output and agency in relation to his society: and Tilak here simply picked up what was to hand and worked with what was emerging, independently, in his milieu. This is relevant for thinking about other aspects of his output, as we shall see.

The rationale for Tilak's first championing the *utsav* in September 1893 in *Kesari* chimed exactly with that of the Hindu mass meeting he had coorganized the previous week, in response to the Bombay riots. This precise concurrence has been overlooked.[38] 'The riots originate amongst the masses', said Tilak at the meeting; thus community meetings like this, for which he was criticized by Ranade and others for their communal exclusivity, were 'emergently wanted' to help conciliate members of the two communities.[39] Tilak even absolved the promoters of a Muslim committee meeting to raise funds for their coreligionists caught up in the violence at Prabhas Pathan of any responsibility for exciting the Hindu community in opposition to the Muslim.[40] But the conditions of communal tension which had given rise to such organization continued into the summer of 1894. This informed the *utsav* planning that year. A month after the 1893 riots the procession for the Balaji festival in Yeola

---

[35] Note by a member of the Bombay Executive Council, H. M. Birdwood, ibid., dated 2 September.

[36] Kaur, *Performative Politics*, 34.

[37] See, for instance, the short 'Character Sketch' by N. C. Kelkar in Kelkar (ed.), *Trial (1908)*.

[38] Cashman, strangely, states that the real reason for convening this meeting—to promulgate a 'Hindu view' of the riots—was 'not publicly stated', and treats it with some detachment from his subsequent study of the *utsav*. *Myth*, 70.

[39] *Mahratta*, 10 September, 3; 17 September, 3 (editorials).

[40] *Mahratta*, 20 August, 4 (editorial notices).

had been pelted with stones as it passed a mosque; the following February in the same town a mosque was burned down and a temple attacked in further disturbances. Indeed, the Bombay Government's files on the Ganapati 'festival' formed part of its sequence on Hindu-Muslim riots in Poona.[41] In Tilak's view, the Bombay Government's reaction to this pattern of disturbances was one-handed, failing consistently to uphold the right of Hindu processions to play music in front of mosques. This led him to a position of outright boycott of Muslim festivities by Hindus as an assertion of community identity and solidarity, vis-à-vis the Muslim community, and in the eyes of the Government.[42] From the beginning, the organization of the enhanced Poona Ganapati *utsav* was associated with the Hindu boycott of Muharram (the anniversary in Shia Islam of the martyrdom of the Imam Hussein Ibn Ali) in Poona in July 1894. One Ganapati handbill mentioned above began by quoting the Bhagavad Gita that 'an alien religion is a source of danger', and indicated the Ganesh festivities would substitute for Muharram *melas* (quoting the Bhagavad Gita, Ch. iii, v. 35); another pointedly likened Hindu dharma to 'the chastity of a woman'. The week following Muhurram, Tilak expressed his satisfaction in *Kesari* over its boycott. Typically, said Tilak,

> every year there are around 140–150 processions out of which 100 belong to Hindus and around 40–50 belong to Muslims. But this time there were only 25 from Hindus and 60 from Muslims.[43]

No Hindu drummers played, a boycott that cost them financially, and Hindu labourers refused to carry the symbolic corpses of Shia martyrs on their shoulders. Tilak said, 'the current political climate necessitates registering such lawful dissent; otherwise no one will care for our rights'. It was necessary, he said, to 'let the Government know that we still have our self-esteem alive', adding: 'Hindus and Muslims have equal rights in this country. And I appreciate their being treated as equal'. He would not suffer his community being mistreated, as if to follow the 'impractical

---

[41] MSA JD 1894, 286, 287.
[42] *Mahratta*, 18 March 1894, 3 (editorial), 'The Bombay Government on the Yeola Riots'.
[43] *Kesari*, 17 July 1894, SLT 5, 81, 'Muharram and the attitude of the Hindus'.

Christian scriptural advice' that 'if you are slapped on one cheek' you should 'present the second'—advice, indeed, he recurrently deplored.[44]

Correspondingly, the Ganapati celebrations in September were designed to be exclusively Hindu. Another petition of Poona Muslims at this time decried the 'wanton mimicry of the time-honoured usages' of the Muslims in elements of the forthcoming festival.[45] The public processions to immerse the idols of Ganesh on the final day of the festivities certainly appear to echo the immersion of *tabuts* representing the martyrs' tombs. However insulting this was intended to be, it certainly seems a form of aggressive substitution, through which the celebrations of the two communities, hitherto in a measure syncretic, could be segregated. Of course, it should be acknowledged that this overtly 'communal' response, of vying public demonstrations of community identity, could be violently antagonistic, as shown by the festive *sloka* sung, by his own account, by Damodar Hari Chapekar—whom we will meet again claiming *Kesari* as inspiration for violence—referring to the 'monstrous atrocity' of the 'wicked' killing kine, and calling for redress.[46] The more militant anti-Islam of some of the Ganapati *melas*, associated with Poona figures such as *Tatyasaheb* Hari Ramchandra Natu, was a corollary of the form of organization Tilak stood for—even if his own tone and language was distinct from it.[47] And it is worth considering Tilak in relation to other movements at almost exactly the same moment further north in the United Provinces to cohere Hindu communities locally, or indeed pan-regionally, while maintaining a commitment to a pluralistic national polity, from the Madhya Hindu Samaj in Allahabad, set up in 1884 and conjoined to the Congress nationalism in the region which emerged around the same time, to Bharatendu Harischandra's seminal speech of the same year in Ballia, 'How Can India Progress', with its call for unity among Hindus and its assumption of the social and historical constitution of India by 'Hindu' and 'Muslim'.[48] Most strikingly, M. M. Malaviya's

[44] Ibid. Tilak would similarly criticize this ethical exhortation in the *Gita Rahasya*, as we shall see in the next chapter.

[45] 'The humble memorial of the Musulman inhabitants of Poona city', n.d. [August?] MSA JD 1894, 287, 419–420.

[46] *Sedition Committee Report*, 2. Chapekar claimed *Kesari* as inspiration for his murder of the British officials Rand and Ayhurst in June 1897; Tilak's subsequent trial is discussed in Chapter 5.

[47] On Natu's *mela*, see Cashman, *Myth*, 92 ff.

[48] See C. A. Bayly, *The Local Roots of Indian Politics: Allahabad, 1880–1920*, 106–109; Pandey, *Construction*, 214–218 and Appendix II.

work to found the Hindu Boarding House at Allahabad, cofound Benares Hindu University, and strengthen and 'uplift the Hindus' through the Prayag Hindu Samaj, coexisted with his emphasis that 'Hindus' and 'Musalmans [sic]' were 'sons of the same Motherland', showing a conception of service to country through community while emphasizing the strength and cohesiveness of the latter as an essential element.[49]

Tilak expounded a rationale for the Ganapati festivals as germinative of a national consciousness, and a unified national culture, in *Kesari* in 1896, likening them to the Olympic games in ancient Greece. Cashman footnotes that 'this was written two years after the reorganised Ganapati festival', explaining that the 'rhetoric of politicisation was not clearly enunciated until this time'.[50] There was in fact a chronological lapse, unnoted here, between the establishment of the festival, born of one set of concerns, and the nationalist rationalization. Of course, this does not minimize the fact that Tilak did, indeed, choose to rationalize the festival as a national celebration in 1896. By this date, of course, the festival had assumed a momentum of its own, and was a fixture in the public culture of Maharashtra. Tilak thus looked to rationalize it in a new way, the imperatives of 1893–1894 having been superseded. It is worth adding that if Tilak's contribution to the 'Ganapati festival' had its genesis in a desire to cohere the Hindu community of Maharashtra at a particular moment in the colonial politics of western India, the unity of the Hindu community was indeed an enduring concern, exercising Tilak in contexts where protest to government was a more remote concern—as, for instance, it was an important impulse behind the *Gita Rahasya*—according to the communal logic we discussed in the section above. And in his choice of Ganesh as a rallying point, Tilak not only selected a deity who had considerable following among lower-caste Hindus in Maharashtra.[51] He deliberately counter-attacked against non-Brahmin protest; the *Satyashodhak Samaj* of Jotirao Phule from the 1870s had specifically urged the boycott of the Chaturthi in favour of worshipping only the Supreme God.[52] Thus his pan-Hindu celebration would necessarily undermine the efforts of non-Brahmin protest to cleave Hindu society.

---

[49] Pandey, *Construction*, 211–213.
[50] Cashman, *Myth*, 78 fn.
[51] On Ganesh see Robert L. Brown, *Ganesh: Studies of an Asian God* (Albany, 1991).
[52] O'Hanlon, *Caste*, 240.

Tilak after Mandalay: finding the Luck
in Lucknow, sidestepping the Khilafat

The position taken by Tilak at the Lucknow Congress of December 1916,[53] in which he had a vital role in drafting the joint resolution on self-government between the Congress and Muslim League, is the culmination of Tilak's communitarian vision of the polity, its expression in political terms. The recognition of the demands of the League, and the principle of separate Muslim representation on the Central and Provincial Councils, did not merely reflect his expanding political base and changed political priorities; this principle of recognition of a minority community that requires distinct representation demonstrates a conceptual consistency with his 'community-based' politics of the 1890s, in a new political context, to which he was able to adapt himself.[54] Tilak of course needed after his release in 1914 to appeal to Gokhale-influenced moderates in the Congress to effect his readmission after the violent debacle of the 1907 Congress session at Surat and his subsequent expulsion; the Lucknow session of 1916 would be the first the readmitted Tilak would attend. And the terms of debate within the Congress in terms of religious community had been radically altered by the changed framework of colonial politics since Tilak's imprisonment. The Indian Councils Act of 1909, conceived by the Viceroy Lord Minto along with his Secretary of State John Morley, along with introducing elections to the imperial and local legislative councils, enshrined separate electorates with separate representation for Hindu and Muslim communities. The measure is generally interpreted as an attempted bulwark against representative nationalist politics on the part of Minto (as well as representing an essentialized colonial understanding of India's society); and the pact therefore represents a moment in which this was transcended in nationalist politics.[55] The Congress had been moving towards doing so since at least the Presidential statements of 1912; and further rapprochement between the Congress and Muslim League had been fostered by maladroit British imperial policies towards

---

[53] The pun in this section's heading is Tilak's. ('Speech on the self-government motion at the 31st Indian National Congress, Lucknow' in *Bal Gangadhar Tilak, His Writings and Speeches*, 3rd ed. (Madras, 1922), (hereafter, *Speeches*), 202.

[54] Cashman, *Myth*, 193, expounds the former view.

[55] Metcalf, *Ideologies*, 224, sees this in particular as Minto's intention.

Muslims within and outside India from 1911, culminating with war with the Ottoman Empire in 1914.[56] Gokhale had already, by the time of his death in February 1915, been drafting combined resolutions with the Aga Khan, President of Muslim League.[57]

From Tilak's perspective, a convergence of such societal understandings facilitated this nationalistic counter-affirmation of colonial attempts to cleave nationalist agitation; but the terms on which it was applied represent a significant statement of Tilak's position. Asserting at Lucknow that absolute statutory majorities in the councils of Bengal and Punjab would be denied to the Muslims while offering over-representation in Muslim minority states showed Tilak to be careful to offer compromise in the name of this pluralistic polity, within a framework that was strictly Hindu majoritarian in all-Indian terms. The resolution at Lucknow stated that 'the great communities of India are the inheritors of ancient civilisations and have shown great capacity for Government and administration.'[58] Tilak's own speech in moving the resolution at the Congress gives us a direct insight:

> I am sure I represent the sense of the Hindu community all over India when I say we could not have yielded too much. I would not care if the rights of self-government are granted to the Mohamedan community only ... I would not care if they are granted to the lower and the lowest classes of the Hindu population, provided the British Government considers them more fit than the educated classes of India for exercising those rights. I would not care if those rights are granted to any section of the Indian community. The fight then will be between them and other sections of the community and not, as at present, a triangular fight.'[59]

Tilak's stance was in direct opposition to the incipient forum of later Hindutva politics, the Hindu Mahasabha, which agitated against them from within the Congress at Lucknow.[60] Indeed the Hindu Sabha

---

[56] Hugh F. Owen, 'Negotiating the Lucknow Pact', *Journal of Asian Studies*, 31/3 (1972), 561–587 (hereafter, Owen, 'Lucknow Pact'), 567 ff.

[57] Ibid., 570.

[58] SLT 8, 'Appendices' (1375 ff).

[59] *Speeches*, 202–203, 'Self-Government' (28 December, speech on the main resolution).

[60] Cf. Rao, *Foundations*, 314–315, 318; and particularly 313, for an unreferenced remark that Tilak 'criticised the communal representation scheme'.

movement had emerged in the context of fears over separate Muslim representation in the Punjab in the first decade of the century (growing out of that region into the Hindu Mahasabha by 1915). The hostility to separate representation in public life for Muslims—evidenced in the words of one of the early Sabha's leading lights, Lal Chand, in 1909, that through appointments to High Courts in India 'both in theory and practice the Hindus have been reduced to a position as if they formed 50 per cent of the population'—was crucial for its early organization.[61] As has been noted, the Sabha derived its 'proto-Hindu nationalist' ethnic definition of Hindus as a nation (though without making claims on the state in those terms) from the ideas of the Arya Samaj, whose understanding of Aryan identity, as we have seen, differed so substantially from Tilak's own.[62] Despite this, both Lala Lajpat Rai and Malaviya, two of its leading figures, voiced, as we have seen, a classic 'compound', pluralist idea of the Indian nation with a strengthened Hindu community within it; and indeed, in this the Mahasabha itself, operating as a pressure group within Congress for 'Hindu' interests, can be seen as an extension of these 'strengthening' activities.[63] Indeed, even in the mid 1920s Rai would describe the (refounded) Mahasabha as having no political aims but to 'define the position of the community in relation to other communities'.[64] Having been outfought at Lucknow over concessions to the Muslims, it was temporarily eclipsed by the resolution and pact—though, significantly, the reborn Mahasabha would feed off dissatisfaction with it.[65] In both its mode of articulating Hindu community and the mode of its integration into the Indian polity, Tilak's differences with it were striking—even before its turn to a more clearly 'Hindu nationalist orientation' (in Christophe Jaffrelot's terms) shortly after Tilak's death.[66]

Tilak's stance on the *Khilafat* movement towards the very end of his career offers a final reflection on the nature of community and its political mobilization. The threat to the Ottoman Empire during the First

---

[61] Jaffrelot, *Reader*, 48–49 (extract from *Self Abnegation in Politics*); Owen, 'Lucknow Pact'.
[62] Jaffrelot, *Movement*, 18–19, citing the prominent Samajist Sabha member Lala Lajpat Rai.
[63] See Rai quoted in Jaffrelot, *Movement*, 84 n.
[64] Jaffrelot, *Reader*, 71.
[65] Richard Gordon, 'The Hindu Mahasabha and the Indian National Congress, 1915 to 1926', *Modern Asian Studies*, 9 (1975), 157, and Owen, 'Lucknow Pact', 578 (using slightly different nomenclature to Gordon).
[66] Jaffrelot, *Movement*, 19.

World War, and most especially as its peace terms were being negoti-ated, formed a well-documented and crucially important rallying point for Indian dissent against British rule, exploited by its new driving force, M. K. Gandhi.[67] The peace terms threatened the dismemberment of the Ottoman Empire, and its Sultan's position as Muslim *khalif* (leader of the *ummah*, or faithful). Many Indian Muslims to varying degrees protested against both the prosecution of the war and the emergence of the peace terms. It was the latter that Gandhi exploited from early 1920, declaring himself against the *Khilafat* 'wrong' and thus leveraging Muslim support within India for Congress, which could thus call upon pan-communal loyalties. The descent of the movement into violence, in particular the Mappila uprising in India's southwest in later 1921, would colour percep-tions of it strongly, and do much to encourage the stance of Savarkar in his 1923 pamphlet *Essentials of* Hindutva, and his pointed definition of a Hindu as one who 'regards his land of Bharat-Varsha from the Indus to the Seas as his father-land as well as his Holy-land', implicitly denigrating South Asian Muslims' spiritual attachment to the 'cradle' of their reli-gion.[68] Even Annie Besant, Tilak's Home Rule collaborator and Congress President in 1917, who had heralded the Lucknow Pact, was now 'forced to see that the primary allegiance of Musalmans is to Islamic countries, not to our Motherland'.[69]

Tilak, notably, was largely silent on the issue; and he was, in the words of Gail Minault, 'conspicuous' by his absence from meetings on the topic, including the Allahabad meetings of the All-India Khilafat Conference in June 1920, at which Gandhian non-cooperation in the face of the Government's policy was on the agenda.[70] Direct evidence of Tilak's stance is indeed scarce. But such as exists does not foreshadow the Besant-Savarkar view. In an interview with the *Bombay Chronicle*, he later explained his absence from the Conference:

---

[67] Judith M. Brown, *Gandhi's Rise to Power: Indian Politics, 1915–1922* (Cambridge, 1972) (hereafter Brown, *Rise*)

[68] V. D. Savarkar, *Hindutva*, 5th ed. (Bombay, 1969) (hereafter, Savarkar, *Hindutva*), frontmatter.

[69] Annie Besant, *The Future of Indian Politics* (Adyar and Benares, 1922), 302 (hereafter, Besant, *Future*).

[70] Gail Minault, *The Khilafat Movement: Religious Symbolism and Political Mobilization in India* (New Delhi, 1999), 101.

> My idea is that the Mahomedans themselves should take the initiative
> in the matter. After full discussion they must come to a definite decision
> in the matter, and it is for the Hindus to support them in whatever de-
> cision they might arrive at.[71]

Tilak was vague about the nature of the 'support' that would be offered,
but it can be inferred that as it was not a matter that touched upon the
whole political community of India, but upon one of its discrete parts, the
negotiations over Indians' general non-cooperation with the Government
in direct response to it were superfluous, and should be avoided. So far
from dismissing the propriety of the mobilization of the Muslim community around the *Khilafat* question, though, Tilak's view was that it was
an issue for that community's deliberation. It was a view consistent with
Tilak's long-held notion of a fairly stark delineation of community identities and political mobilization associated with them, within the context
of an emerging Indian national identity.

Imagining India

The emblem of Tilak's Home Rule League—the semiotic expression of
the Lucknow Pact's communal conception—was a badge emblazoned in
red for the Hindus, and green for the Muslims.[72] For Tilak, as for other
nationalists attempting to fashion a national symbology from this characteristically late-nineteenth-century 'compound' view of community-
based Indian nationality, imagining an India that comprehended yet
transcended community identity, here vividly discrete and colour-coded,
was a major area of experimentation and effort, a project of realization
implied in his 1908 statement at his sedition trial that India was 'not yet a
nation'.[73] But for all that Tilak asserted a communally pluralistic vision of

---

[71] Reprinted *Mahratta*, 13 June 1920, 280, 'Moslems Should Decide First'.
[72] IOR/R/2/745/298 'Indian Home Rule League' (Kathiawar Political Agency, circular from
the special dept., Poona, 5 June 1916), 1. The League, and Tilak's propaganda for it, is described
further below.
[73] 'India is not yet a nation in the sense in which it is understood in western communities.... When communities take part in a discussion, Anglo-Indians, Mahomedans, Hindus, and
Parsees each discuss the matter in their own way ... In India which is divided into communities
public opinion is not represented by parties formed on principles, but parties formed more or

the Indian polity, it seems reasonable to assert that he was unsuccessful, because of the nature of his imaginative resources and preoccupations, in imagining a common Indian identity capable of reflecting it. History was the crucible for his efforts. Tilak drew upon Maratha history to inculcate a modern national consciousness, a predictable and natural reaction from a Maharashtrian Chitpavan whose own family history had been directed by its flow and ebb. Foremost among the Maratha symbols he employed is, of course, Shivaji. His interpretation of the career of this 'Hindu king in Islamic India' was ambivalent.[74] Yet it is hard to maintain that Tilak's invocation of Shivaji's memory was intended to assert that the nation was synonymous with the Hindu community, as for many others up until today. Tilak, rather, offers a problematic emblem of Indianness, equally visible in his attempts to make this quintessentially Maharashtrian hero an all-Indian national symbol. This section will examine Tilak's employment of Shivaji from the 'communal' perspective, describing his positionality and his intentions in his statements upon him, before briefly examining these tensions between regional and all-Indian 'nationalism'. It will then briefly assess the relevance of Tilak's interest in 'Aryan' history, with its implicit 'degenerationist' narrative, and the relevance of this to Tilak's nationalist project.

Tilak's involvement in the movement to memorialize Shivaji seems to date from 1895, when he exhorted *Kesari*'s readers to 'vindicate the name of Shivaji' by repairing his tomb, and was instrumental in arranging an unprecedented meeting at Hirabag to formalize the existing movement to do so, being appointed one of the three secretaries to the overseeing committee. Once more, Tilak seized upon the activities of his immediate milieu, which was reviving and reworking under changing conditions the memory of a major regional patriotic figure.[75] Tilak was thus active in the first full-blown festivities to celebrate Shivaji's birthday in 1896, at which he spoke, and again at the celebration of his coronation in 1897.[76] Though

---

less by different communities'. Kelkar (ed.), *Trial (1908)*, 82. The speech, directed as much to Indian opinion at large as to his jury, is discussed in Chapter 5.

[74] The designation is taken from James Laine, *Shivaji: Hindu King in Islamic India* (Oxford and New York, 2003).
[75] *Kesari*, 23 April 1895, 4 June 1895. See C. A. Bayly, *Origins of Nationality in South Asia: Patriotism and Ethical Government in the Making of Modern India* (New Delhi 1998), 116–119, (hereafter, Bayly, *Origins*), 21–26.
[76] *Kesari*, 21 April 1896.

his incendiary words in June 1897, which led to his conviction for sedition, are best remembered, this obscures what has rightly been described as his moderate tone before this, and, in particular, its inclusive and catholic tenor.[77] Indeed, it should be noted that Tilak's engagement with Shivaji was a distinct effort to the community mobilization achieved by the Ganapati festival, with its own focus. A quite deliberate acceptability of the celebration for the region's Muslims seems to have been an element in this. Tilak editorialized in June 1895 about the Hirabag meeting, emphasizing that 'ruling chiefs and Sardars of the Deccan, many of whom hold their Jahagir from the great Shivaji' and his successors, attended—a point which underscores not only his apparently inclusive aims, but carries a historical conception of Shivaji's inclusive polity.[78] His stance was not without ambiguity: it was also 'the duty of every Hindu to celebrate the festival of Shivaji', he stated, in a line reported in *Kesari* but not apparently in *Mahratta*.[79] *Kesari*, preparing for the following year's celebrations, asked

> Should we not always cherish him in our hearts who has removed this disgrace from us? ... who laid the foundation of our empire, who gave a particular direction to our religion?[80]

If this could be read as a strategic ambiguity in Tilak's use of Shivaji's imaginative appeal, Tilak's language at the festival in 1897, above all, casts his treatment of Shivaji's career in an anti-Islamic light. His rhetoric in celebrating the controversial episode of Shivaji's killing under parlay of the Bijapuri Sultanate's general Afzhul Khan in 1659 is especially notable. Shivaji's cause was just, said Tilak, because 'God had not given to the *mlecchas* [outsiders] the grant inscribed on a copper-plate (*tamprapat*) of the kingdom of Hindustan'; Shivaji 'strove to drive them away from the land of his birth.'[81] This turn can be contextualized by the conditions of June 1897, as plague swept Poona, and the Government's anti-plague

---

[77] Cashman, *Myth*, Ch. 5.
[78] *Kesari*, 4 June 1895.
[79] Ibid.
[80] *Kesari*, 14 April 1896.
[81] His actions were also just through purity of motive; his justification for political violence and its place in the polity are discussed in Chapter 5.

measures included the forcible searching and clearance of private homes, measures Tilak and others had roundly condemned. In this atmosphere, Tilak's exhortation to 'burn alive' thieves who 'enter our house' was intended, and taken, as a threat to the British as the un-named *mlecchas*. As we shall see in 'The Conduct of Politics', these words in particular led to his trial and imprisonment for sedition three months later, the colonial authorities sufficiently alarmed that Tilak spread disaffection for the British through his invective. Tilak here perhaps has something in common with other colonial Indian political agitators who used the divisive polemical analogy between British and Muslim despotisms as a mask, in John Pocock's terms, for criticism of the colonial state, though this does nothing to obviate the divisiveness and its contradiction of Tilak's more inclusive language earlier and elsewhere.[82]

What is notable, and perhaps needs explaining, is in fact the prevalence—voiced from various political standpoints in Maharashtra's political culture during this period—of views of Shivaji as a fighter for Hinduism. The work of Ekanath Joshi in the 1870s set a recent precedent for this, viewing Shivaji as a saviour of orthodox Hinduism from the threat of Islam.[83] V. K. Rajwade, a more prominent Maharashtrian historian whose work we will revisit in the next chapter, in his writings from the 1890s saw Shivaji's *Swarajya* as explicitly Hindu, and the rationale for Maratha expansion as beating Muslims out of India.[84] Rajwade was also archetypical in making Shivaji the protector of cows and Brahmins, the *go-Brahman pratipalak*, a defender of orthodox Hinduism who wished to spread this vision of *Maharashtra dharma* abroad. Even in accounts of ostensible 'moderacy', Shivaji's is the spirit of resistance to an Islamic polity. Thus in the work of Ranade, the moderate par excellence, Islam was a coercive force. His *Rise of the Maratha Power* (1900), seen as the foremost expression of liberal nationalism in Maharashtra in this period, devotes space to a celebration of the syncretic religious culture of

---

[82] This is discussed in C. A. Bayly, *Recovering Liberties: Indian Thought in the Age of Liberalism and Empire* (Cambridge University Press, 2012) (hereafter, Bayly, *Recovering Liberties*), 8.

[83] Rosalind O'Hanlon, 'Maratha History as Polemic: Low Caste Ideology and Political Debate in Late Nineteenth- century Western India', *Modern Asian Studies* 17/1 (1983), 1–33 (hereafter, O'Hanlon, 'Polemic'), 25 ff.

[84] Prachi Deshpande, *Creative Pasts: Historical Memory and Identity in Western India, 1700–1960* (New York and Chichester, 2007), 132 (hereafter, *Creative Pasts*). The term is discussed further below.

Maharashtra, and its 'reconciliation of the two races in mutual recognition of the essential unity of Alia with Rama'.[85] Yet Maratha history was for him 'the history of the formation of a true Indian Nationality, raising its head high above the troubled waters of Mahomedan confusion'. Employing that most commonplace of metaphors for oppression and imprisonment, he referred to Islamic rule as the 'Mahomdean yoke'.[86] Clearly, Ranade's hostility is not meant (as perhaps in Rajwade) to imply Shivaji's a seventeenth-century Hindu *rashtra* and a precedent for the future. Indeed it may be precisely because the notion of historical resistance against a Muslim power was not so contested as were the historical roles of western India's various caste communities, as we shall see, that an antipathy to it was almost universal in these accounts. There was a much clearer sense for these writers of what it meant to advocate the contribution of a particular caste community in contemporary terms than Hindus of the Maratha state on the whole—and a greater sense of precedence.

Indeed, even in so far as Shivaji may have given Hinduism in Maharashtra a 'particular direction', Maharashtra retained for Tilak its sense of place, and its peculiar traditions, in relation to the rest of India. In the aftermath of the riots in 1893, as we have seen, he referred to the 'historical traditions of these parts'; for 'we, in the Deccan, never lived by the sufferance of the Mohamedans'.[87] Not only was it quite alien to Tilak's vision to see Shivaji's as aimed at defeating Islamic power throughout India per se, the way in which Tilak employed Shivaji at the all-India level, in carrying the Shivaji movement to Bengal and elsewhere, was almost scrupulously communally inclusive. Speaking in Calcutta at the Shivaji celebrations there in 1906, Tilak stated 'it is the spirit which actuated Shivaji in his doings that is held forth as the proper ideal … we hope and trust that our Mahomedan friends will not be misled'. Now, 'the Mahomedans and the Hindus stand in the same Boat'.[88] Tilak further urged that the 'lesson which the Mahomedans and the Hindus have to learn from the history of the great Mahratta [sic] Chief' is that 'Indian races do not so

[85] M. G. Ranade, *Rise of the Maratha Power* (Bombay, 1900) (hereafter, Ranade, *Rise*), 284.
[86] Ibid., 126.
[87] *Mahratta*, 20 August 1893, editorial, 3.
[88] Tilak, *Speeches*, 49, 'Is Shivaji not a National Hero?'. Cf. Rao's description of this speech marking an opportunistic divergence from his position on Shivaji hitherto (*Foundations*, 213).

soon lose the vitality which gives them able leaders at critical times', a deliberate inclusion in his memorialization.[89]

This same regional specificity to Tilak's historical imagination is perhaps crucial for thinking about Tilak's employment of Shivaji. Tilak's was an effort, somewhat haphazard, to furnish symbols for an all-Indian nationalism from the imaginary of this regional *patria*.[90] In selecting Shivaji, he employed, as many others in the period, what Milinda Banerjee has described as a royal-nationalist imaginary, in which kingly figures (drawing on divine sanction) signified national sovereignty—something that coexisted with Tilak's own commitment to popular and representative government.[91] But Tilak himself seems to have acknowledged the awkwardness of the fit at times. His Calcutta speech of 1906, given during the Swadeshi agitation that pointedly straddled a 'Bengal' and 'all-India' focus, while showing the consistent influence of Thomas Carlyle upon his project for imaging the nation—and reflecting how well suited the 'heroic' mode of such visible sovereign figures was to the leadership aspirations of male nationalists—stated that

> our political aspirations need all the strength which the worship of a Swadeshi hero is likely to inspire into our minds. For this purpose Shivaji is the only hero to be found in the Indian history ... it matters little that Shivaji was born in Maharashtra.'[92]

The watchful Bombay Government reported that as a result of Tilak's efforts, the Shivaji cult 'spread even to parts of India where the memory of the Mahratta chief could not have been expected to be revered' after 1900.[93] And other Bengali agitators of the period indeed followed suit; Bipin Chandra Pal praised Shivaji (once more, with a clearly different tone

---

[89] Ibid., 50.

[90] Cf. the contradictory notion in Rao, *Foundations*, 269, that Tilak expounds a Hindutva all-Indian nationalism while not in fact extending from a 'Maratha nation' idea.

[91] Milinda Banerjee, *The Mortal God: Imagining the Sovereign in Colonial India* (Cambridge, 2018) (hereafter, Banerjee, *Mortal God*).

[92] Tilak, *Speeches*, 50. In Tilak's earliest editorializing on the Shivaji festival, this sense is present: 'no nation can afford to neglect the memory of its heroes; and Indians are not an exception to the rule', *Mahratta*, 2 June 1895, 3. On this mode, and its prevalence also in Bengal, see Banerjee, *Mortal God*, 162, 178.

[93] IOR/L/PJ/6/877, 'An account of the circumstances which led to the prosecution and conviction of B G Tilak' (from Judicial Dept., Bombay, to the Secretary of State, 15 September 1908).

to Tilak) for giving 'the nation a vision of a Hindu rashtra', and Banerjee's work has outlined the importance to many nationalists there of the tangibility of Shivaji's militant expression of national sovereignty.[94] But Tilak's was a revealing insistence upon the point that it 'mattered little': and even Tilak's other noted Swadeshi collaborator, the Punjabi Lala Rajpat Rai, reflected a very un-Maharashtrian perspective in his biography *Shivaji the Great Patriot* that due to 'selfishness' and power-lust Shivaji 'looted many Hindu chiefs' and 'committed many acts of bad faith'.[95] As C. A. Bayly notes, the inheritance of early modern regional Indian *patrias*— and we shall see more of the Maratha conception of proper government below—was vital in the regions but was drawn on 'in the creation of the wider concept of Indian civilization and polity' in the nationalist period, and Tilak exhibits a classic instance of it here—indeed, for all his insistence on Maharashtra's specific, and special, historical experience, his is not a vision of an alliance of regional cultures, drawn from a conception of Indian history that emphasized regional-communal liberties, as notably in the vision of Aurobindo Ghose, but something that did seek to transcend them in its wider conception.[96]

The tensions inherent in Tilak's employment of Shivaji do not detract from the remarkably sustained attempt he made to make Shivaji a pan-communal rallying point, or the imaginative lengths he went to in doing so. The complicity of both Hindu and Muslim 'communities' in 'Indian' history, their identity with the nation, is also emphasized in his Home Rule League agitation speeches from 1916. These speeches, immediately before and after the Lucknow Pact, in effect form its imaginative counterpart, a construction of a broader historical-national identity that transcended community division. In his celebrated Home Rule speech at Belgaum in May 1916, explicating *Swarajya* ('self-rule', *swa* meaning one's own or one's self, and *rajya* meaning either exercise of sovereign power or polity), Tilak stated

[94] Anil Samarth, *Shivaji and the Indian National Movement: Saga of a Living Legend* (Bombay, 1975), 76; Banerjee, *Mortal God*, 210.

[95] Lala Lajpat Rai, *Shivaji the Great Patriot*, trans. R. C. Suri ([1896] New Delhi, 1980), 52–53. The pitfalls attendant on 'nationalizing' Shivaji are also discussed in Deshpande, *Creative Pasts*, 141 ff.

[96] Bayly, *Origins*, 127; also Sugata Bose, 'The Spirit and Form of an Ethical Polity: A Meditation on Aurobindo's Thought', *Modern Intellectual History*, 4/1 (2007), 129–144 (hereafter, Bose, 'Spirit and Form').

Formerly there were many kingdoms in our India—in some places there was Mohammedan rule, in some places there was Rajput rule, in some places there was Hindu rule and in some places there was Maratha rule—were these *swarajyas* good or bad?[97]

Here, Muslims are included in the Indian self. And this is all the more marked, as *Swarajya* was in fact also conventionally used to describe Shivaji's own rule.[98] The historical acceptance of Muslim *Swarajya* as equally Indian as Shivaji's is a remarkable use of the historical record in the imaginative nationalist project. The contrast with the writings of Bankim in the 1890s—seminal for militant national consciousness in Bengal during the period, and described by Tanika Sarkar as central to 'imagining Hindu rashtra'—on Muslim rule in Bengal, which cost in his imagination 'religion, caste, and honour' to the Hindus, is striking.[99] For Tilak, evoking the Maratha past in particular was not merely a way of writing the 'Muslim period' out of Indian history (something that Ranade, indeed, rather liked to insist on). Maratha resistance and martiality were crucial, as we will discuss, to Tilak's Maharashtrian and Hindu identity; but the uses to which Shivaji's career of conflict was put by Tilak saw no sustained or serialized attempt to demean the position of Muslims in the polity. Tilak's Shivaji memorialization rather represents his imaginative failure to invoke a past that could serve as a rallying point for all sections of Indian society; and this was true in 'communal' as well as, as we shall see, in caste terms.

Tilak's preoccupation with the history of the Aryan race (discussed extensively in Chapter 2), showing itself at its strongest in the 1890s, but never spent in even his later years, also warrants examination for its implication for Tilak's imagining of the Indian nation. As has been noted, accounts of the glories of prehistoric Aryan civilization are often seen to have generated 'Hindu nationalist' understandings of Indian civilization; and certainly, accounts that explain India's decline from greatness, and its renaissance as depending on a revival of Aryan culture in India, distance

---

[97] Tilak, *Speeches*, 105, 'Home Rule Speech at Belgaum', 1 May 1916 (hereafter, 'Home Rule, Belgaum').
[98] Molesworth, 879: '[svarajya] *n* (S Own rule or dominion.) A term applied to certain of the districts possessed by the Marathas'. Ranade, *Rise*, 116, uses it thus. See further below.
[99] Sarkar, *Hindu Wife*, 184.

Indian Muslims imaginatively from the nation. Yet Tilak's work on Aryan history, *Orion* (1893) and *Arctic Home* (1903), had in fact fewer implications for this imagining than may be assumed from existing literature on the 'Aryan idea'. Tilak is silent on the state of India's contemporary society, on the notion of 'decline' and its causes; and although it might be objected that such a notion need not be explicit to nevertheless be meant and powerfully felt, it should be remembered that other writers in this period fastened on other villains in the tragedy of Aryan decline, principally the indigenous Dravidian population. Such understandings may be no less exclusive, or demeaning, to 'non-Aryan' peoples in India, and were not always exclusive of a sense of Muslim historic culpability; but they do not argue for such a vitiating role in Indian history and culture. Thus Tilak's celebration of a Vedic past carries with it no inevitable associations of hostility to the historical role of Muslims in South Asia, intended or understood. His project here is, in any case, not really to 'imagine the nation', as the Aryan people are not understood for Tilak as coterminous with India, or even the category of 'Hindu'; as we shall see, Tilak was in fact mostly concerned to celebrate Brahmin identity and status. Though Tilak's was a 'primordial' view of Hindu community (at least in its near-beginninglessness), there is therefore no engagement with the idea of a Hindu race in these works—as in others of the period on ancient 'Hindu history', noted for their relevance to nationalist imaginings.[100]

The notion that degenerationist narratives were inherently hostile to Muslims is further challenged by Tilak's own clear degenerationist narrative in the *Gita Rahasya*. The invasion of 'intolerant Mohammedans' is indeed cited as an additional reason for Hinduism's descent into a '*moksha marga*' of contemplative or devotional inaction, in the indirect sense that Hindu Kshatriyas were killed off in attempting to resist them, the failure of which further bred passivity. The more profound reason, though, Tilak is clear, is the earlier impact of the 'Buddhist and Jain religions', which 'opened the door of renunciation to all castes'.[101] Such a statement, of course, serves to corroborate the notion that such narratives do lend themselves to stigmatization and the apportioning of historic

---

[100] See Vasudha Dalmia's citation of R. C. Dutt's 'Early Hindu Civilization, 2000 to 320 BC. Based on Sanskrit Literature', in *The Nationalization of Hindu Traditions* ([1888]; Oxford, 1996), 1 (hereafter, Dalmia, *Nationalization*).
[101] *GR*, ii. 622

responsibility. It is the Hindus of India, not Jains or Buddhists, who ensure her prosperity. For Tilak, the problem posed by these entirely indigenous forms of non-Vedic Indian religion would seem to be that they are too close to Hinduism, and thus were capable of sapping Hinduism's strength by their influence. But the contrast with Savarkar's Hindutva is a revealing one. Tilak's Hindutva (a definition of the community of Hindus) excludes Buddhists and Jains, whereas Savarkar appropriated such identities to within Hindutva, arguing its true outsiders were Muslims, or any with sentimental and hence ethnic affinities outside Bharat.[102]

But what Tilak's fleeting reference to the historical role of Buddhism and Jainism demonstrates, like all of his references to the history of Indian civilization, is a view of that civilization in which Vedic Hinduism is preponderant. This preponderance places at a distance from the dominant narrative of Indian civilization—indeed, from the essence of Indian identity—India's minority communities (not to mention, as we shall see, lower caste Hindus), even if their own distinct identity is tolerated or even encouraged. His pluralism was in a sense realist, a recognition of Indian civilization's historic communal pluralism, as discussed above, and he was not imaginatively invested in anything beyond particular manifestations of Hindu-majoritarian culture. And at the same time, it appears that even Tilak's efforts to furnish ways imaginatively in which Indian Muslims could partake of Indian selfhood—as he insisted they should at Belgaum in 1916—were stymied by a lack of imaginative resources—in large measure due to his lifeworld, and particularly his lengthy formation in the Brahminic milieu of Poona (discussed in Chapter 1), in this also perhaps resembling Malaviya.[103] Tilak therefore stands as hemmed in as a spokesman for his conception of Hindu community, emerging from his own region moreover, even as he attempted (admittedly from a majoritarian perspective) to transcend it in the creation of a broader national identity he acknowledged was required. As a new historical context emerged, of the Swadeshi movement and accompanying calls for Swaraj, it was in many ways the old Tilak who struggled to shift from regional and communal articulations to broader national ones in the second half of his career.

---

[102] Savarkar, *Hindutva*, 97, 123.
[103] Bayly, *Recovering Liberties*, 220.

Locating legitimacy and the 'birthright' of self-rule

The political settlement at Lucknow, enshrining the principle of separate representation for historically distinct communities, was also inseparably a demand for 'Home Rule'. Self-government was in effect defined as representative government. In this context, Tilak developed in his agitation for Home Rule a critique of the legitimacy of the colonial state, and a conception of the foundation of legitimate political authority, that emphasized popular sovereignty. Indeed, his explication of this went far beyond echoing the Pact's call for 'as broad a franchise as possible' for representation. For Tilak as anti-colonial nationalist, the discussion of political legitimacy at one level was not a project that occasioned systematic thought: the very obvious 'alienness' of the state registered at an emotional level with his intended audience, and could be sufficient to betoken its illegitimacy. Yet his campaigning, explicitly and with unprecedented prolificity, for the 'Home Rule League' in 1916–1917 (having first established a western Indian branch of the League some months before the Pact in April 1916, as part of a projected nationwide network) occasioned some deeper reflections on this relationship, and thus on political legitimacy itself.[104]

At one level, Tilak seemed to oppose the alienness of colonial rule per se. Employing the homology of the polity as one's household, echoing his famous speech at the Shivaji festival in 1897, Tilak exhorted his audience at Lucknow, just a few days after the Congress-League Resolution: 'Insist on your rights. India is your own house. Is it not?', to which the audience responded with cries of 'Yes'.[105] One's rule in one's own home was invoked as a natural right: 'nobody else can claim to do it', Tilak states, 'unless you are a minor or a lunatic'.[106] This was an emotional appeal to a form of natural order. But it was expressed alongside a slightly different notion: that

---

[104] The best account of the League's foundation and significance is still Hugh Owen, 'Towards Nationwide Agitation and Organisation: The Home Rule Leagues 1915–1918', in D. A. Low, ed., *Soundings in Modern South Asian History* (London, 1968) (hereafter, Owen, 'Towards Nationwide Agitation').

[105] Tilak, *Speeches*, 207, 'Home Rule Conference' (Lucknow, 30 December 1916).

[106] Ibid., 225, 'Home Rule' [n.d.].

alien rule simply fails necessarily to deliver good governance, implying that the basis of legitimacy is a form of social contract.[107] As Tilak stated,

> The difference between aliens and us is that the aliens' point of view is alien, their thoughts are alien, and their general conduct is such that their minds are not inclined to particularly benefit those people to whom they are aliens.[108]

Alienness, he emphasized, 'has to do with interest'.[109] Governing in the interest of the governed was crucial: and this could lead to a startlingly divergent formulation of the nature of legitimacy. Any government,

> whether British or any other, it has, as Government, a sort of duty to perform. Government has a sort of religious duty to perform; a sort of responsibility lies on its shoulders. I say that when a Government evades this responsibility it is no Government at all. Government possesses authority. All the power possessed by Government may be acquired by it by fighting or may be conferred upon it by the people.[110]

But it seems, on balance, that the best way of ensuring the respect of this contractual relationship between government and governed is in fact to have authority conferred by the people. Offering a list of grievances against the colonial government that included the abolition of jury and deficiencies in college education, Tilak states

> if you had been officials in their place or if their authority had been responsible to the public opinion, these things would not have happened ... These things happen because there is no authority in your hands.[111]

---

[107] On this point of the relationship of good governance to imagining sovereignty in the period, see Banerjee, *Mortal God*, 181, once more in the context of Shivaji's memory.
[108] Tilak, *Speeches*, 141, 'Home Rule Speech at Ahmednagar', 31 May 1916 (hereafter, 'Home Rule, Ahmednagar').
[109] Ibid., 142.
[110] Ibid., 144.
[111] Ibid., 113 ('Home Rule, Belgaum').

Tilak refines this sense that good governance is ensured by responsibility to the people, developing an explicit position that legitimacy itself is conferred by popular representation. 'Government has come into existence for giving effect to the things desired by a large number of people'.[112] Hence 'Home Rule', the form of legitimate government he agitates for, in fact 'means Representative Government, Government over which the people will have control'.[113] Power would be put 'in the people's hands, in the hands of good man [sic] viz., in the hands of men elected by the people'.[114] Tilak acknowledges the ironic corollary that foreign rule if responsible to the people would be perfectly legitimate, as in neither its authority nor its 'interest' would it be alien.

> Let there be a Viceroy and let him be an Englishman if you like, but let him act according to the advice of the representatives of the people. Let our money be spent upon us and with our consent.[115]

This is a sense apparently influenced by nineteenth-century liberal thought; the classic statement on the beneficence of representative government is of course by J. S. Mill. Elements of Mill's thesis on *Representative Government* would certainly have struck a chord with Tilak. Representative government is described as best suited to a patriotic people; and criticizing the notion of 'good despotism', Mill suggests of a people living under such a system that

> Their passivity is implied in the very idea of absolute power. The nation as a whole, and every individual composing it, are without any potential voice in their own destiny.[116]

Tilak's own statements on representative government form a contribution to a rich strain of Indian liberal thought in the period that drew on such antecedents, yet had a trajectory of its own, critiquing and reapplying

---

[112] Ibid., 140 ('Home Rule, Ahmednagar').
[113] Ibid., 212, 'Home Rule' (Akola, January [?] 1917) (hereafter, 'Home Rule, Akola').
[114] Ibid., 132 ('Home Rule, Belgaum').
[115] Ibid., 213 ('Home Rule', Akola).
[116] J. S. Mill, *Considerations on Representative Government* (New York, 1875), 56–57 (hereafter, Mill, *Considerations*).

liberal concepts in a new historical environment.[117] It is of course not-able that Tilak here uses the language of the most systematic ideologue of colonial autocracy in order to decry it: Mill's eighteenth chapter is a full-scale justification for the autocratic government of 'Hindoos', who are without 'the knowledge necessary for suspecting the existence' of the causes of wretchedness or prosperity, 'much less for judging of their oper-ation'.[118] His dismissal of Indian intellectual attainment—'nothing better than the mystical metaphysics' of the Vedas, evidencing a singular lack of 'vigorous thinking'—makes his apparently untroubled appropriation in India's political culture seem the more remarkable; it is, to echo C. A. Bayly, an intellectual dismemberment.[119]

Tilak suggests that this sense of Swaraj, as popular and representative—and not merely indigenous—government was exemplified by the 'Village Panchayats, the Councils of Pandits or Elders' in earlier Indian pol-ities, whose counsel effectively ensured rule within the polity was not autocratic; he thus argues for a continuity in Indian conceptions of the polity.[120] *Swaraj*, he told his audience in Yeotmal, 'is a simple Sanskrit word' (an emphasis on its near-beginningless antiquity that was surely not accidental) 'meaning nothing more or less than the power to rule our homes, and hence it is called in short "Home Rule". It is your birth-right to govern your own house or home'.[121] Revising his own words, he con-cluded, 'I said that it was our "right" to have Home Rule but that is a his-torical and a European way of putting it; I go further and say that it is our "Dharma"'.[122]

Ahistoricizing the conception of political rights is a revealing a strategy for Tilak. Rejecting the language of his most celebrated aphorism, and the words most associated with him—'Swaraj is my birthright'—he ob-scures an important part of the historical consciousness that informed it.[123] The notion of self-rule—in whichever formulation, 'Home Rule' or Swaraj—as a 'birthright' surely owes something to English exemplars.

[117] See Bayly, *Recovering Liberties*.
[118] Mill, *Considerations*, 358.
[119] Ibid., 70–71; C. A. Bayly, 'Afterword', *Modern Intellectual History* 4/1 (2007), 165.
[120] Tilak, *Speeches*, 'Home Rule' speech at Yeotmal (? January 1917), 226.
[121] Ibid., 225.
[122] Ibid., 230.
[123] The expression (in English and Marathi) is emblazoned on a plaque by his statue on his cremation ground at Chowpatty beach, Mumbai, and is discussed in Chapter 6.

The expression 'birthright' evokes the English radicalism of the mid-seventeenth century, of 'Freeborn' John Lilburne and his Leveller counterparts like Richard Overton; the word itself is overwhelmingly and indelibly associated with the period, in which it was used as a justification, specifically, for political rights.[124] Tilak indeed seems to borrow the expression. The Marathi phrases *'janmasidha hakka'* or *'janmasidha adhikar'* for 'rights true through birth' (there has, significantly, never been agreement as to its rendering in Marathi, unlike in English) appear to be neologisms.[125] Tilak indeed appears to first use the phrase 'Swaraj is my birthright' in these Home Rule speeches in the immediate wake of the Lucknow Congress, as he expostulates the justifications for Home Rule, and he first justified Home Rule as a 'birthright' in a speech in English at Cawnpore—indeed Tilak was unusually explicit in commenting on his use of the medium. 'Unfortunately not being able to speak in Hindi I have thought it fit to address you in English on this occasion, a few words which relate to a subject in which all of us were engaged at Lucknow' said Tilak:

> unless we get a part of the freedom for which we are trying, for a part of the power which rests in the hands of the bureaucracy at present, it is impossible for us to attain that position to which we are entitled as a birthright.

Later treatments of this idea in Marathi domiciled it into that language; indeed at the first apparent instance of his doing so, in Yeotmal later that month, he was as we have seen above somewhat agonized about it.

It is significant that this concept has such a referent for Tilak. The revolutionary history of England seems to have influenced him significantly, as we shall see in 'The Conduct of Politics', discussing the legitimacy of

---

[124] See the writings collected in Andrew Sharp (ed.), *The English Levellers* (Cambridge, 1998).

[125] Molesworth's definition of 'Adhikar' includes the senses 'right' or 'title' (Molesworth, 25); hakka has a similar range of meanings, one of which is 'justness of claim' (ibid., 881). 'Janma' means birth (ibid., 306); siddha means 'proved or true' (ibid., 854). There is no entry for 'janmasiddha', a compound which can be translated as 'true [from or through] birth'. It is a term overwhelmingly associated with Tilak, and this very phrase. Tilak here seems to follow the example of William Tyndale, whose English translation of the Bible coins the expression from existing English words ('birth' + 'right') to express a Hebrew concept in the story of Jacob and Esau (Gen 25:30. See 'birthright, n.', OED Online [Oxford University Press, September 2022. Web. 30 November 2021]). Tyndale's bible translations themselves, of course, were an important intellectual inheritance for seventeenth-century Protestant revolutionaries in England.

violence to establish constitutional rights. It may be that for Tilak as much as for others like Dadabhai Naoroji, whose enunciation of the goal of Swaraj in the Congress of 1906 Tilak referred to often in these speeches, and whose most famous work paid the British the compliment—and thereby employed a sort of moral coercion—of referring to autocratic rule as 'un-British', there was a significant normative power to the example of British historical progress—in constitutional and political liberties in particular—so central, as we have discussed, to colonial education in India, and the historical consciousness it sought to produce.[126] It should not be overlooked that Tilak was explicit in his speeches about the forms of political consciousness 'English education' had produced in India.[127] The political thought that emerged from critical episodes in this history, and its vindication of rights, therefore had a strong influence upon Tilak; and it seems to have mattered much more here than the inspiration of the Irish 'Home Rulers', which as we have seen Tilak's *Mahratta* was fascinated with in 1881, and whose influence on the Indian Home Rule Leagues (via Annie Besant) is clear.[128] At another level, the affinity that Tilak may have felt, in attempting to finesse intellectual responses to English tyranny, with those who had attempted to do the same before, is natural—and accentuated by the notion that the conception of political rights that thus emerged out of the British historical experience was denied to Indians by its bureaucratic rulers. In alluding to a period of revolutionary violence, Tilak reminds us of how Indian 'subjects' often drank deeply from British history—and the depth of its influence on him should not be ignored—but drew, in the view of the colonial educational authorities, all the wrong, most insidious lessons from it.[129]

[126] Dadabhai Naoroji, *Poverty and Un-British Rule in India* (London, 1901).

[127] Tilak, *Speeches*, 57, 'Tenets of the New Party': 'English education, growing poverty, and better familiarity with our rulers, opened our eyes'.

[128] Though Tilak was inspired by the Irish example, the format of the Home Rule League agitation seems mainly to have been Annie Besant's idea, while Tilak was initially preoccupied with readmission to Congress. Although Tilak inaugurated his first, on 28 April 1916, he did so in order to forestall her preannounced efforts, and to establish his regional responsibility for and primacy in Maharashtra. His was a tight, six-branch affair, though with a very healthy 32,000 members by early 1918, more than Besant's sprawling league in the same period. Owen, 'Towards Nationwide Agitation' (figures on 171–172).

[129] This theme is present in Sanjay Seth, *Subject Lessons: The Western Education of Colonial India* (Durham, N.C.: Duke University Press: Chesham; Combined Academic [distributor], 2007).

This is far from saying Tilak is embarrassedly covering intellectual tracks that led back to an English exemplar, for *swaraj* itself had resonances in Marathi that included a coded conception of political rights. It, in fact, had its own rich seventeenth-century history nearly contemporary with the notion of the English 'birthright'. *Swarajya* was understood throughout the nineteenth century in Maharashtra as describing the territories governed by Shivaji, as we have seen. The popular remembrance of '*Swarajya*' and Shivaji's rule as emancipatory by Tilak's time—regardless, indeed, of which of the sharply divergent interpretations of it in this period is taken—was thus significant to the nature of the polity invoked by the use of the term. It certainly implied a resistance to tyranny, and, to some form, at least, of a more representative government. Shivaji's could be read, indeed, as a liberal moment, as Ranade seemed to imply in his emphasis on the agency of the 'whole population' in creating a popular mode of Maratha sovereignty.[130] This conception itself is a peculiar historical construct (indeed Banerjee deftly demonstrates the transnational valorization of kingship in the period which helped inform it). Though it matters less here whether this conception of Shivaji's polity is an example of domiciled liberalism—a rereading of the Maratha past to comprehend new political forms and ideas—or a continuously propagated historical memory. Tilak draws on this contemporary sense, with which his own historical account of Shivaji was consistent, and associates it explicitly with representative government during his Home Rule agitation. The meanings of *Swarajya* he draws from provide corroboration of C. A. Bayly's view that early modern patriotisms and debate in South Asia, and embodied memories, themselves constantly renewed during the encounter with the colonial state, were 'active forces' in the construction of later nationalisms, not mere symbols to be reinvented at will.[131] Indeed as Bayly notes, even among the 'high peaks' of late nineteenth-/early twentieth-century nationalism we see the 'creative enlistment' of older traditions, articulating a nationalism that simultaneously overlapped with European forms and ideas while articulating opposition to

---

[130] Ranade, *Rise*, 6. This is echoed by Banerjee, *Mortal God*, 211, who emphasizes the religious sanction to 'popular and representative government' offered by the model of Shivaji's kingship.
[131] Bayly, *Origins*: see especially 21–25 citing André Wink's work on eighteenth-century 'Swarajya', which Bayly insists emphasized regional patriotism and devotional traditions linked to place rather than merely being a revenue term.

'colonial knowledge', as evidenced by the historical readings of Indian regional and communal liberties by Aurobindo, or the ascription of female
virtue and power to the nation in the thought of Bipin Chandra Pal; and
we should see Tilak's employment of *Swarajya* in this context.[132]

Conclusion

Tilak held to the notion of India as a land of religious communities
throughout his career, one influenced by colonial conceptions of Indian
society and the colonial state's incentivization of communitarian politics. Indeed it has been noted that social and political pressures created a new cohesion that emerged around multiple community foci in
late nineteenth-century India, even as new nationalist consciousnesses
emerged; and we shall pursue some of the tensions created by competing
community mobilizations by examining Tilak's relationship with caste in
the next chapter.[133] The Tilak of the Lucknow Pact was not the result of
the rupture of exile or the maturing of his stance as all-Indian politician.
Indeed, although we have noted his clear movement towards greater
national rather than regional prominence from around the turn of the
century, it should be remembered that from the inception of *Mahratta*
in 1881, he consciously aimed at the development and strengthening of
a pan-Indian political community, and his conception of communities
in the early 1890s was of course pan-Indian. There is of course nothing
inherently benevolent to such a conception of community. Tilak's attempts to mobilize communally were strident enough; but though we
shall see the value he put on physical strength and 'warriorness' in the
next chapter, his most consistent calls for violence—again in contrast to
Bankim's 'new Hindu'—were in response to the autocratic, colonial government, not in defence of the interests of his primordial community
(as discussed in Chapter 5).[134] It is also clear that the Indian National

---

[132] Ibid., 116. Indeed, Tilak's similarity to Aurobindo's historicist thought on the modern
polity, which drew on constraints on autocratic power observed in the history of the Indian
polity, is striking: see Bose, 'Spirit and Form', 140–141, discussing in particular his writings in
Arya between 1914 and 1921.

[133] Pandey, *Construction* (see esp. 159), is not clear about how such potential contradictions in
mobilization were negotiated.

[134] Sarkar, *Hindu Wife*, 182.

Congress was by default, in some measure at least, 'Hindu' in relation to the League according to the logic of the 1916 Pact.[135] But Tilak is misrepresented as seeing Hindu society's claims over India as integral, in the mode of Savarkar. What is implied, rather, is a majoritarian form of pluralism in which the consolidation of the Hindu community of India would cement it into a dominant numerical position; but it remains a more universalist conception of nationhood than the ethnic one that emerged among Savarkar and others in the 1920s in Maharashtra, for all its exponents succeeded in linking Tilak to it (as we shall see in 'Remembering Tilak').

Tilak was also predominantly drawn to the historical and cultural symbols of the Hindu community, placing other communities, intentionally or otherwise, at a significant distance from the narrative of India's national civilization. It might be interpreted as a realist vision of distinct communities whose existence the political actor must be reconciled to, without emotional investment in their imaginative integration. The Brahmin-centricity of his view is also notable, visible in his treatment of Maratha history, which we shall explore more in the next chapter; yet the notion that this connotes a dismissal of 'tolerance and plurality' and compels an 'essentially Hindu' national vision should be treated with caution, a symptom of essentializing an inclusively liberal historiographical approach and stigmatizing its alleged opposite.[136] Tilak's oeuvre shows that it was quite possible to argue for a special Brahminic position and yet still believe in the religious pluralism of India (unlike such figures as Rajwade). In the same way, his account of Aryan history, for all its supremacist chauvinism and scapegoating of Buddhism and Jainism for sapping India's strength, actually eschews the standard demonization of Islam in South Asia. His all-Indian Shivaji memorialization exemplifies perfectly both his desire to conceive of broadly acceptable historical symbols, and his essential imaginative limitations to the Maharashtrian-Hindu-Brahminic. In imagining India's polity, Tilak drew on a conventional, communal intellectual framework for understanding her society—the same that for figures such as Pal suggested a federal vision—and his political responses

---

[135] See Pandey, *Construction*, 222, on this broader point.
[136] Deshpande, *Creative Pasts*, 134; Deshpande identifies in general a distinction between 'reformist' and 'militant' approaches.

diverged from the Hindu Mahasabha's (which itself under Malaviya maintained a sense of India's basic pluralism).[137] Indeed we shall also see in the following chapter how his ideas for the unity of the Hindu society differed sharply from the Hindu Sangathan (Organisation for Unity) that emerged just after his death.

As for the question of legitimate authority within the polity, it was vested in the representative government of these communities, as an expression of popular sovereignty. At one level, his use of *Swarajya* in connection to representative government might be seen as the kind of vernacularization of liberal concepts in India that C. A. Bayly sees as so important but touches on relatively briefly.[138] But more deeply than this, Tilak conceived of self-government as a natural right—as birthright or dharma—and thus adduced a model of rights formed independently of the ruling power of the state. We can indeed relate these natural rights to his Vedantic conception of the identification of the self with all created things (discussed in Chapter 2), in which could also be found the 'divine in every self', a basis (as has also been noted in relation to contemporary Bengal) that could readily be used to contest absolute kingly power, as Tilak so enthusiastically did over Charles I.[139] His aphorism 'Swaraj is my birthright' showed his mode of finding analogies for his conception of natural rights from diverse cultural locations (specifically the revolutionary Leveller rhetoric of seventeenth-century England); what mattered here for Tilak was the articulation of a universal idea of natural rights, as well as its specifically revolutionary and anti-colonial force. But no less important is the historical Maharashtrian expression of these rights, encoded in the word Swaraj itself, with its remembrance of Shivaji's emancipatory rule, in providing a historical continuity to draw from. And thus for Tilak, just as has been argued of earlier periods regarding the thought of Rammohun Roy, older Indic concepts of selfhood (for the power of such Vedantic arguments over the longue durée is notable) and right (for Roy *adhikara* was a crucial concept) and models of participatory governance were hybridized with Western-origin notions of rights and liberties,

---

[137] Hansen, *Saffron Wave*, 76 n; this was despite what Hansen describes as Pal's sense of Hinduism's 'ideal of nationhood' through integralist tendencies, tending to full social harmony (71).

[138] See Bayly, *Recovering Liberties*, vii, for a justification of this.

[139] Banerjee, *Mortal God*, Ch. 1, esp. 85–87.

to create a deterritorialized conception of rights, and the self as rights-bearing.[140] And it was in defence of these against autocracy that Tilak would support the use of bullet and bomb, as we shall see. Tilak's articulation of this 'birthright' in 1916–1917 was a significant development in terms of political rhetoric in modern India, and in fact perfectly anticipated and fed into the supposedly germinative 'Wilsonian moment' of transnational anti-colonial self-determination movements.[141]

---

[140] See Milinda Banerjee, ' "All This is Indeed Brahman"': Rammohun Roy and a "Global" History of the Rights-Bearing Self', *Asian Review of World Histories*, 3/1 (January 2015), 81–112 (hereafter, Banerjee, 'Rights-Bearing Self'); Roy's own rich deployment of Advaita Vedanta is discussed at 92 ff. Indeed it is remarkable that Tilak here alludes to such 'disenfranchised' figures as the Levellers, exactly the kind of community whose 'global' conceptions of rights are described here as overlooked.

[141] It is not surprising that Tilak enthused over President Woodrow Wilson's 14 Points, alluding to them in his farewell speech as he left for England on 27 March 1918 (Tilak, *Speeches*, 310, 'Self-Government'). Tilak was frustrated in his desire to represent India at the Paris Peace Conference the following year, though he sent a written representation to Wilson and Georges Clemenceau (SLT 7, 262–273). Cf. the emphasis of Erez Manela, who emphasizes the effect of the peace conference itself in giving a transnational location to anti-colonial nationalist movements including Gandhi's Rowlatt Satyagraha (*The Wilsonian Moment: Self-Determination and the International Origins of Anticolonial Nationalism* [Oxford: Oxford University Press, 2007]). Manela gives insufficient consideration to the Home Rule movement, or indeed to the rhetoric of Swaraj in general before that point.

4

Reforming Hindu Society

This chapter will study how Tilak conceived of a revivified Hindu society, refashioned for the historically specific challenges of modernity.
It examines questions of identity, authority, and power within the caste
structure of Hindu society. The title of this chapter might carry a suggestion of the oxymoronic, such is Tilak's reputation—and, as we shall
see, his own position—as an opponent of major social reform initiatives
throughout his career. But on questions of social reconstruction, Tilak
was in some ways an avid reformer—indeed he reminds us of the difficulty of attaching a distinct 'reformist' label to Hindu thinkers of the
period, in contradistinction to some putative opposite.[1] This can be illustrated most clearly by his desire to inculcate martiality and manliness
in Hindu society, in Tilak's words *'kshatriyatva'*, which can be rendered
'warriorness'—a reformist agenda that runs through his career. This
agenda sought to remedy perceptions of India's weakness and emasculation, specifically that of Hindu society. In this it was a response to the
colonial predicament, and echoes the self-reproach of effeminacy most
classically associated with colonial Bengal. Indeed while current work
discusses the popularization of body-building and the aspiration to become one with the 'stronger' races on account of a 'self-image of frailty'
in colonial Bengal, less attention has been paid to this in Maharashtra
in particular—despite the noted influence of Tilak's writings upon
Bengali militant nationalists who emphasized physical culture, such as
Sarala Debi.[2] Tilak's vision also incorporated a valorization of martiality,

---

[1] See Dalmia, *Nationalization*, 7 ff, noting that social reform is in fact common to the various
movements she surveys, albeit with different emphases, despite her description of one important
strain (to which Tilak can be related particularly in terms of his drawing on *Shruti* and *Smriti*
texts) as 'traditionalist'.

[2] Indira Chowdhury, *The Frail Hero and Virile History: Gender and the Politics of Culture in
Colonial Bengal* (Oxford: Oxford University Press, 2001), 21–22; John Rosselli, 'The Self-image
of Effeteness: Physical Education and Nationalism in Nineteenth-century Bengal', *Past &
Present*, 86/1 (1980), 121–148 130.

The Thought of Bal Gangadhar Tilak. Robert E. Upton, Oxford University Press. © Robert E. Upton 2024.
DOI: 10.1093/oso/9780198900658.003.0005

something not only of all-India relevance in the period, but reflected in other Asian societies (and more broadly) in this period of intensifying European encroachment and the 'New Imperialism' in particular.

This chapter will begin by giving a brief account of the sources of Tilak's anti-reformism, in order to establish, by way of a prelude to what follows, that despite Tilak's ostensible pessimism over the revival of Hindu society under colonial conditions, there was considerable scope for it. It will then look at that aspect of revival which was in effect a precondition for an escape from the colonial predicament: his agenda of martiality and manliness. This will be traced from his first substantive contribution to the Indian National Congress, his speech on arms and military service at Nagpur in 1891, to the intense phase of his advocacy of enlistment to the Indian army from 1916 to 1918, as he implored youths to fight for the King-Emperor, even absent the enhanced political rights which he had suggested enlistment should be conditional upon. It will examine how the urging an ideal of a generalized 'kshatriyatva' coexisted for Tilak with an inalienable sense of caste hierarchy, which influenced his sometimes selective calls for the opportunities of military service. The chapter will then examine the implications of Tilak's texts on Aryan history for caste status and Brahmin prestige, and similarly his treatment of Maratha history in connection with the Shivaji festival; and then apply the same questions to the *Gita Rahasya*—an enigmatic text in some ways on this point. Moving to the final phase of Tilak's career, it will look at his hostile response to low-caste/non-Brahmin agitation for separate political ('communal') representation, an especially vital issue in Indian politics from August 1917, and which naturally threatened the authority of revivified Brahminic political authority. His coolness to the eradication of untouchability and hostility to inter-caste marriage in this same final period of his career showed Tilak committed to the integrity of discrete varnas, a system in which a Brahmin community assuming elements of Kshatriya dharma—detached from the varna and reconstituted as 'kshatriyatva' for their uptake—would have a natural position of leadership.

Tilak as an anti-reformist

At the close of his career, looking back in review, Tilak restated the perennial justification for the opposition to reform which had often marked his career.

I don't hold that social reconstruction must be undertaken prior to political emancipation. I attach greater importance to the latter. Without the power to shape our own destiny, our national regeneration, in a large sense, cannot in my opinion, be effected ... when I opposed the Age of Consent Bill I did so mainly on this ground. I did not think nor do I think now that a legislature which is not wholly responsible to the public is competent to deal with social questions.[3]

Tilak spoke here as if he had a single ground for the opposition to reform that appears to characterize his political practice.[4] In fact, he here implies two: firstly, that political emancipation was a prerequisite of social regeneration, releasing society's suppressed energies and enabling Indians to reclaim their agency; secondly, the lack of competence, or perhaps legitimacy, of the colonial state to reform society. It is this second question of legitimacy that dominates Tilak's opposition to reform, most clearly seen in the controversy over the Age of Consent Bill in 1890–1891.[5] For even on the issue of child marriage itself—the most celebrated, signal instance of Tilak's conservatism—Tilak, as we have seen, as early as 1881 in *Mahratta* called for Hindus themselves, rather than (humiliatingly) the government, to banish this 'evil'; just before the bill was moved, Tilak emphasized how Brahmin agency could effect reform: 'such efforts to mould people's minds have been made by the Brahmins for thousands of years', only now, with telling irony, they might need a reformist institution 'like that of the missionaries', to propagate their ideas.[6] His opposition to reform led by the colonial state, though, was absolute. At the same time he could urge Brahmin-led reform, he scorned the notion of applying to government for new laws, and, moreover, minimized the necessity of such change, as the forty cases of rape of minor girls reported in a century in two Indian provinces was 'not a terrible statistic'.[7] This opposition to the principle of alien legislation to amend Hindu social

---

[3] SLT, 7, 40. Taken from Tilak's letter to the *Bombay Chronicle*, 12 December 1919. This reflects his discussion with Agarkar reproduced in Tahmankar, *Tilak* (appendix).

[4] The reactionary impulse is emphasized in Rao, *Foundations*.

[5] For a fuller treatment of Tilak's involvement in this controversy, see Robert E. Upton, *Lokmanya Tilak as Writer and Intellectual in the Political Culture of Late Colonial India*, D.Phil thesis, University of Oxford (2013) (hereafter, Upton, *Lokmanya*).

[6] *The Mahratta*, 22 May, 29 May 1881; Tilak's speech at Joshi Hall, 1 November 1890, reported *Mahratta*.

[7] *Kesari*, 30 September 1890, SLT 5, 51, 'Application form asking for law'.

practice dragged Tilak, by the height of the age of consent controversy in 1891, into a position where Hindu dharma was text-bound and immutable: the *garbhadana* (conception ceremony), he stated on a reading of Hindu law *shastras*, had to be performed on the occasion of a girl's first menstruation, according to all authority: 'from the earliest times of the Sutras down to the present day ... this has been our Shastra and practice'; 'take it as it has been and as it is'—and inescapably, as it shall be.[8] Thus the character of Hindu society itself was redefined according to the need to defend it against intervention: the practices of Hindu society were rooted to texts by Tilak in 1891, the better to withstand attack, but which gave no scope for reform. It should not surprise that elsewhere, notably in the *Gita Rahasya*, away from the fray of such reformist controversy, Tilak outlines a view of Hindu dharma which is altogether more accommodating of changing social customs, encapsulated in his quotation in the work's conclusion '*acaraprabhavo dharmah*' ('Morality springs from custom').[9] And effecting change in customary behaviour was elsewhere a central concern of Tilak.

Of arms and the man

As we alluded to in Chapter 2, the 'activist' dharma that Tilak expounds in the *Gita Rahasya*—that is, the dharma of *karmayoga*—is heavily inflected with Kshatriya virtues. Therefore it is not simply a case of urging Hindus to worldly action, a dharma they have apparently forgotten; Tilak is also urging in the text a revival of Kshatriya dharma, primarily its martial aspect. As we saw, in his conclusion Tilak urges *karmayoga* for the welfare of the Indian nation. Tilak specifies the action that he considers necessary by illustrating his point. The tendency to renunciation rather than action had led to India being overrun by the armies of Islamic invasion; thus the specific action that is wanting historically in India is belligerence, a point underlined by the prominent position of Ramdas, guru to a warrior king, as an exemplar of activism. Tilak pins responsibility for

---

[8] Tilak, *Express Texts from the Shastras Against the Age of Consent Bill* (Poona, 1891?). IOR, Tr. 711.

[9] (Mahabharata, Anusasana: CXLIX, 137), *GR*, ii, 701. This is Sukthankar's translation.

the initial triumph of renunciation upon the development of Buddhism and Jainism in India, and singles out the problem that they opened the door of renunciation to all castes, including her warrior Kshatriyas.[10] The final, enduring shift to renunciation had, further, only occurred after her Kshatriyas had been killed in warfare. For Tilak, it seems, to be active was to fight. He also asserts that Brahmins before him have expounded *karmayoga*; but his illustration is significant:

> even learned Brahmins like Vyasa have written the biographies of great *kshatriyas*. In writing these biographies, would it not be necessary to explain the keynote of the character and lives of those men? This keynote was *karmayoga*.[11]

These statements underline that for Tilak, Kshatriyas were the natural custodians of *karmayoga* virtue.

But there is a sense for Tilak that this virtue can be generalized, and other Hindus act like Kshatriyas. Nowhere is this more clearly or keenly emphasized than in his description of the fighting Peshwa Madhavrao I (ruled 1761–1772). Madhavrao was renowned in Maharashtra for his rebuilding of Maratha fortunes, in particular in his campaigns against Hyder Ali of Mysore, after the Third Battle of Panipat in 1761 had dealt a shattering blow to the Empire's ambitions in northern India. Tilak in fact alludes to a famous anecdote in which Madhavrao sets aside his religious observances to take up the sword; it had become a celebrated part of historical memory in Maharashtra, as can be demonstrated by the seminal 'Gleanings from the Maratha Chronicles' by K. T. Telang. This was in fact first contributed to the same Ninth Congress of Orientalists as Tilak's *Orion*, and was reprinted in Ranade's *Rise of the Maratha Power*. For Telang, who like Tilak and others of his generation wrote in the shadow of Grant Duff, Madhavrao was 'that excellent Peshwa', a status not in the least undermined by the 'great violation of religious rules which was involved in the Brahman Peshwas taking to the military profession' which he had to undertake as his duty to the state; his advisor Ramshastri counselled him, Telang notes, against his 'devoting too much time to religious

---

[10] *GR*, ii, 704–705.
[11] Ibid., 666–667.

observances', being incompatible with those duties of Kshatriyas which the Peshwas had undertaken'.[12] For all Tilak's defence of Brahminic ritual had seen to his earlier spat with Telang over the importance of ritual penance (specifically *prayaschitta*), it is notable that he shared Telang's approval of Madhavrao's pragmatic assumption of the Kshatriya role.[13]

This agenda to generalize a revived Kshatriya dharma throughout Hindu society—with a special focus on its applicability to Brahmins—is visible in many areas of Tilak's political practice. His invocation, and attempted capture, of the memory of Shivaji from the 1890s is notable in this regard; so too is the physically performative masculinity encouraged in both the Shivaji and Ganapati festivals.[14] But in the space available here, it is more useful to go into an under-explored area of Tilak's thought: this relates to his views on martiality, expressed in his hostility to the disarmament of the Indian people through the Arms Act of 1878, and the progressive restriction of opportunities for military service among Indians—in short, the comprehensive demartialization of India, a term (of some broader currency in western India) Tilak used from his earliest journalism.[15]

Indeed some of Tilak's earliest journalistic statements were on the Arms Act, an effective disarmament of the population of British India.[16] And it was always in the context of the lost 'valour of Hindus', as much as the potential to undertake violent insurrection itself, that Tilak couched such statements.[17] At the height of the 'native volunteering movement' occasioned by the apparent Russian military threat in 1885, and which it should be noted animated other Congress nationalists from the

---

[12] K. T. Telang, 'Gleanings from the Maratha Chronicles' in Morgan (ed.), *Transactions*, i. 252-281 (254, 268). For Duff, the anecdote was 'creditable to the good sense of himself and his pupil', for 'Brahmins have departed from the ordinances of their faith and assumed the office of Rajas', a sense that Telang echoes. Duff, *History*, ii, 150.

[13] Telang, an authority on Hindu law, had written a tract during the age of consent controversy pointing out how 'the "sin" ' of not consummating a marriage upon first menstruation can, according to custom, 'in practice be washed away by the expenditure of a few Annas'; Tilak's objections were scathing. K. T. T[elang], *Notes on the Age of Consent Bill*, Poona [?] (1891).

[14] See also Kaur, *Performative Politics*, Ch. 3, and Radhika Singha's review of Mrinalini Sinha, 'Nationalism, Colonialism and the Politics of Masculinity', *Masculinity, Studies in History*, 14/1 (1998), 127–146.

[15] The Arms Act was hastily passed in 1878 ('Indian Arms Act', Act XI of 1878 of the Governor-General's Legislative Council), prompted most immediately by the Deccani revolt in 1878–1879. See *Mahratta*, 16 February 1881.

[16] For example, *Mahratta*, 10 April 1881.

[17] See *Mahratta*, 12 March 1881, for an early complaint of this.

Congress's very inception that year (a point often overlooked), he stated in *Mahratta* that 'what we want is the free use of arms and a little training in the handling of warlike weapons', the present 'slenderness of frame and want of hardihood', which may have discouraged the authorities, being in fact 'the result of a neglect of physical training'.[18] Tilak would go on to move his first Congress motion at Nagpur in 1891 on the Arms Act Rules. Quite apart from the Act itself—for in fact the motion connected the rules to other concerns regarding martiality—the vital context for Tilak's statements here was the progressive restriction of military recruitment in India, coinciding with the start of his career. Such restriction was in large measure due to prevailing colonial conceptions of martiality—often referred to as the 'martial races theory'. Though less uniform and systematic in conception than this title might suggest, these ideas were both powerful and consequential, and in shaping Tilak and his engagement on the issue are worth exploring here. The notion that only certain of India's peoples were fit to bear arms was pervasive from around the 1880s, both among military recruiters and in 'popular imperial culture'.[19] Its most influential patron was perhaps Frederick Roberts, from 1885 to 1893 Commander-in-Chief, India. Roberts expressed its most consistent features:

> no comparison can be made between the martial value of a regiment recruited amongst the Gurkhas of Nepal or the warlike races of northern India, and of one recruited from the effeminate peoples of the south.[20]

This preference for the north was prevalent, as we shall see, though the defining feature of the 'theory' was that martiality was innate to only some peoples, and their precise identity was a matter of dispute. The new

[18] SLT, 8, 861, 26 April 1885 ('Natives as Volunteers'). On early Congress resolutions, see Robert E. Upton, '"It Gives Us a Power and Strength Which We Do Not Possess": Martiality, Manliness, and the Indian Army's Great War Enlistment Drive', *Modern Asian Studies*, 52/6 (November 2018), 1977–2012 (hereafter, Upton, 'Power and Strength'). Sugata Bose and Ayesha Jalal, *Modern South Asia* (Routledge, 2017), 94, for instance note the early Congress's primary concerns as the elective principle in councils and the Indianization of administration, economic demands, and control of the budget: martial questions are conspicuously absent.
[19] Heather Streets, *Martial Races: The Military, Race and Masculinity in British Imperial Culture, 1857–1914* (Manchester, 2017) (hereafter, Streets, *Martial Races*), 13.
[20] Frederick Sleigh Roberts, *Forty-one Years in India: From Subaltern to Commander-in-Chief* (London: Richard Bentley and Son, 1898) (hereafter, Roberts, *Forty-one Years*), 532.

conceptions of martiality that Roberts encouraged and exemplified (for he acknowledged in fact that he had to fight against prevailing ideas of balanced recruitment of diverse races and castes) were bolted on to existing perceptions of who the martial peoples of India were, going back to the days of Company rule; and they were, indeed, also susceptible to communities' self-perceptions.[21] And these conceptions, it should be noted, were in the public intellectual space, and not merely the official deliberative one, where they were propagated in administrative memoranda and handbooks.[22] Roberts's own views were expressed in his memoirs, which had gone through twenty-nine editions within eighteen months of their publication in 1897. In looking at the contours of the theory, this section will focus on expressions in the public domain that were a contribution to the intellectual milieu, rather than merely an expression of policy.

The intellectual climate of the 1880s saw to it that these ideas of martiality were heavily imbricated with conceptions of the Aryan race; and indeed race essentialism was probably a large factor in bringing the martial race theory per se back in vogue, though the relationship between the two should not be seen as deterministic.[23] The 1911 work *The Armies of India* by Lieutenant-General Sir George MacMunn, a work which popularized for a metropolitan audience the now entrenched set of official assumptions on martiality in India, held that 'presumably the great conquest of India away back in the mists of time, by the Aryan race' was responsible for the impossibility of a 'levy en masse' there:

---

[21] See David E. Omissi, *The Sepoy and the Raj: the India Army, 1860–1940* (London, 1994) (hereafter, Omissi, *Sepoy*), 8 ff. on the aftermath of the Peel commission. Kaushik Roy, 'Recruitment Doctrines of the Colonial Indian Army: 1859–1913', *Indian Economic Social History Review*, 34 (1997), 321, 339; Mary Des Chene, 'Military Ethnology in British India', *South Asia Research*, 19/2 (1999), 121–135 on older conceptions of martiality, especially 124 (hereafter, Chene, *Ethnology*). Philip Constable, 'The Marginalization of a Dalit Martial Race in Late Nineteenth- and Early Twentieth-Century western India', *The Journal of Asian Studies*, 60 (May 2001), 439–478, on the idea that self-identifying Kshatriyas developed an exclusive vision of their fitness for enlistment, which the state responded to (hereafter, Constable, 'Marginalization').

[22] The latter are discussed extensively in Chene, *Ethnology*.

[23] Other factors in fostering martiality were explicitly developed by the colonial state, from a 'pure' monotheistic Sikhism to a cold climate and an open frontier. George Fletcher MacMunn, *The Armies of India Painted by Major A C Lovett Described by Major G F MacMunn With foreword by Field-Marshal Earl Roberts* (London, 1911) (hereafter, MacMunn, *Armies*), 132; Metcalf, *Ideologies*, 128.

the subjection of the original inhabitants [is] at the bottom of this. Only certain races were permitted to bear arms, and in course of time only certain races remained fit to bear arms.[24]

The Aryanization of existing martial race notions of course refashioned the perceptions of which races were martial (much as it could also merely assume Aryanness on the basis of previously assessed martiality). Not all authorities agreed precisely on which Indian peoples were Aryan, and there was rarely absolute assertion that only Aryan recruits should be taken. Nonetheless, the outcome of the rough consensus that emerged was, in MacMunn's words, that

the people by tribes from whom we take soldiers in India itself are as follows … The ancient Aryan races, Rajput (lit. sons of princes) and Brahman; Jats and Gujars; Pathans and Moguls.[25]

The provenance of the 'ancient Aryan races' is the history of Aryan origins in Central Asia, and their subsequent invasion of India 'with which we are all familiar'.[26]

It is also important to note that these notions of martiality often continued to assume a commonality of race between Englishmen and Indian martial races themselves, long after the notion had been assailed by metropolitan ethnographers. In this, they reflected and reinforced the conceptions of Anglo-Indian ethnographers like H. H. Risley, as discussed in Chapter 2. By the time of the martial race theory's late nineteenth-century flowering, as we saw there, the ethnographical notions of the true 'Aryan' locus in India had swung to the northwest; and this is another important, and understated, reason why the locus of recruitment became so geographically focused.[27] It has been noted that late nineteenth-century colonial ethnography often emphasized the

---

[24] MacMunn, *Armies*, 129–130.

[25] Ibid., 131.

[26] Ibid., 155.

[27] The sense that Aryan influence in the Deccan was limited is borne out by J. A. Baines' remarks on caste in the Bombay Presidency in the 1881 census: India Census Commission, *Report on the Census of British India taken on the 17th February 1881*, 3 vols (London, 1883), iii. Appendix H, xcv–xcvii.

miscegenation of the Aryans within India, to explain their degradation and their difference-despite-unity with the British Aryans.[28] But locating the Aryans exclusively in the northwest represented an alternative, complimentary strategy. Aryans were segregated physically and psychologically, to a stratum of loyal military peoples. This treatment reflects Thomas Metcalf's conception of 'the creation of difference' between the ruling British and their Indian subjects.[29] Indeed this most likely ensured the relationship between martiality and Aryanness operated both ways—the preference for the Sikhs of the Punjab as fighters and subjects burnished their claim to be not merely martial, but therefore Aryan.

All of this had tangible effects on recruitment to the Army in western India from 1880 to 1914. Roberts set the tone: 'The first step to be taken', recalled Lord Roberts, was 'to substitute men of the more warlike and hardy races for the Hindustani sepoys of Bengal, the Tamils and Telagus of Madras, and the so-called Mahrattas of Bombay'.[30] Although such a shift was never complete, the status of some of the Bombay Presidency's would-be martial communities was indeed considerably undermined in the new definitions of martial peoples. The elite Maratha claim to Kshatriyahood earlier noted, which incorporated a claim to be a true martial people of Rajput descent, softened this effect, and saw to it that 'genuine Marathas', not lower-caste Deccanis attempting to pass as them, would continue to be recruited.[31] But all the communities of western India were affected. In 1879, recruitment of the Bombay Army was localized to the Bombay Presidency and areas of Central India, Rajputana, and Sind, the addition of the last two areas to the Army's recruitment sphere signalling the northwards push.[32] Thus at one level in the Bombay Presidency, Brahmins were frozen out of a local Maratha Kshatriya warrior tradition, which increasingly defined itself exclusively; while at another all Maharashtrian warriorhood itself was progressively denigrated, if not dismissed, in the late nineteenth century, in favour of recruitment from elsewhere.

---

[28] Ballantyne, *Orientalism*, 50–51.
[29] Metcalf, *Ideologies*, Ch. 3.
[30] Roberts, *Forty-one Years*, 531–532.
[31] R. M. Betham, *Marathas and Dekhani Musalmans: Compiled under the Orders of the Government of India* (Calcutta, 1908), 49.
[32] Ibid., 21.

Figures for the Bombay Army for 1891, the year Tilak spoke at Nagpur, are telling. Of 124 'native' cavalry officers, 79 were Muslim officers, just 2 were 'Dakkhani' Brahmins, 6 were Mahrattas, and 17 were Sikhs; in all ranks, there were 2,484 Muslims out of a total of 4,437, with only 5 Dakkhani Brahmins and 257 Hindustan Brahmins, 245 Rajputs and 336 Mahrattas, 362 Jats, and 321 other Sikhs.[33] Similar figures pertained in the artillery ranks (there were, of course, no native officers, a policy consequential of the memory of 1857). The infantry ranks showed a higher proportion of Mahrattas, with 6,697 as against 5,046 Muslims, with Sikhs, Parwaris, and Hindustan Brahmins also well represented. There were only 24 'Dakkhanis'—and in the last year they were in fact to be recruited at all, 34 Mangs and 13 Mahars.[34] There was one Dakkhani officer, as compared to 115 Mahrattas and 119 'Muhammedans', and 32 Sikhs.[35] The entry records eight categories of Muslims, and five of Punjabis, and within that, three categories of Sikh. The picture overall was of a modest position for Marathas, historically identified as a warrior people, while the Brahmins of western India were almost utterly ignored. This regional context is vital for understanding Tilak's particular concerns for and preoccupations with questions of martiality in India as a whole, even when he was speaking of the broader all-India level, or to all-Indian or non-Maharashtrian audiences—and indeed, Maharashtrian ones continued to be important even up to his First World War recruitment efforts described below. In an important sense, Tilak would have understood the Bombay Presidency as representative of the experience of much of India in its near-complete demartialization, much as his understanding of the historic martial qualities of Maharashtra gave him a particular impetus to propagate them. And the sense that the armies of India were disproportionately non-Hindu, in favour of Muslim and Sikh communities, was of course vital.

Tilak made his first major statement on an all-India platform on these very issues of the Arms Act and recruitment. At the 1891 Congress in Nagpur, Tilak, who had been a member of the Indian National Congress

---

[33] IOR/L/MIL/7/17081—annual caste return of the Bombay Army on 1 January 1891, 5.

[34] Ibid., 17: 34 Maungs, 13 Ramusis, 1,780 Parwaris, 107 Baidurs, 750 Sikhs, 1,091 Hindustan Brahmins, 660 Rajputs, 290 Christians, 167 Jews.

[35] Ibid. 20 Parwaris, 3 Baidurs, 32 Sikhs, 22 Hindustan Brahmins, 12 Rajputs, 8 Christians, 21 Jews.

since 1889, moved his first resolution on the 'Arms Act Rules', a matter that he argued to be of paramount importance.[36] In moving it, Tilak stated 'it is desirable that the Government should conciliate Indian public opinion and encourage and qualify the Indians to defend their homes and their Government'. There were four clauses to the resolution. The first alone spoke to the Arms Act Rules themselves, noting 'wild animals habitually destroy human life, cattle or crops', necessitating the right to arms; the second called for the establishment of military colleges, whereat natives 'may be educated and trained for a military career'; the third urged the organization 'throughout the more warlike races of the Empire a system of militia service'; the fourth urged 'authorising and stimulating a wide-spread system of volunteering, such as obtains amongst the people of Great Britain'. The resolution was thus one calling for a general martialization, in a way now in fact well established for the Congress.[37] But for all that, Tilak, perhaps surprisingly, seemed to disavow such martiality for his own class, and confine it to specific others:

> here we have a resolution in which we men—those of us who do really belong to the literary classes—have but little direct concern; it is a resolution directly in the interest of the more warlike races.

The 'argument usually put forward', added Tilak, 'is that the Bengali Babus do not belong to the martial race'. But Tilak did not dissent from the view; he simply emphasized that 'here are millions who do belong to military races, who are asking for their privileges that have been enjoyed by their forefathers'. Thus it was a note of protest on the part of certain communities that Tilak did not necessarily identify with—those, as we have seen, who were being side-lined included Hindustani Muslims and to a lesser extent Marathas. 'We do not mean that everybody, indiscriminately, is to be permitted to volunteer', Tilak added in reassurance; as previously, the demand was made 'under such rules and restrictions as may be necessary'. Tilak's resolution, indeed, appears no more than a broadening of

---

[36] *Report of the Seventh Indian National Congress held at Nagpur on the 28th, 29th and 30th December, 1891* (London: British Committee of the Indian National Congress, 1892), 38 ff.
[37] See Upton, 'Power and Strength', 2010.

the existing pattern of colonial recruitment, with its emphasis on martial traditions, and its mistrust of those of very low status.

Tilak turned to a bodily image, urging the development of the 'sinews of the country' in addition to its intellect. And yet, recruitment should 'be confined to those who are to a certain extent educated', said Tilak, 'and, hence, necessarily belong to the party of order'. Others in the Congress at other times argued very differently: Tilak's perennial rival Gokhale urged universal conscription, specifically so that some communities did not miss the privilege, or escape the burden, of service.[38] Indeed the contrast highlights that while Tilak was in important senses typical of a desire— which crosses boundaries of 'conservative'/'reformer' or later 'moderate'/ 'extremist'—to reinvigorate India martially, other elite figures expressing similar self-perceptions of effeminacy were not, in Mrinalini Sinha's terms, also urging the hegemonic aspirations of those elite groups within colonial society, which Tilak, as we shall see further below, was more concerned to do.[39] Highlighting a perennial concern, Tilak demands that after they have been given arms and 'taught their use', Indians should 'get higher appointments in the military service', suggesting a conception of military virtue that incorporates its deliberative elements and qualities of leadership, and depends upon a cadre of people of some appreciable status.

Of course, the colonial state's 'emasculating the more warlike tribes' was inseparable for Tilak from 'the whole nation ... being demilitarised and enervated'. Tilak anticipated the official objection: 'Has not the British Government undertaken to defend you from attacks of a foreign power, to keep you in peace and prosperity?' But simply being defended against the 'wild beasts of the North'—the Russians—crushes 'the life out of the country'. The people per se should rather be associated with the defence of their country. Though Tilak did not invoke the varna, his resolution spoke to Kshatriya dharma. Its concern with the defence of home and polity, its explicit reference to military vocation, its delimiting to certain classes of people, and its concern with leadership in the field reflect the

---

[38] Omissi, *Sepoy*, 28.
[39] Mrinalini Sinha, *Colonial Masculinity: The 'Manly Englishman' and the 'Effeminate Bengali' in the Late Nineteenth Century* (Manchester: Manchester University Press, 1995) (hereafter, Sinha, *Masculinity*), 91.

spectrum of ideas associated with the varna in classical *dharmashastra*. As the Gita has it, 'Valour, glory, Courage, dexterity, not slinking away from battle, gifts, exercise of lordly power, this is the natural duty of *kshatriyas*'.[40] What is different, and particular to the late colonial period, is that the diminishing of Kshatriya dharma was associated with the de-militarization of the whole of society; and so too did this sharpen the felt need for the resurrection of Kshatriya dharma per se, not necessarily confined to identified *jatis* of the Kshatriya varna. This was to become more urgent and clearer in Tilak's subsequent statements on the theme.

Twenty-five years later, Tilak's statements encouraging enlistment to the Indian Army during the First World War show a remarkable similarity in the structure of their arguments, and in their language, adapting to a changed all-Indian and international political environment.[41] The message of the Commander-in-Chief, Willcocks, to the soldiers at the outbreak of war was that they were to show 'that the sons of India have lost none of their ancient martial instincts'.[42] And it is likely that enlistment in India, and its encouragement by leaders like Tilak, specifically echoed the cult of masculinity and patriotic self-affirmation that swept so many into enlisting in Britain at the outbreak of war. Anglo-India, long seen by Tilak as complacent and dismissive of Indians' capabilities, spoke reverently: according to the *Times of India*,

> when one speaks of the brave doings of the British soldier the praise must be distributed over the widest possible field. Indian, Australian and New Zealander alike share in the glory as they shared in the danger and the daring.[43]

Germans, meanwhile, were 'always glad of an excuse to express their contempt and resentment at the employment of Indian troops against them'. But they 'found out the quality of the men sent to fight them'. Awards

---

[40] Gita 18.43. I use here K. T. Telang's near contemporary translation in vol. VIII of *The Sacred Books of the East* series: *The Bhagavad Gita with the Sanatsugatiya and the Anugita* (Oxford, 1882)(hereafter, SBE VIII), 126–127. Cf my rendering of Tilak's own translation of this verse, below (173).

[41] The Presidency armies had been merged into the Indian Army in 1895.

[42] George Sydenham Clarke, George MacMunn, and Alfred Crowdy Lovett, *India and the War* (London: Hodder and Stoughton, 1915), 76

[43] *TOI*, 4 August 1915, 6.

such as the Indian Order of Merit were bestowed upon soldiers who had shown the 'greatest gallantry under fire': those are men 'of whom the Empire is proud'.[44] That the dignity and worth of Indians were spoken of in the same way as the young men of the white colonies likely accentuated the appeal of Indian military service and its promise of personal and national revival: thus a string of pronouncements in 1917 and 1918 encouraged Indians to enlist.

The pressures of the war, meanwhile, led to changed requirements and expectations regarding Indian recruitment. Indian troops (and labourers and other non-combatants) were deployed in campaigns on the Western Front, in the Middle East, German East Africa, and even at the siege of Tsingtao.[45] Such demands saw the Army expand from 115,423 to 573,484 combat troops by the war's end.[46] Combined with wartime attrition, this increase made the normal peacetime recruitment of 15,000 per year grossly inadequate.[47] In April 1918, recruitment targets finally peaked at 47,000 per month; a grand total of 1,272,460 were recruited during the war.[48] For the first two years of the war, remarkably, the old system remained largely intact: regiments, or individual companies within them, retained unity of class—that is 'ethnic' or caste—composition, and regiments recruited through direct enlistment and class recruitment.[49] In January 1917, though, territorial recruiting was introduced, with regiments simply given a tract of territory to quarry for recruits.[50] The exigencies of war, notably the disaster of the surrender of an Indian Army to the Turks at Kut in Mesopotamia in April 1916, also led to the recruitment of those 'other than those recruited under normal conditions', in the words of the Adjutant General in India, Lieutenant-General H. Hudson.[51] Hudson's dread of the Indian 'conscientious objector' with his religious

[44] Ibid., 14 June 1915, 8.
[45] S. D. Pradhan, 'Indian Army and the First World War', in DeWitt C. Ellinwood and S. D. Pradhan, eds, *India and World War 1* (New Delhi; Manohar, 1978) (hereafter, Pradhan, 'Indian Army').
[46] *India's Contribution to the Great War* (Calcutta, 1923).
[47] IOR/L/MIL/17/5/2396, 'Memorandum for the Indian Representatives at the Forthcoming Imperial War Conference', 27–29 April 1918, Annexure 1, 5 (hereafter, 'Memorandum').
[48] IOR/L/MIL/17/5/2152, 'Recruiting in India Before and During the War of 1914–1918', (hereafter, 'Recruiting'), 22, 26.
[49] Pradhan, 'Indian Army', 56–57.
[50] Memorandum, Annexure 1, 5.
[51] Ibid., 3.

scruples, and of the enervating climate raising men fit only for the 'arts of peace', is visible even in April 1918.[52] But necessity insisted: new 'classes' in Bombay included Berads, Bhandaris, Bombay Telegus, Chambars, Bombay Christians, Guzeratis, Jamkhandis, Kathiawar classes, Khandesh Bhils, Kolis, Lingayats, Mahars, Mahratta Brahmans, and Sindis.[53]

At around the moment that Hudson was casting the net for recruits more widely, Tilak spoke on the 'Loyalty Resolution' at the Bombay Provincial Conference at Belgaum in April 1916. To 'strengthen and consolidate the British rule', said Tilak, 'we have shown our willingness to sacrifice to the utmost our blood and our purse', thus revoking the Arms Act now, or 'at the termination of the war', should surely follow.[54] Some bureaucrats had asked:

'Why do you want arms? We are here to protect you from foreign invasions as well as from internal violence'. I ask, however, why should we go to the District Superintendent of Police to request him to protect us from the depredations of a tiger in the jungle?[55]

Granting the privilege of carrying arms would 'not only promote our welfare', but 'go to strengthen the empire as well. It will further secure the peace of the country' by deterring foes, and 'make the people strong, bold and manly', the 'pernicious Arms Act' having 'eaten into the vitals of our country'.[56] And in this very same speech, characteristically, Tilak specifically addressed the question of military enlistment as well, arguing that it would be encouraged by the concession. Indeed, such encouragement was perhaps necessary, as for all the efforts to enjoin enlistment in the Presidency, the Government of India noted after the war that it was perennially 'hopeless' to expect full numbers.[57]

Efforts to encourage Indians' enlistment grew more strident in the ensuing months, as much from India's intelligentsia as from the colonial authorities themselves.[58] Nowhere was this more marked than in the

---

[52] Ibid., 1.
[53] 'Recruiting', Appendix XIII, 75.
[54] Tilak, *Speeches*, 405.
[55] Ibid., 409.
[56] Ibid., 409–410.
[57] 'Recruiting', Appendix XIII, 25.
[58] See Upton, 'Power and Strength'.

Bombay Presidency, with its pattern of demartialization and its subsequent sluggish enlistment; and at one level it seems Tilak was convinced that changes to social and political rights were necessary to encourage it. But if this was indeed Tilak's logic, it quickly hardened into a political bargain of quid pro quo, which split Tilak from others, such as M. K. Gandhi, who went further in unconditional support for enlistment in the period. 'What does it matter if the country be in possession of the Turks or the possession of the English?', Tilak asked, in one of his final speeches on the matter at the Kirloskar Theatre in Poona in June 1918.[59] What, he asked, are we to tell would-be recruits? 'Join the army to strengthen the *zulum* [unjustness] of these English people?'; why 'should we come forward to protect that India in which we have no rights' and in which 'we are treated like slaves?'[60] As he put it in *Kesari* around the same time, 'give us *Swarajya* and we will be obliged to protect our land; we will not be too enthusiastic to go to war if we do not have *Swarajya*.'[61] As these late statements suggest, it was a line that Tilak stuck to: he castigated the Delhi War Conference of April 1918 for offering 'hot air' (*bhapaka*) rather than substantive change on political issues, despite the same conference witnessing support for enlistment from, among others, Gandhi and Surendra Nath Banerjea.[62] And Tilak himself was ruled out of order by the Governor of Bombay at the subsequent Bombay War Conference for attempting to proffer some views on how 'Home Defence and Home Rule must go together' while speaking on the motion of loyalty to the King Emperor; frustrated, Tilak left (followed by others, including the editors of *Young India* and *Kesari*, and the Parsi industrialist S. R. Bomanji).[63] Tilak's message to fight, under conditions, was intended therefore both for official and popular audiences, and might appear to show Tilak as preoccupied with the conditionality of political rights, to the detriment of his remartialization agenda. Indeed Gandhi explicitly disagreed with

---

[59] 'Speech at Kirloskar Theatre, Poona, 22 June 1918' (enclosure to Cresar to District Magistrate, Poona, 31 July 1918), MSA, Government of Bombay Home Department (Special), 398J (1918) (hereafter, 'Kirloskar Theatre').

[60] Ibid.

[61] SLT, 4, Ch. 25, 'Swarajya, protecting one's country and enlistment in the army' (2 July 1918).

[62] SLT, 3, Ch. 179, 'What happened at Delhi...?' The Conference, from 27–29 April, was at the invitation of the Viceroy, Lord Chelmsford, and aimed at maximizing India's war contribution.

[63] Jamndas Dwarkadas and N. C. Kelkar respectively. Bombay Judicial Department Confidential Proceedings, 1918 (IOR/P/Conf/36).

Tilak for his attaching conditions to his support, saying he would 'not whisper "Home Rule" ' as long as the war lasted; and he promised to the Government that he would 'rain men on you', as an expression of 'ungrudging and unequivocal support to the Empire'.[64]

But even among these statements of Tilak, we see the value he attached to military service per se, and a notable slippage in Tilak's own conditions for supporting enlistment. Elsewhere Tilak asserted that he would

> give up the Home Rule movement if you do not come forward to defend your Home. If you want Home Rule be prepared to defend your Home ... You cannot reasonably say that the ruling will be done by you and the fighting for you.[65]

This contradicts his quid pro quo logic, that the Government's assurances are a prerequisite for full cooperation in the war effort; rather, Indian manhood had to prove itself worthy of being the guardian of a nation. Even more explicitly, Tilak segues between his conditional support for recruitment and his metaphysical justification for martiality:

> who can expect any people on the surface of the earth to fight for a country unless the fighter hopes that he will improve his material position in this world? The Bhagavad Gita has beautifully expressed that if you die on a battle-field there are gates of heaven open to you.[66]

The value of fighting, it seems, is never far from Tilak's mind, and could create such a jarring non sequitur. The pattern of Tilak's statements shows that the strength that could be inculcated through the experience of war took precedence over the conditions which he so prominently attached to them. This experience was never entirely instrumental to gaining Home Rule, even when it was couched as a condition (or indeed, absent such a concession, if Tilak had hoped that political rights could be wrested by the capacities of a remartialized populace). They were complementary aims, the end of which was a strengthened and

---

[64] *TOI*, 13 August, 8; Gandhi to Maffey, 30 April, *CWMG*, vol. 17, 12; Gandhi to Viceroy, 29 April 1918, ibid., 7.
[65] *Speeches*, 309, 'Speech at Poona' (n.d.).
[66] Ibid., 340, 'Home Rule' (n.d.).

self-governing India. Tilak in fact shared with Gandhi to a remarkable degree the insecure sense of a Hindu population which lacked
the requisite strength for self-government; indeed, while for Gandhi
fighting was a means to gain the moral courage necessary to win this
through satyagraha, he also specifically echoed Tilak's language of a
lack of physical courage: but whereas Tilak had been concerned that
demartialization rendered his audience helpless against tigers, Gandhi
told his in a speech on enlistment in neighbouring Gujarat in 1918 that
they were 'people afraid of even a squirrel', who 'had much better think
of improving their own condition than of getting Swaraj'.[67] This wartime agenda to strengthen Hindus through modern combat is visible
in other movements of the period besides. One such was that promoted
by Madan Mohan Malaviya, with his insistence on extensive physical
training and wrestling at the proposed Hindu University at Banares, a
drive for 'national efficiency', in Carey Watt's terms, partly in response
to a transnational turn to Darwinian social ideas (which Tilak had reflected in the *Gita Rahasya*), and relatedly to the ever-harsher realities
of international competition, leading ultimately to global conflict.[68]
Tilak's own thought, consistent in his concern for remartialization,
comprehended the sense of ever-growing international threat: as we
have seen, though in June 1918 he questioned the significance of the
identity of India's rulers if they were not Indians themselves, a few
days later he enjoined his readership in the *Kesari* to enlist, naming
Persia and Turkistan as Germany's props for a likely assault on Asia 'in
future'.[69]

In that same June 1918 speech at the Kirloskar Theatre, which ultimately caused an end to his recruiting statements through its prompting
an order by the Bombay Government upon him against public speaking,
Tilak bemoaned the current recruiting regime for its acceptance of the
lower castes: the 'recruits who are enlisted in the Bombay Presidency', he
said, are of the kind that has 'his eye of the rupees', in particular the Mahar
and Berad communities, who were ill-suited to military discipline,
and who would return to their occupation of 'thieving' and 'receiving

---

[67] *CWMG*, vol. 17, 171 (Speech at Surat, 1 August 1918).
[68] Carey Watt, 'Education for National Efficiency: Constructive Nationalism in North India,
1906–1916', *Modern Asian Studies*, 31/2 (1997), 339–374, esp. pp. 367–368.
[69] SLT 4, Ch. 25, 'Swarajya, protecting one's country and enlistment in the army' (2 July 1918).

beatings' for it after the war.[70] The Berads, or Ramoshis, are defined in Molesworth's classic nineteenth-century dictionary—in the preparation of which he was assisted by Maharashtrian Brahmins—as a 'class of professional robbers'.[71] Tilak endorsed this conception, which saw to it that the Ramoshis were categorized as a criminal class by the Government.[72] Meanwhile genuine Brahmins of the region were to be excluded from the army: 'This is unjust'. Yet Tilak's hostility towards Berad and Mahar recruitment is significant, as it is sympathetic to elite Maratha claims to exclusivity as Kshatriyas. This claim to social and occupational distinctness from Mahars and others had helped their own recruitment to continue at the latters' expense.[73] Such privileging of elite Marathas was, as we have seen, a perennial concern of Maharashtrian Brahmins (one Tilak shared, as his own stance over the 'Vedokta' dispute concerning the ritual status of the 'Kshatriya' Maratha royal house of Kolhapur showed).[74] Tilak's statements here speak powerfully of the limits of Hindu society that are susceptible in his mind to renovation and the assumption of Kshatriya dharma, to the degree that he aligns with the elite Maratha stance.

And allied in this speech to this fear of untouchable mobilization was an articulation of Tilak's long-standing demand that Indians be given full commissions as officers. Indeed, this form of conditionality seems to have distracted Tilak from the political conditions which, as we saw, he simultaneously placed on enlistment. The British, it appeared, 'want mercenaries who will work under them', a traducing of the true military spirit; if appointments were opened, giving Indians 'the same rights as Europeans, two or ten lakhs of people would this day be ready to die'.[75] As a measure of his personal investment in this issue, a few days earlier

---

[70] 'Kirloskar Theatre'. Cf. *Kesari*'s report of the speech on 25 June (see pages 13–14) which merely had Tilak stating that 'paid mercenary soldiers were recruited and this was partially responsible for the destruction of the Peshwas [chief ministers of the Maratha Empire]', after which the British 'started keeping paid soldiers', whose only qualities were 'following orders and being loyal' (my translation). The file indicates that two CID shorthand reporters took the speech down; in his own protest to the Governor of Bombay, Tilak did not dispute the words (SLT 7, 381). This is further discussed in Upton, 'Power and Strength'.

[71] Molesworth,590.

[72] Bombay (Presidency) Police Department, *Notes on Criminal Classes in the Bombay Presidency: With Appendices Regarding Some Foreign Criminals Who Occasionally Visit the Presidency Including Hints on the Detection of Counterfeit Coin* (Bombay, 1908). The Criminal Tribes Act was passed in 1871, and extended over all India in 1911.

[73] See Constable, 'Marginalization'.

[74] See 'Tilak as a Writer', in this volume.

[75] *Kesari*, 25 June 1918; 'Kirloskar Theatre'.

he had stated that, were this granted, he could guarantee 25,000 recruits from Maharashtra, and offered to personally give 100 rupees for every recruit short of 5,000 enlisted within six months.[76] It was not the only time during these weeks he would adopt such a dual stance on the necessary conditions of enlistment.[77] Tilak had in fact the previous year already bemoaned the discussions in the Legislative Council on the commission of Indians; Willcocks claimed that it would merely be a temporary wartime measure, but 'a couple of years' was not sufficient to train a man to be a Major or Colonel, the ranks that Tilak had in mind.[78] Once more, colonial statements of eastern incapacity—that, as Lord Roberts had put it, 'eastern races ... do not possess the qualities that go to make leaders of men, and that Native officers in this respect can never take the place of British officers'—only sharpened Indian nationalist demands on this score.[79] In any case, Tilak's concern over Mahar and Berad recruitment was likely only heightened by his sense, as he explained in *Kesari*, that the middle class ('*madhyam varga*')—a term for him synonymous with the 'learned class'—would not enlist just 'like day labourers on tea plantations'; and the withholding of commissions explains his complaint in his Kirloskar speech that the government did not want '*jaanati*' (intelligent) people in the army.[80] Tilak may have feared that, under these conditions, the invigorating effects of military service would not be felt by educated elites, a destabilizing prospect. Specifically, Tilak was anxious that these elites experience leadership in war, which he viewed as the preserve of educated Indians; and their inability to assume authority over rank-and-file recruits in war would, of course, imperil their claim to social authority in peace. Tilak perhaps also echoes his earlier statement at Nagpur, in implying that the educated classes—as per the classic figure of colonial stereotype, the Bengali babu—have become particularly bodily weakened, and are most greatly in need of the revivifying effects of military service. And these fears imbricated, of course, with Tilak's concern for the reinvigoration of the Brahmins as a varna, a category that overlapped,

---

[76] Speech at Girgaum, 16 June 1918; *Mahratta*, 23 June 1918.
[77] SLT, 4, Ch. 25, 'If not *Swarajya*, the bureaucracy should at least be ready to give military rights'.
[78] *TOI*, 3 March 1917, 10.
[79] Roberts, *Forty-one Years*, 533.
[80] SLT 4, Ch. 25; *Kesari*, 25 June 1918.

tacitly, with the 'learned', and would naturally assume leadership in peace and war: it was as Brahmin specifically that Tilak derided untouchable recruitment.

If the 'military' condition of full commissions, with its pertinence for educated Brahmin leadership, therefore took priority over that of the concession of political rights as regards Tilak's encouragement of enlistment (and he placed his own money as surety of it), his earlier response to the announcement of the (ultimately derisory) domestic Indian Defence Force in February 1917 is also instructive.[81] Amid widespread calls in the Indian press that enlistment to the force (somewhat inaccurately seen as an extension of the regular Army) should depend upon the removal of any restriction on Indians in higher military posts within it, no such positive official offer was forthcoming.[82] Tilak editorialized for *Kesari* mildly in response that the Government 'could have been more open and welcoming', but abjured boycotting the force: 'many believe and argue that until there is no distinction between black and white in the military, no thinking and patriotic ('*deshabhimani*') black soldier will feel like joining the army'. But 'it is not correct to hold this bias and stay away'; Indians should 'join the army without reservations', he said, in a phrase which captures the sense of opportunity Tilak felt the war offered to reinvigorate demartialized India, because 'this time will not come again and again'.[83]

This was an opportunity for the resuscitation of premodern martial traditions under enervated colonial conditions, which Tilak had wished for since the 1880s, and also more. Chris Pinney notes that the experience recognized as modernity involved 'an extension of the power and productivity of the human body' and 'a consequent transformation of the body through new thresholds of demand and danger', and that this 'enchanted' Tilak.[84] But Pinney does not acknowledge that Tilak may have aimed to effect such a transformation of Indian (specifically Hindu male) bodies through an engagement in a modern war carried out by

---

[81] The Indian portion of force was only 2,672 in April 1918: 'Memorandum', Annexure 1, 12.

[82] On this response, see Upton, 'Power and Strength', 2006.

[83] SLT 4, Ch. 20, 'This is the time, join the army' (27 February 1917). Tilak used the same coterminous words *sainya* and *lashkar* for both the regular army and the defence force.

[84] Christopher Pinney, 'The Tiger's Nature, but Not the Tiger: Bal Gangadhar Tilak as Mohandas Karamchand Gandhi's Counter-Guru', *Public Culture*, 23/2 (2011) (hereafter, Pinney, 'Tiger's Nature'), 412.

the colonial state.[85] Such seductions of modernity, at no time more in-triguing than during the mechanized conflict of 1914–1918, gave an extra dimension to the desire to self-consciously revive older Indian modes of martiality, and helps explain the particular modality of Tilak's desire to resurrect lost Kshatriya dharma in Hindu society at this moment. And those demands and dangers of modernity were only underlined by the sense of 'Darwinian' struggle of the international order in the period. Tilak indeed, in these 'recruitment' statements, invoked the Gita's explicit veneration of Kshatriya virtues, in a context that echoes the *Gita Rahasya* in invoking external threats to modern India. Though presumably not in-tended (Tilak apparently did not significantly revise the manuscript after his release from Mandalay in July 1914), the *Gita Rahasya* stands at the beginning of a consistent set of wartime comments upon military ser-vice.[86] Similarly, his demand that higher appointments in military ser-vice be opened up to Indians fulfils part of the resurrection of Kshatriya dharma. Tilak's conception of it is not merely of belligerence, strength, courage, or such muscular qualities. As Tilak had translated the Gita verse encapsulating the 'inherent natural duty (*karma*) of the Kshatriya', they were also to show 'intentness' and 'exercising authority (over subject people)'.[87] Military leadership was quintessential to the dharma to be cap-tured by the emboldened Hindu people at large.

This concern to resurrect lost Kshatriya virtues sits paradoxically with the Brahminic notion that all non-Brahmin caste Hindus were Shudras in the *Kaliyuga*—which Tilak's historical account of Kshatriya death in the *Gita Rahasya* in fact seems to echo. Tilak demonstrates the tension: Brahmins assumed greater ritual and social authority through the denial of *dvija varna* (that is, the status of the 'twice-born' *Arya* varnas, whose ritual initiation was their second 'birth') to would-be Kshatriyas, but at the same time a need was felt to make good the loss of the Kshatriya varna. The tension is resolved for Tilak by his ideal that Kshatriya dharma be (differentially) generalized in society,

---

[85] Indeed, Pinney describes how Gandhi's assassin Nathuram Godse saw himself as a Tilakite in his advocacy of military training for Indians during the Second World War, but sees Tilak himself as hoping for a liberation of Indians from the 'complex of instruments, men and arms' (*Zeugganze*, in Heidegger's terminology) at the command of the colonial state. Ibid., 401, 413.

[86] The circumstances of the *Gita Rahasya*'s composition are discussed in Chapter 2.

[87] Bhagavad Gita 18.43. Cf. *GR*, ii. 1195.

and not confined to a residual or submerged Kshatriya varna. Most decidedly, Brahmins in Tilak's scheme were to have a prime portion of resurgent Kshatriya dharma, as his preoccupation with Brahmin recruitment in the infamous Kirloskar Theatre speech shows. Indeed, the *Kaliyuga* idea thus provided exactly the space in which Brahmins could assume Kshatriya dharma. But Tilak was indeed in an unlikely relationship of sympathy with the claims of elite Marathas: his invocation of a warrior ethos in Maharashtra, coupled with his disdain for the military service of lower-caste Ramoshis, echo elite Maratha claims to hereditary Kshatriya status in the period, much as the general undermining of such traditions of martiality in Maharashtra likely emphasized for Tilak the decay of Kshatriya dharma which urgently needed to be made good. In particular, for Tilak no less than these self-identifying Kshatriya Marathas, the distinction between caste Hindus and 'untouchables' remained important; and his statements here directly contradict the binary vision of *Arya*/Shudra in society, securing however modestly a position of greater dignity for 'Shudra' Marathas. In his statements on untouchable recruitment here, Tilak in fact reflects colonial neuroses about criminal classes and the destruction of order—conceptions which themselves fed off Brahminic notions.

It was during this period of simultaneous campaigning for the Home Rule League and for military enlistment that Tilak gave the name Kshatriyaness to his renewed martial spirit, and made the call explicit. In a speech of January 1917 in Cawnpore, Tilak explained that the vision was of a blend of *varnadharma* in each man, with a special, significant emphasis on 'kshatriyatva' (literally, Kshatriyaness):

> Muscle or the capacity for labour and bravery every Indian must develop … He must be ready to put his hands even to 'shudra' work. And he must rouse up and foster *Kshatriyatva* in himself for, in the new world every one must be a soldier on pain of national ruin.[88]

To the Shudra-Kshatriya training one may add either 'the Brahmin or the vaishya education', or 'a suitable admixture' of the two. 'Thus equipped',

---

[88] *Mahratta*, 7 January 1917.

states Tilak in a heavily gendered exhortation, 'let every Indian place himself at the service of the motherland'.[89]

The maintenance of Brahminic social authority

Even as Tilak imagined a generalized *kshatriyatva*, then, it was not undifferentiated, but comprehended and alloyed itself to the existing hereditary qualities of each varna. And it must be emphasized that this differentiation of varna, its qualities and its roles, was rigorously defended, even as Tilak exposited *kshatriyatva* in this final phase of his career. They were always defined as central to the proper functioning of Hindu society. And just as Brahmins would be prominent in partaking of this emerging, general *kshatriyatva*, they would remain 'standing highest' in the 'ideal hierarchy' of *chaturvarna* (the state of four varnas). It is worth surveying now Tilak's approach to the roles of different varnas in society, from the 1890s to the end of his career.

We have seen that Tilak asserted the Brahmin claim to exercise authority through techniques of historical remembrance. Tilak's forays into India's history, described in Chapter 2, were unavoidably, and deliberately, also statements on the status of India's various caste communities. There is now a rich historiography on the non-Brahman movement's employment of historical symbols to constitute their claim to high political status in contemporary India.[90] Thus when Tilak evoked historical symbols—Ramdas the Brahmin guru to Shivaji, or the ancient Aryan rishi—he engaged in their field, to an extent that made any statement on Indian history loaded with implications for the position of his community. Maratha history was the site for a proxy political war on caste issues in late nineteenth-century Maharashtra. After 1895, indeed, non-Brahmin contestation of the institutions of nationalist politics declined: along with the social reform and an educational agenda, history

---

[89] Ibid. That this term, of apparent novelty in Marathi, was tied to claims of royal descent by martial-peasant communities in Bengal (in a transregional relationship to those claims to Maratha Kshatriya status resisted by Tilak) makes his alignment with them here all the more striking. See Banerjee, *Mortal God*, Ch. 4.

[90] See O'Hanlon, *Caste*; Deshpande, *Creative Pasts*.

was their political front.[91] Combined, these factors do much to explain the prolific outpouring of historical writing, particularly on Shivaji, in this period. Tilak's statements on Maratha history were therefore situated in a field of competing imaginings of the Indian polity. Prachi Deshpande points out that the Brahmin Peshwas and Ramdas provide a 'perfect example for the natural social leadership of Brahmans in Maharashtrian society'.[92] E. A. Joshi's Brahminic account of Shivaji's career from the 1870s asserted the importance of his Brahmin advisors in the growth of the Maratha Empire; we have seen too the polemic that in part inspired it, Jotirao Phule's claiming of the Maharaja as a representative of the region's common non-Brahmin identity.[93] The role of Shivaji's Brahmin advisors had thus become by 1880 a touchstone for the expression of caste identity and views on the position of Brahmins in Maharashtrian society.

Tilak, by his own account, wished the figure of Shivaji to be a rallying point for 'all castes' in Maharashtra. Yet this clashes with his clear choice to emphasize the role of his guru Ramdas, a classic example of what Deshpande refers to as the 'contributions' approach to Maratha history, in which those of one's own community are underlined, and with it a claim to higher contemporary status. From the beginning of his contribution to Shivaji's memorialization in the 1890s, he placed a strong emphasis on Ramdas' role, describing him in his editorial commenting on the Hirabag meeting of 1895 as 'the Guru of the great Shivaji'.[94] Perhaps Tilak's clearest statements on this are actually found in his references to Maratha history in the *Gita Rahasya*. To an extent not realized, the *Gita Rahasya* is, as we shall see, strikingly casteless in its message, given the importance of varna in Krishna's instruction contained within the Gita itself. In his concluding chapter, though, where he extols Ramdas' *Dasbodh* as the torchbearer for a true, all-but-lost activist *karmayoga* interpretation of Hinduism, Tilak nevertheless maintains that 'Shivaji Maharaj was blessed by the advice of Sri Samarth Ramdas'.[95] Similarly, though Tilak also gives prominence

[91] See Gail Omvedt, *Cultural Revolt in a Colonial Society: The NonBrahman Movement in Western India, 1873–1930* (Berkeley, 1976). (Hereafter, Omvedt, *Revolt*), 183.

[92] Prachi Deshpande, 'Caste as Maratha: Social Categories, Colonial Policy and Identity in Early Twentieth-century Maharashtra', *Indian Economic Social History Review*, 41/1 (February 2004) (hereafter, Deshpande, 'Caste as Maratha'), 14 and n.

[93] Both texts are discussed in O'Hanlon, 'Polemic'.

[94] *Mahratta*, 2 June 1895, 3.

[95] *GR*, ii, 706.

throughout his text to Ramdas' close contemporary, the poet-saint Tukaram, remembered as an assailant of caste division and a hero to the non-Brahmin movement of the nineteenth century, Tukaram's ultimate inferiority and, indeed, deference to Ramdas is emphasized. Tukaram is described as 'that highest among the devotees of the Blessed Lord', who taught Ramdas of the non-dualism of the cosmos.[96] But his 'inclination was towards abandonment of action'; and so if one requires a true exposition of the Gita religion, 'he must turn' to Ramdas, the 'venerable preceptor' to whom Saint Tukaram himself directed Shivaji to 'surrender himself'.[97] There is, indeed, a non-Brahmin community of obsequiousness to Ramdas here invoked.

Tilak can be related to other Brahminic celebrations of Shivaji at the close of the nineteenth century, many of them more explicit and exclusive. The Shivaji club, established in Kolhapur in 1893, became a centre for Brahmin social organization and militant politics. It ultimately clashed with the Maharaja of Kolhapur, Shahu IV, as he implemented his own non-Brahmin movement in the state (Shahu, on slender evidence, claiming Tilak's involvement with these 'dacoits').[98] The outstanding example of pro-Brahmin historical writing, meanwhile, is Rajwade's work. For Rajwade not only was Ramdas Shivaji's driving moral and spiritual inspiration, he also made Shivaji, as we have seen, a protector of Brahmins; his 'national vision' avoided the chaos of the earlier Bhakti saints by preaching social behaviour based upon caste.[99] V. D. Savarkar also contributed to this memorialization, his preface to his 1906 Marathi translation of Mazzini's autobiography comparing Ramdas to Mazzini in their roles in their respective movements for national realization. Savarkar elsewhere made explicit, exactly like Rajwade, the relationship between Ramdas as ideologue and Shivaji as agent.[100] In urging Ramdas's contribution, Tilak thus reflects the concerns of the times, a counterblast

[96] *GR*, i, 320, 543.

[97] Ibid., 611.

[98] This centred on a photograph showing Tilak associating with some of the 'militant' party. A. B. Latthe, *Memoirs of His Highness Shri Shahu Chhatrapati Maharaj*, 2 vols (Bombay, 1924)(hereafter, Latthe, *Memoirs*), 271.

[99] Deshpande, *Creative Pasts*, 130.

[100] E. Fasana, '*Deshabhakta*: The Leaders of the Italian Independence Movement in the Eyes of Marathi Nationalists', in N. K. Wagle (ed.), *Writers, Editors, and Reformers: Social and Political Transformations of Maharashtra, 1830–1930* (Delhi, 1999).

to non-Brahmin polemic. His choice of Brahmin hero reflects the milieu, too: Joshi's work had focused on the contribution of Dadoji Kondadev, whereas Brahmins of the 1890s chose Ramdas. The *Satkaryottejak Sabha* was an important institutional part of this renewed propagation of Ramdas' memory. Founded in Dhulia in 1893, it became like Rajwade's later *Bharat Itihas Samshodhak Mandal* a major institutional centre of conservative Brahmin opinion in Maharashtra in the ensuing years.[101] Its activities certainly exercised an influence on Tilak, who would later use the Sabha's edition of the *Dasbodh* in preparing the *Gita Rahasya*.[102]

Indeed, even historical accounts often labelled 'liberal' on account of their ostensible inclusivity tended to assert a special Brahminic contribution as well (just as they tended to emphasize the invidious nature of Muslim overlordship).[103] Bhagwat emphasized in his *Shivaji Charitra* of 1889 Shivaji's Brahmin advisors like Raghunath Hanmante.[104] Ranade too unequivocally states Ramdas to be 'the spiritual adviser of the great Shivaji' who instructed his son to follow in his footsteps, and emphasizes the contribution of Brahmin '*karkuns*', or administrators, like Abaji Sondev and Raghunath Ballal.[105] This prominence perhaps indicated an assumption of a natural Brahmin leadership in a unified national movement—and as such it may have been perceived by some non-Brahmins as all the more insidious.[106] Thus the differences between the Brahmin 'contributions' mode of Maratha history and the 'liberal', 'inclusive' one are easy to exaggerate in caste terms. The latter's self-conscious breadth distinguishes them from both Brahmin and non-Brahmin polemic; yet the place they gave to Brahmins was generally a specially honoured one, an expression of their authors' own assumptions about their own community and society more broadly. They converged to a great degree with Tilak's own assumptions on natural Brahmin spiritual and moral leadership in the polity.

---

[101] Deshpande, *Creative Pasts*, 184. On the history of Ramdas's reception, see Wibur S. Deming, *Ramdas and the Ramdasis* ([1928] Gurgaon, 1990).

[102] *GR*, i, xix.

[103] See, for example, Deshpande, *Creative Pasts*, 180; Malavika Vartak, 'Shivaji Maharaj: Growth of a Symbol', *Economic and Political Weekly*, 34/19 (1999).

[104] O'Hanlon, 'Polemic', 21–25.

[105] Ranade, *Rise*.

[106] Deshpande, *Creative Pasts*, 180, records such negative reactions.

There was another important impulse behind Tilak's emphasis on the Brahmin contribution. It allowed Brahmins to partake of qualities in historical Maratha identity identified with masculinity, specifically Kshatriya martial valour.[107] Brahmin insistence on their historical role was also, of course, conditioned by non-Brahmin attempts to freeze them out of Maratha identity entirely, emphasizing the foreign origins of the region's Brahmins, and restricting the use of the term Maratha to some formulation of the region's non-Brahmin castes.[108] This perhaps was important in polarizing and aggravating the debate, goading Brahmin writers to a sharper assertion of their historical role.

Tilak's writing on Aryan history in 1893 and 1903, as we saw in Chapter 2, carefully avoids statements on the prestige or status of any specific caste communities on account of their descent from the Vedic Aryans. In this, he contrasts starkly with other Brahmin voices, from M. M. Kunte to the 'moderate' Ranade. Tilak, though, as we have seen, lauds the achievements of the Indo-Aryans in prehistoric times, and by extension the Brahmins, the keepers of the Vedas, those most sacred of texts that provide evidence of the Indo-Aryans' precocity. This special link to the texts and their Brahminic language, Sanskrit, conferred tremendous prestige on Brahmins in contemporary India. It is, in effect, a Brahmin claim to a position of high eminence in the Indian polity on the basis of historical achievement. Tilak's texts do not provide an assertion that the Brahmins were the exclusive descendants of Vedic Aryans (rather than as one of the three *Arya* varnas), as deliberate as Phule's inversive assertion that the Brahmins alone deserved historical opprobrium for their expropriation of India. Yet as we saw in Chapter 2, it is strongly implied; and the large Brahminic portion of Tilak's audience would probably have assumed such an exclusive link. As we see below, though, other self-identifying *Aryas* tended to look for different constructions of Aryan prehistory than this narrative which emphasized quintessential Brahminic 'Aryanness', and could only include other *Arya* varnas (Kshatriya and Vaishya) in supporting roles.

The *Gita Rahasya* seems at one level to herald a striking turn to casteless egalitarianism: Tilak urges that castes have fallen away from

---

[107] Ibid., 190.
[108] See Deshpande, 'Caste as Maratha', 15–16.

their original purpose, and thus he fashions the landscape for a general adoption of Kshatriya dharma, as posited by the requirements of modernity. But it is worth looking in more detail at this question—and the assumption of Brahminic superiority that may underpin it—for it is perhaps the Brahmin assumption of Kshatriya duties that Tilak is most deeply invested in. The text, as has been noted, is absolute in asserting the Bhagavad Gita's 'conservative' interpretation of *varnashrama dharma*. Indeed, in the Gita, says Tilak, as well as the *Manu Smriti* and other *Smritis*, 'the word "dharma" has been used as meaning "the duties of the four castes in this world"'; for substantiation, he quotes Gita 3.35, translated as 'it is better to die performing one's caste duties; following the duties enjoined on another caste is dangerous'.[109] The 'ancient *rshis*', he goes on,

> had created the institution of the four castes—which was in the nature of a division of labour—in order that all the affairs of society should go on without a hitch, and that society should be protected and maintained on all sides, without any particular person or group of persons having to bear the whole burden.[110]

Caste, according to Tilak's interpretation, is laid out in the Gita as elsewhere for perfectly natural and utilitarian reasons. Even in contemporary societies without caste, its essential functions are fulfilled in the pattern of professional associations and guilds.[111] The 'welfare of society (*lokasamgraha*) has become a very important science at the present day in Western countries', giving rise to questions as to which arrangement is the best 'or, whether this goodness of arrangement is relative; and whether there can be a change in it by reference to change of times'. But, says Tilak,

> It cannot be doubted that at the time of the Gita, the arrangement of the four castes was rigidly enforced, and that it had originally been given effect to for the welfare of society. Therefore, I have to mention here emphatically, that *lokasamgraha* according to the Gita means, giving

---

[109] *GR*, i. 89–90.
[110] Ibid., 90.
[111] Ibid.

to other people a living example of how one can perform desirelessly all the various activities, which are allotted to one, according to the arrangement of the four castes.[112]

Thus Krishna exhorts Arjuna to engage in the warfare according to his caste duty, for in doing so, he will not incur *adharma*. And one 'does not find that the work of destroying the world has been entrusted to Visnu': for gods and men, there is, for Tilak, a proper calling. And for the latter, this role is in fact defined by their inherited nature, in effect by their blood-as-destiny. The duty imposed upon someone by caste 'has been based on inherent qualities' (Tilak uses the term *adhikara* for these inherent 'high or low qualifications of every kind'), 'because, it is likely that he will be an adept in that business alone'. And as Paramesvara 'created man simultaneously with society, and society simultaneously with man', every human being 'acquires, by birth' such qualifications corresponding to their varna—intellectual, authoritative, financial, or physical.[113] Such a conception has much in common with conceptions of race from the later nineteenth century—which is exactly how caste was, as we have seen, commonly interpreted in this period.

If this is a vision of a timeless model of society, ironically chiming with modern essentializing racial theory that perhaps informed it, it is couched in the quintessential language of industrial modernity. 'Just as extremely small wheels are necessary along with large wheels in order that any machine should work properly', so also is it the case with 'commonplace' and 'superior' persons, 'in order that the immense and ponderous activity or mechanism of the Cosmos should continue to work in a properly regulated manner'. As if to underscore that this institution of timeless antiquity is essential for the conditions of modernity, Tilak adds, in language so different from that employed by Gandhi some years later,

if the most insignificant pointsman or cabinman in a railway administration does not properly perform his duty, it will not be possible for the railway train to rush along with safety and with the speed of wind, both during the day and during the night, as it now does.[114]

[112] Ibid., 43.
[113] Ibid., 344.
[114] Ibid., 465.

This seems a striking modernist modification of a Spencerian, organicist, and evolutionist advocacy of caste—and as such a rebuttal to so many attempts by Indian reformists around this time to employ evolutionist thought to 'purge' India of caste.[115] But this is not, in fact, the sum of Tilak's commentary on the Gita's meaning for the institution of caste. On several occasions in his chapter on worldly conduct, Tilak refers to the duty to perform actions according to one's 'status in life', with a strong implication that this connotes varna.[116] But Tilak's concluding chapter recontextualizes this instruction from the rigid defence of caste encountered in his discussion above. Tilak begins by stating that one should go on performing 'whatever portion of action has fallen on one's shoulders, for the maintenance of the world, according to one's status in life'.[117] But he then qualifies this by stating that 'social duties' are allocated according to caste in the Gita, because of the historical context in which it was written, in which the institution was strongly in vogue: it 'applied to the circumstances of that particular age'.[118] But *varnashrama dharma* is not enjoined per se by the Gita. Tilak also concludes that duties arising on account of the prevailing structure of society are not, in fact, the be-all and the end-all. According to 'any arrangement' of society, 'that duty which has fallen on one's shoulders or which, being possible, may be taken up by one as a duty, of one's own choice, becomes a moral duty'.[119] Self-chosen duties can become the highest moral duties, departing from which is *adharmic*. Startlingly, he concludes that 'this is what is meant' by the verse he earlier quotes to demonstrate that the Gita 'emphatically' enjoins varna duty, that following the duties enjoined on another caste is dangerous.[120]

There is, indeed, an implicit egalitarianism to this statement. In terms of its reference to individual choice, it even reads like a liberal conception of political duty. Those following Krishna's call to action need not necessarily follow the prescription that 'bravery, brilliance, courage, intentness, not running away from the battle, generosity, and exercising authority

---

[115] See, for example, T. V. Vaswani's speech to the Sind Social Conference of 1909, quoted in Susan Bayly, *Caste, Society and Politics in India from the Eighteenth Century to the Modern Age* (Cambridge, 1999) (hereafter, Bayly, *Caste*), 156–157.

[116] *GR*, i, 556.

[117] Ibid., 696.

[118] Ibid.

[119] Ibid., 696–697.

[120] Bhagavad Gita, 3.35.

(over subject people)' is 'the inherent natural *karma* of the Kshatriya'.[121] For Tilak, the Gita's ultimate message is that such 'power' and 'leadership' can belong to others, too. The 'casteless' liberalism of Tilak's sentiments is part of his agenda to inculcate a generalized Kshatriya-redolent dharma among all varnas. Tilak may, though, have been mostly concerned with allowing Brahmin involvement, as is underlined, as we have seen, by his choice of the Maratha Peshwa Madhavrao, his own caste-fellow who took up the sword, as an example. Brahmin political conduct is also a subtext to his citation of the spiritual authority of Ramdas. His dismissal of the relevance of varna has the function of negating the Kshatriya claim to ownership of these virtues, and to the role in the polity they bestow. It is perhaps this implication that is more important to Tilak, once more decimating the claim to authority of self-identifying Kshatriyas, and thus buttressing Brahminic authority by default.

Indeed, in his same '*Kshatriyatva*' speech of January 1917 at Cawnpore quoted above, there is a strong sense of a general uptake to *kshatriyatva* which would augment the Brahminic position most of all:

> we have need to-day and there always is, if a nation is to prosper con-
> tinuously, of scholarship, undaunted bravery, sagacious enterprise as
> well as tough and sturdy muscle. These are severally the distinguishing
> marks of the true representatives of the four classes which constitute the
> ideal *chaturvarna*.[122]

Within this 'ideal *chaturvarna*' hierarchy, the Brahmins 'stand highest'; and Tilak was explicit that his vision of generalized *kshatriyatva* was not a vision without varna distinctions:

> whatever the future of the caste system, it is obvious that if members of
> the four main castes ... develop the excellent qualities which tradition
> gives their forefathers the credit of having possessed in happy abun-
> dance much good will be done to the national cause.[123]

---

[121] Gita 18.43. Cf. *GR*, ii. 1195.
[122] *Mahratta*, 7 January 1917.
[123] Ibid.

Thus *chaturvarna* would survive, with Brahmins assuming their highest ritual status; the significant difference would be that now Brahmins would also be able to assume the Kshatriya attribute of profane leadership as well. Generalized *kshatriyatva* simply added to the existing stock of the Brahmin; it added less to self-identifying Kshatriyas, except, while allowing that they might themselves act as Kshatriyas, denying them their monopoly of that conduct, or even their distinctive claim to it.

This might, then, suggest that the implicit egalitarianism of the *Gita Rahasya* is either unintended or else superficial. And such an interpretation would certainly fit with his subsequent rhetorical efforts against non-Brahman agitation in the succeeding months, especially after the Montagu Declaration of August 1917. For the non-Brahmin movement, the Declaration of ultimate self-government for India provided a major challenge, apparently giving a fillip to the very Brahminic nationalism they contested. It occurred against the background of assertive Non-Brahman caste associations which Susan Bayly sees as active especially from the 1880s—themselves often partly prompted by colonial administrative categorization and hence potential access to boons such as military service or even political participation.[124] The most prevalent non-Brahmin response—notable in Madras, but nowhere more so than in Maharashtra—was to press the colonial authorities for separate electorates for non-Brahmins in any constitutional reforms. One prominent advocate was Bhaskarrao Jadhav, a Maratha leader and ex-official of Kolhapur state, who argued to the reforms committee that, all of society being in thrall to Brahmin influence, Jains, religious minorities, and non-Brahmins needed separate electorates.[125] The Deccan Ryots Association, set up in September 1917, argued similarly.[126] Tilak's response to this demand was unambiguously hostile. In a revealing modification of the language in favour of 'communal' representation at Lucknow in 1916 (and Tilak did not use this term in relation to separate Muslim electorates), Tilak now, referring to caste, stated that

[124] Bayly, *Caste*, 160.
[125] Rosalind O'Hanlon, 'Acts of Appropriation: Non-Brahmin Radicals and the Congress in Early Twentieth-Century Maharashtra', in M. Shepperdson and C. Simmons, eds, *The Indian National Congress and the Political Economy of India* (Aldershott, 1988). (hereafter, O'Hanlon, 'Acts'), 109.
[126] Discussed in Omvedt, *Revolt*, 185.

Communal jealousies and caste rivalries are the weak points in our ar-
mour ... If every caste and community were to ask for separate electorates and separate representation then the administration would be
a chaos. Religion has no place in [the] modern polity ... [Communal
representation] would sap up the very foundations of unity in India.[127]

Separate representation for Indian Muslims had been conscionable; representation for lower castes was not. Tilak's (ultimately unsuccessful)
rear-guard action against this 'communal representation' is indicative of
an assumption of Brahminic leadership of the Hindu community, which
the demands of 1917 rudely shook.

The future of *chaturvarna*

The very survival of *chaturvarna* was a live political issue in the last three
years of Tilak's life. His responses to controversies centring on it give us
further insights into his commitment to discrete varnas, and hence, ultimate Brahminic primacy. The non-Brahmin movement for separate
political representation from 1917 was also, conversely, for the dilution
or extinction of caste distinctions per se, a long-cherished reformist goal,
as per the National Social Conference's declaration in 1909 that caste was
a national 'problem', and endorsing 'depressed classes' (or 'untouchable')
uplift—the latter influentially advocated by Samajists increasingly concerned by the size and cohesive vigour of the Hindu 'nation'.[128] These two
distinct strategies were simultaneously pursued: the Maratha League,
established in early 1919, for instance, campaigned for inter-dining and
separate electorates. Two issues in particular exercised Tilak: inter-caste
marriages, and the removal of untouchability.

Tilak engaged directly with the first question in response to a Bill in
the Legislative Council in September 1918, moved by the Gujarati reformer Vithalbhai Patel.[129] Its aim was summed up by Tilak in *Kesari* as

---

[127] *Speeches*, 306–307, 'Speech at Athani'.
[128] Bayly, *Caste*, 157, 161.
[129] Rao, *Foundations*, 307, notes that Tilak wrote that it was 'invalid according to Hindu law',
and added 'I shall develop on this view in the next Kesari', citing Tilak to Khaparde, 9 September
1918. 'Soon after', adds Rao, 'Tilak left for England'. The article was nonetheless written as promised, something Rao has not noticed.

'to allow inter-caste marriages between Hindus to be legal, even if they are not accepted by the religion'.[130] Tilak claimed, or perhaps threatened, that it would 'create a great deal of uproar in the Hindu community'. His concern for *chaturvarna* underpins this: 'now-a-days many people want inter-caste marriages', he says, 'because they believe that will destroy caste'. Tilak acknowledges that 'it was prophesised in Puranas that the *Kaliyuga* will see caste-intermixing'. There is a measure of acceptance, rather than resistance, implicit in this statement. But Tilak pinned his resistance to the prevailing attitudes of Hindus, which must be respected: 'marriage is a religious ritual and not a mere pact or an entry with the marriage registrar'; therefore even if sanctioned by law, it would not be by society. Tilak's argument that society was not ready to accept reform was time-honoured: he had argued similarly over the Age of Consent Bill. But any notion that Tilak could assume a position of leadership over reform, educating opinion—as he had laid out in 1890—is conspicuously absent. And in fact mixed marriages, he goes on, a little contradictorily, would not be accepted by society, even if they were sanctioned by religious ritual: certain castes and sub-castes do not intermarry, though there is no religious proscription he says, citing the example of Deshastha and Chitpavan Brahmins. This appears by any measure an inconsistent position; Tilak strains to furnish one to support his refusal. The new law was merely made 'for the convenience of those few who want to intermarry' who, in marrying so selfishly, would prevent their offspring inheriting from 'pure-caste' relatives, thanks to the prevailing societal taboo. The broader problem seems to be that such 'offspring miss out on the castes of both the mother and father ... One can enjoy his personal freedom but then he cannot expect others to agree to consider him as one of their own'.

At this point Tilak buttresses this idea with another distinct argument: that the proscription of mixed marriages within Hindu society is itself anthropologically useful, and derived from the highest scriptural authorities. In the *dharmashastra*, the *Manusmriti* being a seminal text, '*pratiloma*' marriages (literally, 'against the hair', in which a woman of higher ritual status marries a man of lower) were particularly censured.[131] Tilak notes (continuing the habit of citing European thinkers

---

130 SLT V, 40, 17 September 1918, 'Inter-caste Marriages'.
131 Kane, *Dharmashastra*, ii, Ch. 2.

as corroboration for his interpretation of Hindu dharma we saw in connection to the *Gita Rahasya*), 'a German scholar Nietzsche also finds this system useful for the society. Manu and Nietzsche believe' that such marriages 'do not result in the offspring with good qualities'. He adds that in current times, even the converse, '*anuloma*' marriages are forbidden. Once more, therefore, while resisting reform, Tilak holds that Hindu social practice has in fact kept alive the beneficent strictures of the *dharmashastra*. 'Current trends in society', he suggests, are in line with Manu. It was a position, in its allusion to eugenics, that showed Tilak converged on a set of criteria in common with National Social Conference reformers of the preceding decade, and indeed it shows Tilak's desire to engage with them on these terms, as well as a desire to rearticulate existing forms of Brahminic thought in new terms in order to support Brahminical norms.[132] Tilak was fleet-footed enough, having been indicted for his reactionary chauvinism in the *Bombay Chronicle* the following year by reformer R. P. Paranjpye, to cover his tracks, stating that 'as for the Patel Bill my opposition does not rest on social or religious grounds but on the economic law of succession'.[133] This statement is strongly redolent of whitewash: in his *Kesari* article, he held that Patel's Bill was 'not just insufficient, but against Hindu dharma'.

The notion of untouchability remained, to some extent, outside all these deliberations of the future of varna. Those with no varna at all, *ati-Shudras* (literally, 'beyond shudras'), were not alluded to in Tilak's call for caste Hindus to develop a judicious blend of the characteristics of the four varnas. Yet the notion was at this time becoming highly politicized as well, thanks to the efforts of sections of the non-Brahmin movement. By 1918, all-Indian organization of lower castes had begun in earnest, and the all-India Depressed Classes Mission Conference held its second session in Bombay. Tilak, perhaps needing to draw the sting of the movement, attended, and spoke out against the degradations of untouchability: the *dharmashastras*, he said, 'do not support the notion of treating any class of human beings as untouchables'.[134] Engaging directly

[132] In terms of reformers, see, for instance, Justice C. Sanakaran Nair, discussed in Bayly, *Caste*, 159.
[133] SLT 7, 48. Tilak's response took the form of a 'Review' of his life, contributed to the *Mahratta* and the *Bombay Chronicle*, reprinted here. It is from this document that the opening quotation of this chapter is taken.
[134] *Mahratta*, 31 March 1918, 145.

with the Aryan invasion, castigated ever since Phule as a brutal and demeaning subjugation of the indigenous inhabitants of India, expropriated
by the Aryan Brahmins, he acknowledged that Aryans in their progress
through the country 'met the original inhabitants of the country, and,
having conquered them, began to look upon them as inferiors'. But this
'did not continue for long', and 'soon enough began the policy of bringing
the non-Aryans within the fold of the Aryans by extending to them the
right of the *Vedic Samskars*'. The tragedy was that this wise work of 'uni-
fication somehow came to a stop' and some groups remained beyond the
pale of Aryan civilization. What was thus needed was a culmination of
the Aryans' unificatory policies; invoking the Gita, he went so far as to say
all should be looked upon as equals. Deflecting fire towards the treatment
of all Indians by the British bureaucracy, he stated that the Brahman bureaucracy 'of old' behaved in the same way, but that the more enlightened
Brahmins of today would rectify their error.

What was not reported in *Mahratta* was Tilak's refusal to personally
sign a motion condemning untouchability. Defending his decision the
following year, in the same encomium of his conduct in which he minimized his opposition to the Patel Bill, Tilak stated 'I am not prepared to
take up the work of actual propaganda as my own', adding that signing the
petition would have thrown the responsibility on him.[135] The matter, he
suggested, must be looked after by those best placed to deal with it. Would
we 'ignore all the good work of statesmen just because they won't take a
role in the emancipation of Negroes?' Thus, though neutralizing the implications for the lower castes of the Aryan history he had so celebrated in
Orion and *The Arctic Home*, by suggesting that the truer Aryan heritage
was in fact inclusivity, Tilak would not go far towards making this a lived
reality. We can infer, further, that the distinction between caste Hindus
and untouchables retained genuine salience for Tilak, something we met
above in his hostility to 'untouchable' recruitment to the Indian Army
at around the same time. Though wishing to garner lower-caste support,
or at least minimize lower-caste hostility, Tilak's (in)action suggests his
uninterest in the reform of untouchability, and his view that it had, in
some form, like all varna distinctions, a structural role within Hindu
society.

[135] SLT 7, 46.

Conclusion

Tilak, therefore, despite his noted record of hostility to reform in some of the major controversies of his time, should not merely be considered a conservative thinker on Hindu society, for all he always sought to up-keep structures of social authority to the benefit of the Brahmin *varna*. In common with many others who sought to reshape Hindu society under late colonial conditions, he sought to strengthen Hindu society in a physical-moral sense, through the embrace of a *karmayoga* and a fighting *kshatriyatva*, and the experience of military combat. Such a move to Hindu self-strengthening, it has been noted, was prevalent in both Bengal and Maharashtra, and was associated with the 'extremist' politics we shall investigate in the next chapter in relation to Tilak—and it should be further noted that the sense of demartialization that was a note in both regions stimulated the highly gendered sense of insecurity that gave rise to it.[136] In Maharashtra, this imbricated with a particular set of martial traditions that Tilak was keen to extend the Brahmin claim to. This move to Hindu self-strengthening, as evidenced by a new growth in *akharas* around the turn of the century, with their blend of group physical exercise and ritual, reached a new peak just after Tilak's death with the Hindu Sangathan and more particularly the RSS, which of course took inspiration from Tilak's concern for muscular Hinduism—though the RSS's sectarian character (in Jaffrelot's terms), and its discrete character as a collective within Hindu society emphasizing world renunciation, and with an organizational structure to match, were quite alien to his thought.[137] More revealingly, the more overtly mimetic forms of 'British' physical culture noted through the RSS emphasis on team sports and aspects of British elements of drill practice were much less pronounced in Tilak, for whom the modernist rearticulation of what he regarded as pre-modern martial forms traditions was still more characteristic.[138]

Of course, though, the explicit colonial British rationale of restricting recruitment to the 'martial races', that is, that effeminacy of the Hindu population (unlike sturdier Sikhs and Muslims), contributed to this

---

[136] Jaffrelot, *Movement*, 36.
[137] Ibid., 33–45.
[138] Joseph S. Alter, 'Somatic Nationalism: Indian Wrestling and Militant Hinduism', *Modern Asian Studies*, 28/3 (1994), 557–588.

gendered insecurity as much as the fact of demartialization; and indeed the explicit connection of manliness and martiality in colonial recruitment literature noted by Heather Streets—a 'martial race masculinity', with such peoples 'manly in their warlike creed'—only cemented this correlation in Tilak's mind, as in others', an influence broader perhaps than Streets imagines.[139] This association valorized martiality still further. It was a conception Tilak shared to a remarkable degree with M. K. Gandhi, who similarly, and in collaboration with Tilak, advocated military enlistment during the First World War, and for whom it was (as preparation for satyagraha) also a matter of both moral and physical strengthening, specifically aimed at Hindu society. In colonial conditions, such self-strengthening would ultimately enable resistance to the autocracy of colonialism and the gaining of Swaraj, as we shall see further in the following chapter—but it was for Tilak (as for Gandhi) a requirement for genuine national political emancipation, a quality without which self-rule could not be exercised, rather than something instrumental to its winning, and this helps explain Tilak's slippage from his ostensive 'conditions' of political rights in exchange for military enlistment. Such a concern for self-strengthening, often inflected with Social Darwinism, was of course far from unique to India in this period, forming a part of the experience of other societies experiencing or fearing greater encroachment during the period of the 'New' European imperialism, such as China, or in the case of the Ottoman Empire, a state which conceived itself to be facing an existential threat from predatory powers, to which the 'Young Turks' responded with 'militaristic attitudes' and a drive to gain military experience, including through service in the Japanese army.[140] Indeed, the hyper-competitiveness and militarism of the contemporary international order, and the global prevalence of Social Darwinist thought, both contributed to valorization of martiality in India as elsewhere in this period. Tilak showed himself well aware of aggressive, self-interested, and technologically advanced states in his *Gita Rahasya*, itself redolent of Social Darwinism; it stands among his statements on military enlistment

---

[139] Streets, *Martial Races*, 12.
[140] Arthur Waldron, 'The Warlord: Twentieth-Century Chinese Understandings of Violence, Militarism and Imperialism', *American Historical Review*, 96/4 (1991), 1073–1100, (hereafter, Waldron, 'Warlord'); M. Sukru Hanioglu, *Preparation for a Revolution: The Young Turks, 1902–1908* (Oxford: Oxford University Press, 2001) (hereafter, Hanioglu, *Revolution*), 304.

for this and other reasons. In his speeches on recruitment, menace at the strength of global adversaries looms large.

Tilak was committed to the maintenance of a varna structure as integral to Indian society's strength in the modern world, in the context of which appears a sense of natural Brahmin preponderance. Indeed Brahmin agency, as he made clear in the debate over Hindu marriage customs, was the appropriate vehicle for effecting reform to Hindu customs in general. And the strengthening of Brahmin leadership claims through their assumption of *kshatriyatva* in particular reflects in the Maharashtrian context Tanika Sarkar's idea of the 'new Brahmin' imagined in Bengal in the late nineteenth century as the 'ideal patriot and nation builder', with Brahminic authority revived as a hegemonic aspiration, cultivated through a reinterpreted Hindu knowledge and physical strengthening; and this Brahminism, reflective of Maharashtrian understandings, encapsulating 'kingly and priestly' aspects, has been observed as centrally important to the subsequent Brahminism of the RSS.[141] The long-standing Maharashtrian Brahmin understanding of the absence of the Kshatriyas in the *Kaliyuga* was likely reified further by the colonial conditions in which their claims to 'secular' leadership had been undermined by the colonial bureaucracy in addition to their military role. It was not just, to adapt Nicholas Dirk's observation, that the Kshatriya's crown was hollow in the colonial period; this further reflected for Tilak and others how it rested upon the heads of hollow men.[142] A vital part of this understanding was the need to revive absent Kshatriya dharma, as well as the acceptance of a mutability in the *Kaliyuga* to *varnashrama* dharma per se: and in Tilak's scheme, Brahmins assumed the leadership role, revived by *Kshastriyatva*.[143] Indeed this imbricated with a sense of historical continuity with Mahrashtrian political traditions, in which the worldly authority of the Brahmin Peshwa was exercised as a tangible reflection of the dharma of the *Kaliyuga*. The way in which the conditions of colonialism instantiated those of the *Kaliyuga*, to structure

---

[141] Sarkar, *Hindu Wife*, 175–176; Walter K. Andersen and Shridhar D. Damle, *The Brotherhood in Saffron: The Rashtriya Swayamsevak Sangh and Hindu Revivalism* (Boulder, 1987).

[142] Nicholas B. Dirks, *The Hollow Crown* (Cambridge, 1987).

[143] *Kshatriyatva* also related to sovereignty, as Milinda Banerjee has discussed, which was therefore diffused for Tilak through society (as we saw in the last chapter). See *The Mortal God*, Ch. 4, esp. 319 ff.

Tilak's thought according to a dharma appropriate to it, is seen in the next chapter in his thought on ethics as much as it is here in relation to varna— and in both cases Tilak hoped an appropriate dharmic response would galvanize Hindu society for the challenges of that age. The general revival of Hindu society had its limits, though, as Tilak's hostility to Mahar recruitment shows; his ironic alignment here with elite Maratha claims to *Kshtatriya* status shows the importance to him of the distinction between caste Hindus and *ati-Shudras* in his conception of Hindu society and its modes of regeneration. And his disavowal of 'untouchable' uplift and denigration of inter-caste marriage shows another important departure made by 'Tilakites' like Savarkar and B. S. Moonje in their drive for Hindu unity in the 1920s.[144]

Before we leave this chapter it is worth engaging directly with Tilak's 'Hindutva'—for his was among the pioneering uses of it, two decades before Savarkar's pamphlet of that title appeared—and how it was defined, specifically in relation to the reform of Hindu society.[145] In one of the first articles in which Tilak used it, he directly tackled the relationship between '*Hindutva* and Reforms'.[146] For Tilak, Hindutva here connoted not just the quality or condition of being a Hindu (for which as with *kshatriyatva* Tilak employed the suffix *tva*, or 'ness', to form the abstract noun), but went further in having it denote what we might call a community of resistance.[147] That is, it referred to those who drew on Hindu dharma to defend dharma from attacks from outside Hindutva. Members of this community may in fact aim for the same reform of social practices; but they would do so in contradistinction to those doing so from outside, most notably to those Tilak views as a class of persons inspired by their English education, and effectively deracinated. The Arya Samaj fought for reform from 'within Hindutva', as did the reformists of the Bhagavata sect; the Social Council, and Buddhists, were outside Hindutva. Luther, Tilak observed, was a devout Christian; such veneration for their traditions

---

[144] Jaffrelot, *Movement*, 19 ff.

[145] This is not least because (see Rao, *Foundations*, 282 ff) his conception of 'Hindutva' has been recently critiqued as resisting any undermining of caste strictures, even through the extension of lower-caste education, as a 'loss of nationality', something which contributes to Rao's sense that he anticipates later Hindutva formulations (319).

[146] SLT V, 62, '*Hindutva* and Reforms'. *Kesari*, 12 January 1904, Editorial.

[147] See Richard Fox Young, *Resistant Hinduism: Sanskrit Sources on Antichristian Apologetics in Early Nineteenth-century India* (Vienna, 1981).

did not mark many reformers. This community would further ideally be defined by its control by Hindu institutions, which would govern Hindu society as a ruler governs a polity. This concern here with Hindutva as a signifier of Hindu status, of effective membership of Hindu society, was a function of Tilak's overwhelming preoccupation with a distinct Hindu identity, and reviving Hindu society through defining it. In speaking to identity—Hinduness, those features in fact associated with Hindu status—he of course necessarily spoke to the issue of those who could claim that status; and this involved a particular vision of Hindu dharma, which, indeed, he even uses Hindutva explicitly as a synonym for. But the use of 'Hindutva' to refer to that community also explicitly foregrounded the differences in identity which marked those outside it, a difference in essential qualities that substantiated this demarcation.[148] A defensiveness towards that group's autonomy, in the heat of reformist controversy, is clear to see in this stark tendency to exclusion—but so too is the sheer importance of the attempts to define Hindu dharma that Tilak was engaged in, and their implication for status as part of Hindu society.

---

[148] The title given to the 1928 reprint of Savarkar's work *Hindutva: Who is a Hindu?* makes clear a similar dual concern, though with a very different mode of definition.

5

The Conduct of Politics

This chapter studies Tilak's thought on the techniques of political practice. It reveals Tilak as a theorist of opposition to autocracy, developing
legitimations for political violence and civil disobedience that rest upon
the principle of popular representative government—the 'Birthright' of
Swaraj or self-rule that we saw outlined in the third chapter. His legitimation of political violence should be understood in that context, not as a
break with liberal thought in advocating loyalty to the primordial community over obedience to the state. Existing literature often sees Tilak as
legitimating anti-Muslim violence in the Shivaji festival in Maharashtra,
and in the *Gita Rahasya*.[1] The anti-state elements of Tilak's rhetoric
have, though, been underplayed, a reflection of broader trends within
the historiography of modern South Asian politics, with its (not unnat-
ural) focus on inter-community, and majority-minority violence, and its
traditional focus on the modes of non-violent resistance to colonialism,
only recently complemented by a renewed interest in violence against
the colonial state.[2] Tilak's agonistic notion of violence could of course be
applicable to the relationship of the 'primordial' Hindu and Muslim communities discussed earlier; and there are moments when this application
is suggested by Tilak, in the wake of the 1893 Bombay riots, for instance.[3]
Yet Tilak's most consistent and explicit calls for violence were not in the
furtherance of the interests of his community against a Muslim 'other',
but were mostly directed against state autocracy. This was a point noted

---

[1] Kuruvachira, *Hindu Nationqlists*; Shruti Kapila, 'A History of Violence', *Modern Intellectual
History*, 7/2 (2010), 437–457 (hereafter, Kapila, 'Violence').
[2] William Gould, *Religion and Conflict in Modern South Asia* (Cambridge, 2011), and
Gyanendra Pandey, *Routine Violence: Nations, Fragments, Histories* (Stanford, 2006) (hereafter,
Pandey, 'Routine Violence') are notable recent efforts; see in particular Ghosh, *Gentlemanly
Terrorists*, for its interest in the question of anti-colonial violence.
[3] *The Mahratta* (20 August, 1893, 1) stated that the Hindu reprisals were excusable 'if not to be
justified'; while regrettable 'on the whole', they had a salutary effect, and minimized the 'contin-
gency of similar outbreaks in the future'.

The Thought of Bal Gangadhar Tilak. Robert E. Upton, Oxford University Press. © Robert E. Upton 2024.
DOI: 10.1093/oso/9780198900658.003.0006

by his contemporary official antagonists. Even his declaration of loyalty after his final release from imprisonment for sedition in 1914 did nothing to dampen official hostility.[4] And the *Sedition Committee Report* (1918) emphasized in its summary Tilak's 'casuistical apology for political assassination' and 'praise to the bomb', building on claims by *The Times'* foreign editor Valentine Chirol a few years earlier that Tilak's influence was behind anti-state violence, even accusing him of organizing gymnasia to equip Indian youth to expel the British by force.[5] However paranoiac this response could be, it was not awry in the direction of its concern.

Tilak's legitimation of political violence during the 'Swadeshi' agitation of 1905–1908, in which the Viceroy Curzon's decision to partition Bengal occasioned a multifaceted mobilization of radical political thought and action in different parts of India, identifies Tilak with other 'extremist' (to use contemporary parlance) nationalist figures such as Lala Lajpat Rai, Bipin Chandra Pal, and Aurobindo Ghose. Yet for Tilak specifically, the consistency of his stance on violence between his first sedition conviction in 1897 and his agitation of 1908, and indeed onwards to that of the *Gita Rahasya*, is striking. It should also be noted that while the question of violence is justifiably central to many critiques of Tilak, it is seldom noted as merely one of a repertoire of techniques for him, as for others such as Aurobindo. Indeed Tilak advocated plural means for the attainment of what he defined as the 'constitutional' rights of representative self-government (Swaraj), and was explicit that there was no difference as to the 'constitutionalism' of any techniques thus used, or, therefore, their legitimacy. Tilak was wedded to the technique of press agitation, the British historical example of which, as much as its espousal in classic works of British liberals whom Tilak adapted and reconfigured, seems to have influenced him (as indeed did the example of violence in Britain's political history). The weaponization of a common conception of British historical 'progress', and facets of British liberal thought which had drawn from it, in his intellectual contest with the colonial bureaucracy, and particularly

---

[4] The Secretary to the Bombay Government Special Department noted after it that he continued as ever to promote the use of force against the Government with 'grandiose phrases', while 'cynically' claiming to be horrified when 'misguided students' put them into action. L. Robertson (n.d.), MSA HD (Special) 376 (1915).

[5] *Sedition Committee Report*, 4, 6. Valentine Chirol, *Indian Unrest* (London, 1910). Chirol famously claimed Tilak was the 'father of Indian unrest' (ibid., 41). Tilak sued Chirol for libel over this and other specific allegations in the book, unsuccessfully.

in his 1908 sedition trial, further reified it as a component of his political thought, and gave it a characteristic radical edge. And Tilak's espousal of the freedom of the press while on the stand accused of sedition has resonance in the arguments of those threatened in contemporary India by Section 124A of the Indian Penal Code—what Gandhi called the 'prince' among those sections 'designed to suppress the liberty of the citizen': the colonial-era law still wields power.[6]

Tilak was, in particular, a pioneer of passive resistance in the Indian context, a contribution dating in a fully-fledged form to 1907, and urged through Tilak's 'New Party' in the Congress. For this, as much as anything else, was the 'extremist' Tilak met with such hostility by the 'moderates' at the infamous 1907 session of the Congress at Surat. Passive resistance, like the obverse use of political violence, had a role largely dependent on political circumstance, a dyadic relationship of political techniques he shared in common with other 'extremists' of the period. It should be noted that Tilak's justifications and advocacy of political techniques always rested on ethical justifications; and these could claim authority on the basis of terms and concepts with well-established prominence within the *dharmashastra*. Above all in the *Gita Rahasya*, Tilak elaborated these, and in so doing offered a distinctive Hindu language for political ethics in the modern age, in parallel undertaking with other nationalist figures of the period who urged the same range of tactics.[7]

Tilak's explicit reflections upon the conduct of politics are the subject of this enquiry, not inferences which could be drawn from aspects of an analysis of his political practice (particularly, perhaps, time-honoured accusations—or accreditations according to taste—that Tilak was involved in violent conspiracies against the government during his career).[8] Of course, this distinction is valuable only when taken so far. These reflections of Tilak were not leisured or detached; even a text as contemplative as the *Gita Rahasya* was itself part of Tilak's political practice. But it is these texts' explicit comment on the nature of political practice that

---

[6] On the Section see Abhinav Chandrachud, *Republic of Rhetoric: Free Speech and the Constitution of India* (New Delhi, 2017); 'Sedition Law a Tool against Free Speech?', *The Hindu*, 15 January 2019, https://www.thehindu.com/.

[7] See especially Bose, 'Spirit and Form', on the Hindu moorings of Aurobindo Ghose's political ethics.

[8] Wolpert, *Tilak and Gokhale*, 88–102, and Peter Heehs, *India's Freedom Struggle 1857–1947: A Short History* (Delhi, 1988) argue particularly for his involvement in secret terrorist activities.

distinguishes them, and defines their interest for us here. By the same token, they must be read in the light of his political practice; and—in particular ensuring that the *Gita Rahasya*, an exceptionally discursive text within his output, is related properly to the rest of it—we can thus interpret them as a series of responses to political circumstances which reveal the development of his thought in its context.[9]

This chapter will begin by looking at Tilak's trials for sedition in 1897 and 1908, from the perspective of Tilak's legitimation of violence, for the 'disaffection' for which he was convicted in each case took the form of apologias for violence printed in *Kesari*.[10] It will then take these same questions in examining the *Gita Rahasya*. Before examining that text, it will also study Tilak's conception of the role of the most important mode of political conduct in his career: a free press. Tilak's widely publicized 1908 trial was an opportunity for him to underscore this, as much for his own countrymen as for his own liberty's sake, once more urging its role as a bulwark against autocracy. We shall end by considering Tilak's conception of 'passive resistance', tracing the vagaries of Tilak's views on it from 1907 when he pioneered the concept in Congress politics, through to the last months of his life when he conversely offered 'responsive cooperation' to the Government of India in a new Indian political environment, and the teeth of Gandhian civil disobedience.

The bullet and the bomb in politics

During the Shivaji festival of 1897, in a febrile and plague-stricken atmosphere, Tilak took a violent turn in his rhetoric that stands in contrast to the self-conscious moderation that had characterized his memorialization of Shivaji since 1895. The content of *Kesari* under his editorship was the cause of his first trial and imprisonment for sedition that year.

---

[9] The comprehensiveness of many accounts is severely compromised by failing to incorporate the *Gita Rahasya*, for example Jai Narain Sharma, *The Political Thought of Lokmanya Bal Gangadhar Tilak*, Encyclopedia of Eminent Thinkers, vol. 24 (New Delhi, 2009). Cashman, *Myth*, focused more explicitly on Tilak's political techniques rather than his thought, is silent on the *Gita Rahasya*.

[10] Tilak was charged under Section 124A of the Indian Penal Code in 1897 (under chapter 6, 'Offences Against the State') and under the same in 1908, in addition to Section 153A (in chapter 8, 'Offences against the Public Tranquility'), thus additionally being accused of 'promoting enmity and hatred between different classes' of the Queen-Empress' subjects.

The prosecution was almost certainly prompted by the assassination of two plague officials, W. C. Rand and his lieutenant Charles Ayerst, shortly after the festival, on Queen Victoria's Diamond Jubilee, 22 June; the Anglo-Indian press blamed Tilak's words, and probably more pertinently the House of Commons heard the following month that Tilak at the Shivaji festival had counselled the 'murder of Europeans': twelve days later he was arrested.[11] For *Kesari* articles, including a report of his festival speech, Tilak was charged under Section 124A of the Indian Penal Code, for exciting and attempting to excite disaffection against the Government.[12]

Tilak was closely enough involved in the public memorialization of Shivaji by 1897, as we saw Chapter 3, to preside over one of the main events of the three-day festivities, a lecture on Shivaji by another notable Poona intellectual, C. G. Bhanu, Professor of History at Fergusson College.[13] This occasion gave Tilak an opportunity to engage directly with the violence that so marked Shivaji's career. His disquisition here on political violence, in lauding Shivaji's actions, invoked the Gita's moral system (just as fifteen years later, as we shall see, he would, conversely, invoke Shivaji's actions in his *Gita Rahasya*). Tilak's espousal of political violence is contained above all in his statement in response to Professor Bhanu's lecture on one of the most famous moments in Shivaji's career, his killing of the Bhijapur Sultanate's General Afzal Khan in 1659 during a parlay. Considerable controversy had raged historically over whether Shivaji struck the first blow, thus implicating him in a premeditated and unethical assault; Bhanu himself suggested that Afzal Khan did so.[14] Tilak, for the sake of argument, assumes this to be a premeditated murder; and his subsequent justification is worth quoting at length:

---

[11] IOR/L/PJ/6/451, File 1386. Question by Sir Mancherjee Bhownaggree, 15 July 1897.

[12] The judge in fact made clear that no connection was sought to be made between Tilak and the assassinations: S. S. Setlur K. G. and Deshpande, *Full and Authentic Report of the Trial of Bal Gangadhar Tilak: At the Fourth Criminal Sessions 1897 of the Bombay High Court before Justice Strachey and a Special Jury* (Bombay, 1897) (hereafter, Setlur and Deshpande (eds.), *Trial (1897)*, Charge to the Jury, 17. The second 'sedition' article of 1897, a poem entitled 'Shivaji's Utterances' (purportedly by Shivaji himself, and almost certainly not by Tilak) has less relevance to this study, but is productively treated in Sukeshi Kamra, 'Law and Radical Rhetoric in British India: The 1897 Trial of Bal Gangadhar Tilak', *South Asia: Journal of South Asian Studies*, 39/3 (2016), 546–559, DOI: 10.1080/00856401.2016.1196529.

[13] On Bhanu's career see Deshpande, 'Pandit'.

[14] *Kesari*, 15 June 1897, (Setlur and Deshpande (eds.), *Trial (1897)* Appendix A (prosecution exhibits), Exhibit C).

Was this act of the Maharaja good or bad? The question ... should not be viewed from the standpoint of even the Penal Code or even the *smritis* of Manu or *Yagnavalkhya* or even the principles of morality laid down by the western and eastern ethical systems. The laws which bind society are for common men like yourselves and myself ... Great men are above the common principles of morality. These principles fail in their scope to meet the pedestal of great men. Did Shivaji commit a sin in killing Afzulkhan, or how? The answer to this question can be found in the *Mahabharata* itself. Srimad Krisna's advice in the Gita is to kill even our teachers and our kinsmen. No blame attaches to any person if he is doing deeds without being actuated by a desire to reap the fruit of his deeds. Shri Shivaji Maharaja did nothing to fill the small void in his stomach. With benevolent intentions he murdered Afzulkhan for the benefit of others. If thieves enter our house and we have not strength in our wrists to drive them out, we should, without hesitation, shut them up and burn them alive ... Do not circumscribe your vision like a frog in the well; get out of the Penal Code, enter into the extremely high atmosphere of *Srimad Bhagavadgita* and then consider the actions of great men.[15]

A striking qualification here is the distinction between Shivaji, as the 'great man', and 'yourselves or myself'; Shivaji's example is not one, ostensibly, to be followed by Tilak or his audience, the justification of his actions not applying to those in everyday life, as laudatory but not exhortatory. But the speech nonetheless contains a contradictory exhortation to violence in the statement that 'we' should burn alive thieves who enter 'our house'. Moreover, the invocation of the selflessly disinterested 'Gita morality' by which great men live seems contradicted by the obvious self-interest of the defence of hearth and home. The contemporary context for this imagery made its relevance even more immediate: June 1897 saw the plague outbreak in Poona close to its height, and widely protested sanitary measures undertaken by the Government included the occupation and clearance by soldiers of private homes. Tilak thus offers an apparent remedy for a very tangible violation, on the authority of Shivaji. The citizens of Maharashtra should justify their actions by the

[15] Ibid.

Gita morality, though they may not in fact attain it as did their exemplary historical hero.

Bhanu's speech on 'The Killing of Afzul Khan', which provided Tilak's immediate context, helps further explicate his statements. Bhanu suggested that Shivaji's aggression, if proved, would have been excusable; he made special reference to historical conditions in which a weak and decaying system of government could justify recourse to actions beyond the pale of ordinary morality, provided that the agent behaved unselfishly, was divinely inspired, and passed the crucial test of being successful.[16] Yet Bhanu elsewhere acknowledged his initial unwillingness to 'take any part in the Shivaji festivities' because he agreed with their organizers 'in no point except in admiring the great Shivaji': he identified himself with the reformist faction in western Indian politics, against the ostensible reactionary Hindu-Brahminic chauvinism of Tilak and his associates, the two camps split over questions on the reform of Hindu social customs, and over attitudes towards Hindu-Muslim tensions, especially those centred on religious processions.[17] Yet Bhanu's alignment instead with the 'liberal nationalism' of such figures as M. G. Ranade, and the remarkable mirroring of his and Tilak's views here, helps to situate Tilak's own remarks. For Tilak, the historical cause of the Maratha nation need not be explicitly stated, after Bhanu's remarks—especially as the 1897 festival marked the anniversary of his coronation, a symbolic moment of state foundation—despite Tilak's apparent concern with metaphysical and non-historical justifications. As the founder of the Maratha state, Shivaji was the nineteenth-century nationalist's hero because he was seen to represent nationalism, and thus in hearing Tilak speak on him, we can gauge his conception of the legitimacy of violence undertaken for the national community, under the 'moral sovereignty of the nation' (in Thomas Blom Hansen's terms).[18] It was a common good; to be animated by it against the rapacious colonial state in 1897, mirroring the conflict of 1659, was still, implicitly, an abnegation of self-interest.

---

[16] Ibid.

[17] Setlur and Deshpande (eds.), *Trial (1897)*, Appendix B (defence exhibits), number 16 (from *Times of India*, 8 July 1897, letter to the editor, 'A Speech at the Shivaji Meeting').

[18] Thomas Blom Hansen, 'Sovereigns beyond the State: On Legality and Public Authority in India', in Ravinder Kaur, ed., *Religion, Violence and Political Mobilisation in South Asia* (London, 2005); see also Banerjee, *Mortal God*, 211, on Shivaji serving as the 'iconisation' of a nationalist social contract based on the threat of force more broadly in the period.

The attempted assassination of the Chief Presidency Magistrate of Bengal, Douglas Kingsford, at Muzaffarpur in April 1908 by a bomb thrown by a Bengali youth, Khudiram Bose, evidenced a new historical context in India in terms of political action; and it prompted new reflections upon the legitimacy of physical violence in politics, not least because the new technology heralded diversified opportunities for it.[19] Responding in *Kesari* to what he viewed as the autocratic policy of the Bengal partition, Tilak did not disguise his historical conclusion that violence can beget liberty, or his application of this to current Indian conditions. Invoking the course of English historical progress, and the mid-seventeenth century triumph of Parliamentary government, Tilak echoed in the *Kesari* that

> At one time such oppression gave rise to small insurrections in England; and it was only when the people of that country rose in rebellion, and, after dethroning the King, introduced constitutional rule that no occasion was left for them to resort to violent means for effecting administrative reform.[20]

Most strikingly, Tilak offers, in precisely this context, a further justification for the assassination of the Poona plague officials of 1897, which his words at the Shivaji festival were said to have inspired.[21] The assassination of W. C. Rand affected the Government exactly as a stumble while walking affects an individual: it may have been unwelcome and even harmful, but it reminded the Government 'to make use of the eyes while walking'.[22] Violence succeeded in causing the Government to reform the plague administration, as 'the light dawn[ed] on their heads owing to the murder'. What, asks Tilak, 'was there amiss' in violence thus rectifying misgovernment? 'When is this lesson to be learnt if not when one has actually stumbled?'[23]

---

[19] Bose's coassailant was armed, more conventionally, with a revolver; but it was the fact of the bomb itself which seems particularly to have fascinated Tilak.

[20] *Kesari*, 12 May 1908. Kelkar (ed.), *Trial (1908)*, Prosecution Exhibits [E], 27.

[21] Subsequent to Tilak's 1897 trial, Damodar Hari Chapekar, Rand's assassin, himself had cited *Kesari* as inspiration: *Sedition Committee Report*, 1–2.

[22] *Kesari*, 2 June 1908, 'The Secret of the Bomb'. Kelkar (ed.), *Trial (1908)*, Prosecution Exhibits [H], 53.

[23] Ibid.

It is 'despotic bureaucracy' (the meaning he imputed to the phrase *zulmee adhikarivarga*)—for Tilak here, rule without regard to the sentiment of the ruled—that begets violence, which in turn acts as its corrective.[24] Tilak made this relationship plain in one of his most famous articles, 'The Country's Misfortune'. India's bureaucratic government is necessarily despotic, states Tilak, because the English bureaucracy 'does not at all take the advice or opinion of the subjects or their leaders in the matter of our administration'.[25] It is as a result of the 'exasperation produced by the despotic exercise of power' that Bengali youths had taken to arms. The significance of the image of a government using its 'eyes when walking' lies in just this notion of watchfulness to popular feeling. More specifically, it is the crises of autocratic government that cause and legitimate violence—euphemistically described as the 'stumble'. The context for the violence of 1908 is set squarely in the autocratic crisis of the partition of Bengal, foisted upon an unwilling Bengali population, who are unable to find redress from a government acting with a deliberate blindness to them. They act 'just as a deer attacks a hunter, totally regardless of its own life, after all means of protection have been exhausted' (and Tilak distinguishes this reaction from self-interest).[26] This in turn is situated in a concept central to Tilak's political ethics, that of reciprocity. For Tilak, 'the scripture laying down the duties of kings is declaring at the top of its voice' that government must fulfil its obligations to govern consensually for the ruled to fulfil theirs of loyalty. Thus, the Government of India must understand plainly that if they resorted 'to oppressive Russian methods, then the Indian subjects, too, would be compelled to imitate, partially at least, (the methods of) the Russian subjects!' It is a 'well-known maxim' says Tilak, 'As you sow, so you reap'.[27]

The capacity of the population to effect violence, therefore, is crucial for a society to live freely. Here, Tilak makes it explicit in commenting, once more, on the Arms Act. Why, he asks 'did the English commit' this 'great sin of emasculating a nation?' The answer is that

---

[24] As against the official translation, 'oppressive official class'. Ibid., 108.
[25] *Kesari*, 12 May 1908, 'The Country's Misfortune' (hereafter, 'Misfortune'). Kelkar (ed.), *Trial (1908)*, Prosecution Exhibits [C].
[26] Ibid.
[27] Ibid.

the manliness of the nation was slain by the Arms Act in order that the authority exercised even by petty officials from day to day should be unopposed and that the selfish administration might be carried on all right without any hitch and without granting the subjects any of the rights of *Swarajya*.[28]

The threat of violence is necessary to ensure responsive government, and violence itself to achieve redress from an autocratic one, and ultimately the constitutional representative self-government encoded in his conception of *Swarajya*. This relationship underpins one of Tilak's most controversial statements on the bomb, that it is a 'kind of magic, it is a charm, an amulet'.[29] As it could be produced relatively easily by small groups or individuals without relying upon the techniques of modern factory production, it restored a balance to the polity lacking since the introduction of the Arms Act. The technological superiority of the modern state had augmented the effect of the Act, to grant a monopoly of coercion to the colonial state in India; now another feature of technological modernity had remedied the situation. Ironically, it is thus the inherently modern diffusion of technical knowledge of explosives that enables the kind of small-scale non-industrial (and non-state) acts of force that Gyanendra Pandey sees as representative of so-called violence, a pre-modern, residual term.[30] Tilak characteristically bemoans the state of affairs ushered in by the disarmament of the peoples of India as an 'emasculation', as he articulates the propriety of force being diffused throughout society. In this, he carries a memory of a pre-1857 India, and echoes a mode of thinking about the conduct of politics that developed in the longer term in conditions in which such a diffusion of force was a lived historical reality. It has been noted that the coercion of absolutist states in Europe led to the development of theories justifying political violence, whereas the diffusion of such power in Indian societies did not compel it.[31] Such theorizing as Tilak's was therefore a new departure in the colonial period,

---

[28] *Kesari*, 9 June 1908, 'These remedies are not lasting'. Kelkar (ed.), *Trial (1908)*, Prosecution Exhibits [D], 18. Swaraj is a contraction of the longer Sanskritic term.

[29] Ibid., 19.

[30] Pandey, *Routine Violence*, 3.

[31] J. J. L. Gommans, 'The Embarrassment of Political Violence in Europe and South Asia, c. 1100-1800', in Jan E. M. Houben and Karel R. van Kooij, eds, *Violence Denied: Violence, non-Violence and the Rationalisation of Violence in South Asian Cultural History* (Leiden, 1999).

a fact underlined by his apparent coinage in *Kesari* of *ekmukhi* (literally, of one mouth or aspect) as a Marathi term for 'absolute'.[32] At the same time, Tilak's theory was not only relevant to the colonial conditions he invoked, of a disarmed population and an (alien) government. Any state per se enjoying a monopoly on violence—even, implicitly, one that had obtained those constitutional rights that apparently ended the relationship of violence between state and society he described—would put itself in the same privileged position vis-à-vis society, and could behave autocratically. Tilak, indeed, universalized his point: it was not only Bengalis, but all who do not wish to remain 'perpetually in slavery' that must thus be fierce or timid as the occasion demands.[33]

The freedom of the press

Tilak's second trial for sedition forced—and gave an ideal platform to— Tilak to expound and justify his broader conception of the conduct of politics. This is an opportunity he took full advantage of, specifically in his extraordinary four-day speech in his own defence in the High Court in Bombay. It is not merely that Tilak offered a disavowal of violence, as he was sure to do (among other things, and despite suggestions to the contrary, acquittal being on his mind). Tilak was able to articulate the legitimacy of the form of constitutional political activity he was engaged in, his work as a writer and editor, and its importance as a check upon the exercise of autocratic rule (whose very illegitimacy would then be demonstrated to the whole of India through its rejection in the trial and his conviction).[34] This was not purely a profession of innocence; and the points of interest are not of the legality of this agitation, but Tilak's statements on its underlying historical importance. In making this point about the press's role in the necessary progress of India, Tilak perhaps had an eye to the sentiments of his jurors, both 'European' and Indian; and his citation of English legal and constitutional history can particularly

---

[32] Kelkar (ed.), *Trial (1908)* 69.
[33] 'Misfortune', 3.
[34] This latter point is substantively argued in Mithi Mukherjee, 'Sedition, Law, and the British Empire in India: The Trial of Tilak (1908)', *Law, Culture and the Humanities* (January 2017), https://doi.org/10.1177/1743872116685034.

be read as an appeal to the formers' sentiment. It would be a mistake, however, to reduce Tilak's statements to such narrow courtroom instrumentality. Tilak would have been well aware of the coverage of the case throughout India; his trial in fact gave him probably the largest audience for his words that he had ever known, even greater than that for his statements at the stormy Congress sessions of 1905 and 1906. Its very vehicle was the press; thus Tilak issued a call to his own community of newspaper editors and writers, officially threatened by prosecution and imprisonment in the wake of Lala Lajpat Rai's deportation without trial in May 1907 (following the prosecution of his weekly newspaper *The Punjabee*), and more immediately the prosecution of Aurobindo Ghose beginning in May 1908 (itself in connection with the Kingsford assassination attempt), and the new Press Act of 1908, to gird themselves to a political duty that he saw as crucial to the development of more representative government in India.[35] For Tilak, the press would bring about progress in the administration of the country, being a counterweight to autocratic power, and ensuring it became more representative; and in making his case through analogy, Tilak implies its universality.

Tilak's statements in court commanded a huge audience. They were commented upon in England by, for example, *The Times*, *The Manchester Guardian*, and *The Labour Leader*; more pertinently, he achieved an all-India reach in vernacular and English-language publications.[36] The *Phoenix* of Karachi stated upon his sentence that '[this] much is certain that the entire country, from Dan to Beersheba, watched with admiration the able and elaborate defense which he made'; as far afield as Rangoon, *United Burma* stated that 'the whole country is stunned to hear that Maharaja Tilak is transported and breathe heavy sighs at so dramatic a trial'; *Bande Mataram* of Calcutta saluted the 'brilliant address to the jury which will for ever enrich our patriotic literature'; and even *The Mussalman* of Calcutta reflected on 'the ability with which Mr Tilak defended himself'.[37] Tilak would have been well aware of the interest his trial generated from all quarters, and surely directed himself to public opinion as well as to the jury in the case.

---

[35] Under the terms of the Newspaper (Incitement to Offences) Act, District Magistrates were empowered to confiscate printing presses on suspicion of incitement to acts of violence.
[36] An account of the press coverage of Tilak's trial is given in Kelkar (ed.), *Trial (1908)*, 121 ff.
[37] See ibid., 127–140.

Tilak elaborates a theoretical distinction between 'government' and 'bureaucracy' in order to justify the legitimate right to protest the Government's actions. The 'Government established by law' refers to government 'in the abstract'; 'Government' pure and simple refers to all the Government's officials: 'any officer, even a police constable'. Clearly, it cannot be 'that if I say a police man is not doing his duty I am guilty of sedition'; and on a grander scale, arguing for a whole new system of government does not betoken sedition against the 'Government established by law'. Tilak thus establishes the parameters for political polemic. But more significant is the instrumental value that Tilak places on this freedom. 'I have to express my opinion', and 'I am allowed to express it freely. There can otherwise be no progress'.[38] Tilak, overtly turning from journalist to political philosopher, defends the value of his journalistic reflections on the system of government:

> Now if we were philosophically discussing the point, and Section 124A were strictly applied, every philosopher in the world to whom we owe this progress will have to be sent to Jail.[39]

Provided their views are simply motivated by the desire for reform of institutions, writers, says Tilak, as a duty, 'have to try to convert the majority to our views'. If a writer

> is trying to secure constitutional rights of the people ... he is entitled to express his views fully and fearlessly. It would not be fair to obstruct him in expressing these views. It would be coming in the way of the progress of the country to do so.[40]

The free press's role was to guarantee progress towards the rights of constitutional self-government, substantially through its influence of popular opinion. There was, of course, another, related sense that under current administrative conditions, a free press mitigated the abuse of autocratic power (just as the employment of violence would both achieve

---

[38] Ibid., 80.
[39] Ibid., 81.
[40] Ibid., 98.

redress and lead to improvements in the administrative framework of the country):

> newspapers stand between the arbitrary power and people, and the press represents public opinion to Government and this is particularly necessary in the administration of the country.[41]

This recalls, of course, Tilak's very first journalistic foray: the editorial in the first issue of *The Mahratta* in January 1881.[42] It was the desire to place before Government the views of his community that had prompted the publication of the articles of sedition in 1908; of other constitutional means, like making statements in council, Tilak stated 'we might as well cry in the wilderness'.[43]

Tilak cited the example of Britain, which had 'sacrificed some of its best men' in the fight for press freedom.[44] Tilak strikes a familiar note of agitators for political freedoms in India: 'These are your traditions. We admire them. So long as we admire them you are pleased, but as soon as we begin to imitate them you call it seditious'.[45] This may be read as a rhetorical ploy, of mixed shaming and flattery, to his jury (in the manner Bayly refers to as 'counter-preaching').[46] Indeed, Tilak states the whole freedom of the press would depend on the legal safeguard—'the safeguard of liberty'—of trial by jury, operating equally in India and in England, their common-sense view on the bounds of legitimate complaint acting as people-derived law. But Tilak's statements, ironically referencing British liberties while prosecuted by British autocracy, warrant more careful examination. Tilak's citation of the celebrated defence by Thomas Erskine of Thomas Paine *in absentia* in 1792, for criticizing the constitution of the United Kingdom in the *Rights of Man*, would even support a reading that Tilak's is a universal conception of political progress drawn from the British historical example applied in a didactic and linear fashion to his own conditions: the approving citation of Erskine himself aligns Tilak

---

[41] Ibid., 102.
[42] See the discussion of *The Mahratta* in Chapter 2.
[43] Kelkar (ed.), *Trial (1908)*, 120.
[44] Ibid., 99.
[45] Ibid., 98.
[46] Bayly, *Recovering Liberties*, 9.

with an English Whig conception of history that itself had strong univer-
salizing tendencies.[47] Tilak in fact went further in this direction in the defence he offered of his *Kesari* article condemning press repression in the
wake of the Bengal bomb blast. 'Liberty of speech and liberty of the press
give birth to a nation and nourish it', *Kesari* had stated.[48] Now at trial,
in justification he cited its intellectual antecedents: 'this is an historic[al]
truth put in to show that by passing the Press Act, you retard the growth of
a nation. It is not my own phrase. It is quoted from English works.'[49] These
included a passage from *The Science of Politics* (1883) by the English Jurist
Sheldon Amos:

> An untrammelled press, security against police despotism, an unre-
> stricted right of orderly public meeting, and ungrudged opportunities
> for the announcement of wishes and opinions in an organised form to
> the heads of Government Departments, all operate in one and the same
> direction of calling into mature existence political conceptions and in-
> stincts of the highest order.[50]

It should be noted that Amos was indeed an authority for Tilak in his
understanding of constitutionalism—being cited by Tilak on exactly that
question in *Mahratta* the year previously.[51]

As we saw in Chapter 3 while discussing Tilak's debt to the ideas of
English radical tradition in relation to the British historical example,
the latter's normative power clearly influenced Tilak, as his writings in
Kesari discussed here make clear; and the thought of Erskine and Amos,
emerging from and articulating aspects of that experience (not to mention Mill, whose classic use of the term despotism in *Representative
Government* likely influenced his understanding of it and preference for
the term over its near synonyms), did similarly. Such statements of Tilak's
at trial, then, were not merely a set of knowing references, aimed at the

---

[47] Erskine (a Scot) was heavily involved in the Whig radicalism of Charles James Fox. See
David Lemmings, 'Erskine, Thomas, first Baron Erskine (1750–1823)', *Oxford Dictionary of
National Biography*, https://doi.org/10.1093/ref:odnb/8873.
[48] *Kesari*, 9 June 1908, 'These remedies are not lasting'. Kelkar (ed.), *Trial (1908)*, Prosecution
Exhibit [D], 16.
[49] Ibid., 147.
[50] Sheldon Amos, *The Science of Politics*, 3rd ed. (New York, 1897), 210.
[51] *Mahratta*, 24 February 1907 (SMT 8, 71, 'Constitutional or Extra Constitutional I').

moral persuasion or embarrassment of his European jurors and Anglo-Indian opponents. But that is not to say that arguments for the freedom of the press in India were drawn from a British liberal blueprint: they comprehended older traditions of intellectual exchange and patterns of social communication, as has been noted: the ready propagation of information and ideas was always understood in India to have a political value.[52] In Tilak's statements, we see this liberal ideal domiciled into an environment which had already given rise to a vital press and which was therefore conducive to its theorization; as we have seen, the press in western India was hugely important as a vehicle in the heavily conflicted intellectual milieu from the 1840s. And the act of thus resisting colonial autocracy with these intellectual materials saw to not only their prominence in the construction of his political thought, which emerged from this political context, but a genuine radicalism in their application, which can in fact be seen as a characteristic of his thought. What emerged, further, was a conception of political conduct that transcended the autocratic political conditions of early-twentieth-century India from which it was derived.

The *Gita Rahasya's* vision of politics

As we saw in detail in Chapter 2, Tilak's *Gita Rahasya* emphasized that *karma* (action) rather than *bhakti* (devotion), or *jnana* (knowledge), beloved of other commentaries on the Gita, was the manner of achieving *moksha*. Thus his own text was a study of the science of proper action ('*karmayoga shastra*'), an explicitly ethical idea. The nature of the dilemmas of action that the Gita discusses meant its espousal of action was relevant to political action in his own time: how to act when faced with the dilemmas of a time of conflict, and when faced with action that could accrue *adharma*. Declaring it not seditious, the Bombay Government's official translator may have declared it 'free from objectionable matter', because though dealing with practical ethics, Tilak had 'exclude[d] all references to politics'.[53] But this section will underscore rather the continuities of the *Gita Rahasya* with the rest of Tilak's political thought,

---

[52] Bayly, *Empire and Information.*
[53] MSA JD 1703 (1914).

and the clear resistance to the colonial state it sought to justify.[54] It will focus on Tilak's disquisition on political conduct contained in the twelfth chapter of this philosophical exposition, which deals with proper worldly conduct in general, and the manner of knowing dharma from *adharma* in such conduct.[55] This chapter can really be said to be the keystone of the entire 1,200-page edifice: indeed, it provides the science of proper conduct that is the text's main import.[56]

Tilak begins his twelfth chapter with a lengthy exposition on the metaphysical basis for ethical conduct. The title of the chapter demonstrates this concern with *Siddhavastha*, or the state of that perfect or accomplished *siddha*, and its relation to quotidian worldly activity, or *vyavahara*.[57] For Tilak, the figure of the perfected *siddha*—or *jnanin* (Tilak in fact prefers this term above all others in the text)—is invoked at the beginning as a model of conduct: all must consider the way in which the *jnanin* 'performs the activities of his worldly life'.[58] He describes the state of the *jnanin*'s metaphysical understanding: he is one 'whose Pure Reason has become steady by means of control', capable of realizing 'that "there is only one Atman in all created things"', and whose desire is also, perforce, pure. On account of this, 'it is impossible that he should commit any sin or any action obstructive of Release'.[59] It is this frame of mind which Krishna exhorts Arjuna to achieve in the Gita. The *jnanin* is synonymous for Tilak with another term he uses: *sthitaprajna*, or 'steady in mind'. Tilak uses *jnanin* in place of other terms for 'the wise' in the Gita, conflating many other terms and concepts under its banner. Thus Aristotle's *Ethics* holds to an analogous doctrine (predated by the Gita) that 'the decision given by the *jnanin* is always correct'; and Tilak goes on to state that Ramdas' *Dasbodh* calls on us to emulate the indifference to the world of the *jnanin*, whereas Ramdas instead uses the term *jaanata*, simply meaning knowledgeable.[60] In thus imposing his own carefully

---

[54] Cf. Kapila's approach in 'Violence', urging its divorce from his political conduct hitherto.

[55] Tilak, *GR*, i, 510–565.

[56] Kapila, 'Violence', 445 fn, notes its importance but does not exploit it.

[57] The English translation of this mistransliterates the title as 'siddhavastha and siddhavyavahara', that is, 'the state and worldly activities of the perfected person'. Though an error, it does not in fact misrepresent the chapter's concern with the conduct of the *siddha* as exemplary. *GR*, i, 510.

[58] Ibid., 511.

[59] Ibid., 513. Tilak's explicit equation of Vedantic and Kantian language is discussed below.

[60] Tilak, *GR*, i, 514, 522; and cf. Ramdas, *Dasbodh*, 18.2.

defined term, Tilak strongly emphasizes his concept of the model of conduct.

For Tilak, the purity of mind, not mere aping of actions, is all: and after this purity of mind is ascertained, somewhat self-contradictorily and circularly, by examining the *jnanin*'s actions, no matter how his actions appear—even if they appear immoral 'from the ordinary point of view'— they must be 'essentially sinless'.[61] The quotidian rules of ethics cannot apply: *jnanins* are 'beyond the bounds of sin and merit'.[62] Ultimately, reflecting his apparent contradictions in 1897, Tilak completes a volte-face to clarify that in fact we do merely need to emulate the actions of the *jnanin*: not everybody is capable of achieving such mental equability anyway, and Arjuna was able to achieve it because he was already self-enlightened (*buddha*)—and had the unique assistance of an explicit articulation of the device by Krishna. For the common human actor, the actions of *jnanins* are literally unquestionably authoritative as laws of conduct.[63] This circularity appears to give ample scope for self-justification; and just as he is poised to demonstrate some such precepts from the lives of the *jnanins*, Tilak adds a new qualification: that we must bear in mind that the *jnanin* 'has to live in a society in this *kaliyuga*', the evil age, the final in the sequence of *yugas*, beginning when Krishna left the earth, and in which dharma has progressively decreased. The *Kaliyuga* is central to his conception of ethics: as almost everyone is steeped in 'selfish interests' in it, no matter what one's equability of mind, 'it will not do if he adopts the practice of harmlessness, kindness, peacefulness, forgiveness'. In short, it is 'necessary to make some changes in the rules of Right and Wrong' which apply in the abstract.[64] Tilak's statement on the mutability of moral rules is a classic statement in defence of Relative Ethics, and Tilak in fact refers to the term, acknowledging that he is indebted to Herbert Spencer for expounding the concept.[65] Tilak acknowledges the adjustment for 'time and place'—to mundane imperatives, including political life—is 'the most difficult question in the *karmayoga*', and proceeds

---

[61] Tilak, *GR*, i, 519.
[62] The Nietzschean overtones of the *jnanin* concept are discussed further on, ibid., 516.
[63] Ibid., 522. It is, further, not clear how, if at all, Arjuna's state differs from that of the *jnanin*.
[64] Ibid.
[65] Ibid., citing Spencer's *Data of Ethics* (1879).

to describe a quotidian ethics of politics through his own characteristic vision of the *Kaliyuga*, and what we might call his *yugadharma*.[66]

All of this has solid political application. There is no reified politics in Tilak's ethical discussion, no citation of *rajniti* or *arthashastra*; but they are simply inferable from worldly ethics. Tilak begins his substantiation of the nature of worldly conduct in the *Kaliyuga* by citing the prestigious Maharashtrian authority of Ramdas, whom he regarded as guru to the seventeenth-century warrior-king Shivaji, specifically a stanza in his *Dasbodh*:

> Boldness with boldness/Impertinence by impertinence/
> Villainy by villainy/Must be met//[67]

This is the 'ultimate advice' of Ramdas, and its reciprocity is invoked, just as in his 1908 articles, as Tilak's own watchword. Tilak describes saintliness as the preferred option; but one must not be afraid to 'take out a thorn by a thorn' (*kantakenaiva kantakam*).[68] Non-enmity (*nirvaira*) may be of 'sacred importance', as is Christ's exhortation to 'turn the other cheek' (Luke 6.29). But they too are consigned their place: they cannot be reconciled with 'worldly ethics', leading Nietzsche to dismiss Christian non-inimicalness as emasculating, and Tilak's agreement in this is clear: indeed his *jnanin* seems to be a fusing of *advaita* Vedanta metaphysics with Nietzsche's Superman.[69] Beyond this, self-preservation is invoked as the highest precept on more than one occasion, again on moral grounds: one must preserve oneself, in the belief that one 'is maintaining and keeping alive his body for the benefit of others'; Tilak later adds that as 'one can bring about universal welfare only if one lives ... this right of self-protection becomes higher than the world'.[70] There is, though, within this, a large scope specifically for a legitimation of violence. When Tilak

---

[66] Ibid., 523. Cf. Kapila's suggestion, in 'Violence', 453, that the *Kaliyuga* may represent a 'perpetual state' of that 'exception' capable of creating the political subject; this is more naturally expressed as a quotidian state of affairs.

[67] Ibid., 524.

[68] Ibid., 554. The expression is proverbial, but Tilak may have been thinking of the sense of '*kantaka*' in the *Manusmriti*, for an enemy or 'paltry foe' (and neatly inverting Manu's sense of it as 'a thorn to the state', 'a seditious person'): M. Monier-Williams, *Sanskrit-English Dictionary*, 245, citing *Manusmriti*, IX, 253.

[69] Tilak, *GR*, i, 519, 524, 545–547.

[70] Ibid., 559, 535

prefaces his concluding chapter with Krishna's exhortation to 'think of me and fight', though he may claim it to synecdochically refer to all action, this may seem to signify a specific priority: to justify violence in the conduct of politics with reference to conditions that call for acts of requital. Tilak's illustration of the justness of setting aside non-enmity is substantially a description of violent conduct.[71] His choice of sanguinary examples, and their frequency, over these pages, is striking: Tilak states that the principle of non-violence, being relative, is not violated by killing evildoers, Paramesvara himself, he of the very purest reason, destroying them.[72] Likewise there is no enmity in a judge directing the execution (Tilak specifies this rather than any other punishment) of the criminal, whose *karma* has caused that harm to himself.[73] Action and reaction being equal in physics, the 'principle of "measure for measure"' is natural and proper in life; the 'counterblow' must be as strong as the 'blow'.[74] Tilak, to underscore the point, euphemistically suggests that there should be no saintly treatment for the villain who comes with the intention of cutting the throats of others. Thus we are left with a saturation of images of violence to demonstrate proper worldly conduct.[75] The summary of the entire teaching of the Gita, indeed, is that 'even the most horrible warfare' is righteous, provided that equability of mind exists.[76] It is hardly surprising to find Tilak cross-referencing here that other Sanskrit epic depicting righteous warfare, the Ramayana: the 'sinless' Rama was meritorious in killing Ravan, on account of the latter's evil-doings.[77] This analogy, indeed, would become popular in justifying the conduct of Indian nationalists who did choose to take up the sword.[78]

It should be emphasized that the colonial state is a vital antagonist in the *Gita Rahasya*. Though war against kin is the basis of the Gita, and one form of action justified in Tilak's commentary, it would be a mistake

---

[71] Ibid., 547–554, contains this account.

[72] Ibid., 548.

[73] Ibid., 549.

[74] Ibid., 551.

[75] The sole exception in this section is Tilak's description of Indra, whose deceit merely is lauded (ibid., 552).

[76] Ibid., 550.

[77] Ibid., 551.

[78] Twenty-five years later, Subhas Chandra Bose's journey to Germany to enlist the armed help of Hitler was condoned, ironically, by the more peaceable Jawaharlal Nehru. Prison diary entry, 11 November 1941. *Selected Works of Jawaharlal Nehru*, ed. S. Gopal, 15 vols (1972–), vol. XI, 252.

to read the violence of the *Gita Rahasya* as exclusively, or even predominantly, 'communal'.[79] Indeed Tilak here resembles, in Ayesha Jalal's re-reading, his younger contemporary 'Maulana' Azad, who, far from abjuring *jihad* for 'secularism', in fact retained an anti-colonialism that was steeped in a 'religious sensibility' expressing itself in a *jihadhi* commitment, all the while consistent with a nationalism of Hindu-Muslim unity.[80] Struggle or violence against the state was still a locus of political action for Tilak, notwithstanding the failure of the Swadeshi movement, and his simultaneous moves to be readmitted to Congress and push for resolutions on Home Rule just as he was bringing the *Gita Rahasya* to publication militate against any interpetation of his detachment from anti-state politics. The fact that Tilak's first sedition conviction in 1897 had rested on a speech invoking the Gita morality to resist foreigners (*mlecchas*) is significant to his choice of material in 1910. The Mahabharata's narrative of political usurpation, which the Gita is situated in, would also surely have been inescapable to Tilak's readers, its metaphorical resonances scarcely needing elaboration; this, indeed, is one reason why the text saw such an intense engagement by Indian thinkers in this period. His references to the aggression of world powers in the *Gita Rahasya*, and the Darwinian struggle of competing, industrialized world powers, whose 'onslaught' *karmayoga shastra* was intended to help India 'resist', according to the *Gita Rahasya*'s concluding chapter, argue similarly.[81]

Tilak, indeed, maintains a privileged status for the nation within his ethical scheme: as one ascends a ladder of self-identification with all things, one does not destroy the rungs of the ladder, for 'pride in one's country' is a virtue through which some countries have now become 'fully advanced'.[82] He later adds that even in the highest stage of equable reason, patriotism is necessary.[83] Slightly paradoxically, then, a disinterested

[79] Kapila, 'Violence', gives an emphatic argument that Tilak's politics here were 'beyond the purview of the state', arguing that the Muslim-Hindu relations are actually understood in terms of kinship, the conversion of which into enmity Tilak describes in the text; this misreads Tilak's understanding of the two communities as historically, even primordially, distinct.

[80] Ayesha Jalal, 'Striking a Just Balance: Maulana Azad as a Theorist of Trans- National Jihad', *Modern Intellectual History*, 4/1 (2007), 95–107.

[81] Tilak, *GR*, ii, 710.

[82] *GR.*, i, 556.

[83] Ibid., 523, 557.

defence of the national community remains a justification for violent conduct, as it had been for Tilak in 1897. But this does not imply that the state, were it to express the nation, can legitimize any conduct. For there are implicit limits laid out to the state's power vis-à-vis the individual. There will always be, Tilak points out, tensions between orders of identification; the solution to this is that 'duties of the lower order should be sacrificed for duties of the higher'.[84] But Tilak's reading is individualist, and he outlines an ethical position in which the needs of the greater number may be resisted by the individual. He quotes the Mahabharata:

> for protecting a family, one person may be abandoned; for protecting a town, a family may be abandoned; for the protection of a society, a town may be abandoned; and for the protection of Atman, the earth may be abandoned.[85]

Perhaps surprisingly quixotically, Tilak explicates that the final clause constrains the majoritarian impulse implicit in the first three: the numerical imperative must be followed, but not to the detriment of Atman, which for Tilak carries a connotation of the self. As the same Atman is in each individual, 'the benefit of a larger multitude' is no justification for coercing any individual. Says Tilak:

> ... the fourth part of this stanza says that if people behave unjustly in that way, then the inherent ethical right of everybody of protecting himself is of a higher importance than the benefit of a greater multitude, nay even of the whole world.[86]

In this we can find Tilak justifying a core liberal axiom, through asserting the ontological primacy of the individual.[87] Knowledge of the unity of Atman and Brahman, as we have seen, is the basis for the individual's autonomous action; and the knowledgeful protection of Atman provides

---

[84] Ibid., 557.
[85] Ibid., 558.
[86] Ibid., 559.
[87] On this concept see Anthony Arblaster, 'Liberal Values and Socialist Values', *Socialist Register* 9 (1972).

an ethical basis for protecting the autonomy of the individual within society—like resistance to state autocracy, a quintessential liberal aim.[88]

'An operator, a cooperator, and a non-cooperator'

The last months of Tilak's career, between his return from England in late 1919 to his death in August 1920, were naturally dominated by his relationship with the new Gandhian politics of resistance in the Indian National Congress, witnessed on a large scale with the 'Rowlatt Satyagraha' in April 1919 (the campaign against the extension of repressive war-time legislation through the so-called Rowlatt Acts) during Tilak's absence.[89] Tilak re-emerged onto the Indian political scene in which the terms of debate were permeated by Gandhian conceptions of 'satyagraha', or 'truth force', and its modes of non-violent resistance to the British administration. By early 1920, Tilak was in fulsome disagreement with Gandhi concerning the politics of 'non-cooperation', ironically with Gandhi (temporarily) departing from his previous stance and advocating full cooperation in the workings of the new Government of India Act, and Tilak withholding. This section will examine that disagreement, but will do so by establishing the longer context of Tilak's own pioneering and remarkable thought on non-cooperation and 'passive resistance'—expounded alongside and as complementary to his thought on violence—to see its continuities and apparent ruptures through to the moment he clashed with its historically most celebrated exponent.

Tilak was one of a number of Congress politicians, including his associates Lala Lajpat Rai and Bipin Chandra Pal, as well as Aurobindo Ghose, whose response to the announcement of the Bengal partition in October 1905 was to urge a far-reaching boycott not only of British goods, but of British institutions in India. Rai, in his *Young India* of 1916, gave Tilak primacy among those positing what he termed such 'passive resistance' within the Congress politics, just two months after the

---

[88] Cf. Kapila's contention that the *Gita Rahasya* contains a dismissal of liberalism, 'Violence', and 'Self' esp. 120.

[89] See The heading of this section is the description in Athalye, *Tilak*, 256. On the 1919 campaign, see H. F. Owen, 'Organizing for the Rowlatt Satyagraha of 1919', in R. Kumar, ed., *Essays on Gandhian Politics: The Rowlatt Satyagraha of 1919* (Oxford, 1971).

partition's enactment, in an open conference of younger members in the 1905 Congress in Benares.[90] It was not for another year that Tilak would make his most prominent and full exposition of it, in his famous apologia of this Congress 'extremist' wing, now referred to as the 'New Party':

> We are not armed, and there is no necessity for arms either. We have a stronger weapon, a political weapon in boycott. We have perceived one fact, that the whole of the administration, which is carried on by a handful of Englishmen, is carried on with our assistance.[91]

The Government perpetuated this system by keeping Indians ignorant of the fact that they were 'clerks and willing instruments of our own oppression at the hands of an alien Government'; and Tilak exhorted his listeners to be not so deceived, but to

> realise the fact that your future rests entirely in your own hands. If you mean to be free, you can be free; if you do not mean to be free you will fall and be forever fallen. So many of you need not like arms; but if you have not the power of active resistance, have you not the power of self-denial and self-abstinence in such a way as to not assist this foreign Government to rule over you? This is boycott, and this is what we mean when we say, boycott is a political weapon.[92]

Tilak gives a glimpse in practical terms of what boycott would look like, and the success it could yield:

> We shall not give them assistance to collect revenue and keep peace. We shall not assist them in fighting beyond the frontiers or outside India with Indian blood and money. We shall not assist them in carrying on the administration of justice. We shall have our own courts, and when

---

[90] Lala Lajpat Rai, *Young India: An Interpretation and a History of the Nationalist Movement from Within* (New York, 1916), 162. By Congress's final day's proceedings on the Partition of Bengal resolution, it was named as such, to cheers, by Surendra Nath Banerjea (and later in the proceedings by Rai himself) (*Report of the Proceedings of the Twenty-First Indian National Congress* [&c.], 63, 73).

[91] *Speeches*, 'Tenets of the New Party', 2 January 1907, 64.

[92] Ibid., 65–66.

time comes we shall not pay taxes. Can you do that by your united efforts? If you can, you are free tomorrow.[93]

Gandhi's intellectual antecedents in formulating his conception of 'civil
disobedience' are much noted (though Tilak is not generally counted
among them).[94] Tilak's creditors are more obscure, and neither in his letters nor in the pages of *Mahratta* is there any reference to the formative
influences upon this seminal speech on the issue, some few months prior
to Aurobindo's articles in the influential Calcutta English-language newspaper *Bande Mataram*, which he coedited with Pal.[95] Tilak by his own
account was influenced by J. R. Seeley's account of England's government
of India, which claimed that England must 'succumb at once' to a 'feeling
of nationality' that robbed them of 'the submission of the population'. The
mere feeling that it was 'shameful to assist him in maintaining his dominion' would be enough; not even another mutiny, but the simple impossibility of levying an army. But there is no sense in Seeley that civil
disobedience may be manifest, or how.[96] There is a clue in one of Tilak's
further speeches on the subject, just a few months later, to a possible antecedent, however. 'You must realise', he told his audience at the annual
Shivaji celebrations,

> that you are a great factor in the power with which the administration in
> India is conducted. You are yourselves the useful lubricants which en-
> able the gigantic machinery to work so smoothly.[97]

This seems an echo of perhaps the most noted theorist of civil disobedience in the mid-nineteenth century, and a known influence on Gandhi,
Henry David Thoreau, the American naturalist and transcendentalist
thinker whose *Essay on Civil Disobedience* (1849) was penned out of dis-
gust with the Mexican war and the institution of slavery. Thoreau asserted

---

[93] Ibid., 66.

[94] See, for instance, Vinay Lal, 'Gandhi's West, the West's Gandhi', *New Literary History*, 40/2
(2009), 281–313.

[95] Reprinted in Aurobindo Ghose, *The Doctrine of Passive Resistance* (Calcutta: Arya
Publishing House, 1948).

[96] J. R. Seeley, *The Expansion of England: Two Courses of Lectures*, revised ed. (Leipzig,
1884), 238.

[97] *Speeches*, 'The Shivaji Festival', Poona, 25 June 1907, 77.

'the right to refuse allegiance to, and to resist, the government, when its tyranny or its inefficiency are great and unendurable'. The 'mass of men', says Thoreau, serve that state 'not as men mainly, but as machines, with their bodies. They are the standing army, and the militia, jailers, constables, posse comitatus, etc'. Rather than perpetuate injustice in this manner, he exhorts his reader: 'break the law. Let your life be a counter-friction to stop the machine'.[98] Tilak's statement that the 'selves' of his audience are nothing but lubricants to the gigantic machine is one of absolute symmetry, a similarity in modes of expression that is at least highly suggestive of an awareness of Thoreau's work. Tilak's perhaps surprising borrowing from Thoreau's Christian transcendentalism at this juncture would be a further token of his intellectual resourcefulness in devising political strategies at times of considerable stress, and the sheer range of material on which he was wont to draw; and, of course, of the individualistic nature of his applications of it.

Tilak, in *Kesari*, at this moment grappled with the question of the constitutionalism of this mode of agitation—associated, as we have seen, with 'extremist' politics. In an article entitled 'Constitutional and Lawful', Tilak disagreed with the 'moderate' Gokhale to point out that all agitation undertaken in India was in fact unconstitutional.[99] A constitution (*sanad*) ensured that rights limited power: and anticipating exactly his 1908 articles, he again stated that Charles I of England was killed because it was necessary that the country's kingly rule become thus constitutional. There was no influence—a crucial notion for Tilak—on the organs of rule under India's unconstitutional conditions, and Indian press efforts to change public opinion differed from those in England (his examples, notably, being the Liberal radicals John Bright and Richard Cobden) because public opinion was represented there, unlike in India. The Penal Code determined legality; but the new movements of Swadeshi and boycott were therefore not less constitutional. And if such efforts were deemed unlawful, Indians' own sense of justice, morality, and historical progress—towards those constitutional rights—should be the yardstick as to whether they should contravene legality.

---

[98] H. D. Thoreau, *Walden and Civil Disobedience* (London, 1983) (hereafter, Thoreau, *Civil Disobedience*), 370.

[99] SLT 4, 5 March 1907.

After exile, release, and the Home Rule agitation of the war years, the context for the Tilak-Gandhi quarrel on non-cooperation was the passing of the Government of India Act in December 1919, increasing Indian representation in the administration in a limited fashion, under the principle of 'dyarchy' transferring certain competencies such as agriculture and health to provincial governments answerable to enlarged Provincial Councils, whose membership was to be directly elected.[100] This followed from the so-called Montagu Declaration of August 1917 (by Secretary of State for India Edwin Montagu), with its declared aim of progressively making the Government 'responsible' to an Indian electorate, and the subsequent 'Montagu-Chelmsford' report, which, however, the Congress in Special Session at Bombay, with Tilak supporting, in August–September 1918, resolved to be an 'inadequate and disappointing' fulfilment of that aim—*Kesari* memorably describing it as like a 'sunless dawn'—but which nonetheless served as the basis for the 1919 act.[101] The Royal Proclamation which accompanied the Act on 23 December 1919 held it to be a 'historic' measure, which 'points the way to full representative Government hereafter'; and it promised that 'opportunity will now be given for experience to grow and for responsibility to increase with the capacity for its fulfilment.[102] Tilak's policy now towards the Act was described under the name 'responsive cooperation'. According to *Kesari*, 'about two hours' after receiving news of the King's proclamation, Tilak sent telegrams to the Viceroy Chelmsford and to Montagu to convey his message:

Please convey to His Majesty grateful and loyal thanks of Indian Home Rule League and the people of India for proclamation and amnesty and assure him of responsive co-operation.[103]

'It is true', said *Kesari*, that the word 'responsive' does not normally go with 'co-operation'; but it clarified that 'Tilak was of the opinion that the

[100] H. N. Mitra (ed.), *The Govt. of India Act 1919 Rules Thereunder & Govt. Reports 1920* (Calcutta, 1921).
[101] *Kesari*, 'It is morning, but where is the sun?', SLT 4, 26.
[102] Ibid., i–iv.
[103] SLT 4, 28, *Kesari*, editorial 13 January 1920, 'The King's Telegram and its Intoxicated Critics'.

advice' of the King-Emperor for people and bureaucracy to cooperate 'was not necessary to be given to the people, since the people never obstruct any beneficial moves. The bureaucracy so far had raised all resistance and hurdles'. If 'the bureaucracy was disinclined to support the *Badshah* [Emperor] in these matters', the people would 'have to revolt' against the scheme: they would respond therefore to the bureaucracy's level of cooperation.[104]

Ironically, in the light of subsequent developments, Gandhi criticized Tilak for withholding cooperation. Reverting himself to a cooperative attitude to the scheme laid out in the Act, Gandhi proposed an amendment to that effect—accepted by Tilak—as Congress resolved on it at Amritsar a few days later, calling them disappointing but promising cooperation; but Tilak's continued espousal of 'responsive cooperation' over the coming weeks lead to an impugning of his integrity, and suggestions he used his fellow Congressmen as 'tools' at Amritsar. In response, Gandhi commented that Tilak represented 'a definite school of thought of which he makes no secret. He considers that everything is fair in politics'. Gandhi, meanwhile, held that the 'political life of the country will become thoroughly corrupt' if they thus imported what he described as 'Western tactics and methods'.[105] Tilak's response by letter was to situate not only his conduct at the Congress but his entire 'responsive cooperation' policy with reference to the ethic of his *Gita Rahasya*. Responsive cooperation, he stated, was best reflected in the words of Sri Krishna, that '*ye yatha mam prapadyante tams tathaiva bhajamy aham*'.[106] We can identify this as Gita 4.11: 'In that way in which they worship Me, I give them Fruit accordingly'.[107] The implication is that the response must be appropriate for the circumstances, that like must be met with like; this is the essence of his position in the *Gita Rahasya*. Thus responsive cooperation, he implies, is the art of responding in sympathy to the level of generosity displayed by the reforming Government. It comes as no surprise to find the verse quoted in the same section of the *Gita Rahasya* as he cites Manu as prescribing non-enmity merely for the sannyasi, and Nietzsche

104 Ibid.
105 *Young India*, 14 January 1920, *GWMG*, vol. 19, 324, 'The Reforms Resolution in the Congress'.
106 Ibid., 331.
107 This reflects Tilak's own rendering, *GR*, ii. 945.

in suggesting that the same principle has 'emasculated Europe'.[108] But in the longer-term development of Tilak's thought on passive resistance, which he had enthusiastically espoused, this apparently timeless ethical absolute seems a sudden departure.

It does not really appear, though, that the philosophical project of the *Gita Rahasya*, or at least the intellectual convictions of the final phase of his career, determined a change in Tilak's stance, as this tantalizingly implies. The *Gita Rahasya* had in fact emphasized, of course, the importance of the nation for general welfare, as patriotism is crucial for the advancement of society, as well as the illegitimacy of the domination of one country by another. And if Tilak thought it possible to win 'freedom tomorrow' through non-cooperation—as he insisted in 1907 it would be, with sufficient effort—this stance would surely be ethically compelled, rather than be bound by such reciprocity (even if he had not in fact earlier condemned the proposed reforms). At one level, plain political positioning explained his stance: Tilak had to appeal to the reform scheme's supporters in the Congress, while maintaining his freedom of manoeuvre towards a policy of rejection (not least to maintain some support from 'rejecters' like C. R. Das), at a time, following the Rowlatt Satyagraha, when Gandhi had come to eclipse Tilak in prominence.[109]

Further, at the very moment of first expounding passive resistance in 1907, Tilak had in fact referred to the 'compromise' that is necessary with those who had not given 'a full recognition of our principles' in order that the Congress not be 'wrecked'; and this strategic imperative is perhaps as important. In his thought, its utility governed its use. This refers to both the practicality of calling for a plausible campaign of passive resistance and the practical advantages that could conceivably be gained by it. It was the milieu of extreme pessimism with the pliancy of the state ushered in by the announcement of the partition of Bengal that occasioned Tilak's first call to passive resistance; the development of his position was a matter of urgency, as Tilak was forced to think of and espouse new means of applying political pressure because of the sudden change in political circumstances. Evidence abounds that Tilak was pessimistic about the

---

[108] Cited in *GR*, i, 549.

[109] A point also suggested in Jim Masselos, 'Tilak and Gandhi: A Study in Alternatives', in Sibnarayan Ray, ed., *Gandhi, India and the World* (Philadelphia, 1970), 78–79; see Brown, *Rise*, 187 ff.

vigour of nationalist agitation after his release in 1914, and this in part explains his declaration of loyalty to the Raj in August (as well, once more,
as his appeal to Congress 'moderates' as he sought to re-establish himself
there). His turn towards espousing it during the Home Rule League agitation showed his confidence in the growing strength of that movement
and aimed to expedite the principles of the Montagu Declaration, hence
the (at least ostensible) call to resist—and its coinciding with his call to
military enlistment underlines once more the anti-government aspect of
such apparent support for the Empire, as we saw in Chapter 4).[110] By 1920,
in spite of manifest disappointment with it, Tilak wanted to use the constitutional opportunity, and hence responded cooperatively. This logic is
certainly borne out by the Manifesto for the new party Tilak launched
within Congress to push for responsive cooperation in April 1920, when
Gandhi and his followers had made their irrevocable turn back towards
non-cooperation: the Congress Democratic Party, it stated, would 'work
the Montague Reforms Act [sic] for all it is worth, and for accelerating the
grant of full Responsible Government' would 'without hesitation, offer
co-operation or resort to constitutional opposition, whichever may be
expedient and best calculated to give effect to the popular will'.[111] Like
political violence, 'passive resistance' was for Tilak a tactic in which he
reposed moderate enough faith to espouse it in helpless circumstances,
and withhold it when circumstances offered other paths of political progress; his conception was in this sense responsive from its inception. The
distance he perceived himself from influencing the state, paradoxically,
promoted a call for non-cooperation; the rhetoric of boycotting political representation within the framework of the Raj, was, ironically, a response to too little representation within it.

To be sure, Tilak was careful, as we saw in his *Kesari* article on constitutionalism, to justify law-breaking according to the same constitutionalist ethics as in his comments on violence and press freedom. Indeed, he
continued to modify and refine these. A decade after his statements on
India's lack of a constitution, and invocation of justice, morality, and progress towards rights, Tilak in the Home Rule agitation pointed out again

---

[110] Tilak suggested in his speech 'The Present Situation' of April 1918 at Gowri Vilas under
Annie Besant's presidency that passive resistance would make the government 'come down on
its knees'. *Speeches*, 360.
[111] *Mahratta*, 18 April 1920, 185–186.

that, law-making being in the hands of a despotic bureaucracy, laws that contravened 'popular opinion according to the ethics of the 19th and 20th centuries' would be passed; such a law may be strictly legal 'but it was not constitutional'—and indeed the implication of this was that his audience should behave constitutionally, that is, in keeping with progress to just constitutional rights.[112] But this did not mean that such a law must not be obeyed (as, for example, for Thoreau): things need not be done simply because they are just. 'If in their balanced judgment' his audience found 'that the advantages of disobeying it under particular circumstances were greater', they would then be justified.[113] Passive resistance was, for Tilak, the 'means to an end but was not the goal in itself', and in his understanding of this dichotomy can be seen at least a significant Gandhian divergence from him in his conception of resistance in general.[114]

Conclusion

The high degree of consistency in Tilak's anti-autocratic thought, envisioning a series of complementary tactics of resistance under the pressures of his shifting political situation, is shown by his earliest journalism—*Mahratta* in 1881—foreshadowing his famous legitimation of the bomb in *Kesari* in 1908, as a function of autocracy, which begets violence. Moreover, the close relationship of the *Gita Rahasya*'s politics to the rest of his thought, particularly in this regard, is worth noting (especially in the light of the contrary observations made on the thought of Aurobindo, for instance).[115] Tilak publicly declared the Gita morality to be a political touchstone in his speech in honour of Shivaji in 1897, a justification for violent acts with altruistic actions, for the good of the national community; as such it anticipates those aspects of the *Gita Rahasya* closely; and the latter's urging righteous violence against usurpation (and despotism) while expanding the Marathi lexicon of political action ties it to his earlier *Kesari* writing. Indeed, the *Gita Rahasya* is a form of apologia

---

[112] *Speeches*, 262, 'Home Rule' (Allahabad, October 1917).
[113] Ibid.
[114] Ibid., 261.
[115] Cf. Kapila, 'Violence', 444; on Aurobindo see Andrew Sartori, 'The Transfiguration of Duty in Aurobindo's Essays on the Gita', *Modern Intellectual History* 7/2 (2010), 319–334.

for Tilak's career (while of course also looking forwards to the immediate future, and the opportunities for politics opened by the all-Indian mobilization of the Swadeshi campaign, despite its setbacks)—and not only in its deeper philosophical justification of his own writings on violence. Its emphasis on the duty of the political actor to encourage his fellows into higher and higher stages of identification reflects Tilak's own nationalist proselytization.

The ideologies of anti-colonial violence are seen by some as having a brutalizing effect upon the future political development of India.[116] For Tilak, any society must stand in visible readiness for violence to live freely, hence one reason for his recurrent espousal of physical training and *kshatriyatva*, and his love of the improvised explosive device. In this sense there is no clear boundary between violence and its absence.[117] And Tilak thus provides, for all he also drew on precolonial notions on the dispersal of legitimate coercion, a reflection of what Achille Mbembe calls the '*spirit of violence*', which permeates structures and interactions of colonialism, and, for Mbembe, influences the life of the post-colony.[118] And the applicability of Tilak's argument is in other ways broader. Specifically in the *Gita Rahasya*, it is the yuga, not the nature of the administration, that justifies setting aside non-enmity, and the nation, that most timeless of constructs, that offers particular focus; and in foregrounding a literal interpretation of the injunction to kill one's kinsmen, Tilak offers a view of violence in the conduct of politics more broadly applicable within the life of his society than that merely against the alien forces of the colonial state.

Violence, however—a constructive, incremental, rather than necessarily revolutionary force—in fact appears on the reverse side of the coin to Tilak's notion of passive resistance: they were pragmatic and morally legitimate choices for Tilak, and in this regard Tilak has something in common in particular with Aurobindo Ghose, that seminal theorist of the Swadeshi era, who penned his doctrine of passive resistance in the wake of Tilak's 1907 'Tenets of the New Party' speech and who anticipated Tilak's future flexibility in its handling in relation to violence, which he

---

[116] On the enduring pathologies of the colonial state, see Ashis Nandy, *The Intimate Enemy: Loss and Recovery of Self under Colonialism* (New York, 1983).
[117] This point is developed in a different context by Pandey, *Routine Violence*, 11.
[118] Achille Mbembe, *On the Postcolony* (Berkeley, 2001), 175 (italics original).

based upon the 'circumstances of servitude'.[119] Indeed, the falseness of the dichotomy of violence/non-violence for radical Indian nationalists of the early twentieth century is reflected in Faisal Devji's account of Gandhi's satyagraha, coexisting with a countenance of violence as great as any contemporary Indian revolutionary.[120]

In his acceptance of violence and law-breaking in the name of representative government and popular sovereignty, Tilak can be identified with radical aspects of liberal thought, despite Indian liberalism in the period being in fact defined antithetically to his 'violence' in particular.[121] This imbricates, indeed, with the liberal conception of legitimate power and political rights we have already encountered in Chapter 3. Certainly, the constitutionalist element in his desire to establish popular control of government (repeated over the course of his statements in 1907–1908) carries a concern for the protection of the individual from power, and the historical empiricism of his political claims offers some grounds to relate him more closely to the applications of liberal thought noted in India in the period—indeed his discussion of political action in relation to seventeenth-century *Swarajya* (as we saw in the earlier chapter) aligns him with earlier nineteenth-century English (and Indian) liberals' preoccupation with the 'ancient constitution'.[122]

Complementary to his reworking of British liberal thought in contesting colonial autocracy was his drawing on terms and concepts in Hindu ethics, something that should not be read as a mere claim to cultural authenticity, but as a reworking of a corpus of ethical understandings in response to the new pressures of the late colonial period. Tilak's prominent citation of seventeenth-century commentaries like Ramdas' *Dasbodh* reflects Vasudha Dalmia's point on the importance of tracing the usage of the classical Sanskrit terms and concepts in the early modern period, for such traditions were still 'alive and actively known' in the nineteenth century—to be drawn on, it might be added, by an intellectual like Tilak in conscious continuation of a tradition of critical argumentation and revision within the *dharmashastra*.[123] Ramdas' commentary,

---

[119] See Bose, 'Spirit and Form', 133.
[120] Faisal Devji, *The Impossible Indian: Gandhi and the Temptation of Violence* (Harvard, 2012).
[121] Bayly, *Recovering Liberties*, 5.
[122] On this last point see esp. ibid., 50–60.
[123] Dalmia, *Nationalization*, 16–18.

which sprang from a period of conflict, implies the responsiveness of this tradition; and it is unsurprising that Tilak and others cited Ramdas from the 1890s in particular for his germaneness to their own moment—as indeed they increasingly focused on the Gita itself.[124] Tilak only seems to simply indigenize Western philosophy in the *Gita Rahasya*, emphasizing that Kant and Green were anticipated by Vedanta in ancient times, and translating them into the Gita's language. In fact his insistence of self-identification as the fundament of political ethics belies Bhikhu Parekh's notion that colonized Indians, like others in the non-Western world, were prone to import finished concepts from the West wholesale, leaving their own 'indigenous traditions of thought [to] remain unexplored and unfertilised' by their 'novel political experiences'.[125] It seems to be, most especially in the *Gita Rahasya*, exactly what Tilak attempts, in his era of the novel experience of modern anti-colonial nationalism.

---

[124] Savarkar even wrote a 1906 Marathi translation of Mazzini's autobiography with a preface comparing him to Ramdas. Discussed in E. Fasana, '*Deshabhakta*: The Leaders of the Italian Independence Movement in the Eyes of Marathi Nationalists', in N. K. Wagle, ed., *Writers, Editors, and Reformers: Social and Political Transformations of Maharashtra, 1830–1930* (Delhi, 1999).

[125] Bhikhu Parekh, *Gandhi's Political Philosophy: a Critical Examination* (Basingstoke, 1989), 2.

6

Remembering Tilak

This chapter studies how Tilak's memory has been transmitted, contested, and employed in India in the century since his death. Having examined Tilak's output, we will now see how the many and divergent personalities he has in his afterlife emerged, how he has been reworked in various contexts to be relevant to so many causes. It therefore shifts from the intellectual history of Tilak we have followed through previous chapters, to a cultural history, one that helps us to explain the enduring and pervasive legacy of Tilak with which we began this study. Much of this remembrance is of Tilak's ideas, even if Tilak is not mostly remembered as a thinker. And so, his (presumed) ideas are still also a focus, in addition to his symbolic content. It focuses on popular memory. That is, it refers to non-academic accounts and references to Tilak, recorded in the public space and in political life. Its source base reflects the astonishing vibrancy of historical memory in India: Tilak is a subject of, or has appeared in, not just newspapers, magazines, and popular histories, but poems, plays, and novels, and also comic books and feature films—indeed all kinds of visual arts, including, as we have seen, having, for a national audience, his giant likeness paraded on a float.

Having established the contours of Tilak's thought, this chapter is able to view with greater clarity the modes of representation and reimagining that have gone into the remembrance of Tilak; in short, it is able to see crucial developments in India's modern culture more clearly through the way it has remembered Tilak at different moments. Crucial among these are his remembrance among Hindu nationalists; as socially regressive anti-reformist (and the rebuttals to this); as an exponent—celebrated or denounced—of political violence; and his careful handling and various deployments as a patriotic icon, including by left-wing critics of the state. In surveying this range, the chapter builds on Chris Moffat's stimulating argument that the anti-colonial dead remain 'effective and indeed

The Thought of Bal Gangadhar Tilak. Robert E. Upton, Oxford University Press. © Robert E. Upton 2024.
DOI: 10.1093/oso/9780198900658.003.0007

demanding interlocutors for the living'.[1] In addition to this, the chapter aims to demonstrate modes of historical remembrance in modern India, and their interrelation. There is ample scope for scepticism, in the pages that follow, that academic history is cleanly differentiated from popular memory by its rational and critical approaches.[2] The academic memory of Tilak draws on popular memory (as well as influencing it in turn); and this popular memory itself can be demonstrated to be a composite, incorporating elements of official construction.[3] The interrelation of scholarly historiography and popular memory that this chapter deals with, then, helps to explain that historiography's construction, thus providing what Sumit Sarkar describes as a 'social history of historiography'.[4]

This chapter will begin by looking at the initial, startlingly broad response to Tilak's death in 1920, and the importance of Tilak's 'charismatic' suffering to his India-wide valorization and commemoration, suggesting its importance as an embodiment of national suffering under colonialism. It will then look at how Tilak's reputation was canalized by Gandhi as he established his own leadership, effectively reading Tilak as Gandhian—a crucial aspect of how Tilak, as an alternative 'father of the nation' figure, has been accommodated to the subsequent nationalist scheme of an independent state.[5] Surveying the extent of his subsequent celebration and the appropriation of his 'patriotic' memory, it will then turn to the most important controversies, examining these across time. Paramount is his memory as a proto-Hindu nationalist, something which was not obvious in 1920 but which was established by the mid-1920s, a crucial and pivotal moment in his historical reputation. Tilak's claiming by the Hindu right was not without its dissenters, especially connected to

---

[1] Chris Moffat, *India's Revolutionary Inheritance: Politics and the Promise of Bhagat Singh* (Cambridge, 2019), 4, (emphasis original).

[2] On this sense, see the classic Maurice Halbwachs, *On Collective Memory*, ed. and trans. Lewis A. Cose (Chicago: University of Chicago Press, 1992) and Patrick H. Hutton, *History as an Art of Memory* (University of Vermont, 1993).

[3] The construction of popular memory is discussed in Alon Confino, 'Collective Memory and Cultural History: Problems of Method', *The American Historical Review*, 102/5 (December 1997), 1386–1403.

[4] Discussed in Deshpande, *Creative Pasts*. This work endorses Deshpande's interpretation of memory as a modern phenomenon constructed through cultural practices, comprising interacting popular and academic histories (6).

[5] This is in marked contrast to what Cashman, *Myth*, takes to be the content of the Tilak 'myth' during his life: although it is actually ill-defined, Cashman does name his un-Gandhian 'practical, pragmatic approach to politics', emphasizing physical strength.

Congress; but it also provoked bitter hostility in some who associated him with Hindutva: both, as we have seen (the latter more strongly) endure today, and a significant feature of this is his part in India's school textbook wars raging from the 1970s until today. The same is true of Tilak's approach to political violence, celebrated from the 1920s onwards by many as un-Gandhian muscular patriotism; some of its devotees have more recently feared that Tilak's textbook characterization as 'extremist' carries a coded condemnation, and have sought to excise it—and it is this which represents the rising tide in India's contemporary culture, as we saw at the outset. Tilak's putative reactionariness on social matters has led to his condemnation on grounds of gender politics (especially since the 1980s), and (from much earlier) high-caste, *Arya* supremacy. The response of his defenders has increasingly been to define him in those terms he is glowingly referred to by today, as a 'Legendary social reformer Bal Gangadhar Tilak', something revealing of the vigour with which heroes are curated in India, and also of the increased importance of social reformism as an index of historical approbation.

India's victorious victim, and father of the nation

One of the most striking things about the impact of Tilak's death is its breadth. His stature close to home was enough to see 'half of the adult population of Bombay' (including a considerable number of women) reported at his funeral there.[6] In Allahabad, meanwhile, *The Independent*, mouthpiece of Motilal Nehru, referred to him as a 'great national hero'; mocking a sour obituary by the Anglo-Indian *Statesman*, it commented that Tilak's so-called 'malign spirit has to-day possessed every class and section of the Indian people'.[7] In Madras, the *Desabhaktan* bemoaned the death of 'the mighty brain' and 'linchpin' of Home Rule car; *New India* carried Tilak's photograph with a black border, along with an advertisement from a local photographer selling them for one rupee.[8] In Lahore in the distant Punjab, it was decided two days after his death to erect a

---

[6] *New India*, 2 August, 1920, 7
[7] Report on the Native Press in the United Provinces, week ending 14 August 1920.
[8] Madras Press Report, week ending 14 August 1920; *New India*, 2 August 1920, 6, 9.

Tilak hall.[9] Tilak was also held a leader among the Indian diaspora in East Africa, with the *East African Chronicle* (Nairobi) observing in late August that 'no event of late has so profoundly moved the Indian community of East Africa'; the 'local day of national mourning' announced by the East African Indian National Congress was apparently so 'universally obeyed' that the journal itself was delayed.[10] The *Uganda Herald* noted a similar closure of Indian shops in Kampala and Entebbe.[11] The *Chronicle* even reported a private wire claiming a devotee of Tilak had self-immolated on his funeral pyre.[12] The 'Hindustani' community in the USA also communicated its sense of loss.[13] In London, *The Times*, true to its recurrent hostility, celebrated the passing of a 'Baneful Influence on Public Life' with a 1,100-word obituary.[14] As far away as Tokyo, the *Yomiuri* 'sympathise[d] with India for her irreparable loss in the death of this leading light', a hint of the pan-Asian sympathy for Indian nationalism strongly visible in Japan in this period, and a small counterpart to Tilak's long-standing admiration for Japan.[15]

The range of this response within India and its diasporic communities is significant. Much literature on Tilak continues to emphasize his regional power base, even until the end of his career.[16] All-Indian politics during Tilak's prime is seen as a coalescence of regional networks, exemplified by the Lal-Bal-Pal triumvirate of regional leaders in the India-wide Swadeshi campaign from 1905, with the decisive shift to national leadership coming with Gandhi's first satyagraha and non-cooperation campaigns of 1919–1920. Such a picture, though not inaccurate, is complicated by this broad, not to say comprehensive all-India response to Tilak's death, just as Gandhi inaugurated his 1920 campaign, for it can in turn be clearly linked to claims to all-India leadership during his lifetime. A paradigmatic account of Tilak by Aurobindo Ghose links leadership to suffering, and his national leadership to unequalled suffering for the

---

[9] *New India*, 5 August.

[10] *East African Chronicle*, 21 August, 6.

[11] *Uganda Herald*, 20 August, 14.

[12] *East African Chronicle*, 21 August, 6. A similar claim was made on the front page of *Kesari* on 3 August, but wider reportage of this is not apparent.

[13] *All About Lok. Tilak, etc.* (Madras: V. R. Sastrulu & Sons, 1922).

[14] *The Times*, 2 August 1920, 7.

[15] Reported in *Japan Times*, 25 August 1920, 4.

[16] Cashman, *Myth*, is typical, resting on, for example, Owen, 'Nationwide Agitation'.

nation. Deeply expressive of Aurobindo's broader sacrificial doctrine, to 'suffer so that' the motherland 'may rejoice', it was first published in 1918 as an 'Appreciation' of Tilak, in the wake of his release from imprisonment and subsequent all-Indian campaigning.[17] His imprisonments were the 'seal of the divine hand upon his work; for there can be no diviner seal than suffering for a cause'.[18] Further, as Aurobindo emphasized, that 'no prominent man in India has suffered more for his country' was actually 'the reason of his immense hold on the people', the reason why he was treated as leader, and he charted Tilak's rise to national prominence through his imprisonments: that of 1897 'left him an uncrowned King' of Maharashtra, and that of 1908 'sent him back … adored and followed by the whole nation'.[19] This Appreciation is a perennial. It was much quoted, and reprinted in 1940 and 1947, and it seems to have been plagiarized for a centenary memorial piece in the *Times of India* by the celebrated author D. G. Tendulkar.[20] The recent popular account described in the Introduction in fact uses it as the framework for the entire discussion.[21] As described by Ghose, Tilak's suffering has a charismatic quality, in the Weberian sense. It is worth recalling Weber's famous definition of charisma as 'a certain quality of an individual personality, by virtue of which he is … treated as endowed with supernatural, superhuman, or at least specifically exceptional powers or qualities' which 'are regarded as of divine origin or as exemplary', and on the basis of which 'the individual concerned is treated as a leader'.[22] The appreciation of Tilak as marked by suffering has proved remarkably widespread, and it has often been associated with the divine. At a Madras memorial meeting in August 1920, S. K. Iyengar said he was 'sanctified by his various sufferings', and the *Uganda Herald* at the same time noted that he was 'counted a martyr'; the following year *The Mahratta* held that he 'sacrificed himself upon the altar' of his motherland, and five years after his death Lala Lajpat Rai remembered

[17] See Bose, 'Spirit and Form', 135.
[18] Ghose, 'Appreciation' 7.
[19] Ibid., 8 ff.
[20] This is included in the celebratory volume Aurobindo Ghose, *Bankim Tilak Dayananda*, 2nd ed. ([1940] Calcutta: Arya Publishing House, 1947): 'No Leader in His Time Suffered More for India', 23 July 1956, 11.
[21] Saraf, *Tilak*.
[22] Max Weber, *The Theory of Social and Economic Organization*, trans. T Parsons (London, 1947), 329.

his possessing a 'halo' of suffering; the President of the Congress U. N. Dhebar called him on his birth centenary the 'embodiment of sacrifice'; the account of Tilak in the 'Builders of Modern India' series is introduced with his imprisonment, which the author states provides the setting for the image of Tilak etched on nation's consciousness.[23]

The celebrated suffering of 1908–1914 is in this context the most important moment of Tilak's career. Tilak himself invoked suffering (and providence) at the consummation of his 1908 trial, the most widely yet propagated instance of the colonial state's victimization of the individual Indian for agitation in the name—so it could be viewed—of the nation.[24] Tilak's defence of himself in court, the mark of a master publicist, ensured his all-Indian association with suffering for India. Reportage of his release in 1914 echoes Aurobindo's claim about it. In Bengal, the *Amrita Bazar Patrika* hailed 'this great Indian patriot ... whose imprisonment convulsed the whole of India and evoked a feeling of pain and indignation which was perhaps never witnessed in this country', and other newspapers there agreed.[25] This study has underlined some of the significant limitations on Tilak's 'national' leadership after 1914. And yet, these acclamations from that period themselves offer evidence for what they describe: an all-Indian following for Tilak created by his charismatic suffering.

The strength of this response to Tilak underlines especially the relevance of suffering for establishing political leadership in colonial contexts, in which the seal of suffering not only provides a leader's credentials, but enables him or her to act as the embodiment of the nation—more so because of the self-conscious sacrifices made by their followers in its name.[26] One of Tilak's biographers at least seems explicitly to agree, referring to Tilak as the 'embodiment of sufferings, struggles and aspirations

---

[23] *New India*, 5 August 1920, 10; 20 August 1920, 14; *Mahratta*, 17 July 1921, 342; ibid., 2 August 1925, 383; *Times of India*, 23 July 1956, 9; N. G. Jog, *Lokamanya Bal Gangadhar Tilak* (Delhi: Publications Division, Ministry of Information & Broadcasting, Government of India, 1962), (hereafter, Jog, *LBGT*), 8.

[24] 'All I wish to say is that in spite of the verdict of the Jury I maintain that I am innocent. There are higher Powers that rule the destiny of things and it may be the will of Providence that the cause which I represent may prosper more by my suffering than by my remaining free'. This was quoted and requoted in the various newspapers that covered the trial, as described in Chapter [6].

[25] Report on the Bengal Native Press, week ending 20 June 1914, 372; week ending 4 July 1914, 659–660; week ending 27 June 1914, 624.

[26] Bose, 'Spirit and Form', 142.

of the people'.[27] Tilak therefore appears a 'victorious victim'. And as such he offers a fresh perspective on victorious victimhood in the construction of national identities, even as far as founding fatherhood: it is not perhaps, as has been argued, such a uniquely European Christian phenomenon.[28] For Tilak, it should be noted, was heralded and remembered, repeatedly and broadly, as the father of the nation. In 1920 in Madras, a meeting at Triplicane Beach saw the chairman C. Vijayaraghava Chariar refer to him as the 'foremost if not the first to start the work of Indian nationalism', adding, more remarkably, that he 'founded the people of India'.[29] Biographers of Tilak have taken up this theme: he is its 'first mass leader', setting the tone for other Asian freedom fighters; or even, to one, not just India's father, but its 'Prometheus'; and he has frequently been compared to other founding fathers such as Mazzini and George Washington.[30] It is not mere decontextualized journalistic enthusiasm, then, that sees Tilak, as we saw in the Introduction, described today as 'the father of the national movement'.

Tilak as Gandhi

Tilak's remembrance as national founding figure from 1920—though of course not comprehensive, and coexisting with strong anti-Tilak sentiment—and his wide national following itself both represented a challenge for the concurrent leadership aspirations of M. K. Gandhi. Gandhi himself in 1920 recognized this in writing on his death that

---

[27] Dhananjay Keer, *Lokamanya Tilak, Father of the Indian Freedom Struggle*, 2nd ed. (Bombay: Popular Prakashan, 1969) (hereafter, Keer, *Tilak*), 453.

[28] See David Martin, 'Charisma and Founding Fatherhood', in *Religion and Power: No Logos Without Mythos* (Burlington: Ashgate, 2014). Such an interpretation rests on assumptions of the cultural impact of Christ-like suffering. This may be less important to the phenomenon than Martin suggests; equally, Martin overlooks the importance of suffering in other belief systems. Indeed of note here are *Nayak*'s words on Tilak in 1914: 'he is an orthodox Hindu who has suffered probably because he was fated to suffer because of his deeds in a previous birth. His compatriots are bound to worship him' (Report on Native Papers in Bengal 1914, week ending 27 June 1914, 62), though that is not to suggest, either, that responses to Tilak depend upon any specific ideas of Hindu dharma.

[29] *New India*, 5 August 1920, 10.

[30] Keer, *Tilak*, 447; S. L. Karandikar, *Lokamanya Bal Gangadhar Tilak; The Hercules & Prometheus of modern India* (Poona, 1957); T. V. Parvate, *Bal Gangadhar Tilak* (Ahmedabad, Navajivan Publishing House, 1958) (hereafter, Parvate, *Tilak*), 527; Tahmankar, *Tilak*, front matter.

236 THE THOUGHT OF BAL GANGADHAR TILAK

'he will go down to the generations yet unborn as a maker of Modern India'.[31] A sense of continuity, that Gandhi, rather than fashioning new and broader constituencies of national leadership, was simply following in a succession from Tilak's national leadership, was present in the early 1920s: Annie Besant held simply that 'Gandhi replaced Tilak' at the head of the nationalist 'revolution'.[32] There is ample, sometimes flagrant, evidence for Tilak being coopted into the Gandhian scheme. Gandhi expended effort to persuade Tilakites in Maharashtra to adopt his non-cooperation programme in the early 1920s, at the Maharashtra Provincial Conference in May 1921 urging his audience to 'prove that you are his worthy heirs' by contributing their share to the programme, to 'either win swaraj this year or die in the attempt'.[33] In a famous passage in *Young India* that July, he recognized the hold of Tilak on the people, and admitted 'my method is not Mr. Tilak's method', and the consequent 'difficulty with some of the Maharashtra leaders' he experienced; but he was also careful to add—referring to a discussion which would provoke much controversy—that '[Tilak's] last word to me in the presence of several friends was, just a fortnight before his death that mine was an excellent method if the people could be persuaded to take to it' (which he acknowledged Tilak doubted).[34] By October, he was becoming bolder, or perhaps more desperate. One need not, he said at a speech in Bombay, read the *Gita Rahasya* to learn the 'Tilak Gita': Tilak had supplied the first half, 'Swaraj is our birthright'; Gandhi would supply the second: 'the spinning-wheel is the means to attain it'.[35]

Tilak's name was quickly attached to the Gandhian agenda by Gandhi's supporters. An 'All-India Tilak Memorial Swarajya Fund' was set up at the Nagpur Congress in December 1920 'for the purpose of financing the foregoing National Service and the Non-Co-operation movement in general'.[36] On this central question of non-cooperation, many Tilakites,

---

[31] *Young India*, 4 August 1920, *CWMG*, vol. 21, 112.
[32] Annie Besant, *The Future of Indian Politics* (Adyar: Benares, Theosophical Publishing House, 1922), 259.
[33] *CWMG*, vol. 23, 120, 'Speech at Maharashtra Provincial Conference, Bassein', 7 May 1921.
[34] Ibid., 427. 'A Confession of Faith', *Young India*, 13 July 1921.
[35] *CWMG*, vol. 24, 402, 'Speech on Working Committee Resolution', Bombay, 9 October 1921.
[36] Indian National Congress Civil Disobedience Enquiry Committee, *Report of the Civil Disobedience Enquiry Committee, 1922* (Madras, 1923) (hereafter, *Disobedience Report*), Appendix IX B, 4.

especially in Maharashtra, remained heartily unconvinced by Gandhi's 'Tilak Gita'. Though there seems, in the first two years after Tilak's death, during Gandhi's first non-cooperation campaign, to have been a period of muted criticism, or judgement withheld, within Maharashtrian political circles. The first anniversary of Tilak's death was met by an editorial in *The Mahratta* quoting Tilak's 1907 speech 'Tenets of the New Party', and noting its continuities with Gandhi in its conviction that India was 'enslaved by her own sons without whose active help' the British could not rule; Tilak had made the Gandhian movement possible, and it 'wholeheartedly' supported him.[37] Many Maharashtrian supporters of Gandhi continued to emphasize continuities between them into the 1930s.[38] Even after many Tilakites took the opportunity of the suspension of the non-cooperation campaign after the 'Chauri Chaura incident' in 1922 to dissent from Gandhi, others, especially those dominant in Congress, still forcefully invoked Tilak in Gandhi's support: the report of the enquiry into civil disobedience set up by Congress in 1922 noted that in 1907 'Lokamanya Tilak expounded the principle of Non-Co-operation in a remarkable speech', challenging those who invoked his blessed memory to criticize non-cooperators to 'ponder over these noble sentiments'.[39] In some cases a more symbolic elision between Tilak and Gandhi was visible. Already in September 1920 work stoppages in honour of Tilak were being referred to by the notably Gandhian term *hartal*; and the Tilak fund was ultimately swelled after Gandhi's 1922 conviction by donations on the eighteenth of each month, renamed 'Gandhi Day'.[40]

Such an interpretation of Tilak's stance on non-cooperation continued—not without reason—to have force after the battles of the 1920s were long passed.[41] In many of Tilak's biographies, though, the broader similarities between Tilak and Gandhi suggest a thirst to see the latter in the former. An outstanding example of this is the 1958 biography by T. V. Parvate. Devoting a whole chapter to 'Tilak and Gandhi', Parvate

---

[37] 17 July 1921, 341, 343. Tilak's speech is discussed in Chapter 5.
[38] M. J. Kanetkar, *Tilak and Gandhi: A Comparative Character Sketch* (Nagpur: Author, 1935), 69.
[39] *Disobedience Report*, 11.
[40] *East African Chronicle*, 4 September 1920, 3; IOR/L/PJ/12/129 [1925], 'Histories of the Non-cooperation and Khilafat Movements', f. 76.
[41] *TOI* (23 July 1956, 6), for instance, editorialized on his centenary that he had anticipated Gandhi (before diverging from him).

sees Tilak fitting seamlessly into the tradition of Gandhi and Vinoba Bhave, centred around Gandhi's concept of *Sarvodaya* ('universal up-lift'); even the violence which, Parvate explains, Tilak condones is seen as an 'aberration indulged in out of curiosity' in the context of a forty-year career of consistent constitutional agitation.[42] More generally, in Tilak Parvate sees a 'kindred spirit'. Tilak would have presumably have gone further with his earlier version of satyagraha had he not 'realized that he himself was not a proper person' for the message.[43] Ultimately the differences between them are summed up: 'Gandhi is essentially and basically a universalist, a humanitarian; Tilak is overwhelmingly a patriot and a Nationalist': while 'Tilak must be classed with DeValera ... and Mazzini', Gandhi 'has to be classed with Buddha and Christ'.[44] It is this which forces their divergent approaches: Tilak's 'intellectual perception' is of a non-violent struggle, the way to take humanity to a 'higher cultural level'; but it would take a Christlike figure to lead it.[45] Thus Gandhi merely fulfilled Tilak's work. Noting a point of great controversy already alluded to, Parvate added 'it is a thousand pities there was not a dictaphone' to record the Gandhi-Tilak dialogues and prove these speculations correct. Most revealing of all, perhaps, is Parvate's insistence not only on Tilak's asceticism (which is significantly often noted), but also his would-be celibacy: 'if left to himself' he would have remained celibate to dedicate himself to work: if not quite a Gandhian sentiment, it significantly nudges Tilak in that direction.[46] Thus is Tilak, a rival national founding father, accommodated to a nationalist pantheon so dominated by Gandhi.

The many ways of celebrating Tilak—patriot, theologian, communist

Disputes as to the meaning of Tilak and his relation to Gandhian nationalism for a moment aside, the scale and variety of his remembrance in India, and its durability, are remarkable. His statue at Chowpatty beach

---

[42] Parvate, *Tilak*, 51.
[43] Ibid., 516.
[44] Ibid., 526–527.
[45] Ibid., 530.
[46] Ibid., 536.

in Bombay, where he was cremated, 10.5 feet high with a 14-foot plinth, was erected in 1933 at a cost of 30,000 rupees; Maharashtra also boasts a *chowk* (square), a *marg* (street), and a whole district (*nagar*), as well as a hospital and railway terminus named after him in Mumbai; the Tilak Maharashtra Vidyapeeth (university), among many other educational establishments, recalls his own efforts in the field.[47] This form of memorialization is not limited to Maharashtra; Delhi too has its Tilak Nagar, and his statue stands in Delhi, Kolkata, and elsewhere. As well as a prolific outpouring of popular non-fiction (and some imaginative) literature in Marathi, the number of popular biographies published in English has been steady in the years since his death, witnessing a spurt around his birth centenary; some important works have also been published in Hindi.[48] Tilak has also been the subject of a pioneering 1957 biographical feature film (*Lokmanya Tilak*, dir. Vishram Bedeker) in English and Hindi versions, as well as the 2015 Marathi biopic *Lokmanya: Ek Yugpurush* ('The Man of His Age'). The *Lokamanya Tilak* comic book by Amar Chitra Katha (ACK), a series dedicated to giving Indian children 'a glimpse of their glorious heritage', was published in 1980 in Hindi, Marathi, and English. Tilak's fame, indeed, is sufficient to obliterate the historical contributions of contemporaries and collaborators. The outstanding example of this is in 'Tilak's' initiation of a public Ganapati *utsav* in Maharashtra in the 1890s. The understanding that the festival was Tilak's handiwork is practically universal, as we saw in the Introduction. Yet as we have seen, not only was Tilak not responsible for innovations in Ganesh Chaturthi in 1893 (or those of the immediately preceding years), he was not any more associated with the efforts to popularize them in Maharashtra's first large public Ganesh festival in 1894 than collaborators such as Badekar and Namjoshi.[49] Not only his devotees but also his critics, in academia as much as anywhere, demonstrate this apparent fixation on historical celebrity in negating the corporate nature of the festival's organization and propagation in 1892–1894; its crude assumption of the agency of 'memorable' figures is not an isolated solecism.[50]

---

[47] *TOI*, 27 July 1933.

[48] For instance, the version of Ram Gopal's biography, *Lokamanya Tilaka* (Bombay: Esiya Palisinga Hausa, 1965).

[49] See the discussion 'Tilak and Ganapati' in 'The Nature of the Indian Polity', this volume.

[50] The tendency to refer to *Kesari* and *The Mahratta* as 'Tilak's' papers from their inception, noted earlier, also reflects this focus.

Press accounts during Tilak's lifetime (Tilak's own, of course, and his sympathizers' and allies': a reflection of power within the print culture of Maharashtra in the 1890s and 1900s), burnishing his credentials and celebrity, were, it seems, then constitutive of the 'popular' account of Tilak; and both press accounts directly and (more so, given the appalling survival rate and state of preservation of most regional newspapers of the period) this broader popular belief in general inform academic accounts. It is worth reiterating that the notion of Tilak's authorship of the *utsav* does not originate in 'the archives'; rather, in showing the permeability of the boundary between popular memory and academic history, this case thus demonstrates a recurrent theme, not only in writing on Tilak, but also in the broader historiography of modern South Asia (indeed, historiography more broadly).

Tilak is not predominantly remembered as a thinker (despite the remembrance of the assumed content of his thought). But it would be a mistake to assume that this role is entirely subsumed into Tilak the freedom fighter. Some of his newspaper obituaries specifically refer to him as a political and religious thinker. Almost twenty years later, Bhulabhai Desai, himself a noted man of letters (who would go on to be one of the defence counsels in the first 'Red Fort Trial' of three Indian National Army officers in 1947), claimed in an address at Congress House in Bombay for Tilak's death anniversary that 'Tilak will go down as the Voltaire and Rousseau of India' for his explication of the idea of Swaraj.[51] This may not have happened, though he is sometimes lauded as both patriot and thinker, and his biographies often credit him as a thinker on constitutionalism, for instance—and it has been recently argued that his agitation for self-government drew from and contributed to emerging 'Wilsonian' norms of legitimacy.[52] His full-scale treatments often give a substantial, though as we have seen too discrete, place for his major scholarly works, Bedekar's *Lokmanya Tilak* for instance noting the *Arctic Home* to be 'a

[51] *TOI*, 2 August 1938, 8.
[52] Chief Minister of Maharashtra, Davendra Fadnavis, on the renaming of the garden around Tilak's Chowpatty statue as 'Swaraj Bhoomi', *TOI*, 18 March 2015 (see Introduction); Indira Gandhi also made a point of praising his studies of the Vedas and Gita while garlanding his statue in 1980, *TOI*, 2 August 1980; Tahmankar, *Tilak*, particularly; Miloon Kothari, 'Remembering India's Contributions to the Universal Declaration of Human Rights', *The Wire*, 20 December 2018, https://thewire.in/rights/indias-important-contributions-to-the-universal-declaration-of-human-rights.

remarkable piece of research' for its time. Indeed his immediate obituaries as far away as The Hindu Mandal Ashram of Dar es Salaam noted
the 'greatness' of his works on Hindu scripture.[53] His work on Aryan history has continued to garner public notice: the *Times of India* reported
in 1959 that 'Science Confirms Tilak's Theory' on Arctic origins, and in
recent times Tilak's works have been cited both by popularizing Russian
and Ukrainian scholars to indicate that theirs are antique, white, Aryan
cultures.[54]

His thought on Hindu dharma, as distinct from history, is perhaps the
most important element in his remembrance as a thinker. There has been
a curious tendency to emphasize the profundity of the *Gita Rahasya* by
emphasizing how 'moved to raptures' F. Max Muller was by it, a classic
reversion to foreign authorities to assert the greatness of Indian achievement (it will be recalled that Tilak himself had written an obituary for
the noted Sanskritist fifteen years before the *Gita Rahasya*'s publication),
and its focus on action has been seen as giving 'a political twist to a philosophical theme'.[55] Most significant of all, though, is the state's citation
of the *Gita Rahasya* to provide its definition of Hinduism in the post-
independence period. As mentioned in the Introduction, the Indian
Supreme Court's 1966 definition of Hinduism is taken from Tilak's *shloka*:

Acceptance of the Vedas with reverence; recognition of the fact that
the means to salvation are diverse; and realization of the truth that the
number of gods to be worshipped is large, that indeed is the distinguishing feature of Hindu religion.[56]

For this the court in 1966 cited, without edition or page number, 'B.
G. Tilak's Gitarahasaya' and accepted it as a 'working formula which
may be regarded as fairly adequate and satisfactory'. It was recapitulated

---

[53] *Dar es Salaam Times*, 28 August 1920, 4.

[54] 'Arctic Home of the Aryans: Science Confirms Tilak's Theory' (the interpretation of article's
author Mohanlal Gandhi), 2 August 1959, 8; *TOI*, 25 February 2003, 14, article by Kalpana Sahni.

[55] The phrases are Frank Moraes's, *TOI*, 23 July 1956, 6.

[56] The 1966 case was Sastri Yagnapurushadji vs Muldas Brudardas Vaishya [1966 SCR (3) 242]
(known as the 'Satsangi case', concerning Swaminarayan's followers' claim to have their religion considered distinct from the Hindu religion). Judgement given 14 January 1966. See also
Ronojoy Sen, 'Defining Religion: The Indian Supreme Court and Hinduism', *Heidelberg Papers
in South Asian and Comparative Politics*, 29 (2006).

in a highly controversial judgement in 1995, in which the Ramakrishna Mission was defined, against its own petition, as Hindu (just like the 'Satsangis' in the 1966 case); and ultimately later that same year it underpinned the Supreme Court's milestone judgement that no abstract meaning could confine the terms 'Hindu', 'Hindutva', or 'Hinduism' to the limits of religion, exclusive of the broader 'content of Indian culture and heritage'.[57] As we have noted, this description of Hindu religion is not in fact to be found in the *Gita Rahasya* at all.[58] Extraordinary as it is that the Supreme Court provided an erroneous citation for its definition of the majority religion of India, more interesting, perhaps, is speculation as to its genuine provenance. As it obviously did not come from consultation of the text, the intriguing probability, therefore, is that one of the Justices in 1966 simply remembered this definition as a form of slogan—just as Tilak intended when he composed and promulgated it to consolidate the Hindus of western India in 1900—and, associating it with Tilak, gave it a scholarly attribution to the most famous of Tilak's works.[59]

Most consistently, Tilak has been remembered as an Indian patriot. This prevalence is not unanimity, as we have seen; and still less is this response normative. Powerful, and powerfully felt, rebuttals have always been advanced against the content of his patriotism. But 'Swaraj is my birthright and I will have it' is the legend under his statues at Chowpatty, Ahmedabad, and (placed after independence) in Kolkata; it was also emblazoned on a second commemorative Tilak postage stamp in 1988 (see Figure 6.1) designed by the illustrious M. F. Husain, and is as we have seen a feature of state celebration today.[60] The image evoked is, to use the title of the Amar Chitra Katha comic, the 'Firebrand Nationalist'— and it is remarkably popular, as its echoes in film and print up to today

---

[57] Bramchari Sidheswar Bhai & Ors. etc. vs State of West Bengal etc., 2 July 1995 [1995 SCC (4) 646]; Justice J. S. Verma's judgement in Ramesh Yeshwant Prabhoo vs Shri Prabhakar Kashinath Kunte [1996 SCC (1) 130], concerning electoral 'corrupt practices' regarding appealing for votes on the ground of religion.

[58] See the discussion of the *Gita Rahasya* in Chapter 2.

[59] The antecedent of the Chief Justice during the 1966 case, Pralhad Balacharya Gajendragadkar, born in 1901 and schooled at Satara and at the Deccan College, is perhaps noteworthy here. 'P. B. Gajendragadkar', at https://www.scobserver.in/.

[60] *TOI*, 28 January 1963, 7; the first was a 'birth commemorative stamp' released some years later (see *TOI*, 6 January 1963, 8); 'Tilak Remembered', 23 July 2016 (see Introduction). The history of the expression and its origin in 1916–1917 are discussed in Chapter 3.

भारत INDIA   60
स्वराज्य

स्वराज
मेरा जन्मसिद्ध
अधिकार है ।
बाल गंगाधर
तिलक

60

भारत INDIA   SWARAJ IS MY BIRTHRIGHT
BALGANGADHAR TILAK

Figure 6.1 'Swaraj is my Birthright': Tilak's most famous phrase
is commemorated through M. F. Husain's artwork on this 1988
commemorative postage stamp. Image by author.

suggest (see Figure 6.2).[61] It was tightly associated with the nation, and
the state, in newly independent India. Close to the end of the proceedings
of India's Constituent Assembly in 1949, assembly member S. M. Ghose
from West Bengal took the moment to offer a peroration on 'our journey
which was commenced by the Indian sepoys in 1857', stating that 'I would
be failing in my duty' to not list 'those great leaders, and martyrs': Tilak
was the first on his list.[62] Bedekar's *Lokmanya Tilak* (commissioned by
the Ministry of Information and Broadcasting) assured its audience that

[61] Indu J. Tilak, et al., *Lokamanya Tilak* (Mumbai: Amar Chitra Katha, 1980) (hereafter ACK
Lokamanya Tilak).
[62] Monday 21 November 1949 (Constituent Assembly Debates [Proceedings], vol. XI), https://
loksabha.nic.in/writereaddata/cadebatefiles/C21111949.html, accessed 30 October 2023. He
also credited Aurobindo with instigating the freedom movement, and Gandhi as father of the
nation.

Figure 6.2 Tilak's apotheosis: the July 1908 sedition trial, as rendered on the front cover of Amar Chitra Katha's 'Lokamanya Tilak' children's comic (1980). Image courtesy of Amar Chitra Katha Pvt Ltd.

Tilak's memory remains, 'nourishing the mind and heart of free India', and that his Congress Democratic Party's manifesto anticipated the Indian Constitution. The Home Minster in the same Government dated India's national revival to Tilak's Ganesh Chaturthi instigation.[63] It is unsurprising that this memory could even have been used by Maharashtrian politicians and journalists to instil unity against what they saw as 'insidious forces' such as linguistic separatism in the era of the emergence of the 'pro-Marathi' Shiv Sena in the mid-late 1960s—as much as anything to prevent his appropriation as a Maharashtrian separatist icon.[64] This official insistence is certainly one reason for the continuing popular hold of the idea. Emphasizing the potency, and official endorsement, of this fame as a freedom-fighting patriot, it was the First President of Ghana, Kwame Nkrumah, who unveiled the plaque to Tilak at his London residence, 10 Howley Street, in 1961.[65]

As we saw in the Introduction, Tilak's patriotic memory has also been employed, particularly recently, to buttress subversive critiques of the state—and, further, those finding themselves in opposition to the state are naturally apt to invoke Tilak in support, pointing up how the state in India rests on anti-colonial acts of resistance. Yet it is only partly this that explains the attraction of Tilak to Indian Marxists, as we noted there— despite his opposition to the regulation of land ownership and the protection of tenants, and defence of the interest of Brahmin moneylenders, which saw one academic study of Tilak suggesting that 'he identified himself with the feudal landlord class'.[66] The Marxists' is a wholehearted embrace: and around the same time that study was published, Shripad Amrit Dange, founding member of the Communist Party of India and its leading light in Maharashtra, declared himself Tilakite.[67] Dange himself

---

[63] Kailash Katju, *TOI*, 13 September 1953, 11.

[64] The Bombay Pradesh Congress Committee (BPCC) invoked his 'unforgettable lesson of unity' in August 1967: 'People Urged to Stand by Tilak's Unity Aim', *TOI*, 2 August 1967. See also 'Tilak's Vision', *TOI*, 30 July 1967, 6. Equally, he is taken by Indian officialdom to have endorsed linguistic state boundaries, at least when they were a fait accompli—see D. P. Karmarkar, *Lokmanya Tilak, A Study* (Bombay: Popular Book Depot, 1956), xiv.

[65] *TOI*, 2 March 1961, 7.

[66] N. V. Sovani, 'Economic Thought of Tilak', in N. R. Inamdar, ed., *Political Thought and Leadership of Lokmanya Tilak* (New Delhi: Concept, 1983), 153.

[67] 'Our Comrade in India', *TOI*, 5 April 1981, A1. J. V. Naik cites Dange's admiration in an overdrawn argument of Tilak's Marxism, 'Lokmanya Tilak on Karl Marx and Class Conflict', *EPW*, 34/18 (1 May 1999) 1023–1025.

was in good company here, for Vladimir Lenin had appropriated Tilak in his turn during his life, commenting on the strikes of the Bombay mill hands in July 1908 at the conviction of this 'Indian democrat'.[68] Lenin's own canonical endorsement naturally cast its own shadow. And we may also observe the self-reinforcing nature of his historical fame, as Tilak becomes a figure to attach to a cause in order to burnish it, regardless of his historical content. Thus Indira Gandhi claimed on Tilak's death anniversary in 1976 that the 'India of Tilak's dreams' could only be achieved through a twenty-point economic programme of her government during the Emergency; or, in a revealing and even touching scene, Tilak's statue at Chowpatty was almost overloaded with garlands, from G. L. Reddy of the communist party, the Bombay Pradesh Congress Committee, Praja Socialist, and others at his death anniversary in 1969.[69] These garlands serve as party emblems, and Tilak in death suffers the patriot's curse of having to wear an uncomfortable number.

Tilak and Hindutva

Historically, most controversy has attached to Tilak as an apparent Hindutva forerunner—again, as we saw at the outset, in both academic and popular conception, with both apologists for Hindutva and its opponents sharing the assumption regarding Tilak's stance. Maharashtra was the crucible of Hindutva in the decade after Tilak's death. It was the next generation of ostensibly Tilakite Brahmins who finessed Hindutva in the 1920s, and a succession of Maharashtrian Brahmins (Savarkar, Moonje, Golwalkar, Hedgewar), who interpreted and claimed his legacy, were its fathers. Hindutva, in this critical period of the mid 1920s, thus came to accommodate Tilak, with his self-professed supporters within it claiming that he had anticipated and informed its ideology and organization—but it should be emphasized that this process was neither seamless nor instantaneous. From thenceforth, though, he was largely

---

[68] 'Inflammable Material in World Politics', *Proletary*, 33 (July 23 [August 5] 1908), Marxists Internet Archive, https://www.marxists.org/archive/lenin/works/1908/jul/23.htm, accessed 11 September 2023.

[69] *TOI*, 2 August 1976, 5; *TOI*, 2 August 1969, 5.

viewed from within the Hindutva tradition as one of its own; and it is this process of remembrance that set the tone for how he has been seen since.[70]

As we have seen, Tilak had through his career been indicted as an 'anti-Muslim' communalist, including notably by those associated with the colonial state; Chirol's *Indian Unrest* (1910) underlined the impression. Organized Hindutva was merely incipient by the end of Tilak's life, and indeed his death closely coincided with a pivotal moment in the development of the Hindu right (and, partly correlatively, with Gandhian nationalism). The aftermath of the Mappila revolt of 1921, as has been noted, was significant, giving a spur to the reorganization of the Hindu Mahasabha within the new framework of the 'Hindu Sangathan' movement; 1923 saw the publication, too, of that central text, Savarkar's *Hindutva*. It is not merely, though, that organized Hindutva of the early-mid-1920s was able to take Tilak's output and place it in its new contexts and frameworks, which it was said to support: that is, that the changing content of his remembrance was a function of new political developments. It should be recalled that the Hindu Mahasabha had actually decried Tilak's stance at Lucknow in 1916. Those very developments of post-1921 had, in some measure, by the Mahasabha and others, been anticipated. And later yoking Tilak to them meant a substantial reworking of his legacy, from his attested hostility to their earlier expressions to something new.

The early part of the 1920s saw a notable celebration of Tilak as an explicit secularist. Indeed it also saw some sympathetic response to him by Indian Muslims, which was in turn read as indicative of Tilak—as shown by the enthusiastic noting in the press of Muslim speakers at his 1920 memorials. A revealing statement of remembrance from this period was from Maulana Mohammad Ali, before his alienation from the Congress politics and ultimate espousal of the Muslim League, referring to Tilak as his 'guru' (he had yet to fall under Gandhi's own spell) in his reply to a Gandhi speech marking Tilak's anniversary in 1921.[71] For Tilak's fellow former 'extremist' Bipin Chandra Pal, speaking in the heat of the *Khilafat* agitation the following year, Tilak would have stood against it, not for reasons of Hindu sentiment, but because he understood that to

---

[70] For 1920s Hindutva, see Jaffrelot, *Reader*, 17 ff.
[71] *Mahratta*, 24 July 1921, 357.

'mix up nationalist politics with mediaeval religion' would be dangerous; thus Tilak never appealed to 'his Brahmin sanctity' among the Hindu masses (a position contrasting with 'the new leadership in the country'). Tilak rather stood against this for a fully-fledged 'secular state' independent of any 'credal and denominational peculiarities'.[72] The Bombay Government, meanwhile, noted that a different interpretation stalked the land: during 1922 a fraud was apparently spreading selling 'Muslim Unity Bonds' with Tilak's image on them, an overt visual appropriation of Tilak to *Khilafat*, perpetrated by 'plausible scoundrels', in the words of the Sind Police Gazette.[73]

Such views could not last unchanged as the 1920s progressed, and the communal atmosphere deteriorated. Within Maharashtra, Tilakites associated him increasingly with Hindu nationalist politics, as it emerged strongly in the region. A new note is detectable within the defences of Tilak as a figure of communal unity by 1924: one writer in *Mahratta* held that such a principle had indeed been 'taught' by Tilak, but it was unity 'with honour'; the dishonouring of Hindus by Muslims was said, with a hint of menace, to be intolerable to Tilak (as would be Hindus dishonouring Muslims—which 'fortunately they have not hitherto done').[74] On the other hand, that April one Subedar Abdul Hamad told an 'Enquiry Committee for ascertaining the rights of Hindus and Moslems regarding the playing of music opposite mosques' in Nagpur that Tilak first 'sowed discord between the Hindus and Muslims' by inciting propaganda and organizing Ganapati processions.[75] By 1925, a wholesale change in Tilak's perspectives had occurred as far as *Mahratta* was concerned. In a commemorative editorial that August, the paper hailed Tilak as 'The Unerring Statesman' and noted India was heading 'at breakneck speed to communalism of the worst type', sarcastically noting, with not a word regarding the Lucknow Pact, that separate electorates and separate representation were essential 'if poison can ever be nectar'.[76] An account by

[72] *Mahratta*, 30 July 1922, 361.
[73] MSA HD (SPL) 355 (20) (A) 1921–1923, 'Tilak swaraj fund' (Sind Police Gazette, 1 December 1922).
[74] V. M. Bhat, *Mahratta*, 3 August 1924, 389.
[75] *TOI*, 2 April 1924, 10; *TOI*, 7 April 1924, 10.
[76] *Mahratta*, 2 August 1925, 374.

Mavji Govindji published in a Marathi-English collection of reminiscences in 1925 described Tilak as a protector of Hinduism, and as such a representative of Maharashtra, the 'safest asylum of Hindu culture' and the 'strong protecting arm of Hindu liberties', a place where the zenana and other Muslim corruptions were unknown.[77]

One crucial element in this Maharashtrian milieu was Hindutva's shaping ideologue, V. D. Savarkar. Indeed, Savarkar embraced Tilak in the very issue of *Mahratta* just discussed. Under a heading labelling Tilak 'The Foremost Forerunner of Hindu Sanghatan' [sic] (a subsequent vehicle for the Mahasabha's politics, meaning 'Hindu Organisation for Unity'), Savarkar urged that Tilak 'did not ask Hindus to go in sackcloth and ashes for the crime of defending themselves' against the swaggering Muslims, but rather rejoiced at their 'virility, communal strength and courage'.[78] Tilak's rousing of Hindudom through the Shivaji festival (setting the tone for a 'racial tribute at the feet of our racial Heroes'), as well as the 'great racial festival' of Ganapati, and the *Gita Rahasya*'s 'broad and deep foundations', were credited as the three great wellsprings of Sanghatan. Savarkar retained his reverence for Tilak. In his address to the 21st Session of the Hindu Mahasabha in 1939, Savarkar reminded his audience that it was in spite of the warnings of 'the Great Tilak' that Gandhi committed Congress 'to the purely communal, religious and extra-territorial Khilafat'; and he exhibited fury at the deceitful use of Tilak's name for the Swaraj fund, half of which 'was spent in vilifying and exterminating the Tilakite principles' and to 'enrich the Moslem purse to drive the propaganda for "Khilafat"'.[79] That is not to say that Tilak had successfully pre-empted Savarkar's own definition of a Hindu in *Essentials of Hindutva* (1923). It was, for Savarkar, merely a very large 'sect of Hinduism or Hindu Dharma which the late Lokamanya Tilak framed in the famous verse'; 'excellent so far as it goes, [it] is in fact not a definition of Hindu Dharma, much less of Hindutva'.[80]

[77] S. V. Bapat (ed.), *Lokmanya Tilak yanchya Aathavarnee va Aakhyaayika* ('Reminiscences and Anecdotes of Lokamanya Tilak') (hereafter, Bapat (ed.), *Reminiscences*), v. 2 (Poona: Author, 1925), 627.

[78] *Mahratta*, 2 August 1924, 375–376.

[79] Reproduced in *Hindu Rashtra Darshan: A Collection of the Presidential Speeches Delivered from the Hindu Mahasabha Platform* (1949), https://savarkar.org/en/pdfs/hindu-rashtra-darshan-en-v002.pdf, 54–55; 'The Hindu Sanghatanists [sic] should not contribute a single pie to the congressite Kasturba fund', 14 May 1944, reproduced in *Historic Statements by Savarkar* (1967), https://savarkar.org/en/encyc/2017/5/23/2_12_15_55_historic_statements_by_savarkar.v001.pdf_1.pdf, 71.

[80] Savarkar, *Hindutva*, 109–110.

The subsequent tradition of Maharashtrian Hindutva ideologues invoked Tilak, and has largely been seen as Tilakite. Keshav Baliram Hedgewar, founder of the Rashtriya Swayamsevak Sangh ('National Volunteer Association', or RSS) in Nagpur in 1925, as we saw in the Introduction, is simply referred to in a post-2014 Government-published biography as a disciple of Tilak.[81] Hedgewar's own self-designated successor after 1940, M. S. Golwalkar, referred to Tilak as 'great *karmayogi*'.[82] Tilak's emphatically non-Hindutva interpretation of Aryan origins in *The Arctic Home* (as discussed in Chapter 3, the favoured interpretation is that Aryans were autochthonous to India) required some artful recasting, which Golwalkar provided in *We or Our Nationhood Defined* (1939):

> We may agree with him that originally the Aryans i.e. the Hindus lived in the region of the North Pole. But, he was not aware that, in ancient times, the North Pole and with it the Arctic Zone was not where it is today.[83]

Citing some modern authorities, Golwalkar concludes:

> in a nutshell ... the North Pole is not stationary and quite long ago it was in that part of the world, which, we find, is called Bihar and Orissa at the present ... If this be so, did we leave the Arctic Zone and come to Hindusthan or were we all along here ... ?

Had Tilak known this, he would have declared ' "The Arctic Home in the Vedas" was verily in Hindusthan itself'.[84]

In the post-independence phase, with the dominance at the centre of the Congress party, and the decline of the Hindu right in general in the wake of Gandhi's assassination, most prominent celebrations of Tilak emphasized his commitment to communal unity and harmony. Ram Gopal's 1956 biography, insisting in its preface that Tilak had 'no communalism in him', is typical.[85] Indeed, this became something of an 'official'

[81] Sinha, *Hedgewar*. Its publication date of 2015 is relevant due to the coming to power of the BJP in 2014.
[82] M. S. Golwalkar, *Bunch of Thoughts* (Bangalore: Vikrama Prakashan, 1966).
[83] M. S. Golwalkar, *We or Our Nationhood Defined* (Nagpur: Bharat Publications, 1939), 44.
[84] Ibid., 45.
[85] Gopal, *Tilak*, vi.

view: D. P. Karmarkar, a minister of state in the Congress Government, commended in a 1956 Tilak study his religious impartiality and 'completely secular' outlook; N. G. Jog's 1962 biography (published by the Ministry of Information and Broadcasting), in discussing the 'national festivals', highlighted 'social consolidation'—though also noted that Tilak was fighting against anti-Hindu attitudes which coloured the Muslim 'suspicious' response to both.[86] Into the 1980s and 1990s, works from a Congress perspective had similar emphases, noting for instance his role in the Lucknow Pact.[87] Such a view naturally has broader purchase, too: the ACK Tilak comic book (1980) stated the Ganapati festival was a 'forum for bringing people of various communities together', and added the perennial story of a Muslim warder slipping Tilak extra food supplies to keep up his strength during his 1897 imprisonment; and, as we have seen, some more recent studies have argued similarly.[88]

The resurgence of the Hindu right in Indian politics from the mid-1970s brought with it other interpretations of Tilak. As it claimed power in the form of the ascendant Janata Party (forerunner of the BJP), it laid renewed claim to Tilak itself: on his death centenary in 1977, the Prime Minister Morarji Desai urged people to implement the patriotism he taught, adding 'now we have to go from Swaraj to Ram Rajya [the rule of Ram]'.[89] At the corresponding event the following year, G. B. Kanitkar of the Janata party in Maharashtra recalled that during the initial stages of the Emergency (lasting 1975–1977) several parties opposed to the ruling Congress organized a clandestine meeting at the Tilak statue 'out of reverence', in defiance of a ban on assemblies, showing the power of Tilak as a symbol of patriotic resistance under these circumstances for the Hindu right in particular, at a crucial moment in its revival.[90] Of course, this celebration of Tilak as proto Hindu nationalist led to a corresponding renewed scrutiny and criticism of him. By the mid-1990s, press opposition to once again resurgent Hindutva

---

[86] Ibid., xiii; Jog, *LBGT*, 47, 51.

[87] G. P. Pradhan, *Lokmanya Tilak* (New Delhi: National Book Trust, 1994), 115 emphasized that Tilak was the deciding factor in bringing Hindus on board. See also the Congress Centenary Committee's publication, Nihar Nandan Singh, *Lokamanya Bal Gangadhar Tilak: The Life and Achievements of a Mass Leader and Fighter for India's freedom* (New Delhi, 1985), which declared he 'was not a communalist' (103).

[88] ACK *Lokamanya Tilak*, 14, 22. See also Sorab Ghaswalla, *Lokmanya Tilak: Symbol of Swaraj* (New Delhi, 2003), 25.

[89] 'Follow Tilak's Footsteps, says Morarji', *TOI*, 2 August 1977, 4.

[90] *TOI*, 2 August 1978, 4. See Jaffrelot, *Hindu Nationalist Movement*, 272.

politics, in the wake of the destruction of the Babri Masjid at Ayodhya, was a mature phenomenon; one representative writer in the *Times of India* in 1995 claimed that the 'BJP is using a fascist ideology to cause social divisions', using the methods of 'Tilak and other militant nationalists who mobilised the masses for the freedom struggle by invoking Vande Mataram'.[91] Even on the left of Indian politics, though, there has sometimes been a move to spare Tilak the worst ire: the veteran commentator Praful Bidwai for instance blamed Tilak simply for defeating the reformism of Agarkar and thus opening the space 'for his epigones—narrow-minded, xenophobic counter-reformist Hindus who sought to pervert Tilak's own politics' and 'hijack the Congress towards political Hinduism': the RSS and Hindu Mahasabha were among the 'legatees' of that perversion.[92] The renewed vigour of Hindutva politics leading to and following from the BJP's election victory of 2014 similarly provides the context in terms of the use of Hindutva symbols—like Gandhi's killer Nathuram Godse—to which, conversely, Tilak is consciously linked.[93] And, of course, in this context too, Tilak remains a symbol to evoke and control for the Hindu right.

Because of this capacity to legitimize or delegitimize trends in current politics, Tilak, prominent among other figures, has been the subject of bitter politicized rows about the content of school textbooks in India since the 1970s. Once more it was the Janata Government in 1977 that ushered in a new phase of such contestation: Bipan Chandra's *Modern India* (1971), published by the National Council of Educational Research and Training (NCERT), a body of the Government of India, was indicted in a note sent by the Prime Minister's principal secretary to the Education Minister, claiming the work held 'nationalists' like Tilak and Ghose 'responsible for creating disunity between Hindus and Muslims' and urging consideration of withdrawal of the work and closer scrutinization of publications by the ministry.[94] Chandra, while very complimentary about

---

[91] 'Democracy devalued by money and muscle', Gurmukh Singh, *TOI*, 28 February 1995, 16. The patriotic song 'Vande Mataram' (usually translated 'Mother I bow to thee!'), originating in Bankim Chatterjee's *Anandamath*, is commonly criticized for equating Hinduism with the nation.

[92] *TOI*, 13 November 1990, 12.

[93] This is discussed in the Introduction in this volume.

[94] Lloyd I. Rudolph and Susanne Hoeber Rudolph, 'Rethinking Secularism: Genesis and Implications of the Textbook Controversy 1977–1979', *Pacific Affairs*, 56/1 (1983), 25 ff; see also Sylvie Guichard, *The Construction of History and Nationalism in India: Textbooks, Controversies and Politics* (London: Routledge, 2010).

Tilak's bravery and service, does note that 'unfortunately while militant nationalism was a great step forward in every other respect, it was a step back in respect of the growth of national unity', decrying the strong 'religious and Hindu tinge' of this politics, and citing the Shivaji and Ganapati festivals in particular: to declare 'Shivaji a "national" hero was to project into past history the communal outlook of 20th century India.'[95] Such disputes reached another high point with the coming to power of the BJP in 1998, and the publication by NCERT of the National Curriculum Framework for School Education (2000), which was criticized as a vehicle for Hindutva cultural politics.[96] In the ensuing years, what William Dalrymple has described as a 'passionately contested battle' raged over India's history.[97] In relation to Tilak, the most heated was not over NCERT books propagating Hindutva, but over their alleged spurious secularism. NCERT's Class X social science textbook *India and the Contemporary World II* (2007) contains a chapter on 'Nationalism in India' stating that 'nationalism spreads when people begin to believe that they are all part of the same nation', and reproduces an early twentieth-century print of a 'secular' Tilak with the caption: 'Notice how Tilak is surrounded by symbols of unity. The sacred institutions of different faiths (temple, church, masjid) frame the central figure.'[98] The 'Hindu Janajagruti Samiti', an organization established in 2002 to 'reinstate Dharma, that is, to establish the Hindu Nation', and claiming (as of 2017) 160 educational centres throughout India, published an online critique of this 'wrong history', refuting the 'so foolish' attempt to show Tilak as secularist, and noting he 'tried to bring Hindus together' with Ganapati and Shivaji festivals and the *Gita Rahasya*, 'but there is no mention of it anywhere in the chapter'; 'propagation of equality of all religions and secularism' it insisted, was undertaken by Gandhi, an unadmired figure for the Samiti.[99] And these

---

[95] Bipan Chandra, *Modern India* (New Delhi, 1971), Ch. 12, 196 ff, 252–253.

[96] S. U. Khan, *Saffronisation of Education* (Delhi: Institute of Objective Studies, 2004) is an indictment of the Framework.

[97] 'India: The War Over History', *New York Review of Books*, 7 April 2005, https://www.nybooks.com/; the essays in *Communalisation of Education: The History Textbook Controversy* by the Delhi Historians' Group (2001[?]), http://www.sacw.net/India_History/DelHistorians.pdf, offer a largely Indian liberal perspective on the controversy up to 2001.

[98] Reprinted November 2013, 70.

[99] https://www.hindujagruti.org/hindu-issues/distortion-of-history/school-textbooks/ncert-textbook-controversy/controversial-matter, accessed 30 April 2017. It also complained of the description of the Taj Mahal as a Muslim symbol.

attitudes were reflected in increasingly bold activism over subsequent years from those identifying with Hindu nationalism to contest the content of educational materials, notably in the case of the University of Mumbai textbook proscribed in 2016 (ironically) for implying Tilak was 'anti-secular'.[100]

Such textbook controversies over Tilak have had their counterpart in Pakistan. A widely noted Islamization of Pakistan's public culture, also occurring from the 1970s and associated with the aftermath of the Bangladesh War and the coming to power of Zia-ul-Haq, has led to what has been described as a 'political abuse of history' operating broadly in modern times, in which an Islamized version of it serves to confer legitimacy on the state.[101] Within this framework, Tilak is seen as an irreconcilably violent Hindu chauvinist. The *History of Pakistan* by Rafiullah Shehab (1989) blames Hindus' attitudes in general for communal ill-will from 1861, leading ultimately to the necessity of separatism: the 'Hindu revivalist movements reached their climax and took militant force under the leadership of Mr B. G. Tilak who espoused Shivaji cult and Sangathan movements', the latter being a 'paramilitary organisation, the purpose of which was to train a group of people in handling the light weapons efficiently to fight against Muslims'.[102] Jinnah, meanwhile, was wholly responsible for the Lucknow Pact.[103] M. A. Aziz's *History of Pakistan* (1979) concurs that Tilak 'initiated the cult of Shivaji to bring violence in the [Congress nationalist] movement'.[104] This is testament to the power of politics to inflect memory: the father of Pakistan, after all, had chaired Tilak's Bombay memorial meeting in 1920, describing him as 'the greatest political and social figure in this country', 'sagacious and far-seeing', 'worshipped by hundreds, followed by thousands and admired by millions'.[105]

---

[100] See Introduction in this volume.

[101] See Marie Lall, 'Educate to Hate: The Use of Education in the Creation of Antagonistic National Identities in India and Pakistan', *Compare*, 38/1 (2008), 103–119; see also the Sustainable Development Policy Institute Report, *The Subtle Subversion: the State of Curricula and Textbooks in Pakistan*, ed. A. H. Nayyar and Ahmad Salim (Islamabad, 2003 [?]), https://sdpi.org/. I am indebted to Dr Tania Saeed for sharing her expertise on this issue.

[102] Rafiullah Shehab, *History of Pakistan* (Lahore: Sang-e-Meel Publications, 1989), 103.

[103] Ibid., 112.

[104] M. A. Aziz, *A History of Pakistan: Past and Present* (Lahore: Sang-e-Meel, 1979), 132.

[105] M. A. Jinnah, reported in *TOI*, 9 October 1920, 10.

Non–Gandhianism, violence, and 'extremism'

Entwined with discussions over Tilak's communal politics is an en-during controversy over his attitude to violence. Many of the same ex-ponents of Hindutva, like Savarkar and Moonje, opposed non-violence, and associated Tilak with that opposition. And it is also associated, for them and more broadly, with a Maharashtra-specific, non-Gandhian, self-consciously 'muscular' patriotism. Opponents of Hindutva have also been at the forefront of criticizing Tilak's violence—although the insistence by some that Tilak is thus criticized is more visible than that criticism itself. The half decade immediately following his death, as we alluded to above, saw disputes as to the direction of Indian politics under Gandhian leadership, in which Tilak ultimately became a rallying point for those opposed to Gandhian non-violence and non-cooperation. Already in August 1920, the author of an open letter in the *Times of India* to Lala Lajpat Rai, the President of the forthcoming special Congress ses-sion, suggested another dialogue between Gandhi and Tilak had taken place: 'I understand from hearsay (I would be very sorry if it is not a fact) that he on his deathbed told Mr. Gandhi to give up non-Cooperation as it is bound to fail'.[106] Maharashtra, with its self-conscious and carefully nurtured (not least by Tilak) martial traditions, was at the forefront of this.[107] The *Mahratta* in July–August 1921, as we have seen, editorialized in support of Gandhi, but this support appears to have been on a knife-edge. In its pages Kelkar anxiously assured Gandhi that Maharashtra had 'faith' like the 'religious saints of Maharashtra' in non-cooperation, but insisted that Tilak would have taken Gandhi aside and have him mod-erate his programme: its aim was too broad to hit its mark.[108] Joseph Baptista, another former Tilak lieutenant, remained all for Tilak's 're-sponsive cooperation', and Kelkar noted 'the great democracy in India' would have to decide who was right.[109] By the following year's Tilak death centenary, following the crisis of the campaign after the incident at Chauri Chaura, *Mahratta* was calling for a return to Tilak's way, as

---

[106] Letter to Lala Lajpat Rai from 'Vencam', Special Session Congress, *TOI*, 5 August 1920, 11.
[107] This expands on Cashman's observation that many Maharashtrians, such as the Tilakite M. R. Jayakar, saw a non-Gandhian 'Maratha mind' at work. Cashman, *Myth*, 211.
[108] *Mahratta*, 24 July 1921, 358.
[109] Ibid., 359.

'Non-cooperation has not fulfilled its solemn purpose'; it defied reason to give up the 'captured strongholds' of the councils by refusing to cooperate in elections to them.[110] G. S. Khaparde talked of 'the Tilak party' and its distinct policy based upon the Congress Democratic Party's manifesto, and of Maharashtra as the crucible of the coming change; others spoke of the wisdom of this vilified 'Maharashtra party'.[111] The paper regretted the un-Tilakite 'dilettante nationalism' of deferring to Gandhi in 1920 to see if he could redeem his promise of Swaraj within a year.[112] Agreeing, V. M. Bhat added he was present at the Tilak-Gandhi meeting and remembers 'as clear as anything' that Tilak was against non-cooperation.[113] Such a shift is more broadly visible by 1922. Besant's *Future of Indian Politics*, published that year, queried the Gandhian leadership: it was the 'queerest revolution that ever was', since Gandhi replaced Tilak, with the 'queerest leader, and has now the queerest collapse'; a Tilak memorial compilation noted that Tilak would not have turned opponent of non-cooperation, but would have 'never have allowed it to run along channels of metaphysical abstractions', nor would it have 'deviated from normal political activity' or 'degenerated into a personal religion—a peculiar type of fetishism characteristic of the primitive ages'.[114]

This set the pattern for the mid 1920s. By 1924 Tilak's anniversary was hailed by Motilal Nehru, who noted how in his 'Tenets of the New Party' speech 'we have the ground fully prepared for Mahatma Gandhi', but added significantly that Tilak 'eschewed religion in politics' and disbelieved in 'avoid and suffer', his Maratha blood rebelling at the thought of the 'pseudo asceticism'.[115] Reminiscences in Marathi published in 1924 contained many accounts emphasizing Tilak's enthusiasm for violence: G. V. Ketkar gave another version of the Tilak-Gandhi dialogue in which Tilak specified 'I consider armed rebellion also to be constitutional' and asked only for an 'eight anna guarantee' for him to then 'trust in God for the other eight annas and rise in rebellion'; V. M. Potdar insisted Tilak specified he needed to see 25,000 men ready to rebel before

[110] 30 July 1922, 358.
[111] Ibid., 360; For example, one K. R. Bodas, ibid., 368.
[112] Ibid., 362.
[113] Ibid., 365.
[114] Annie Besant, *Future of Indian Politics* (Adyar; Benares: Theosophical Publishing House, 1922), 259; *All About Lok* (biographical sketch by S. Airavatam, cxii).
[115] *Mahratta*, 27 July 1924, 364.

he did so, while G. S. Marathe said he asked only for 500; V. M. Bhat recorded him bragging about having attempted violence when younger.[116] At the same time, *Mahratta* published a sonnet by one Raoji Bin Ramji, an extrametrical adaptation of 'London, 1802' by Wordsworth:

> Lokamanya! Thou shouldst be living at this hour; Hind sorely needs thee ... Foul times we are in, while maudlin Ahimsa—/ Deaf to Lord Shri Krishna's words of wisdom—/ Bestrides the robust spirit of puissant Hind![117]

Romain Rolland's *Mahatma Gandhi*, published the same year, apparently drew a favourable response in Maharashtra, and *Mahratta* echoed it that Gandhi's leadership was fundamentally spiritual, Tilak's political, even wishing—somewhat surprisingly, given previous 'Tilakite' insistence on Swaraj before reform—that Tilak and Gandhi had led sister movements for political and social renewal.[118] *Mahratta*, issuing the call 'Back to Tilak', underlined that Tilak believed in violence if possible and necessary because he 'was a hero born on the lap of Maharashtra'.[119] The gendered critique became explicit: his death anniversary in 1925 was marked in its pages by one by Tilakite Chitpavan, noting Tilak's espousal of 'manly retaliation', and underlining his point: 'the creed of Lokamanya was manliness; the creed of Mahatmaji is non-violence'.[120] The Gita, which he described as 'the common prayer-book of Lokamanya's school', denounced the Gandhian preference for death over lifting a hand against violence, as 'not a soldier's death'.[121] Dissent from Gandhian priorities through the 1930s, especially in Maharashtra, continued to cohere around the issue of violence, and use Tilak as a touchstone.[122]

Accounts of Tilak since have strongly tended towards emphasizing Tilak's realist approach to politics and acceptance of non-violence.[123]

---

[116] Bapat (ed.), *Reminiscences*, i. 21 ff (Ketkar); 77 (Potdar); 66 ff (Marathe); 71 ff (Bhat)

[117] *Mahratta*, 27 July, 374. Bin Ramji appears not to have published poetry again.

[118] *Mahratta*, 3 August, 383.

[119] Ibid.

[120] R. V. Patavardhan, 'The True Non-Violence', *Mahratta*, 2 August 1925, 378–379.

[121] Ibid.

[122] See Savarkar's and Moonje's speeches on the Arms Act, and Maharashtrian military volunteering and non-acceptance of non-violence, on Tilak's birthday in 1938: MSA HD (SPL) 953 A (1938).

[123] Exceptions are rare: but the noted post-independence journalist and editor Frank Moraes referred to the 'unusual blend of the conservative and the revolutionary' (echoing contemporary

Parvate's biography is exemplary, devoting a special section to Tilak's 'attitude to [the] cult of violence': arguing Tilak's unconcern for 'conscience and scruples' and exclusive focus on Swaraj, Parvate nonetheless is clear that he preferred the steady technique of non-violent agitation, rather than 'short cuts' with their attendant risks.[124] Though he is explicit that Tilak did not share Gandhi's doctrinaire opposition to violence, the notion that the careful legality (in Tilak's own view) of his writings was only a cloak to his complicity in secret violent conspiracies is dismissed as a psychologically comforting confection.[125] Parvate's conviction is occasionally buttressed by an apparent naïvety in interpreting Tilak's interest in physical violence, suggesting that he was merely 'curious to know what a bomb was like, what a machine gun looked like'.[126] This interpretation, rather like that regarding his communal inclusivity, was also favoured in demi-official accounts, such as Jog's state-published biography, in which Tilak's pragmatic eschewing of violence coexists with a 'benevolent interest' in armed Indian revolutionaries.[127] Within this broad consensus, a Maharashtrian non-Gandhian note is detectable. R. P. Paranjpye (who was generous despite their sharp disagreements during Tilak's life) marked Tilak's centenary in the *Times of India* by noting Tilak's 'severely practical' approach, to politics as to violence, though adding in a coda that Tilak was 'fortunate in the time of his death' as it saved him from having to go against Gandhi.[128] Keer's biography also states that Tilak was plotting an armed revolt; and the pragmatism of Tilak's use of Congress-based agitation instead is placed in sharp contrast to Gandhi, with the time-honoured barb noting that 'Tilak did not make a fetish of non-violence'.[129] One further notable feature of Tilak's remembrance over the long-term is its association with physicality as distinct from violence: the 1957 *Lokmanya* film, for instance, associates the 'political awakening' of the Ganesh festival visually with a scene of physical training and

---

British critiques), comparing him to Vallabhbhai Patel. Moraes's statement that he believed in 'political terrorism' is especially atypical. *TOI*, 23 July 1956, 6.

[124] Parvate, *Tilak*, 499.
[125] Ibid., 501.
[126] Ibid., 506.
[127] Jog, *LBGT*, 179.
[128] 23 July 1956, 10.
[129] Keer, *Tilak*, 2nd ed., Preface, 448.

wrestling, and Tilak's personal valuing of physical strength is noted here and elsewhere.[130] A point about the physical energies of Tilak's politics is thus suggested.

Many of these debates about the violence of Tilak's politics express themselves in contests over the term 'extremist'. From the very beginning, this term, of impeccable colonial pedigree in describing an undesirable, was a point of tension: the Reuters newswire announcing Tilak's death was taken to task for calling him an 'extremist leader'.[131] During his career, Tilak tackled the delegitimizing insult, most famously in his 'Tenets of the New Party' speech: 'Extremist is an expression of progress' said Tilak; and thus 'we are Extremists to-day and our sons will call themselves Extremists and us Moderates'.[132] Yet this tendency to take ownership of the term and define its meaning has not been consistently taken up by Tilak's proponents. Controversy over the term flared again from the mid-2000s, when the labels given to his politics in school textbooks, particularly labels carrying connotations of physical violence, became—like his description as 'anti-secular' (or alternatively as secular)—a significant issue. Indeed, many of the same forces were ranged on the same sides in each of these debates. In textbooks in use in the 1980s and 1990s, 'extremist' was commonly used interchangeably with nationalist and/or militant, in contrast to 'moderate', to describe the distinctions in Indian politics during Tilak's career: Tilak is captioned in one 'addressing a meeting of the Nationalists (Extremists)'; Chandra's *Modern India* (discussed above) meanwhile discusses 'militant nationalism (also known as Extremism)'.[133] Yet in August 2006, a BJP member of the Rajya Sabha objected (once more) to Chandra's work, not apparently accurately, for calling Tilak along with Aurobindo Ghose and Bipin Chandra Pal 'terrorists', an early salvo in a tediously repetitive dispute.[134] Apparently this particular objection rests on the conflating of the terms 'extremist' and 'terrorist' in the minds of some readers of such works, in an era when 'extremism' was a term routinely

---

[130] See, for instance, the account of Tilak's youth in ACK *Lokamanya Tilak*.

[131] *East African Chronicle*, 21 August, 7.

[132] 'Tenets of the New Party', 2 January 1907, *Speeches*, 55.

[133] *India's Struggle for Independence* (Delhi, NCERT, 1985); Chandra chapter 14 p. 235 and ff.

[134] The member was Ravi Shanker Prasad: 'Noisy scenes in RS over distorted textbooks', *Financial Express*, August 18th 2006 https://www.financialexpress.com/archive/noisy-scenes-in-rs-over-distorted-textbooks/174685/.

attached in the global news media and elsewhere to the Islamist-inspired terrorism of Al Qaida and related groups. Thus the implicit acceptance of the colonial meaning of 'extremist' was echoed by the up-take of the same globally used term for illegitimate political (Islamist) violence, and this gave extra urgency to its rebuttal. Hence the RSS ideologue Devendra Swaroop in July 2006 diagnosed a group of what he labelled 'Marxist' historians in India who 'still love to use the language of their colonial masters': citing the NCERT social science textbook *Modern India*, which stated that Tilak, Lajpat Rai, and Ghose, 'came to be known as extremists', Swaroop claimed it is 'beyond our imagin-ation' that patriots could thus 'be termed as terrorists'.[135] It was in an escalation of such tendencies that serial objector Dina Nath Batra of the RSS education wing Vidya Bharati petitioned the Delhi High Court in 2011, as we saw in the Introduction, stimulating the ministerial inter-vention of Smriti Irani on his side. The proscription of the language of 'extremism' for Tilak et al., as such cases show, is consistently associated with the BJP and the Hindu right, often in stated opposition to leftist or 'neocolonialist' viewpoints. This proscription of language which the Hindu right's ideological opponents might use to connote disapproval is a strategy to deny them rhetorical space, though it commensurately forecloses interrogation of the legitimacy of the violence of Tilak's pol-itics, enlarging its scope for influence on Indian society. The eclipse of Congress in Maharashtra and the growth there of the Hindu right, meanwhile, also coincides with the new flowering of Maharashtra's per-ennial celebration of Tilak's muscular patriotism, with, as seen in the Introduction, Pehlwani wrestlers accompanying him on Maharashtra's 2017 Republic Day parade float, and his endorsement of political assas-sination being celebrated in *Ek Yugpurush*.[136]

---

[135] By Arjun Dev & Indira Arjun Dev (Delhi, NCERT 1989, reprinted 2002). This should not be confused with Chandra, *Modern India*, criticised similarly. Davendra Swaroop, 'They baffle us with their Goebbelsian mischief' *Organiser*, 2nd July 2006 https://organiser.org/

[136] The BJP and Shiv Sena between them won forty-one out of forty-eight seats in the Lok Sabha in the 2014 general election, and the BJP subsequently gained a plurality in the Maharashtra Legislative Assembly.

Gender, caste, and *Arya* supremacy: criticisms and responses

Unsurprisingly given the animus exhibited by non-Brahmin political organizers and spokesmen in Maharashtra during his lifetime, Tilak consistently continued to attract similar criticism for his views on caste and *Arya* supremacy. Indeed, much of this grew out of the increased vigour of non-Brahmin political agitation, and Tilak's dismissal of it, between 1917 and 1920. As has been demonstrated, dalit criticism of Tilak continued strongly in the 1920s, and included efforts spearheaded by figures such as Keshavrao Marutirao Jedhe to prevent his memorialization.[137] Out of this Maharashtrian dalit milieu sprang the politics of B. R. Ambedkar, acknowledged by the Round Table Conferences from 1930 as the foremost spokesman for 'untouchable' political demands. Ambedkar's furious attack on Congress nationalism, *What Congress and Gandhi Have Done to the Untouchables* (1946), lists Tilak as first among the Congress villains, setting the tone for its politics: his 'antipathy to the servile classes was quite well known'.[138] Raising a perennial criticism of Tilak, his pressuring to have the Social Conference removed from the Congress pandal in 1895, Ambedkar sees him as representative of a type of Congress nationalist, the 'social Tory and political radical'.[139] Maharashtrian dalits perennially invoke the position taken by Tilak's son Shridharpant, who became an admirer of Ambedkar before killing himself in 1928, his state of mind apparently much affected by the injustices of society and the conservative attitudes, reflecting those of his own father, which prevented their remedying.[140] Keer, Tilak's overwhelmingly sympathetic Maharashtrian Bhandari biographer, chides Tilak's evasiveness on social reform issues, witnessed by for example his refusing a memorial on temples being opened to untouchables, and especially his refusal to put his name to the untouchability motion at the Depressed Classes Conference in March 1918: 'he had nothing to do with such problems which clamoured

[137] See Omvedt *Revolt*; also O'Hanlon, 'Acts'.
[138] B. R. Amedkar, *What Congress and Gandhi Have Done to the Untouchables* (Bombay: Thacker, 1946), 221.
[139] Ibid., 13.
[140] Sanjay Paswan and Paramanshi Jaideva (eds), *Encyclopaedia of Dalits in India*, vol. 13 (Delhi: Kalpaz, 2003), 124.

for social justice and equality'; though a great fighter for freedom, like Winston Churchill he had a blind spot (racism against Indians in the case of Churchill, casteism for Tilak).[141]

Tilak's name has also been anathematized by non-Brahmin politicians in other parts of India, nowhere more so than in the Bahujan Samaj Party (BSP, its name referring to 'people in the majority'), the Uttar Pradesh-based party founded on Ambedkar's centenary in 1984, famed for its agitation against Brahmin societal dominance. For Kanshi Ram, its founder, speaking at a rally in Lucknow district in 1996, 'upper caste'-dominated parties, which deserved to be routed for their corruption, still drew on the philosophy of Tilak, who had opposed the enfranchisement of the lower castes, won for them later by Ambedkar.[142] It is not a surprise, then, that one of the slogans most associated with Ram and his protégé Mayawati has 'Tilak' standing for all the hated Brahmins: 'Tilak, Traju aur Talwar—inko maro jute char' (beat the Brahmins, Banias and Thakurs with shoes).[143] Tilak's 'Arya' chauvinism naturally saw him criticized by 'Periyar' E. V. Ramasami, the leading light of the 'Self Respect' movement from the mid-1920s and the later Dravida Kazhagam (Dravidian Association), both of which were concerned with the burnishing of lower-caste and Dravidian non-*Arya* identities. Taking aim at the great slogan of Tilak's Swaraj politics, Periyar stated in 1927 that since Tilak was a varnashrama Brahmin, belief in superiority to others was his 'birthright'; his Swaraj was a hoax, only the birthright of 'self-respect' giving rise to true Swaraj.[144] Tilak's conception of Aryan history has also been contested by dalit activists. The perennial insistence on the autochthony of dalits carries an implicit rebuttal of Tilak's prestigious Brahmin origin story, and in this connection his name need not be mentioned for his memory to be evoked.[145] Indeed, it sometimes is: Kanshi Ram's 1996 speech mentioned

[141] Keer, *Tilak*, 387, 449. The Bhandaris were listed as one of Maharashtra's Other Backward Classes in 1993, see http://www.bcmbcmw.tn.gov.in/obc/faq/maharashtra.pdf (Government of Tamil Nadu, Backward Classes and Most Backward Classes Welfare Department).

[142] Speech at Mohanlalganj, *TOI*, 22 March 1996, 9.

[143] Mayawati has recently—unconvincingly for many—attempted to deny the slogan. See 'Mayawati is Suddenly on the Defensive. Is BSP Trailing in UP Elections?', *India Today*, 5 September 2016, http://indiatoday.intoday.in.

[144] *Kudi Arasu*, 9 January 1927, cited in Periyar E. V. Ramasami, *Words of Freedom: Ideas of a Nation* (New Delhi: Penguin, 2010), 3.

[145] See Kancha Ilaiah, 'Towards the Dalitization of the Nation', in Partha Chatterjee, ed., *Wages of Freedom: Fifty Years of the Indian Nation-state* (Delhi; Oxford: Oxford University Press, 1998) on the resilience of the trope of autochthony among dalit activists.

above included a reference to the BSP being composed of the 'indigenous people', since cheated of their rights by 'wily Brahmins', and it is perhaps not coincidental that he singled out Tilak among those who had done so. Around the same time, one historical account, *Autochthon of India and the Aryan Invasion* (1995), by S. K. Biswas, President of the dalit network the D. R. Ambedkar Vichar Manch, mocked Tilak by pointing out the absence of horses in the arctic.[146] The hostility to Tilak's memory among many lower-caste spokespeople, and many others professing their commitment (as we saw in the Introduction) to the Indian Constitution's concept of 'Social Justice', has, then, been resilient.

One area that has seen marked increase over the last thirty or so years relates to criticisms of Tilak's views on women. Such reproaches were often associated with the general 'anti-reformist' charge of R. P. Paranjpye and others during his life described above; indeed, non-Brahmin activists were instrumental in Tilak having to be escorted away from a meeting under police guard in Poona in February 1920, after he had been shouted down by reformers as he tried to express his views on female education.[147] As we have seen, lower-caste agitation in Maharashtra from before Tilak's career had always attacked perceived Brahminic norms relating to women. But given the volume of hostility to Tilak's 'orthodoxy' in evidence today, it is notable how little criticism was offered from female articulators of women's roles in nationalist politics in the pre-independence period or immediately after. Sarojini Naidu, the first woman Congress President and first female governor of an Indian state after independence, and commonly referred to as a feminist activist, poetically extolled Tilak on his death anniversary in 1927, assuring him that 'your ashes are our children's heritage'.[148] Hansa Mehta, who as Indian delegate to the UN Human Rights Commission ensured that the Universal Declaration embraces 'all human beings' rather than 'all men', similarly used Tilak's anniversary to celebrate him in 1930, in order to chastise instead the British

---

[146] S. K. Biswas, *Autochthon of India and the Aryan Invasion* (New Delhi: Genuine Publications & Media, 1995), 186 ff.

[147] *Advocate of India*, 10 February 1920, 7. The incident is discussed in Upton, *Lokmanya*, 196–197.

[148] Satvinder Kaur, *Sarojini Naidu's Poetry: Melody of Indianness* (Delhi: Swarup & Sons, 2003), 172. Academic readings do not diverge from the popular consensus here: see M. Alexander, 'Sarojini Naidu, Romanticism and Resistance', *Economic and Political Weekly*, 20/43 (26 October 1985).

authorities.[149] Tilak's treatment in Venu Chitale's 1950 novel *In Transit*, about a Brahmin family in Poona between 1915 and 1935, is also highly revealing: a lullaby is composed by the village bard for the family's newly born daughter, but in honour of Tilak, and presented as a song of Mother India. Her mother Lopamudra favours this lullaby even over those for Rama and Shivaji.[150] At one level, ignoring Tilak's gender politics might appear an obvious concession to the requirements of a nationalist agitation, or a reflection of the loyalties it secured. But the blitheness of this remembrance does hint at the broader capacity of such 'nationalist' loyalties to normalize (as well as to legitimize) and hence more deeply entrench patriarchal attitudes and structures.[151]

Such a tendency has been increasingly vigorously resisted, with female Indian activists in the van, in recent times—though that is not, of course, to overlook the long Indian and specifically Maharashtrian pedigree of women's criticisms of patriarchy.[152] This resistance is connected to the growth of an organized postcolonial 'women's movement', concerting and propagating dissent from perceived patriarchal norms in India; and female Indian scholars have notably straddled the line between academia and public debate in fomenting it.[153] A significant level of criticism of Tilak does issue from the academy into the popular milieu: one recent web article cited in the Introduction, noting Tilak's opposition to female education, and viewing his ideology as the 'source' of 'the marital rape controversy we face today', is notable for its citation of the work of Sudhir Chandra, Uma Chakrvarti, and Sabyasachi Bhattacharya, et al.[154]

And as we saw there, such criticisms of Tilak on such social matters, often bracketed together in a single indictment, have met a vigorous

---

[149] Devaki Jain, *Women, Development and the UN* (Bloomington, 1995), 20. Pattabhi Sitaramayya, *History of the Indian National Congress* (Madras: Indian National Congress Working Committee, 1935), 697.

[150] Eunice De Souza (ed.), *Women's Voices: Selections from Nineteenth- and Early Twentieth-century Indian Writing in English* (Delhi; Oxford: Oxford University Press, 2002), 338–339.

[151] See Partha Chatterjee, *The Nation and Its Fragments: Colonial and Postcolonial Histories* (Princeton, N.J.: Princeton University Press, 1993).

[152] See Rosalind O'Hanlon, *A Comparison Between Women and Men: Tarabai Shinde and the Critique of Gender Relations in Colonial India* (Oxford: Oxford University Press, 1994).

[153] Perhaps the best introduction to the range and tenor of the movement is Radha Kumar, 'From Chipko to Sati: The Contemporary Indian Women's Movement', in Amrita Basu, ed., *The Challenge of Local Feminisms: Women's Movements in Global Perspective* (Oxford: Westview Press, 1995).

[154] 'Teaching English', (https://counterview.org). (Chandra, 'Whose Laws?'; Chakravarti, 'Gendering Caste: Through the Feminist Lens'; Bhattacharya, et al., 'Educating the Nation'.)

response. The dominant form of rebuttal has been to echo Tilak's own self-defence on social matters from 1919, and to find solid grounds to excuse his opposition to reform. Reform is often described as a distraction from the task of gaining Swaraj, or potentially dividing Indians from each other as they strove for it; or it was impossible to accomplish in any case while foreign rule sapped India's culture; in any case Indian reformers were attempting to outpace the mass of Hindu society, demanding sudden reform rather than changing attitudes first; it was not right that a foreign power could sit in judgement upon India's social affairs, still less that it could claim extra legitimacy by reforming them; and Kelkar even makes the remarkable assertion that criticism of the reformers *ad hominem* was a legitimate reason for Tilak's not supporting them.[155] Some justifications seem especially stretched, such as the notion that Tilak was simply too old and tired to support the 1918 untouchability motion.[156] Tilak's own personal life is mentioned in his defence, particularly his decision to educate and delay marrying his daughters.[157] Alternatively, and revealingly, Amar Chitra Katha simply suggests that Tilak had a positive approach to reform, more respectful of Indian customs than other reformers, without mentioning any specific reform issues or controversies at all.[158] But it seems there has been an increased tendency in recent times simply to reinvent Tilak as a leading exponent of reform—the 'legendary social reformer' we met at the beginning of this study. The defences of Tilak's resistance to reform offered above could, of course, be taken as indications of a pragmatic reformer, urging organic and sturdy societal growth.[159] But increasingly it seems possible to deny or ignore the very apparent conservatism that Tilak himself and his advocates sought to justify, and simply baldly state that he was at the forefront of reform. The efflorescence of such readings in the 2010s, which saw him positively namechecked by Aamir Khan in the introduction to his social reform

---

[155] Kelkar, *Tilak*, 201; G. P. Pradhan and A. K. Bhagwat, *Lokamanya Tilak: A Biography* (Bombay, 1959), 54; Athalye, *Tilak*, 51; N. C. Kelkar, *Landmarks in Lokamanya Tilak's Life* (Madras: S. Ganesan, 1924), Preface.

[156] Pradhan, *Tilak*, 120.

[157] *Ek Yugpurush*; cf. Motilal Nehru's comments in July 1924 that Tilak was a 'practical social reformer in his own life, but focused on Swaraj', *Mahratta*, 27 July 1924, 364.

[158] ACK *Lokamanya Tilak*, 12

[159] Jog, *LBGT*, 37, for instance, while noting Tilak's wariness of the 'foreign graft' of customs, has him supporting organic change.

chat show *Satyamev Jayete*, reflects an interesting valorization of social reform in historical judgement in India, perhaps a reflection of contemporary societal pressures and dissent; the patriot, increasingly, must be associated with social reform to have validity, the nation thus associated with social uplift.

Conclusion

That Tilak was heralded as the 'father of the nation' in 1920 is a remarkable, and mostly forgotten, feature of his remembrance, not least for showing the importance of suffering as a foundation of such leadership. The rapidly ascending fame of M. K. Gandhi largely put paid to this, in most quarters, only its distorted echo being resonant today. But ironically Tilak's very prominence necessitated rewriting his contribution and character to be more Gandhian, an attempt to render invisible the specific and un-Gandhian characteristics of Tilak's politics. The vision of Tilak as ascetic and sexually abstinent was the ultimate expression of this. This process, which Gandhi contributed to, was a significant part of the construction of Gandhi's own leadership, and should be noted. Conversely, the scale of Tilak's remembrance contributed to the recently noted, somewhat disguised prominence of Tilak in the formation of Gandhi's political thought.[160] It should not be imagined, of course, that in appropriating Tilak's memory for his own leadership, Gandhi was parasitic upon it: Gandhi's own all-India fame in 1920 probably enabled Tilak to be more broadly celebrated, as a representative of the Congress nationalism that Gandhi had enhanced during the previous two years; and Gandhi, enlisting Tilak's sacrifice and aiming to demonstrate how he built on such precedents, further enhanced Tilak's reputation, Gandhi's fame associating with Tilak's name in the Swaraj Fund. Tilak's fame, once deeply established as a self-sacrificing patriot, had a self-reinforcing character, garnering a limitless number of appropriators, as the suggestions of Tilak's Marxism show. As a patriotic hero, he also has had to (posthumously) adapt. As the endorsement of social reform has become increasingly valorized as an index of historical judgement in India,

---

[160] Pinney, 'Tiger's Nature'.

Tilak-as-patriot has had to assume a new character, intimately connected to the social reform movements he had, in fact, done much to oppose in his life. The contention of this study is that Tilak was, indeed, concerned with reforming Hindu society to promote martiality and manliness. But this does not constitute a standard definition of social reform, or correspond to any reform he is suggested, in recent favourable accounts, to have supported. And so it is markedly ironic that Tilak, who first shot to all-India prominence as an anti-reformer over the raising of the age of sexual consent for girls to 12, is at the time of writing celebrated by Indian newspapers as 'Legendary social reformer Bal Gangadhar Tilak', who specifically 'worked towards social reforms for women'.[161]

Tilak's remembrance also demonstrates the interplay between popular, academic, and official memory. Scholarly accounts can simply reproduce popular ones: the outstanding example of this is the common assumption of Tilak's 'founding' of the revived Ganesh festival in the 1890s, which ignores the corporate nature of the festival's growth, and shows a lack of concern to properly interrogate historical agency. The influence of popular memory on the academy can of course run the other way, as with the example of (mostly female) academics influencing the popular memory of Tilak's attitudes towards gender—though the memory here is still a somewhat marginalized and dissenting one. In any case, such 'popular' influences upon academic writing are not themselves natural or spontaneous: they bear the marks of their construction, imbricated with power relations. Tilak's own publicity, and that of his admirers in positions of control within Maharashtra's print culture, cemented his relationship with Ganapati in the popular mind. The same is true of his fame as a self-sacrificing patriot, which was augmented by his ownership of two newspapers as much as by his skill as a publicist in the courtroom in 1908. It might be noted in this connection that the boundary between official and non-official memorialization is actually quite indistinct, as the influence of political organization and the impact of power relations assert control over memory in the 'unofficial' sphere. The progenitors and organizers of Hindutva themselves in the 1920s, like V. D. Savarkar, informed a more broadly popular interpretation of Tilak's proximity to the

---

[161] '98th Death Anniversary of Lokmanya Bal Gangadhar Tilak', 1 August 2018, *Times of India* website, https://timesofindia.indiatimes.com/etimes.

Hindu Sangathan; it then influenced (perhaps proportionately more in-fluentially) the academic view of Tilak, for as we have seen much schol-arly writing on Tilak's 'Hindutva' situates isolated aspects of his thought in broader assumptions that are not empirically derived, but come from accounts left by later Hindu nationalists as much as this general and (somewhat) popular sense of Tilak's positionality. Non-Brahmin polit-ical organization, meanwhile, also fed popular (often lower-caste) dis-putations on Tilak's caste chauvinism. Continuities, of course, are visible in Congress's remembrance of Tilak, relating to his patriotism and con-gruence to Gandhianism, from 1920, and the official line of the Indian state post-independence. In opposition to the state, or in government, Congress sought to buttress its legitimacy by selecting heroes and man-aging the content of their remembrance. This view in turn was itself contested by a less concerted or broadly influential official 'Hindutva' celebration from the late 1970s, continuing in Prime Ministerial state-ments up to the time of writing. Even official (or official-cum-scholarly) accounts can simply reproduce popular ones: the extraordinary proven-ance of the definition of Hinduism given by the Supreme Court of India in 1966, and upheld since, shows this. It is telling that Tilak's *shloka*, which the court accepted as a working definition of Hinduism, was thought to be textual, and considered by learned judges to find its way into their minds through their learning; in fact, the lettered in this case had their understanding shaped by demotic, oral traditions, something that went unacknowledged and misattributed.

As we saw at the outset, amid the many audible voices commemorating Tilak in India today, the loudest are those suggesting Tilak was a benignly reform-minded, patriotic hero. The commanding heights of popular memory, especially the mass media and television in particular, offer this set vision, apparently amplified by the mass media's propagation through social media. This media-influenced view is also largely expressive of an official view. Such a situation is, in fact, quite naturally, time-honoured. Criticism of Tilak, like other patriots, often has illicit, anti-official con-notations, and is associated with political protest (especially as regards gender politics and caste politics). What does appear novel is the degree of popular pressure on the state to uphold such a laudatory view, through legal challenges to Government-published textbooks, and broader polit-ical mobilization against educational establishments. Criticisms of Tilak or implications of the illegitimacy of his politics, particularly his support for violence, can be thus shut down, in an acrimonious debate increasingly employing the heresy-hunting binary of national/anti-national. Historians should avoid predictions: but it may safely be said that the relevance of Tilak's memory for India will outlive these particular disputes; and the dynamism and plurality of the culture that remembers him has always managed to express itself through its remembrance of him before.

Conclusion

Running through Tilak's output is a self-conscious construction of an Indian modernity, despite the overt concern with cultural authenticity which is often seen to define him. The major strands of this, and his positions in articulating it—as a majoritarian pluralist in inter-community terms, a radical liberal in his political ethics, and in social terms as both self-strengthening reformer and Brahmin supremacist—we shall revisit shortly. Before doing so, it might be apposite to reflect on what this suggests of Tilak as an intellectual, and in turn what reflections Tilak prompts on the concept and practice of global intellectual history relating to modern South Asia.

At one level, the pervasiveness of some colonial conceptions of Indian society and culture in Tilak's thought is remarkable. The notion of caste as graded subordination of the non-Aryan to the Aryan races in India was formed, in a way which has never been fully appreciated, by Free Church of Scotland missionaries in Bombay around the time of Tilak's birth. Conceptions of India as a land of primordial and unitary Hindu and Muslim communities, drawing on the comprehension of India by East India Company servants in the mid-seventeenth century, and hardening thereafter, were an important part of the colonial state's understanding of India. They find an echo in Tilak's conception of the polity as a site of contest between discrete, ancient communities, ultimately expressed at Lucknow in 1916, as Hindu and Muslim communities were drawn in political distinction. Tilak's reversion to a narrow conception of the sources of dharma, as exclusively drawn from *Smriti* texts, during the age of consent controversy of 1890–1891 was likely prompted by the textual citations of his reformist opponents who were themselves responding to colonial jurisprudence's privileging of textual authorities. His perception of Hindus as prone to lapsing into apathetic renunciation, so keenly felt in the *Gita Rahasya*, which was above all written to rouse them from it,

The Thought of Bal Gangadhar Tilak. Robert E. Upton, Oxford University Press. © Robert E. Upton 2024.
DOI: 10.1093/oso/9780198900658.003.0008

owes too a great deal to Western conceptions of Hindu indolence, and his specific understanding of *sannyasa*—the final stage of life during which a Hindu may abandon worldly concerns like family and home—seems to have been informed by such criticism, Tilak describing *sannyasa*, against the evidence of its precolonial realities, as a path of utter renunciation of action. For all the varied agency of Tilak as an intellectual, which we shall recapitulate below, the influence of Tilak's educational milieu, shared with so many of his early colleagues especially, in the English-medium High School, and at the Deccan College, must be remembered as centrally important. Indeed, we see Tilak is conscious of the influence of western Indology in his historicization of the Vedas, and of the priorities and assumptions of academic Indology, as much as the substance of its critical approaches. Even the *Gita Rahasya*, a notable reversion to a venerable tradition of *bhasya* or commentary (though in this instance vernacular) devotes some discrete space to an examination of the text's history and provenance, as if to recognize an imperative. Prominent from Tilak's high schooling was a carefully inculcated 'Anglicized' historical consciousness, and it is remarkable how explicitly he drew upon the pool of historical and intellectual antecedents it provided, even in his vernacular journalism in *Kesari*—something again surprising given his major achievement, as Aurobindo has it in his 'Appreciation' of Tilak, was to broaden the nationalist appeal to the sentiments of the non-English-educated populace through comprehending their ancestral culture. Especially in his English-language journalism, and above all in the Bombay High Court in 1908, Tilak could employ this learning knowingly for its rhetorical edge; but in for example his 'weaponizing' of liberal thought in defence of press freedom in the latter case, we see these elements of his thought reified in polemical use: they existed as both thought and strategy, and his relationship with them was deeper than can be reflected by the language of 'appropriation'.

At the same time, Tilak's output demonstrates the importance of being aware of moments of imbrication between 'exogenous' ideas and those precolonial and often microregional argumentative forms and understandings which were foregrounded in the context of new and pressing socio-political concerns (specifically the multiple crises of negotiating rights under the conditions of colonialism). The signal example is Tilak's conception of the 'birthright' of Swaraj, a notion of the natural right to self-rule which rested on Vedantic understandings while being articulated in an idiom of English political thought; and Tilak's drawing on older arguments and stances concerning the Brahmin role of political leadership, or on the *karmayoga* of Ramdas, or on the ethical implications of Hindu notions of cosmic time (specifically the *Kaliyuga*), show an engagement across time with contested and living Indic traditions, in a new environment in both intellectual and socio-political terms (indeed, the two cannot be separated). And in this, Tilak's own conceptions of the 'global' also show him drawing on Indic terms and concepts: the application of Vedanta to create a universalizable model of sovereignty in relation to that of selfhood in his definition of Swaraj underlines that the 'global' itself is a notion of multiple provenances across time and space, offered here in resistance to a global network of imperial power.[1] It should be noted in addition that Tilak was consciously a transnational intellectual, who intended to imbibe and contribute to global intellectual trends. *The Arctic Home* engaged with a major cosmopolitan intellectual framework of the period, deliberately contributing to current debates on Aryan origins, and indeed his correspondence with the Oxford Sanskritist Friedrich Max Muller shows a seeking for global connectedness. This same sensitivity to global intellectual trends also in some measure explains his turn to the Bhagavad Gita, a text of global significance by 1910. Tilak's application of the thought of Mill and Carlyle for instance in explicating his vision for India was also a quite deliberate undertaking. But there was more to it than this. His pattern of explicit analogies—ranging from those between India's position and England's history, to the analogies between the Vedanta of the Gita and the thought of Immanuel Kant—show in fact that Tilak conceived of Indian society as partaking in unfolding historical-intellectual processes that were not peculiar to her, in which India gave rise to ideas of global importance, and imbibed them. It was with this sense that Tilak embraced the role of a transnational intellectual; and it might be added that this consciousness in the mind of the historical agent of this role as actor in a global exchange of ideas, is an important component of 'global intellectual history'.[2]

---

[1] See also Banerjee, 'Rights-Bearing Self', 106 ff.

[2] Samuel Moyn and Andrew Sartori, 'Approaches to Global Intellectual History', in Samuel Moyn and Andrew Sartori, eds, *Global Intellectual History* (New York: Columbia University Press, 2013) (hereafter, Moyn and Sartori, 'Approaches').

Indeed despite that 'global' self-consciousness, Tilak's relationship to existing, precolonial understandings in the *dharmashastra*, one conditioned by the colonial political and intellectual milieu, repays attention. Tilak's own contributions were to a living and intensely self-critical tradition of thinking about dharma: it might be added that it does not aid our understanding of that tradition to hold that Tilak or others like Vivekananda (who influenced Tilak greatly) played fast-and-loose with it, where we see them reinterpreting concepts and applying them in different contexts than those of a reified 'classical' *dharmashastra*. More importantly, Tilak clearly conceived of himself as profoundly rooted within such concepts. The case of Tilak's thought on *advaita* Vedanta is a case in point, contained most fully in the *Gita Rahasya*. This non-dualist understanding of the cosmos posited that there was only one irreducible reality in the universe (Brahma) and that the visible and constantly changing world of discrete things was in fact *maya*, or illusion. For Shankara and his followers, in the dominant school of so-called classical Vedanta, this understanding of existence was the supreme goal in itself, leading to *moksha*. For Tilak, an *advaitin* awareness was the basis for unselfish ethical action towards others, for the knowledgeable *jnanin* and for those who follow his visible behavioural example. The problematic relation of this logic to classical *advaita*, in which the existence of 'others' was merely illusory, was not remarked upon by Tilak; but his determination to root his own ethical positions within such a cosmology is plain. At the same time, his conviction that the path to *moksha* lay in conducting proper action (*karmayoga*) rather than in devotion (*bhakti*) to Brahma or to its knowledge (*jnanin*) was one traceable to the earliest Vedic exegesis—and was expounded, as Tilak enthusiastically pointed out, in early modern India by figures such as Ramdas; and thus under the political and intellectual pressure of late colonial conditions was Ramdas and his existing, vernacular Maharashtrian vision of dharma foregrounded in Tilak's thought.

Another very important part of Tilak's ethical scheme deriving from as far back as the *Manusmriti* and Mahabharata was the *Kaliyuga*—the current, evil stage of cosmic time that precedes the destruction of the universe. Once more, we can see Tilak also give this concept a new, ethical application: even acting with the perfect even-handedness of the *advaitin*, one should reply to the villainy of the *Kaliyuga* with villainy. This sense is hugely important to the ethical scheme of the *Gita Rahasya*. But a much greater relevance of the *Kaliyuga* is in fact discernible throughout Tilak's thought. It can be seen to silently shape his assumptions in many areas, an influence Tilak does not appear to explicitly acknowledge. This influence is both pervasive and fascinating, because it suggests a deep relevance for cosmology in political thought even in the mind of an intellectual who gently scoffed, in *The Arctic Home*, at the 'orthodox' desire to establish the veracity of the *Kaliyuga's* traditional *puranic* dating of 3201 BC— something that was important to many of Tilak's contemporaries. Indeed Tilak's prescriptions for Indian society, polity, and politics can be read as a *yugadharma*. We can see structural similarities between Tilak's agenda to reform Hindu society and the conditions of that society in the *Kaliyuga*, as described in the *dharmashastra*. It is described as a period in which changes in dharmic practices occur, while at the same time all varnas have fallen away from their proper duties, and all have become confused; the flexibility of Tilak's conception of *varnashrama dharma* in his late speeches, and his embrace of a generalized '*kshatriyatva*' (Kshatriyaness) to galvanize society for the challenges of the age, is an accommodation to these conditions, creating out of them a dharmic response that can help to defend Hindu society. Most pointedly, Kshatriya dharma, in the prevalent Brahminic conception that Tilak was heir to, had disappeared from the earth in the *Kaliyuga*, as recorded in the Puranas—and thus needed to be recreated. For Tilak, all society would partake of Kshatriya virtues, with Brahmins specifically exhorted to do so.

What we may take to be the relevance of the *Kaliyuga* to Tilak's view of India was anything but a device to demonstrate cultural authenticity. The very fact that Tilak did not invoke it in connection with views on *kshatriyatva*, for instance, shows this. It was a pervasive assumption, whose presence suggests that it retained a prominence in the minds of Indian intellectuals because of current social and political conditions— broadly, those of colonialism—that were a manifestation of the *Kaliyuga's adharma*. Indeed, Tilak's bemoaning the demilitarization of contemporary India, a central strand of his reform agenda, appears a substantiation of the death of Kshatriya dharma in the *Kaliyuga* described in the *dharmashastra*. More fundamentally, the *Kaliyuga* described in therein as a time when India would be overrun by outside, *mleccha* rulers. Colonial rule brought an expression of some of the assumptions of the *Kaliyuga* in the social and political thought of Brahmin intellectuals of the period (perhaps even more than in the thought of precolonial Maharashtrian Brahmins, whose historical precedent was of course independently directly inspirational to Tilak), something indeed that may have operated unconsciously. The 'reformist' or 'revivalist' assertion that current social practices departed from those of the Vedic 'golden age' was also a reflection of this same *Kaliyuga* sensibility, and not entirely a function of new 'Aryan' racial theories of the nineteenth century, which in India were rather parasitic upon it. Gail Omvedt in her study of the non-Brahmin movement in Maharashtra also notes a parallel assertion to Tilak's: the lower castes rejoiced that the *Kaliyuga* had come, 'untouchable' Mahars and Mangs were reading religious books, and the Bhats (a common Brahminic surname in Maharashtra) were losing their position.[3] Thus the upheaval of society from the mid-nineteenth century, and its current conditions, seems to have inculcated the *Kaliyuga* in diverse minds.[4] It provided an organizing principle for coming to terms with the conditions of colonialism; yet at the same time it was not an expression of despair, but suggested strategies of accommodation, and ultimately reassured that current conditions were in fact dharmic, and of redemptive significance for Hindu society, and the individual or community within it. Late colonial conditions thus gave rise to a historical reification of the *Kaliyuga*, providing a comprehending framework for India's historical condition, though it is beyond the scope of this enquiry to trace how this sense relates to conceptions of the *Kaliyuga* in India's early modern intellectual culture.

In terms of Tilak's aims, expressed in the thought which emerged at this conjuncture, the construction of an Indian modernity, and the burnishing of the Brahminic place within it, are central. This tendency may seem surprising; yet modernity was a preoccupation of Tilak's, and shaped his responses in creating a society, polity, and politics apt for it. Modern Western scientific and industrial developments were something both materially threatening (as implied in the *Gita Rahasya*) and

---

[3] Omvedt, *Revolt*, 143.

[4] The *Kaliyuga* motif as expressing the social pessimism of the Bengali bhadralok in nineteenth-century Bengali literature, in the context of colonial rule and its imposition of 'clock time' in particular, is discussed in Sumit Sarkar, ' "Kaliyuga", "Chakri" and "Bhakti": Ramakrishna and His Times', *Economic and Political Weekly*, 27/29 (18 July 1992), 1543–1559, 1561–1566.

attractive to him, necessary of emulation, while not threatening to the rootstock of Indian civilization. In *The Arctic Home*, science was put at the service of the Vedas, establishing through a modern geological understanding of earth's history the viability of a prehistorical Arctic habitation, whose discernible traces encoded in their Samhitas demonstrate the extreme antiquity of Aryan civilization and the precocity of the Indo-Aryan branch in propagating it. 'Modern science is gradually justifying and vindicating our ancient wisdom', said Tilak to the Bharata Dharma Mahamandala in 1906, referring to understandings of the cosmos. 'Our enemies are fast disappearing before the teachings of modern science, take courage and work hard for the final triumph.'[5] And Tilak was also much attached to machine metaphors, seeing Hindu society as a railway, as well as explicitly calling for mechanization in India.[6] Tilak's attachment to machines and to progress, and as we shall see to physical force and courage, points to under-explored parallels between Indian intellectual life in the period and European Futurist thought.[7] The contrast with Gandhi, for whom the *Kaliyuga was associated* with machinery (*kal*), and whose *yugadharma* thus entailed a strong note of rejection, is notable. For Tilak, the *Kaliyuga* clearly allowed for material and industrial progress, which he encouraged.[8]

Tilak's call during the Home Rule movement was to 'raise your status to that of a civilized nation according to the modern standard'.[9] This stands as a kind of summation of his aims, and its modernity was clearly linked to a deeply historicist sense and a (universal) political conception of emerging democratic nationalism, deepening Tilak's attachment to representative forms of government (which comprehended in addition precolonial Maharashtrian as much as revolutionary English intellectual and moral influences). At the same time, this therefore sharpened his

---

[5] Tilak, *Speeches*, 40.

[6] See speech on 'National Education', *Speeches*, 81 ff.

[7] This analogy was made explicit in Tilak's own lifetime by the Bengali political thinker Benoy Kumar Sarkar. An admirer of Tilak, he referred to Kautilya as the 'Bismarck of India', his *arthashastra* being a 'code of militarism'; 'It is on such historic truths that the futurism of Young Asia is nurtured', he claimed. 'The Futurism of Young Asia', *International Journal of Ethics*, 28/4 (July 1918), 521–541 (527–528). See also his 'World Culture in Young India', in *The Future of Young India and Other Essays* (Berlin: Julius Springer, 1922), 321. The relevance of the Japanese example was not lost on Tilak, who cited it often as inspiration.

[8] Pinney, 'Tiger's Nature', 412.

[9] *Speeches*, 217, 'Home Rule Conference'.

anti-autocratic politics, in defence of print journalism and modern forms of political violence: Tilak embraced the home-made bomb, the 'charm' and 'amulet' of modern politics, as an anti-autocratic weapon with such fervour because it could right the imbalance of modernity in India; the state presently governed modernity, and so it must be embraced in turn by Indians. And while India was 'not yet a nation' as it was understood in Western countries, but was rather divided into ancient communities, creating a national identity for it was a consciously modern project, for which he deployed the figure of Shivaji under the influence of modern transnational thought, in which Thomas Carlyle was prominent. And it was 'on pain of national ruin' that a muscular Kshatriya dharma in every Indian must arise, indeed that *karmayoga* must be embraced, explicitly in each case contextualized by the materially threatening conditions of modern international politics with its 'advanced nations'. By the same token, modern, mechanized war would help to forge that society, inculcating courage and also giving a bodily experience of modernity for Indian manhood, an agenda underpinning his persistent calls for military enlistment from 1916. The uncredited influence of Spencerian evolutionism, and preoccupation with national efficiency, is traceable here; but so too is a conscious reflection by Tilak of the contemporary experiences of other societies. The global turn to militarism in the period served as direct inspiration for, as well as providing a transnational context to, Tilak's self-strengthening efforts. Of particular note is Tilak's taking inspiration from Japan's modern experience, in which, it has been noted, martial arts classes were sanctioned in schools as part of a 'Spencerian struggle', and a deliberate effort was made to make military values dominant in society.[10] A similar trend is indeed visible in other societies fearing of experiencing domination or dismemberment by European imperialism in the period, such as China, or the Ottoman Empire, hence the 'Young Turks'' adoption of 'militaristic attitudes' inspired by Social Darwinism, and indeed the service of many in the Japanese army.[11] This was the historically specific context in which Tilak called for a revival of a historical Maharashtrian tradition of physical force and martiality; his

[10] Denis Gainty, *Martial Arts and the Body Politic in Meiji Japan* (London: Routledge, 2013); Sandra Wilson, 'Rethinking Nation and Nationalism in Japan', in Sandra Wilson, ed., *Nation and Nationalism in Japan* (New York: Routledge Curzon, 2002), 1–20.
[11] Waldron, 'Warlord'; Hanioglu, *Revolution*, 304.

positioning of himself within the tradition indicates not its unchanging historical reality, but the imperatives of his own time, something he was conscious of.

Within this India, its Brahmin communities, Tilak asserted, had a natural position of eminence. India's peculiar modernity must accommodate such social realities (as also the immemorial religious communities of India) in Tilak's mind. Yet there was an unacknowledged and unresolved tension in Tilak's thought between natural Brahmin hegemony and the democratic nationalism that Tilak aligned himself with during his Home Rule agitation. In the *Gita Rahasya*, Tilak expresses a casteless vision of dharma, in which any duty may be taken upon one's shoulders as a matter of choice, not for egalitarian reasons so much as to justify the Brahminic leadership role in the polity, which a conventional reading of the *varnashrama dharma* of the Bhagavad Gita might otherwise suggest belongs to Kshatriyas. The emphasis on the Brahmin guru Ramdas in the text serves to underline this. The threat to the unitary Hindu polity posed by the demand for separate non-Brahmin electorates in Maharashtra provoked an acerbic response in Tilak not only because it suggested fragmentation of the polity, but because it endangered the Brahmin leadership position within it. Nor was it simply a matter of political roles. Tilak also expressfed an inherited sense of the role of Brahmin as arbitrator of dharma, which the state must defer to. His vision of the reform of Hindu society was that it would be Brahmin-led (not only was he explicit on this point, he played the role himself); and his hostility to the state's interference over the age of consent owes something to this. Tilak's opposition to the Patel Bill concerning inter-caste marriage also displays a concern as to the stability of the discrete Brahmin community, whose jeopardy would weaken leadership within society and polity. There is also a divergence here, too, with Tilak's radical liberal thought in defence of natural rights in political terms. Tilak shares more than has been acknowledged with Indian 'liberal' thinkers of his time in this, and even his 'communitarian' definition of the nation is harmonizable with what C. A. Bayly notes as the 'global drift' towards such forms of liberalism, more focused on society than the individual, from 1860, and associated with such figures as T. H. Green; in India especially, representative government had to be made safe (as elsewhere) by comprehending its society, and the reality of power-holding by the 1890s in India foregrounded the issue, which

saw even 'archetypical late-liberals' support separate 'communal' electorates.[12] But the social texture that Tilak imagines, specifically in relation to
the Brahmin varna, is a critical impediment to his assumption of either
fully democratic or more programmatically liberal thought.

Tilak asserted Brahminic status by engaging in the atavistic contest
over authority with Maharashtra's non-Brahmins, particularly her self-
identifying Kshatriyas, in which he reasserted a historical Chitpavan
Brahmin role: this was seen in his handling of the polemic battle over the
relationship between Shivaji and Ramdas for instance, with its implications for the prestige and authority of the communities they represented.
But this provides perfect exemplification of how Tilak's regional antecedents informed his growing articulation of all-Indian nationalism, as
indeed nationalist articulations became a more credible and prominent
feature of Indian politics in the course of Tilak's career, just as, relatedly,
he also grew in all-India prominence. This study has underlined the consistency in Tilak's thought, remarkably evident in his views on religious
communities within the polity, and on martiality, for instance; and indeed there is no sharp discontinuity between Tilak's regional conceptions
and his ideas of the Indian nation. As Tilak articulates his imagined India,
Tilak's particular Maharashtrian Brahminism informs his solutions in
the realm of all-Indian politics, just as the modes of his use of Shivaji as a
model of indigenous sovereignty see markedly little change between his
employment of them in Maharashtra and outside.

Tilak's remembrance in the century since his death is deeply revealing,
firstly of the extraordinary early prominence of this alternative 'father of
the nation', and the substantial efforts by Gandhi to coopt him posthumously to his own emergent leadership, a vital part of its construction.
The scale of Tilak's remembrance doubtless had its impact on Gandhi's
political solutions on the whole, which have been noted to have a kind of
mirror-like symmetry to Tilak's own positions. The power of Tilak's own
pen in achieving his historical celebrity, shown in the misremembrance
that he initiated the enlarged Ganapati festival of the 1890s, also gives
rise to an example of the permeability of the boundary between popular
conceptions and academic history, which as regards Tilak in fact accepts

---

[12] See Bayly, *Recovering Liberties*, Ch. 9; and cf. Pandey, *Construction*, simply viewing commu-
nitarianism as a 'weakness' of liberalism (231).

so many of the former's assumptions. This unmediated impact of Tilak's journalism decades later is also visible in his citation in the Supreme Court of India's 1966 definition of Hinduism, misattributed to the *Gita Rahasya*, but traceable to a popular definition promulgated in *Kesari*. In recent times, the surprising heralding of Tilak as a prominent social re- former also highlights the striking increase in the importance of social reformism as an index of historical approbation in contemporary India.

At the time of writing, Tilak is once more relevant to pressing debates relating to cultural politics in contemporary India, particularly in con- nection to Hindu nationalism. His relationship to Hindutva is broadly assumed in academic writing. But it was in fact historically constructed in the unique and fraught circumstances of the 1920s, whereas he had, in his own lifetime, stood askance the Hindu Mahasabha—and even there- fore to such similar articulations of a self-strengthened and majoritarian Hindu nationalism, such as Malaviya's, as could still comprehend reli- gious pluralism despite their opposition to the separate Muslim electoral representation which Tilak supported. Indeed, the timing of Tilak's in- tegration into the Hindutva narrative, from around 1925, gives insights into the historical construction of the relationship between Hindutva and violence. Though violence in defence of the Hindu community had been a celebrated component of 'proto' Hindu nationalism (in Bankim's Anandamath, for instance), the association of opposition to non-violence and growing opposition to Gandhi's 'anti-Hindu' politics, with their al- leged deference to Indian Muslims, by the mid 1920s, appears to have cemented the prominence of violence in Hindutva's political repertoire. And it was in these conditions that the memory of Tilak's 'Maharashtrian' physically violent politics eased his acceptance as a Hindutva hero— particularly among pro-Hindutva Brahmins, for whom his violence al- ready exerted an appeal. As the association of Tilak and Nathuram Godse shows, it is still Tilak's advocacy of physical force which leads to pre- sumptions of his character as a proto-Hindu nationalist. This study has shown that specific elements of Tilak's output are commonly misunder- stood in relation to a whole that is rather assumed than studied; whilst others seem misread under the weight of a Hindutva teleology. Tilak's treatment of symbols and ideas of utmost relevance to contemporary Hindu nationalism—the precocity of Vedic civilization, or the greatness of Shivaji—shows the variety of purposes to which they have been put in modern India, not their deterministic production of Hindu nationalist politics. Crucially, Tilak's stances underline the novelty of the forms of Hindutva politics that emerged in Maharashtra in the 1920s, and the enduring importance of tracing them.

For the historian at least, the problems with this misreading are not merely that Tilak is misrepresented as a linear ancestor of contemporary Hindutva, though. He is reduced to this role, and his complexity as a thinker on modern India is reduced accordingly; his role as a kind of historical connective tissue becomes the dominant way of thinking of him. Yet Tilak's vision for modern India, his unique response to the challenge of constructing an inclusive polity with a vital politics, and a revived Hindu society within it, was on its own terms fully-fledged, and expressive of its particular historical conditions, which it thus helps us understand more fully, over a forty-year period that was pivotal in the formation of India's modern political culture. It is for these reasons that Tilak's influence on his successors in all-India politics has been pervasive, and that his continued importance to our understanding of modern India, and his continued significance as a symbol within it, are assured.

Bibliography

i) Manuscript and archival sources

Bodleian Library, Oxford:
Papers of Friedrich Max Müller and of his wife Georgina Adelaide, 1794–1919 [various shelfmarks]

British Library, India Office Records, London:
George Harris Papers [Mss Eur B206]
Papers of Quaid-i-Azam Mahomed Ali Jinnah [IOR Pos 10760-826]
Reports on the Native Press [IOR/L/R/5]
Records of the Military Department, Military Collections [IOR/L/MIL/7]
Military Department Library, Indian Army [IOR/L/MIL/17/5]
Proceedings of the Legislative Department for April 1891 [IOR/P/3951]
Public and Judicial Departmental Papers, Annual Files [IOR/L/PJ/6]
Indian States Residencies, Record Confidential Files [IOR/R/2]
Reports on the Proceedings of the Indian National Congress

The National Archives, London:
War Cabinet and Cabinet: Memoranda (GT CP and G War Series) [CAB 24]

Nehru Memorial Museum and Library, New Delhi:
Tilak, B. G. Collection

Kesari-Mahratta Trust, Pune:
Tilak Papers

Deccan College Library, Pune:
Lokmanya Bal Gangadhar Tilak Vedic Collection

Maharashtra State Archives, Mumbai
Judicial Department (JD)
Educational Department (ED)
Political Department (PD)
Home Department (HD & HD (SPL)

National Archives of India, New Delhi:
M. R. Jayakar Papers

ii) Printed primary sources

Works and statements of Tilak:

Speeches of Srj. B. G. Tilak Delivered at Bellary (Bellary, 1905).
Speeches Delivered during 1889–1918, etc. [With a portrait] (Madras, 1918).
A Step in the Steamer [speeches] (Bombay, 1918).
Bal Gangadhar Tilak, His Writings and Speeches, 3rd ed. (Madras, 1922).
Letters of Lokamanya Tilak, ed. M. D. Vidwans (Poona, 1966).
Samagra Lokmanya Tilak, ed. B. K. Kelkar, D. N. Shikare, and B. D. Kher, 8 vols (Pune, 1974–1995).
Lokmanya Tilak in England, 1918–19: Diary and Documents, ed. V. D. Divekar (Pune, 1997).
B. G. Tilak, *Express Texts from the Shastras Against the Age of Consent Bill* (Poona, 1891).
B. G. Tilak, *The Orion: Or Researches into the Antiquity of the Vedas* (Bombay, 1893).
B. G. Tilak, 'A Summary of the Principal Facts and Arguments in *The Orion: Or Researches into the Antiquity of the Vedas*', in E. D. Morgan, ed., *Transactions of the Ninth International Congress of Orientalists*, 2 vols (London, 1893), i. 376–383.
B. G. Tilak, *The Arctic Home in the Vedas* (Poona; Bombay, 1903).
B. G. Tilak, *Vedic Chronology and Vedanga Jyotisha* (Poona, 1925).
B. G. Tilak, *Sri Bhagavadgita-Rahasya: Or Karma-Yoga-Shastra*, trans. Bhalchandra Sitaram Sukthankar, 2 vols (Poona, 1935).
B. G. Tilak, *Brahmasutra Vriti* (Pune, 1947).

Newspapers and news magazines:

Advocate of India
Bombay Chronicle
Bombay Guardian
Dar es Salaam Times
Dawn (at https://epaper.dawn.com/)
East African Chronicle
Financial Express at https://www.financialexpress.com/)
The Hindu (at https://www.thehindu.com/)
Hindustan Times (at https://www.hindustantimes.com)
Indian Express (at https://indianexpress.com/)
India Today (at https://www.indiatoday.in/)
Japan Times
Kesari (print edition, and at http://www.dailykesari.com/)
Mahratta
Mid-Day (at https://www.mid-day.com/)
Mint (at https://www.livemint.com/)
New India
Organiser (at https://organiser.org/)
Outlook (at www.outlookindia.com)
The Times
Times of India (print edition, and at https://timesofindia.indiatimes.com/)
Uganda Herald

Census reports:

Census of India 1871–1872: Bombay Presidency, 3 vols (Bombay, 1875).

Imperial Census of 1881: Operations and Results in the Presidency of Bombay, Including Sind by J. A. Baines [With maps], 2 vols (Bombay, 1882).

Report on the Census of British India taken on the 17th February 1881, 3 vols (London, 1883).

Census of India, 1891, 33 vols (London, 1891–1894).

Census of India 1901. Vol. 1, India. Pt. 1, Report (London, 1903).

Other sources:

Ambedkar, B. R., *What Congress and Gandhi Have Done to the Untouchables* (Bombay, 1946).

Amos, Sheldon, *The Science of Politics*, 3rd ed. (New York, 1897).

All About Lok. Tilak (Madras: V. R. Sastrulu & Sons, 1922).

The Atharvaveda, trans. Maurice Bloomfield (Strassburg, 1899).

Bain, Alexander, *Mental and Moral Science: A Compendium of Psychology and Ethics* (London, 1879).

Bapat, S. V. (ed.), *Lokmanya Tilak yanchya Aathavarnee va Aakhyaayika* ('Reminiscences and Anecdotes of Lokamanya Tilak'), 3 vols (Poona, 1924–1928).

Bart, A. Grant, *Catalogue of Native Publications in the Bombay Presidency Up to 31st December 1864*, 2nd ed. (Bombay: Byculla, 1867).

Berriedale, Keith A. (ed.), *Speeches and Documents on Indian Policy, 1750–1921*, 2 vols (London, 1922).

Besant, Annie, *The Bhagavad Gita, or the Lord's Song*, trans. Annie Besant (London, 1896).

Besant, Annie, *The Case for India: The Presidential Address Delivered by Annie Besant at the Thirty-second Indian National Congress Held at Calcutta 26th December 1917* (London, 1918[?]).

Besant, Annie, *The Future of Indian Politics* (Adyar and Benares, 1922).

Betham, R. M., *Marathas and Dekhani Musalmans: Compiled under the Orders of the Government of India* (Calcutta, 1908).

The Bhagavad Gita with the Sanatsugatiya and the Anugita [Sacred Books of the East], vol. 8, trans. K. T. Telang (Oxford, 1882).

The Bhagavad Gita, trans. W. J. Johnson (Oxford, 1994).

Biswas, S. K., *Autochthon of India and the Aryan Invasion* (New Delhi, 1995).

Bhandarkar, R. G., *Collected Works of Sir R. G. Bhandarkar*, ed. Narayana Bapuji Utgikar and Vasudev Gopal Paranjpe, 4 vols (Poona, 1927–1933).

Bhandarkar, R. G., *First Book of Sanskrit*, 8th ed. (Bombay, 1883).

Bhandarkar, R. G., *Note on the Age of Marriage and its Consummation According to Hindu Religious Law* (Poona, 1891).

Bhandarkar, R. G., *Wilson Philological Lectures on Sanskrit and the Derived Languages Delivered in 1877* (Bombay, 1914).

Bombay (Presidency). Police Department, *Notes on Criminal Classes in the Bombay Presidency: With Appendices Regarding Some Foreign Criminals Who Occasionally Visit the Presidency Including Hints on the Detection of Counterfeit Coin* (Bombay, 1908).

The Bombay Riots of August 1893, Reprinted from The Times of India (Bombay, 1893).

The Bombay University Calendar for the Year 1873–74 (Bombay, 1873 [& c]).

Bonarjee, P. D., *Handbook of the Fighting Races of India* (Calcutta, 1899).

Bonney, T. G., *The Story of Our Planet* (New York, 1893).

Bopp, Franz, *Uber das Conjugationssystem der Sanskritsprache: in Vergleichung mit jenem der griechischen, lateinischen, persischen und germanischen Sprache* (Frankfurt, 1816).

Bowen, George, and Gokhale, Vishnu Bhikaji, *Discussions by the Sea-side* (Bombay, 1857).

Carey, William, *A Dictionary of the Mahratta Language* (Serampore, 1810).

Carlyle, Thomas, *On Heroes, Hero-worship, and the Heroic in History* (Oxford; Berkeley, 1993).

Chiplunkar, Vishnu Krishna, *Nibandhamala* (Pune, 1993).

Chirol, Valentine, *Indian Unrest* (London, 1910).

Church Missionary Society, *Missionary Register for 1833* (London, 1833).

Clarke, George Sydenham, MacMunn, George, and Lovett, Alfred Crowdy, *India and the War* (London, 1915).

Committee for a History of the Freedom Movement in India (ed.), *Source Material for a History of the Indian Freedom Movement in India*, 11 vols (Bombay, 1957–).

Deshmukh, Gopal Hari, *Lokahitavadikritta nibandhasangraha* (Ahmednagar, 1866).

De Souza, Eunice (ed.), *Women's Voices: Selections from Nineteenth and Early Twentieth-century Indian Writing in English* (Delhi; Oxford, 2002).

Deussen, Paul, *The Elements of Metaphysics*, tr. by C.M. Duff. *With an Appendix, Containing the Address On the Philosophy of the Vedanta in its Relations to Occidental Metaphysics* (London, 1894).

Dixit, S. B., *Bharateeya Jyotishashastra*, trans. R. V. Vaidya (Delhi, 1969).

Duff, *History of the Mahrattas*, 3 vols (reprinted Bombay, 1864).

Duff, *Bakhar Marathyanci* [History of the Mahrattas], trans. Capt. David Capon (Bombay, 1830).

Elphinstone, Mounstuart, *Report on the Territories Conquered from the Paishwa* (Calcutta, 1821).

Elphinstone, Mounstuart, *The History of India*, 2 vols (London, 1841).

Fleet, J. F., '[Obituary Notices:] Franz Kielhorn, C.I.E', *Journal of the Royal Asiatic Society of Great Britain and Ireland* (July 1908), 159–163.

Gandhi, M. K., *The Collected Works of Mahatma Gandhi* (Electronic Book), 98 vols (New Delhi, 1999).

Gadre, Narayan Krishna, *Pro. Shridhar Ganesh Jinsiwale Yanche Trotak Charitra* (Poona, 1903).

Gazetteer of the Bombay Presidency, 27 vols (Bombay, 1877–1904).

Geikie, James, *The Great Ice Age and its Relation to the Antiquity of Man* (London, 1874).

Geikie, James, *Fragments of Earth Lore: Sketches & Addresses, Geological and Geographical* (Edinburgh; London, 1893).

Ghose, Aurobindo, 'An Appreciation by Babu Aurobindo Ghose', in *Bal Gangadhar Tilak, his Writing and Speeches* (Madras, 1918), 1–21.

Ghose, Aurobindo, *Bankim Tilak Dayananda*, 2nd ed. ([1940] Calcutta, 1947).

Ghose, Aurobindo, *The Doctrine of Passive Resistance* (Calcutta, 1948).

Gidumal, Dayaram (ed.), *The Status of Woman in India: Or, A Hand-book for Hindu Social Reformers* (Bombay, 1889).

Golwalkar, M. S., *We or Our Nationhood Defined* (Nagpur, 1939).

Golwalkar, M. S., *Bunch of Thoughts* (Bangalore, 1966).

The Govt. of India Act 1919 Rules Thereunder & Govt. Reports 1920, ed. H. N. Mitra (Calcuatta, 1921).

Green, T. H., *Prolegomena to Ethics*, ed. A. C. Bradley (Oxford, 1883).

Hambly G. R. G., 'Mahratta Nationalism before Tilak: Two Unpublished Letters of Sir Richard Temple on the State of the Bombay Deccan, 1879', *Journal of the Royal Central Asian Society*, 49 (1962), 144–160.

Haug, Martin (trans. and ed.), *The Aitareya Brahmanam of the Rigveda*, 2 vols (Bombay, 1863).

Haug, Martin, *Sacred Writings Language and Religion of the Parsees*, 4th ed., ed. E. W. West (London, 1907).

Historic Statements by Savarkar (1967), https://savarkar.org/en/encyc/2017/5/23/2_12_15_55_historic_statements_by_savarkar.v001.pdf_1.pdf.

Imperial gazetteer of India, 26 vols (Oxford, 1907–1909).

Indian National Congress Civil Disobedience Enquiry Committee, *Report of the Civil Disobedience Enquiry Committee, 1922* (Madras, 1923).

The Indian Penal Code (Act XLV of 1860). With Notes by W. Morgan and A. G. Macpherson (Calcutta, 1863).

India's Contribution to the Great War (Calcutta, 1923).

Infant Marriage and Enforced Widowhood in India: Being a Collection of Opinions For and Against, Received by Mr. Behramji M Malabari, from Representative Hindu Gentlemen and Official other Authorities (Bombay, 1887).

Jackson, J. W., *Ethnology and Phrenology as an Aid to the Historian* (London, 1863).

Jacobi, Hermann, 'Beitrage zur Kenntnis der Vedischen Chronologie', *Nachrichten von der Königl Gesellschaft der Wissenschaften* (1894),105–115.Jacobi, Hermann, 'On the Antiquity of Vedic Culture', *Journal of the Royal Asiatic Society of Great Britain and Ireland* (July 1909), 721–726.

Jnanedeva, *The Jnaneswari*, trans. Ranganath Shamachary Lokapur, 3 vols (Belgaum, 1995–1999).

Jones, William, *Discourses Delivered at the Asiatick Society, 1785–1792* ([Calcutta 1824]; London, 1993).

The India list and India Office list [1905] (London, 1905).

Kanetkar, M. J. *Tilak and Gandhi: A Comparative Character Sketch* (Nagpur, 1935).

Kennedy, Vans, *A Dictionary of the Maratha Language* (Bombay, 1824).

Kant, Immanuel, *Critique of Pure Reason*, 2nd, revised ed., trans. F. Max Muller (New York, 1900).

Kant, Immanuel, *Kant's Critique of Practical Reason, and Other Works on the Theory of Ethics*, 2nd ed., trans. T. K. Abbott (London, 1879).

Kelkar, N. C. (ed.), *Full and Authentic Report of the Tilak Trial (1908)* (Bombay, 1908).

Kelkar, N. C., *Landmarks in Lokamanya Tilak's Life* (Madras, 1924).

Kelkar, N. C., *Lokmanya Tilak Yanche Charitra*, vol. 3 (Poona, 1928).

Kelkar, N. C., *Life and Times of Lokamanya Tilak*, trans. D.V. Divekar (Delhi, 1987).

Kielhorn, Franz (ed.), *Paribhashandusekhara of Nagojibhatta*, 2 vols (Bombay, 1868–1874).

Kielhorn, Franz (ed.), *The Vyakarana-mahabhashya of Patanjali*, 3 vols (Bombay, 1880).

Kielhorn, Franz, *A Grammar of the Sanskrit Language*, 3rd ed. (Bombay, 1888).

Kitts, Eustace John, *Compendium of the Castes and Tribes Found in India* (Bombay, 1885).

Kunte, M. M., *The Vicissitudes of Aryan Civilization in India* (Bombay, 1880).

Laing, Samuel, *Human Origins* (London, 1893).

Latthe, A. B., *Memoirs of His Highness Shri Shahu Chhatrapati Maharaj*, 2 vols (Bombay, 1924).

The Legal Proceedings in the Case of Tilak v. Chirol and Another: Before Mr. Justice Darling and a Special Jury, January 29th 1919–February 21st 1919 (London, 1920).

Lemmings, David, 'Erskine, Thomas, First Baron Erskine (1750–1823)', *Oxford Dictionary of National Biography*, https://doi.org/10.1093/ref:odnb/8873.

Lenin, V. I., 'Inflammable Material in World Politics', *Proletary*, 33 (July 23 [August 5] 1908), Marxists Internet Archive, https://www.marxists.org/archive/lenin/works/1908/jul/23.htm, accessed 11 September 2023.

Long, George (ed.), *Penny Cyclopaedia of the Society for the Diffusion of Useful Knowledge*, 27 vols (London, 1833–1858 [& c]).

Lubbock, John, *Prehistoric Times* (London, 1865).

MacMunn, George Fletcher, *The Armies of India Painted by Major A C Lovett Described by Major G F MacMunn With foreword by Field-Marshal Earl Roberts* (London, 1911).

Maharaj Libel Case, Including Bhattia Conspiracy Case (Bombay, 1911).

The Mahomedan and Hindu Riots in Bombay, August 1893, from The Bombay Gazette (Bombay, 1893).

May It Please Your Honour: Statement of Nathuram Godse (Pune, 1977).

Mesopotamia Commission, *Report of the Commission Appointed by Act of Parliament to Empire into the Operations of the War in Mesopotamia* (London, 1917).

Mill, J. S., *Considerations on Representative Government* (New York, 1875).

Mill, J. S., *Utilitarianism*, ed. Roger Crisp ([1863] Oxford, 1998).

Mitchell, John Murray, *In Western India: Recollections of my Early Missionary Life* (Edinburgh, 1899).

Molesworth, James, *A Dictionary, Marathi and English*, 2nd ed. (Bombay, 1857).

Moor, Edward, *The Hindu Pantheon* (London, 1810).

Muir, *Original Sanskrit Texts on the Origin and Progress of the Religion and Institutions of India* (London, 1858).

Muller, Friedrich Max, 'On the Relation of the Bengali to the Arian and Aboriginal Languages of India', *Report of the Seventeenth Meeting of the British Association for the Advancement of Science: Held at Oxford in June 1847* (London, 1848), 319–350.

Muller, Friedrich Max (ed.), *Rig-Veda-Sanhita: The Sacred Hymns of the Brahmans: Together with the Commentary of Sayanacharya*, ed., (London, 1849–1874).

Muller, Friedrich Max, 'The Last Results of the Researches Respecting the non-Iranian and non-Semitic Languages of Asia and Europe, or The Turanian Family of Language', in Christian Bunsen, ed., *Outlines of the Philosophy of Universal History, Applied to Language and Religion*, 2 vols (London, 1854), I, 263–269.

Muller, Friedrich Max, *The Languages of the Seat of War in the East, with a Survey of the Three Families of Language, Semitic, Arian, and Turanian*, 2nd ed. (London, 1855).

Muller, Friedrich Max, *A History of Ancient Sanskrit Literature So Far As It Illustrates the Primitive Religion of the Brahmans*, 2nd ed. (London, 1860).

Muller, Friedrich Max, *On Ancient Hindu Astronomy and Chronology* (Oxford, 1862).

Muller, Friedrich Max, *India: What Can It Teach Us? A Course of Lectures Delivered before the University of Cambridge* (London, 1892).

Naoroji, Dadabhai, *Poverty and Un-British Rule in India* (London, 1901).

Natesan, G. A., *The Indian National Congress: Containing an Account of its Origin and Growth, Full Text of All the Presidential Addresses, Reprint of All the Congress Resolutions, Extracts from All the Welcome Addresses, Notable Utterances on the Movement, Portraits of all the Congress presidents*, 2nd ed. (Madras, 1917).

Nehru, Jawaharlal, *Selected Works of Jawaharlal Nehru*, ed. S. Gopal, 15 vols (Delhi, 1972–).

Nerurkar, M. H., *Vedoktadharmacha Vichara* (Bombay, 1874).

Nesbit, Robert, *The Brahman's Claims*, trans. D. G. Malhar (Madras, 1894).

Nietzsche, Friedrich Wilhelm, *Beyond Good and Evil: Prelude to a Philosophy of the Future*, trans. R. J. Hollingdale ([1886] London, 2003).

Nietzsche, Friedrich Wilhelm, *The Antichrist*, trans. Anthony M. Ludovici ([1888] Amherst, 2000).

'O Empress! Pray do not Interfere with Religion', from the *Bangabasi* (Calcutta, 1891).

Pandurang, Dadoba, *Dharma Vivechan* (Bombay, 1868).

Papers Relating to Infant Marriage and Enforced Widowhood in India. Selections from the Records of the Govt on India in the Home Department, No. 223 Home Dept Serial No. 3 (Calcutta, 1886).

Pavgee, Narayan Bhavanrao, *Bharatiya Samrajya*, 11 vols (place of publication unknown, 1893–1901).

Pavgee, Narayan Bhavanrao, *The Aryavartic home and the Aryan Cradle in the Sapta Sindhus: Or, From Aryavarta to the Arctic and From the Cradle to the Colony* (Poona, 1915).

Phadke, G. S., *Hindudharmatattva* (Poona, 1852).

Potdar, D. V., *Lo. Tilakance Sangati* (Poona, n.d.).

Prichard, J. C., *The Eastern Origin of the Celtic Nations Proved by a Comparison of their Dialects with the Sanskrit Greek Latin and Teutonic Languages* (London, 1831).

Prichard, J. C., *The Natural History of Man: Comprising Inquiries into the Modifying Influence of Physical and Moral Agencies on the Different Tribes of the Human Family* (London, 1843).

Prichard, J. C., 'On the Various Methods of Research which Contribute to the Advancement of Ethnology and of the Relations of That Science to Other Branches of Knowledge', *Report of the Seventeenth Meeting of the British Association for the Advancement of Science: Held at Oxford in June 1847* (London, 1848), 230–253.

Rai, Lala Lajpat, *Writings and Speeches*, ed. V. C. Joshi, 2 vols (Delhi, 1966).

Rai, Lala Lajpat, *Shivaji the Great Patriot*, trans. And ed. R. C. Suri (New Delhi, 1980).

Rai, Lala Lajpat, *Young India: An Interpretation and a History of the Nationalist Movement from Within* (New York, 1916).

Ramasami, E. V, *Words of Freedom: Ideas of a Nation* (New Delhi, 2010).

Ramdas, *Dasbodh: Spiritual Instruction for the Servant*, trans. Shilpa Joshi and Shrikrishna Karve [s.l.] (2010).

Ramdas, *Dasabodha*, S. B. Amarapurakara, et al. ed. (Bombay, 1853).

Ranade, M. G., *Rise of the Maratha Power* (Bombay, 1900).

Ranade, M. G., *Religious and Social Reform: A Collection of Essays and Speeches by Mahadeva Govind Ranade*, ed. M. B. Kolasker (Bombay, 1902).

Ranade, M. G., *The Miscellaneous Writings of the late Hon'ble Mr. Justice M. G. Ranade* (Bombay, 1915).

Rapson, E. J., 'Obituary Notice: Peter Peterson' in 'Notes on the Quarter (July, August, September 1899)', *Journal of the Royal Asiatic Society of Great Britain and Ireland* (October 1899), 915–919, 921–923.

Report of the Director of Public Instruction in the Bombay Presidency (Bombay, 1859–1860 [&c.]).

Roberts, Frederick Sleigh, *Forty-one Years in India: From Subaltern to Commander-in-Chief* (London, 1898).

Samarth, Anil, *Shivaji and the Indian National Movement: Saga of a Living Legend* (Bombay, 1975).

Saraswata Brahmana [IOR VT 2251].

Sarkar, Benoy Kumar, 'The Futurism of Young Asia', *International Journal of Ethics*, 28/4 (July 1918), 521–541.

Sarkar, Benoy Kumar, 'World Culture in Young India', in *The Future of Young India and Other Essays* (Berlin, 1922), 303–307.

Savarkar, V. D., *Hindu Rashtra Darshan: A Collection of the Presidential Speeches Delivered from the Hindu Mahasabha platform* (1949), https://savarkar.org/en/pdfs/hindu-rashtra-darshan-en-v002.pdf.

Savarkar, V. D., *Hindutva*, 5th ed. (Bombay, 1969).

Schleicher, August, *Compendium der vergleichenden grammatik der indogermanischen sprachen* (Weimar, 1861–1862).

Schrader, Otto, *Prehistoric Antiquities of the Aryan Peoples*, trans. F. B. Jevons, London, 1890).

Seeley, J. R., *The Expansion of England: Two Courses of Lectures*, revised ed. (Leipzig, 1884).

Sedition Committee, 1918: Report (Calcutta, 1918).

Setlur, S. S. and Deshpande, K. G., *A Full and Authentic Report of the Trial of Bal Gangadhar Tilak: At the Fourth Criminal Sessions 1897 of the Bombay High Court before Justice Strachey and a Special Jury* (Bombay, 1897).

Shankaracarya, *Gita in Sankara's Own Words*, trans. V. Panoli, 2 vols (Calicut, 1989–1990).

Sharp, Andrew (ed.), *The English Levellers* (Cambridge, 1998).

Smith, George, *The Life of John Wilson: For Fifty Years Scholar and Philanthropist in the East* (London, 1878).

Smith, George, *Stephen Hislop: Pioneer Missionary and Naturalist in Central India from 1844–1863* (London, 1888).

Spencer, Herbert, *The Data of Ethics* (London, 1879).

Strange, Thomas, *Elements of Hindu Law Referable to British Judicature in India* (London, 1825).

John Stevenson, 'Observations on the Marathi Language', *Journal of the Royal Asiatic Society of Great Britain and Ireland*, 7/I (1843), 84–91.

John Stevenson, 'Observations of the Grammatical Structure of the Vernacular Languages of India', *Journal of the Bombay Branch of the Royal Asiatic Society*, 3 (1849–1851), Part 1, 71–76.

Taylor, Isaac, *The Origin of the Aryans: An Account of the Prehistoric Ethnology and Civilisation of Europe*, 3rd ed. (London, 1908).

Telang, K. T., *Notes on the Age of Consent Bill* (Poona [?], 1891).

Telang, K. T., 'Gleanings from the Maratha Chronicles', in E. D. Morgan, ed., *Transactions of the Ninth International Congress of Orientalists*, 2 vols (London, 1893), i. 252–281.

The Tilak Case. Security under Sec. 108 Cr. P. C., 1916. Edited by D. V. Gokhale. (With portraits) (Bombay, 1917).

Thoreau, H. D., *Walden and Civil Disobedience* (London, 1983).

Tilak, Indu J., et al. [Amar Chitra Katha], *Lokmanya Tilak* (Bombay, 1980).

Vedic Hymns tr. by F. M. Müller, H. Oldenberg (Sacred Books of the East, 32 and 46) (Oxford, 1891, 1897).

Vivekananda, *The Complete Works of Swami Vivekananda*, 10th, enlarged ed., 8 vols (Calcutta, 1957–).

Warren, William F., *Paradise Found: The Cradle of the Human Race at the North Pole*, 10th ed. (Boston, 1893).

Weber, Albrecht, *The History of Indian Literature*, 3rd ed. (London, 1892).

Williams, Monier Monier-, A Sanskrit- English Dictionary: Etymologically and Philologically Arranged with Special Reference to Greek, Latin, Gothic, German, Anglo- Saxon, and other cognate Indo- European languages (Oxford, 1888).

Wilson, Daniel, *The Archaeology and Prehistoric Annals of Scotland* (Edinburgh, 1851).

Wilson, H. H., 'Max Müller's Ancient Sanskrit Literature', *Edinburgh Review*, 112 (1860), 361–385.

Wilson, John, *An Exposure of the Hindu Religion, in Reply to Mora Bhatta Dandekara* (Bombay, 1832).

Wilson, John, *India Three Thousand Years Ago* (Bombay, 1858).

Wilson, John, *Indian Caste*, 2 vols (Bombay, 1877).

Whitney, W. D., *Oriental and Linguistic Studies* (New York, 1873).

Yule, Henry and Burnell, Henry Coke, *Hobson-Jobson: A Glossary of Anglo-Indian Words and Phrases, and of Kindred Terms [and c.]* (London 1886).

iii) News websites and online only newspapers/news magazines

https://www.firstpost.com/.

https://india.com.

https://www.indiatvnews.com/.

The Print, https://theprint.in/.

The Wire, https://thewire.in/.

https://www.dnaindia.com/.

Scroll.in https://scroll.in/.

iv) Other primary web resources

Constituent Assembly Debates (Proceedings), https://loksabha.nic.in/writereaddata/cadebatefiles/C21111949.html.

Counterview, Interactive Voluntary E-platform Wedded to Peace, Democracy and Social justice (2022), https://counterview.org.

Government of Tamil Nadu, 'Backward Classes and Most Backward Classes Welfare Department, List of OBS [Other Backward Classes] for Maharashtra', http://www.bcmbcmw.tn.gov.in/obc/faq/maharashtra.pdf, accessed 2 April 2022.

Hindu Janajagruti Samiti, 'Controversial Matter', [in std. 7th NCERT book Beware Parents! The Textbooks of Centre's NCERT Teach Distorted History!] (2014), https://www.hindujagruti.org/hindu-issues/distortion-of-history/school-textbooks/ncert-textbook-controversy/controversial-matter.

National Council of Educational Research and Training, Textbooks and other Resources (version: 2022), https://ncert.nic.in/textbooks.php.

Website of Narendra Modi, Account of Public Meeting in Pune, July 14, 2013, https://www.narendramodi.in/need-of-the-hour-is-to-bid-goodbye-to-the-congress-which-has-failed-on-all-fronts-cm-at-bjp-public-meeting-in-pune-5392.

Supreme Court of India: Ramesh Yeshwant Prabhoo vs Shri Prabhakar Kashinath Kunte, 11 December 1995 [1996 SCC (1). 130], https://main.sci.gov.in/jonew/judis/10197.pdf, accessed November 2022.

Supreme Court of India: Bramchari Sidheswar Bhai & Ors. etc. vs State of West Bengal etc, 2 July 1995 [1995 SCC (4). 646], https://main.sci.gov.in/jonew/judis/10725.pdf, accessed November 2022.

Supreme Court of India: Sastri Yagnapurushadji vs Muldas Brudardas Vaishya, 14 January 1966 [1966 SCR (3). 242], https://main.sci.gov.in/jonew/judis/2757.pdf, accessed November 2022.

Supreme Court Observer, https://www.scobserver.in/, accessed November 2022.

http://twitter.com

Vishva Hindu Parishad (VHP), 'Cow Protection', 2021, https://vhp.org/cow_protection/.

Ministry of Information and Broadcasting YouTube Channel, https://www.youtube.com/@inbministry.

DD News (Doordarshan), YouTube channel, https://www.youtube.com/@ddnews.

Times Now Youtube Channel, https://www.youtube.com/TimesNow.

v) Films and television serials

Me Shivajiraje Bhosale Boltoy (2009, dir. Santosh Ramdas Manjrekar).

Lokmanya Ek Yugpurush (2015, dir. Om Raut).

Lokmanya Tilak (1957, dir. Vishram Bedeker).

Shobhayatra (2005, dir. Vijay Ghatge).

Satyamev Jayete (Aamir Khan Productions, Season 1, 2012, available at https://www.youtube.com/@SatyamevJayate).

vi) Published secondary works

Aarsleff, Hans, *The Study of Language in England, 1780–1860* (Princeton, 1982).

Alexander, Meena, 'Sarojini Naidu, Romanticism and Resistance', *Economic and Political Weekly*, 20/43 (26 October 1985), W68–W71.

Alter, Joseph S., 'Somatic Nationalism: Indian Wrestling and Militant Hinduism', *Modern Asian Studies*, 28/3(1994), 557–588.

Andersen, Walter K., and Damle, Shridhar D., *The Brotherhood in Saffron: The Rashtriya Swayamsevak Sangh and Hindu Revivalism* (Boulder, 1987).

Arblaster, Anthony, 'Liberal Values and Socialist Values', *Socialist Register*, 9 (1972).

'Aryan, adj. and n.', *OED Online* (Oxford University Press, September 2022; Web. 30 November 2020)

Athalye, D. V., *The Life of Lokamanya Tilak* (Poona, 1921).

Aziz, M. A., *A History of Pakistan: Past and Present* (Lahore, 1979).

Ballantyne, Tony, *Orientalism and Race: Aryanism in the British Empire* (Basingstoke, 2001).

Ballhatchet, Kenneth, *Social Policy and Social change in Western India 1818–1830* (London, 1957).

Banerjee, Milinda, 'Sovereignty as a Motor of Global Conceptual Travel: Sanskritic Equivalents of "Law" in Bengali Discursive Tradition', *Modern Intellectual History*, 17/2 (2020), 487–506.

Banerjee, Milinda, '"All This is Indeed Brahman": Rammohun Roy and a "Global" History of the Rights-Bearing Self', *Asian Review of World Histories*, 3/1 (January 2015), 81–112.

Banerjee, Milinda, *The Mortal God: Imagining the Sovereign in Colonial India* (Cambridge, 2017).

Basu, B. D., *History of Education in India Under the Rule of the East India Company* (Calcutta, 1922).

Basu, Tapan, et al., *Khaki Shorts and Saffron Flags: A Critique of the Hindu Right* (Hyderabad, 1993).

Barnouw, V., 'The Changing Character of a Hindu Festival', *American Anthropologist*, 56/1 (February 1954), 74–86.

Bayly, C. A., *The Local Roots of Indian Politics* (Allahabad, 1880–1920).

Bayly, C. A., *Empire and Information: Intelligence Gathering and Social Communication in India, 1780–1870* (Cambridge, 1996).

Bayly, C. A., *Origins of Nationality in South Asia: Patriotism and Ethical Government in the Making of Modern India* (Delhi, 1998).

Bayly, C. A., *The Birth of the Modern World, 1780–1914: Global Connections and Comparisons* (Oxford, 2004).

Bayly, C. A., 'Afterword', *Modern Intellectual History*, 4/1 (2007), 163–169.

Bayly, C. A., *Recovering Liberties: Indian Thought in the Age of Liberalism and Empire* (Cambridge, 2012).

Bayly, Susan, *Caste, Society and Politics in India from the Eighteenth Century to the Modern Age* (Cambridge, 1999).

Benson, James, 'Samkarabhatta's Family Chronicle', in Axel Michaels, ed., *The Pandit: Traditional Scholarship in India* (New Delhi, 2001), 105–118.

Bergunder, Michael, 'Contested past: Anti-Brahmanical and Hindu nationalist recon-structions of Indian prehistory', *Historiographia Linguistica*, 31/1 (2004), 59–104.

Bhagwat, A. K., *Lokamanya Tilak: A Biography* (Bombay, 1959).

Bhatt, Chetan, *Hindu Nationalism: Origins, Ideologies and Modern Myths* (Oxford, 2001).

birthright, n.', OED Online [Oxford University Press, September 2022. Web. 30 November 2021].

Bose, Sugata, 'The Spirit and Form of an Ethical Polity: A Meditation on Aurobindo's Thought', *Modern Intellectual History*, 4/1 (2007), 129–144.

Bose, Sugata, and Manjapra, Kris (eds), *Cosmopolitan Thought Zones: South Asia and the Global Circulation of Ideas* (Basingstoke, 2010).

Bose, Sugata, and Jalal, Ayesha, *Modern South Asia* (Abingdon, 2017).

Bronkhorst, Johannes, 'Traditional and Modern Sanskrit Scholarship: How Do They Relate to Each Other?', in Axel Michaels, ed., *The Pandit: Traditional Scholarship in India* (New Delhi, 2001), 167–180.

Brown, D. MacKenzie, 'The Philosophy of Bal Gangadhar Tilak: Karma vs. Jnana in the Gita Rahasya', *Journal of Asian Studies*, 17/2 (1958), 197–206.

Brown, Judith M., *Gandhi's Rise to Power: Indian Politics, 1915–1922* (Cambridge, 1972).

Brown, Robert L., *Ganesh: Studies of an Asian God* (Albany, 1991).

Bryant, Edwin, *The Quest for the Origins of Vedic Culture* (New York; Oxford, 2001).

Cashman, Richard I., *The Myth of the Lokamanya: Tilak and Mass Politics in Maharashtra* (Berkeley, 1975).

Catanach, I. J., *Rural Credit in Western India, 1875–1930* (Berkeley; London, 1970).

Chandrachud, Abhinav, *Republic of Rhetoric: Free Speech and the Constitution of India* (New Delhi, 2017).

Chandavarkar, Rajnarayan, *Origins of Industrial Capitalism: Business Strategies and the Working Classes in Bombay, 1900–1940* (Cambridge, 1994).

Chandra, Bipan, *Modern India* (New Delhi, 1971).

Chatterjee, Partha, *The Nation and Its Fragments: Colonial and Postcolonial Histories* (Princeton, 1993).

Chatterjee, Partha, 'History and the Nationalization of Hinduism', in Vasudha Dalmia and Heinrich von Stietencron, eds, *Representing Hinduism* (Delhi, 1995), 103–128.

Chowdhury, Indira, *The Frail Hero and Virile History: Gender and the Politics of Culture in Colonial Bengal* (Oxford, 2001).

Cohn, Bernard, 'Law and the Colonial State in India', in June Starr and Jane F. Collier, eds, *History and Power in the Study of Law: New Directions in Legal Anthropology* (London, 1989), 131–152.

Confino, Alon, 'Collective Memory and Cultural History: Problems of Method', *The American Historical Review*, 102/5 (December 1997), 1386–1403.

Conlon, Frank F., 'Vishnubawa Brahmachari: A Champion of Hinduism in Nineteenth Century Maharashtra', in N. K Wagle and A. Kulkarni, eds, *Region, Nationality and Religion* (Mumbai, 1999), 157–184.

Constable, Philip, 'The Marginalization of a Dalit Martial Race in Late Nineteenth-and Early Twentieth-Century Western India', *Journal of Asian Studies*, 60 (May 2001), 439–478.

Courtright, Paul B., *Ganesa, Lord of Obstacles, Lord of Beginnings* (Oxford, 1989).

Dalmia, Vasudha, *The Nationalization of Hindu Traditions: Bharatendu Harischandra and Nineteenth-century Banaras* (Delhi, 1997).

Dalrymple, William, 'India: The War Over History', *New York Review of Books* (7 April 2005), https://www.nybooks.com/.

Dandekar, R. N. (ed.), *Ramakrishna Gopal Bhandarkar as an Indologist: A Symposium* (Poona, 1976).

Dandekar, R. N. (ed.), *Sanskrit and Maharashtra: A Symposium* (Poona, 1972).

Dasgupta, Surendranath, *A History of Indian Philosophy*, 5 vols (Cambridge, 2009–).

Davis, Donald R. Jr, *The Spirit of Hindu Law* (Cambridge, 2010).

Davis, Donald R. Jr, 'A Realist View of Hindu Law', *Ratio Juris*, 19/3 (2006), 287–313.

Delhi Historians' Group, *Communalisation of Education: The History Textbook Controversy* (New Delhi, 2001[?]), http://www.sacwose.net/India_History/DelHistorians.pdf.

Deming, Wilbur S., *Ramdas and the Ramdasis* ([1928] Gurgaon,1990).

Derrett, Duncan, *Religion, Law and the State in India* (London, 1968).

Des Chene, Mary, 'Military Ethnology in British India', *South Asia Research*, 19/2 (1999), 121–135.

Deshpande, Madhav M., 'Pandit and Professor: Transformations in the 19th Century Maharashtra', in Axel Michaels, ed., *The Pandit: Traditional Scholarship in India* (New Delhi, 2001), 119–154.

Deshpande, Madhav M., 'Aryan Origins: Arguments from Nineteenth-century Maharashtra', in E. F. Bryant and L. L. Patton, eds, *The Indo-Aryan Controversy: Evidence and Inference in Indian History* (London, 2005), 407–433.

Deshpande, Madhav M., '"The Arctic Home in the Vedas": Religion, Politics and the Colonial Context', in Vinay Lal, ed., *Political Hinduism: The Religious Imagination in Public Spheres* (New Delhi; Oxford, 2009), 33–57.

Deshpande, Madhav M., 'Kshatriyas in the Kali Age? Gagabhatta and his Opponents', *Indo-Iranian Journal*, 53 (2010), 95–120.

Deshpande, Kusumawati and Rajadhyaksha, M. V., *A History of Marathi Literature* (New Delhi, 1988).

Deshpande, Prachi, 'Caste as Maratha: Social categories, colonial policy and identity in early twentieth-century Maharashtra', *Indian Economic Social History Review*, 41 no. 1 (Feb 2004), 7–32

Deshpande, Prachi, *Creative Pasts: Historical Memory and Identity in Western India, 1700–1960* (New York; Chichester, 2007).

Dev, Arjun, and Dev, Indira Arjun, *Modern India: A History Textbook for Class VIII* [NCERT] (Delhi, 1989; repr. 2002).

Devji, Faisal, *The Impossible Indian: Gandhi and the Temptation of Violence* (Harvard, 2012).

Dirks, Nicholas B., *The Hollow Crown: Ethnohistory of an Indian Kingdom* (Cambridge, 1987).

Dobbin, Christine, *Urban Leadership in Western India: Politics and Communities in Bombay City, 1840–1885* (London, 1972).

Dodson, Michael S., 'Contesting Translations: Orientalism and the Interpretation of the Vedas', *Modern Intellectual History*, 4/1 (2007), 43–59.

Doniger, Wendy, *The Hindus: An Alternative History* (New York, 2009).

Dwivedi, Sharada, and Mehrotra, Rahul, *Bombay: The Cities Within* (Mumbai, 2001).

Ellinwood, DeWitt C., 'Ethnicity in a Colonial Asian Army: British Policy, War and the Indian Army, 1914–1918', in DeWitt C. Ellinwood and Cynthia Enloe, eds, *Ethnicity and the Military in Asia* (London, 1981), 89–144.

Engels, Dagmar, 'The Age of Consent Bill: Colonial Ideology in Bengal', *South Asia Research*, 3/2 (1983), 107–134.

Fasana, E., 'Deshabhakta: The Leaders of the Italian Independence Movement in the Eyes of Marathi Nationalists', in N. K. Wagle, ed., *Writers, Editors, and Reformers: Social and Political Transformations of Maharashtra, 1830–1930* (Delhi, 1999), 42–63.

Flood, Gavin, *The Blackwell Companion to Hinduism* (Oxford, 2003).

Fort, Andrew O., *Jivanmukti in Transformation: Embodied Liberation in Advaita and neo-Vedanta* (Albany, 1998).

Fort, Andrew O., 'Knowing Brahman while Embodied: Sankara on Jivanmukti', *Journal of Indian Philosophy*, 19 (1991), 369–389.

Fraser, James Nelson, *Deccan College: A Retrospect 1851–1901* (Poona, 1902).

Gainty, Denis, *Martial Arts and the Body Politic in Meiji Japan* (London, 2013).

Ganachari, Aravind, *Nationalism and Social Reform in the Colonial Situation* (Delhi, 2005).

Ghaswalla, Sorab, *Lokmanya Tilak: Symbol of Swaraj* (New Delhi, 2003).

Ghosh, Durba, *Gentlemanly Terrorists: Political Violence and the Colonial State in India, 1919–1947* (Cambridge, 2017).

Gommans, J. J. L., 'The Embarrassment of Political Violence in Europe and South Asia, c. 1100–1800', in Jan E. M. Houben and Karel R. Van Kooiji, eds, *Violence Denied: Violence, Non-violence and the Rationalization of Violence in South Asian Cultural History* (Leiden; Boston, 1999), 287–316.

Gordon, Richard, 'The Hindu Mahasabha and the Indian National Congress, 1915 to 1926', *Modern Asian Studies*, 9 (1975), 145–203.

Gordon, Stewart, *The Marathas, 1600–1818* (Cambridge, 1993).

Gole, R. M., *N. C. Kelkar* (New Delhi, 1976).

Gopal, Ram, *Lokamanya Tilaka* (Bombay, 1965).

Gopal, Ram, *Lokamanya Tilak: A Biography* (Bombay, 1956).

Gore, M. S., 'Identifying Maharashtra as a Cultural Region', in N. K Wagle and A. Kulkarni, eds, *Region, Nationality and Religion* (Mumbai, 1999), 1–4.

Gould, William, *Religion and Conflict in Modern South Asia* (Cambridge, 2011).

Gould, William, *Hindu Nationalism and the Language of Politics in Late Colonial India* (Cambridge, 2004).

Guichard, Sylvie, *The Construction of History and Nationalism in India: Textbooks, Controversies and Politics* (London, 2010).

Guha, Ramachandra, *Makers of Modern India* (New Delhi, 2010).

Hacker, Paul, 'Aspects of Neo-Hinduism as Contrasted with Surviving Traditional Hinduism', in Wilhelm Halbfass, ed., *Philology and Confrontation: Paul Hacker on Traditional and Modern Vedanta* (Albany, 1995), 229–256.

Hansen, Thomas Blom, *The Saffron Wave: Democracy and Hindu Nationalism in Modern India* (Princeton, 1999).

Hansen, Thomas Blom, 'Sovereigns Beyond the State: On Legality and Public Authority in India', in Ravinder Kaur, ed. *Religion, Violence and Political Mobilisation in South Asia* (London, 2005), 109–144.

Halbwachs, Maurice, *On Collective Memory*, ed. and trans. Lewis A. Cose (Chicago, 1992).

Hanioglu, M. Sukru, *Preparation for a Revolution: The Young Turks, 1902–1908* (Oxford, 2001).

Harvey, M. J., 'The Secular as Sacred?—The Religio-Political Rationalization of B. G. Tilak', *Modern Asian Studies*, 20/2 (1986), 321–331.

Hasan, Mushirul, 'The Myth of Unity: Colonial and National Narratives', in David Ludden, ed., *Making India Hindu* (Oxford, 2007), 185–208.

Hatcher, Brian, *Bourgeois Hinduism, or the Faith of the Modern Vedantists: Rare Discourses from Early Colonial Bengal* (New York and Oxford, 2008).

Heehs, Peter, *India's Freedom Struggle 1857–1947: A Short History* (Delhi, 1988).

Hewart, E. G. K, *Christ and Western India: A Study of the Growth of the Indian Church in Bombay City from 1813*, 2nd ed. (Bombay, 1953).

Hutton, Patrick H., *History as an Art of Memory* (Hanover; London, 1993).

Ilaiah, Kancha, 'Towards the Dalitization of the Nation', in Partha Chatterjee, ed., *Wages of Freedom: Fifty Years of the Indian Nation-state* (Delhi; Oxford, 1998), 267–292.

Inamdar, N. R. (ed.)., *Political Thought and Leadership of Lokamanya Tilak* (New Delhi, 1983).

Irschick, Eugene F., 'Dravidianism in South Indian Politics', in A. Sjoberg, ed., *Symposium on Dravidian Civilization* (Austin, 1971), 147–169.

Irschick, Eugene F., *Dialogue and History: Constructing South India, 1795–1895* (Berkeley, 1994).

Isayeva, Natalia, *Shankara and Indian Philosophy* (Albany, 1993).

Iyengar, Ramaswami, 'Dr. Buhler', in [editor unknown] *Eminent Orientalists, Indian, European, American* (Madras, 1922), 129–146.

Jaffrelot, Christophe (ed.), *The Hindu Nationalist Movement and Indian Politics, 1925 to the 1990s: Strategies of Identity-building, Implantation and Mobilisation (with Special Reference to Central India)* (London, 1996).

Jaffrelot, Christophe (ed.), *Hindu Nationalism: A Reader* (Oxford, 2007).

Jain, Devaki, *Women, Development and the UN* (Bloomington, 1995).

Jalal, Ayesha, 'Striking a Just Balance: Maulana Azad as a Theorist of Trans- National Jihad', *Modern Intellectual History*, 4/1 (2007), 95–107.

Jog, Narayan Gopal, *Lokamanya Bal Gangadhar Tilak* (Delhi, 1962).

Johnson, Gordon, 'Chitpavan Brahmins and Politics in Western India in the Late Nineteenth and Early Twentieth Centuries', in Edmund Leach and S. N. Mukherjee, eds, *Elites in South Asia* (Cambridge, 1970), 95–118.

Johnson, Gordon, *Provincial Politics and Indian Nationalism: Bombay and the Indian National Congress, 1880 to 1915* (Cambridge, 1973).

Johnson, W. J., *A Dictionary of Hinduism* (Oxford, 2009).

Jones, Kenneth, *Socio-Religious Reform Movements in British India* (Cambridge, 1990).

Jones, Kenneth, *Religious Controversy in British India: Dialogues in South Asian Languages* (Albany, 1992).

Jones, Kenneth, *Arya Dharm: Hindu Consciousness in 19th-century Punjab* (New Delhi, 1976).

Kaiwar, Vasant, 'The Aryan Model of History and the Oriental Renaissance: The Politics of Identity in an Age of Revolutions, Colonialism, and Nationalism' in

Vasant Kaiwar and Sucheta Mazumdar (eds.), *Antinomies of Modernity 'Essays on Race, Orient, Nation'* (2003), 13–61.

Kamra, Sukeshi, 'Law and Radical Rhetoric in British India: The 1897 Trial of Bal Gangadhar Tilak', *South Asia: Journal of South Asian Studies*, 39/3 (2016), 546–559, DOI: 10.1080/00856401.2016.1196529.

Kane, P. V., *History of Dharmashastra (Ancient and Mediæval Religious and Civil Law)*, 5 vols (Poona, 1930–1962).

Kapila, Shruti, 'Self, Spencer, and Swaraj: Nationalist Thought and Critiques of Liberalism, *Modern Intellectual History*, 4/1 (2007), 109–127.

Kapila, Shruti, 'A History of Violence', *Modern Intellectual History*, 7/2 (2010), 437–457.

Kapila, Shruti, 'Preface' [Special issue: 'An Intellectual History for India'], *Modern Intellectual History*, 4/1 (April 2007), 3–6.

Kapila, Shruti, and Devji, Faisal, 'The Bhagavad Gita and Modern Indian Thought: An Introduction', *Modern Intellectual History*, 7/2 (2010), 269–273.

Karandikar, S. L., *Lokamanya Bal Gangadhar Tilak; The Hercules & Prometheus of Modern India* (Poona, 1957).

Karkaria, R. P., *India, Forty Years of Progress and Reform: Being a Sketch of the Life and Times of Behramji M. Malabari* (London, 1896).

Karmarkar, D. P., *Lokmanya Tilak, A Study* (Bombay, 1956).

Kaur, Raminder, *Performative Politics and the Cultures of Hinduism: Public Uses of Religion in Western India* (London, 2005).

Kaur, Satvinder, *Sarojini Naidu's Poetry: Melody of Indianness* (Delhi, 2003).

Kaye, G. R., *Hindu Astronomy* (Calcutta, 1924).

Keer, Dhananjay, *Lokamanya Tilak, Father of the Indian Freedom Struggle*, 2nd ed. (Bombay, 1969).

Khan, S. U., *Saffronisation of Education* (Delhi, 2004).

Kidambi, Prashant, *The Making of an Indian Metropolis: Colonial Governance and Public Culture in Bombay 1890–1920* (Ashgate, 2007).

Kidambi, Prashant, Kamat, Manjiri, and Dwyer, Rachel (eds), *Bombay before Mumbai: Essays in Honour of Jim Masselos* (London, 2019).

Kochhar, Rajesh, and Narlikar, Jayant, *Astronomy in India: A Perspective* (New Delhi, 1995).

Kosambi, Meera, 'Life After Widowhood: Two radical reformist options in Maharashtra', in M. Kosambi, ed., *Intersections: Socio-Cultural Trends in Maharashtra* (New Delhi, 2000), 92–117.

Kosambi, Meera, 'Child Brides and Child Mothers: The Age of Consent Controversy in Maharashtra as a Conflict of Perspectives on Women', in Anne Feldhaus, ed., *Images of Women in Maharashtrian Society* (Albany, 1998), 135–162.

Kothari, Miloon, 'Remembering India's Contributions to the Universal Declaration of Human Rights', *The Wire*, 20 December 2018, https://thewire.in/rights/indias-important-contributions-to-the-universal-declaration-of-human-rights.

Kumar, Radha, 'From Chipko to Sati: The Contemporary Indian Women's Movement', in Amrita Basu, ed., *The Challenge of Local Feminisms: Women's Movements in Global Perspective* (Oxford, 1995), 55–86.

Kumar, Ravinder, *Western India in the Nineteenth Century: A Study in the Social History of Maharashtra* (London, 1968).

Kuruvachira, Jose, *Hindu Nationalists of Modern India: A Critical Study of the Intellectual Genealogy of Hindutva* (Jaipur, 2006).

Laine, James, *Shivaji: Hindu King in Islamic India* (Oxford and New York, 2003).

Lal, Vinay, 'Gandhi's West, the West's Gandhi', *New Literary History*, 40/2 (2009), 281–313.

Lall, Marie, 'Educate to Hate: The Use of Education in the Creation of Antagonistic National Identities in India and Pakistan', *Compare*, 38/1 (2008), 103–119.

Lariviere, Richard W., *Studies in Dharmashastra* (1986).

Lederle, Matthew, *Philosophical Trends in Modern Maharashtra* (Bombay, 1976).

Leopold, Joan, 'British Applications of the Aryan Theory of Race to India, 1859–1870', *English Historical Review*, 89/352 (July 1974), 587–603.

Leopold, Joan, 'The Aryan Theory of Race', *Indian Economic and Social History Review*, 7 (1970), 271–297.

Malik, S. C., *Dissent, Protest and Reform in Indian Civilization* (Simla, 1977).

Manela, Erez, *The Wilsonian Moment: Self-Determination and the International Origins of Anticolonial Nationalism* (Oxford, 2007).

Marshall, P. J., ed., *The British Discovery of Hinduism in the Eighteenth Century* (Cambridge, 1970).

Martin, David, *Religion and Power: No Logos Without Mythos* (Burlington; Ashgate, 2014).

Martin, Gregory, 'The Influence of Racial Attitudes on British Policy towards India during the First World War', *Journal of Imperial and Commonwealth History*, 14/2 (1986), 91–113.

Masselos, Jim, 'Tilak and Gandhi: A Study in Alternatives', in Sibnarayan Ray, ed., *Gandhi, India and the World* (Philadelphia, 1970), 81–98.

Masselos, Jim, 'Some Aspects of Bombay City Politics in 1919', in Ravinder Kumar, ed., *Essays on Gandhian politics: The Rowlatt Satyagraha of 1919* (Oxford, 1971), 161–166.

Masselos, Jim, *Towards Nationalism: Group Affiliations and the Politics of Public Associations in Nineteenth-century Western India* (Bombay, 1974).

Masselos, Jim, 'Tilak, Bal Gangadhar (1856–1920)', in *Oxford Dictionary of National Biography* (2007), https://doi.org/10.1093/ref:odnb/41085.

Mbembe, Achille, *On the Postcolony* (Berkeley, 2001).

Mehta, V. R., and Thomas Pantham, eds, *Political Ideas in Modern India: Thematic Explorations* (New Delhi; London, 2006).

Metcalf, Thomas R., *Ideologies of the Raj* (Cambridge, 1995).

Minault, Gail, *The Khilafat Movement: Religious Symbolism and Political Mobilization in India* (New Delhi, 1999).

Minor, Robert (ed.), *Modern Indian Interpreters of the Bhagavadgita* (Albany, 1986).

Minkowski, Christopher, 'Advaita Vedānta in Early Modern History', in Rosalind O'Hanlon and David Washbrook, eds, *Religious Cultures in Early Modern India: New Perspectives, Special Volume of South Asian History and Culture*, 2/2 (2011), 205–231.

Moffat, Chris, *India's Revolutionary Inheritance: Politics and the Promise of Bhagat Singh* (Cambridge, 2019).

Moyn, Samuel, 'On the Nonglobalization of Ideas', in Samuel Moyn and Andrew Sartori, eds, *Global Intellectual History* (New York, 2013), 187–204.

Moyn, Samuel, and Andrew Sartori, 'Approaches to Global Intellectual History', in Samuel Moyn and Andrew Sartori, eds, *Global Intellectual History* (New York, 2013), 3–30.

Mukherjee, Mithi, 'Sedition, Law, and the British Empire in India: The Trial of Tilak (1908)', *Law, Culture and the Humanities* (January 2017), 454–476.

Naik, Chitra (ed.), *Lokmanya Tilak as Educational Thinker* (Pune, 2004).

Naik, J. V. *The Collected Works of JV Naik: Reform and Renaissance in Nineteenth-century Maharashtra: Edited with an Introduction by Murali Ranganathan* (Mumbai, 2016).

Naik, J. V., 'Lokmanya Tilak on Karl Marx and Class Conflict', *EPW*, 34/18 (1 May 1999), 1023–1025.

Nandy, Ashis, *The Intimate Enemy: Loss and Recovery of Self under Colonialism* (New York, 1983).

Natarajan, S., *A Century of Social Reform in India* (London, 1959).

National Council of Educational Research and Training, *India and the Contemporary World II* (Delhi, 2013).

National Council of Educational Research and Training (NCERT), *India's Struggle for Independence: Visuals and Documents* (Delhi, 1985).

National Council of Educational Research and Training (NCERT), *Our Pasts III* (Delhi, 2021).

Nayyar, A. H., and Salim, Ahmad (eds), *The Subtle Subversion: The State of Curricula and Textbooks in Pakistan* (Islamabad, 2003 [?]), https://sdpi.org/.

Nicholson, Andrew, *Unifying Hinduism: Philosophy and Identity in Indian Intellectual History* (New York, 2010).

O'Hanlon, Rosalind, 'Maratha History as Polemic: Low Caste Ideology and Political Debate in Late Nineteenth-century Western India', *Modern Asian Studies* 17/1 (1983), 1–33.

O'Hanlon, Rosalind, *Caste, Conflict and Ideology: Mahatma Jotirao Phule and Low Caste Protest in Nineteenth-century Western India* (Cambridge, 1985).

O'Hanlon, Rosalind, 'From Ritual Status to Political Conflict: Brahmans and Marathas in Southern Maharashtra Under Early East India Company Rule', in Kenneth Ballhatchet and John Harrison, eds, *East India Company Studies: Papers Presented to Professor Sir Cyril Philips* (London, 1986), 233–254.

O'Hanlon, Rosalind, 'Acts of Appropriation: Non-Brahman Radicals and the Congress in Early Twentieth-Century Maharashtra', in M. Shepperdson and C. Simmons, eds, *The Indian National Congress and the Political Economy of India, 1885–1985* (Aldershot, 1988), 102–146.

O'Hanlon, Rosalind, *A Comparison between Women and Men: Tarabai Shinde and the Critique of Gender Relations in Colonial India* (Oxford, 1994).

O'Hanlon, Rosalind, 'Narratives of Penance and Purification in Western India, c. 1650–1850', *Journal of Hindu Studies*, 2/1 (2009), 48–75.

O'Hanlon, Rosalind, 'Letters Home: Banaras Pandits and the Maratha Regions in Early Modern India', *Modern Asian Studies*, 44/2 (2010), 201–240.

O'Hanlon, Rosalind, and Minkowski, Christopher, 'What Makes People Who They Are? Pandit Networks and the Problem of Livelihoods in Early Modern Western India', *Indian Economic & Social History Review*, 45 (2008), 381–416.

Omissi, David E., *The Sepoy and the Raj: the India Army, 1860–1940* (London, 1994).

Omvedt, Gail, *Cultural Revolt in a Colonial Society: The NonBrahman Movement in Western India, 1873–1930* (Berkeley, 1976).

Omvedt, Gail, *Reinventing Revolution: New Social Movements and the Socialist Tradition in India* (Armonk and London, 1993).

Owen, Hugh, 'Towards Nationwide Agitation and Organisation, the Home Rule Leagues 1915–1918', in D. A. Low, ed., *Soundings in Modern South Asian History* (London, 1968), 159–196.

Owen, Hugh, 'Organizing for the Rowlatt Satyagraha of 1919', in R. Kumar, ed., *Essays on Gandhian Politics: The Rowlatt Satyagraha of 1919* (Oxford, 1971), 64–92.

Owen, Hugh, 'Negotiating the Lucknow Pact', *Journal of Asian Studies*, 31/3 (1972), 561–587.

Paswan, Sanjay, and Jaideva, Paramanshi (eds), *Encyclopaedia of Dalits in India*, 14 vols (Delhi, 2002–2003).

Patterson, Maureen, 'Changing Patterns of Occupation among Chitpavan Brahmans', *Indian Economic & Social History Review*, 7/3 (January 1970), 375–396.

Palshikar, Sanjay, *Evil and the Philosophy of Retribution: Modern Commentaries on the Bhagavad-Gita*, [s.l.] (2015).

Pagdi, Gayatri, *Lokmanya Tilak: The First National Leader* (Delhi, 2019).

Pandey, Gyanendra, *Routine Violence: Nations, Fragments, Histories* (Stanford, 2006).

Pandey, Gyanendra, *The Construction of Communalism in Colonial North India* (Oxford, 1990).

Pandey, Gyanendra, 'Rallying Round the Cow: Sectarian Strife in the Bhojpuri Region, c.1888–1917', in Ranajit Guha, et al. eds, *Subaltern Studies: Writings on South Asian history and Society*, 10 vols (Delhi; Oxford, 1994–1999), ii, 60–129.

Parekh, Bhikhu, *Gandhi's Political Philosophy: a Critical Examination* (Basingstoke, 1989).

Parvate, T. V., *Bal Gangadhar Tilak* (Ahmedabad, 1958).

Parvate, T. V., *Tilak, the Economist* (Bombay, 1985).

Pati, Biswamoy (ed.), *Bal Gangadhar Tilak: Popular Readings* (Delhi, 2011).

Pels, P., 'The Politics of Aboriginality: Brian Houghton Hodgson and the Making of an Ethnology of India', in P. van de Velde, ed., *International Institute for Asian Studies Yearbook* (Leiden, 1994), 147–168.

Phadke, H. A., *R. G. Bhandarkar* (New Delhi, 1968).

Phadke, Yashwant Dinkar, *Shodh: Bal-Gopalancha* (Pune, 1977)

Pinch, W. R., *Warrior Ascetics and Indian Empires* (New York, 2006).

Pinney, Christopher, 'The Tiger's Nature, but Not the Tiger: Bal Gangadhar Tilak as Mohandas Karamchand Gandhi's Counter-Guru', *Public Culture*, 23/2 (2011), 395–416.

Poliakov, Léon, *The Aryan Myth: A History of Racist and Nationalist Ideas in Europe*, trans. Edmund Howard (New York, 1977).

Pollock, Sheldon, *The Ends of Man at the End of Premodernity* (Amsterdam, 2005).

Pollock, Sheldon, 'New Intellectuals in Seventeenth-century India', *The Indian Economic & Social History Review*, 38/1 (2001), 3–31.

Powell, Avril A., 'Muir, John (1810–1882)', in *Oxford Dictionary of National Biography* (Oxford, 2004), [http://www.oxforddnb.com/view/article/19497, accessed 20 February 2010.

Pradhan, G. P., *Lokmanya Tilak* (New Delhi, 1994).

Pradhan, G. P., and Bhagwat, A. K., *Lokamanya Tilak: A Biography* (Bombay, 1959).

Pradhan, S. D., 'Indian Army and the First World War', in DeWitt C. Ellinwood and S. D. Pradhan, eds, *India and World War 1* (New Delhi, 1978), 49–67.

Prior, K., 'Harris, George Robert Canning, Fourth Baron Harris (1851–1932)., Cricketer and Administrator in India', in *Oxford Dictionary of National Biography*, https://doi.org/10.1093/ref:odnb/33724.

Radhakrishnan, Sarvepalli, 'Bal Gangadhar Tilak', in [editor unknown] *Eminent Orientalists, Indian, European, American* (Madras, 1922)

Rao, Parimala V., *Foundations of Tilak's Nationalism: Discrimination, Education and Hindutva* (New Delhi, 2010).

Rao, Velcheru Narayana, Shulman, David, and Subrahmanyam, Sanjay, *Textures of Time: Writing History in South India 1600–1800* (New York, 2003).

Raychaudhuri, Tapan, *Europe Reconsidered: Perceptions of the West in Nineteenth Century Bengal* (Delhi, 1988).

Richards, Graham, 'Bain, Alexander (1818–1903)', *Oxford Dictionary of National Biography* (Oxford, 2004), http://www.oxforddnb.com/view/article/30533, accessed 4 January 2013.

Richman, Paula, ed., *Many Ramayanas: The Diversity of a Narrative Tradition in South Asia* (Delhi, 1992).

Robinson, Catherine A., *Interpretations of the Bhagavad-Gita and Images of the Hindu Tradition: the Song of the Lord* (London; New York, 2006).

Rosselli, John, 'The Self-image of Effeteness: Physical Education and Nationalism in Nineteenth-century Bengal', *Past & Present*, 86/1 (1980), 121–148.

Roy, Kaushik, 'Recruitment Doctrines of the Colonial Indian Army: 1859–1913', *Indian Economic Social History Review*, 34 (1997), 321–354.

Rudolph, Lloyd I. and Susanne Hoeber Rudolph, 'Rethinking Secularism Genesis and Implications of the Textbook Controversy 1977–1979', *Pacific Affairs* 56/1 (1983), 15–37.

Saraf, Nandini, *The Life and Times of Lokmanya Tilak* (New Delhi, 2012).

Sarkar, Sumit, '"Kaliyuga", "Chakri" and "Bhakti": Ramakrishna and His Times', *Economic and Political Weekly*, 27/29 (18 July 1992), 1543–1559, 1561–1566.

Sarkar, Sumit, 'Indian Nationalism and the Politics of Hindutva', in David Ludden, ed., *Making India Hindu* (New Delhi, 1996).

Sarkar, Tanikar, 'Rhetoric against Age of Consent: Resisting Colonial Reason and the Death of a Child-Wife', *Economic and Political Weekly*, 28/36 (4 September 1993), 1869–1878.

Sarkar, Tanika, *Hindu Wife, Hindu Nation Community, Religion, and Cultural Nationalism* (Delhi, 2001).

Sartori, Andrew, *Bengal in Global Concept History: Culturalism in the Age of Capital* (Chicago, 2009).

Sartori, Andrew, 'The Transfiguration of Duty in Aurobindo's Essays on the Gita', *Modern Intellectual History*, 7/2 (2010), 319–334.

Sathe, Shanta, *Lokmanya Tilak, His Social and Political Thoughts* (Delhi, 1994).

Sen, Amiya, 'Hindu Revivalism in Action: The Age of Consent Bill Agitation in Bengal', *The Indian Historical Review*, 7/1–2 (1980–1981), 160–184.

Sen, S. N. and Shukla, K. S. (eds), *History of Astronomy in India* (Delhi, 1985).

Sen, Ronojoy, *Defining Religion: The Indian Supreme Court and Hinduism* (Heidelberg Papers in South Asian and Comparative Politics, Working Paper No. 29 November 2006).

Seth, Sanjay, 'The Critique of. Renunciation: Bal Gangadhar Tilak's Hindu Nationalism', *Postcolonial Studies*, 19/2 (2006), 137–150.

Seth, Sanjay, *Subject Lessons: The Western Education of Colonial India* (Durham, N.C; Chesham, 2007).

Sharma, Arvind, 'Jivanmukti in Neo-Hinduism: The Case of Ramaa Mahari', *Asian Philosophy*, 15/3 (2005), 207–220.

Sharma, Jai Narain, *The Political Thought of Lokmanya Bal Gangadhar Tilak (Encyclopedia of Eminent Thinkers)* vol. 24 (New Delhi, 2009).

Sharpe, Eric J., *The Universal Gita: Western Images of the Bhagavatgita: A Bicentenary Survey* (London, 1985).

Shehab, Rafiullah, *History of Pakistan* (Lahore, 1989).

Singh, Hulas, *Rise of Reason: Intellectual History of 19th-century Maharashtra* (Abingdon, 2016).

Singh, Nihar Nandan, *Lokamanya Bal Gangdhar Tilak: The Life and Achievements of a Mass Leader and Fighter for India's Freedom* (New Delhi, 1985).

Singha, Radhika, 'Nationalism, Colonialism and the Politics of Masculinity', *Studies in History*, 14/1 (1998), 127–146.

Sinha, Mrinalini, *Colonial Masculinity: The 'Manly Englishman' and the 'Effeminate Bengali' in the Late Nineteenth century* (Manchester, 1995).

Sinha, Rakesh, *Dr. Keshav Baliram Hedgewar*, 'Builders of Modern India' series (New Delhi, 2015).

Sitaramayya, Pattabhi, *History of the Indian National Congress, 1885–1935* (Madras, 1935).

Skinner, Quentin, 'Meaning and Understanding in the History of Ideas', in James Tully, ed., *Meaning and Context: Quentin Skinner and His Critics* (Princeton, 1988), 29–67.

Smith, Brian K., 'Questioning Authority: Constructions and Deconstructions of Hinduism', *International Journal of Hindu Studies*, 2/3 (1998), 313–339.

Somwanshi, Gaurav, 'Bal Gangadhar Tilak: Teaching English Would Prove to Turn out Girls to be a Dead Weight on their Husbands', https://counterview.org.

Sovani, N. V., 'Economic Thought of Tilak', in N. R. Inamdar, ed., *Political Thought and Leadership of Lokmanya Tilak* (New Delhi, 1983), 151–154.

Spencer, Jonathan, 'Afterword: We Have Other Ideas', in *South Asian Sovereignty* (Delhi, 2019), 216–226.

Steitencron, Heinrich, *Hindu Myth, Hindu History; Religion Art and Politics* (Delhi, 2005).

Stepan, Nancy, *The Idea of Race in Science: Great Britain, 1800–1960* (Basingstoke, 1982).

Streets, Heather, *Martial Races: The Military, Race and Masculinity in British Imperial Culture, 1857–1914* (Manchester, 2017).

Subrahmanyam, Sanjay, 'Global Intellectual History beyond Hegel and Marx', *History and Theory*, 54/1 (2015), 126–137.

Tahmankar, D. V., *Lokamanya Tilak: Father of Indian Unrest and Maker of Modern India* (London, 1956).

Tejani, Shabnum, *Indian secularism: a social and intellectual history, 1890–1950* (Bloomington, Ind., 2008).

Thapar, Romila [et al.], *India: Historical Beginnings and the Concept of the Aryan* (New Delhi, 2006)

Thapar, Romila, 'The Theory of Aryan Race and India: History and Politics', *Social Scientist*, 24/1–3 (January–March 1996), 3–29.

Tomar, Ankit, and Malik, Suratha Kumar (eds), *Reappraising Modern Indian Thought: Themes and Thinkers* (Basingstoke, 2022).

Trautmann, Thomas R., *Aryans and British India* (Berkeley, 1997).

Tucker, R. P., 'Defence of Dharma in Maharashtra, 1840–1870' in A. G. Pawar (ed.), *Maratha History Seminar* (Kolhapur, 1971), 375–389.

Tucker, R. P., 'Hindu Traditionalism and Nationalist Ideologies in Nineteenth-Century Maharashtra', *Modern Asian Studies*, 10/3 (1976), 321–348.

Tucker, R. P., *Ranade and the Roots of Indian Nationalism* (Bombay, 1977).

Upadhyay, S. B., 'Communalism and Working Class: Riot of 1893 in Bombay City', *Economic and Political Weekly*, 24/30 (29 July 1989), PE69–PE75.

Upton, Robert E., '"It Gives Us a Power and Strength Which We Do Not Possess": Martiality, Manliness, and the Indian Army's Great War Enlistment Drive', *Modern Asian Studies*, 52/6 (November 2018), 1977–2012.

Varma, Vishwanath Prasad, *The Life and Philosophy of Lokamanya Tilak. With Excerpts from Original Sources* (Agra, 1978).

Malavika Vartak, 'Shivaji Maharaj: Growth of a Symbol', *Economic and Political Weekly*, 34/19 (1999), 1126–1134.

Vidyasagar, Ishvarchandra, *Hindu Widow Marriage; A Complete Translation, with an Introduction and Critical Notes, by Brian A Hatcher* (New York, 2012).

Wagle, N. K., 'A Dispute between the Pancal Devajna Sonars and the Brahmins of Pune Regarding Social Rank and Ritual Privileges: A Case-study of the British Adminsitration of Jati Laws in Maharashtra, 1822–1825' in *Images of Maharashtra* (London, 1980), 129–59.

Wagle, N. K., 'Readmission of Sripat Sesadri: dharmasastra vs. Public Consensus, Bombay 1843–54', in A. R. Kulkarni and N. K. Wagle, eds, *Region, Nationality and Religion* (Bombay, 1999), 130–156.

Wagle, N. K., 'Ritual and Change in Early Nineteenth Century Society in Maharashtra: Vedokta Disputes in Baroda, Poona and Satara, 1824–1838', in Milton Israel and N. K. Wagle, eds, *Religion and Society in Maharashtra* (Toronto, 1987), 145–181.

Waldron, Arthur, 'The Warlord: Twentieth-Century Chinese Understandings of Violence, Militarism and Imperialism', *American Historical Review*, 96/4 (1991), 1073–1100.

Watt, Carey, 'Education for National Efficiency: Constructive Nationalism in North India, 1906-1916', *Modern Asian Studies*, 31/2 (1997), 339–374.

Weber, Max, *The Theory of Social and Economic Organization*, trans. T. Parsons (London, 1947).

Wilson, Sandra, 'Rethinking Nation and Nationalism in Japan', in Sandra Wilson, ed., *Nation and Nationalism in Japan* (New York, 2002), 1–20.

Wolpert, Stanley, *Tilak and Gokhale: Revolution and Reform in the Making of Modern India* (Berkeley, 1962).

Young, Richard Fox, *Resistant Hinduism: Sanskrit Sources on Antichristian Apologetics in Early Nineteenth-century India* (Vienna, 1981).

Zavos, John, *The Emergence of Hindu Nationalism in India* (New Delhi, 2000)

vii) Unpublished theses

Angadi, S. S., 'Bal Gangadhar Tilak: A Study of His Role in the Indian Nationalist Movement', PhD thesis, Karnatak University, 1992.

Chirmuley, Parnal, 'Appropriating the Past: European Indology and Conflicting Notions of History in Nineteenth century Maharashtra', PhD thesis, Jawaharlal Nehru University, 2002.

Gumaste, Mangala Bhaskar, 'Tilak's Social and Political Philosophy', PhD thesis, University of Pune, 1981.

Jasper, Daniel Alan, 'Commemorating Shivaji: Regional and Religious Identity in Maharashtra, India', PhD thesis, New School University, 2002.

Rupwate, Daniel D., 'The Lokmanya Bal Gangadhar Tilak's Srimadbhagavadgitarahasya in the Light of the Saintly Tradition of Maharashtra', PhD thesis, McMaster University, 1980.

Thomas, Phillachira Mathew, 'Twentieth Century Indian Interpretations of the Bhagavadgita: A Selective Study of Patterns', PhD thesis, McMaster University, 1974.

Tilak, Rohit, 'Lokmanya Bal Gangadhar Tilak—An Economist (1880–1920)', PhD thesis, Tilak Maharashtra Vidyapeeth, 2012.

Upton, Robert E., 'Lokamanya Tilak as Writer and Intellectual in the Political Culture of Late Colonial India', D.Phil thesis, University of Oxford, 2013.

Index

For the benefit of digital users, indexed terms that span two pages (e.g., 52–53) may, on occasion, appear on only one of those pages.

Notes for the reader:

The heading for 'Bombay' contains references to the city by its Marathi name Mumbai, which it was officially known as from 1995; this negates the confusion and inconvenience of having two headings for the same city, and reflects the historical preponderance displayed in this work. Similarly, the University of Mumbai post-1996 is grouped under 'Bombay, University of'

As there is no index heading for Tilak, topics relevant to his thought are listed independently, and their connection to Tilak is not stated where this is considered superfluous.

Figures are indicated by *f* following the page number